D1570517

America's China Trade
in Historical Perspective

Harvard Studies in American–East Asian Relations 11

The Harvard Studies in American–East Asian Relations are sponsored and edited by the Committee on American–East Asian Relations of the Department of History at Harvard University.

edited by
ERNEST R. MAY
and JOHN K. FAIRBANK

Published by
THE COMMITTEE ON AMERICAN-EAST ASIAN RELATIONS
OF THE DEPARTMENT OF HISTORY
in collaboration with
THE COUNCIL ON EAST ASIAN STUDIES / HARVARD UNIVERSITY
Distributed by the Harvard University Press
Cambridge (Massachusetts) and London   1986

America's China Trade in Historical Perspective

The Chinese and American Performance

382.0973
A51

Library of Congress Cataloging-in-Publication Data
Main entry under title:

America's China trade in historical perspective.

(Harvard studies in American-East Asian relations ; 11)
Bibliography: p.
Includes index.
1. United States—Commerce—China—History.
2. China—Commerce—United States—History. I. May,
Ernest R., 1907– . II. Fairbank, John King, 1928–
III. Harvard University. Dept. of History. American-
East Asian Relations Committee. IV. Harvard
University. Committee on American-East Asian Relations.
V. Series.
HF3128.A62 1986   382'.0973'051   85–29159
ISBN 0-674-03075-3

mR.

Designed by Adrianne Onderdonk Dudden

ERNEST R. MAY

American China policy has figured in a multitude of books and articles, many of which focus on economic motivations, especially on American hopes for commerce and investment in China. Yet, very little research or writing has dealt with the China trade itself, or the actual economic relationships between Americans and Chinese. The Old China Trade from 1784 to about 1860 became a legend in American thinking, but, after that romantic era of tea, silk, and opium, what actually happened? What did Chinese–American economic relations consist of in fact?

This volume explores the commercial realities underlying the rhetoric about the China trade. It began with a conference supported by the national Committee on American East Asian Relations at Mt. Kisco, New York, in 1976. The specialists who contributed were able to penetrate major aspects of the subject as no single author could have done.

Revised and developed, their essays cast glints of light onto this little-explored terrain. Given the sparseness of prior work, the variable quality and availability of the sources, and the usual difficulties inherent in cross-cultural scholarship, these explorations only hint at the overall shape of what future research may eventually disclose. When the history of China's domestic economy still awaits sustained investigation, it is hard to tell now whether the stories told in this volume reflect the main lines of China's entrance into the international trading world or are more superficial. But, even if they are only like the French warships off the coast of Africa that Joseph Conrad described in *Heart of Darkness* as "firing onto a continent," the chapters that follow nevertheless make a much needed beginning. Chinese-American economic relations pose crucial problems for both peoples, and we need to separate myth from fact in their history.

17273

C O N T E N T S

TABLES

KANG CHAO, Professor of Economics at the University of Wisconsin, Madison, is the author of *The Development of Cotton Textile Production in China* (East Asian Research Center, Harvard University, 1977) and *Man and Land in Chinese History: An Economic Analysis* (Stanford University Press, 1985). He is currently doing research on labor supply in China's history.

CHU-YUAN CHENG, Professor of Economics at Ball State University, Muncie, Indiana, served for ten years as a consultant to the National Science Foundation, during which he was chief investigator with the research project on scientific and engineering manpower in China. His most recent books are *China's Economic Development: Growth and Structural Change* (Westview, 1982) and *The Demand and Supply of Primary Energy in Mainland China* (Chung-Hua Institution for Economic Research, 1983). His current research is on the impact of Sinic culture on East Asian economic development.

SHERMAN COCHRAN teaches Chinese history at Cornell University. He has written *Big Business in China: Sino-Foreign Rivalry in the Cigarette Industry, 1890–1930* (Harvard University Press, 1980) and, with Andrew C. K. Hsieh and Janis Cochran, *One Day in China: May 21, 1936* (Yale University Press, 1983).

JOHN K. FAIRBANK is Francis Lee Higginson Professor of History, Emeritus, at Harvard University. He has long been interested in the China trade and, in 1953, published *Trade and Diplomacy on the China Coast: The Opening of the Treaty Ports 1842–1952* (Harvard University Press), developed from an Oxford dissertation of 1936.

ROBERT P. GARDELLA is Associate Professor in the Department of Humanities, United States Merchant Marine Academy, Kings Point. His most recent publications are articles in *Ch'ing-shih wen-t'i* (June 1982) and *The Academy of Accounting Historians Working Paper Series* (August 1983). He is now engaged in a continuing study of Sino-foreign commerce and the socioeconomic history of late Qing Fujian and North Taiwan.

YEN-P'ING HAO is Lindsay Young Professor of History, University of Tennessee, Knoxville. He is the author of *The Comprador in Nineteenth Century China* (Harvard University Press, 1970) and *The Commercial Revolution in Nineteenth Century China: The Rise of Sino-Western Mercantile Capitalism* (University of California Press, 1986), and is currently working with Kwang-Ching Liu on the early history of the China Merchants' Steam Navigation Company.

LILLIAN M. LI is an Associate Professor of History, Swarthmore College. She is the author of *China's Silk Trade: Traditional Industry in the Modern World, 1842–1937* (Council on East Asian Studies, Harvard University, 1981) and is now serving as Assistant Editor of the *Journal of Asian Studies*. Her current research and writing concern food supply and famines in China over the last three centuries.

ERNEST R. MAY is Charles Warren Professor of History at Harvard University. His recent works include *The Making of the*

Contributors** xvii

Monroe Doctrine (Harvard University Press, 1975) and, with several collaborators, *Knowing One's Enemies: Intelligence Assessment before the Two World Wars* (Princeton University Press, 1985). His forthcoming book in collaboration with Richard E. Neustadt, *Thinking in Time: Uses of History for Decision-Makers,* will be published by the Free Press.

BRUCE REYNOLDS is Associate Professor of Economics at Union College, Schenectady. During 1981 he was a visiting research associate at the Chinese Academy of Social Sciences, Beijing, studying Chinese industrial planning. Since then, his research has centered on the relationship of international trade to economic development in China. His most recent publications include "Economic Reforms and External Imbalance in China," *American Economic Review* 73.2 (May 1983) and "China in the International Economy," in Harry Harding, ed., *China's Foreign Relations in the 1980's* (Yale University Press, 1985).

PETER SCHRAN is Professor of Economics and Director of the Center for East Asian and Pacific Studies at the University of Illinois at Urbana-Champaign. His most recent work is a paper on the relationship between China's traditional transportation and railroad development, to appear in a conference volume called *Region, State, and Enterprise in Chinese Economy History, 980–1980,* edited by Robert Hartwell, Albert Feuerwerker, and Robert Dernberger. His current research focuses on the use of price statistics in interpreting economic developments during the period of the Chinese Republic and the transformation of handicrafts during industrialization on the Mainland and in Taiwan.

MIRA WILKINS is Professor of Economics, Florida International University, Miami. She is the author of *The Emergence of Multinational Enterprise: American Business Abroad from the Colonial Era to 1914* (1970) and *The Maturing of Multinational Enterprise: American Business Abroad from 1914 to 1970* (1974), both published by Harvard University Press. She is now engaged in research on the history of foreign investment in the United States.

Patterns and Problems

JOHN K. FAIRBANK

The Old China Trade, down to the time of the American Civil War, had the merit of being both exotic and lucrative. It was a pleasure to make money in it, even though one might die suddenly of ague or colic. Moreover, in the China trade we often got ahead of the British, not so much by Yankee ingenuity as by using the opportunities they made available to us. After 1850, when Britain let us carry teas to London, our newly designed clippers sometimes got there first. Because the British did not open the India-China trade to us, we did less well in supplying opium to China; but that only enhanced our sense of moral superiority. It was not Americans who fought the Opium War of 1839–1842 and the second war that finally opened China in 1860. Our conscience could be clear.

From that experience between 1784 and the 1860s we inherited a national image of the China trade as a good thing, an American success story.[1] This idea remained untarnished by the fact that, during the next hundred years, the American trade with China never amounted to much. China might take no more than 2 to 4 percent of total American foreign trade, but never mind, it was surely a great *potential* market, and indeed so it remains to this day.

The idea of the China trade has thus had a long and distinctive career in the American public mind. Some have seen it as a national concomitant of the westward course of empire that brought American settlers into this virgin land and on across the Pacific. In this view, trade with China was our manifest destiny under the invisible hand of divine providence. In the expansive enthusiasm of the 1890s, as the United States emerged into power politics, the vision of the China trade gained new currency in capitalist America. At the same time China's weakness and the European scramble for concessions in 1898 set China up as a primary target of international rivalry. Soon the Leninist and other theories of imperialism linked America's economic expansion with the lure of the China market, and a great deal has since been written about the influence of economic interests on our China policy.

This is a large subject that does not diminish with time. Trade in hand with Taiwan and potential trade with the People's Republic figure in our current counsels. The one thing that seems to be lacking is a concise and coherent picture of what the American China trade actually amounted to. Knowledge of the facts is needed.

Once one begins to seek the facts, it becomes apparent that both sides must be studied, and our picture of Sino-foreign relations must be considerably revised. The traditional picture of Western enterprise and Chinese passivity must be abandoned. For far too long, Westerners, aware of their own vigor and informed from Western records, have retained a one-sided view of the Sino-Western encounter. It is now evident that the conservative policies of the Chinese state before and after 1800 were superficial to an economy and society undergoing extensive growth and change.[2] China in the eighteenth century was already a country in motion, in the process of doubling its population and therefore its production and trade. The international trade at Canton, which the Americans joined in after 1784, was only an offshoot of China's burgeoning domestic commerce. The teas and silks that went abroad were only a part of the growing domestic product. After all, while the merchants who took the initiative in the Canton trade came from Europe and America, the staple goods of the trade came mainly from China.

The American trade at Canton began under the same compulsion that pressured British India into the opium trade—how to lay down funds at Canton with which to buy China's teas and silks. For Yankee merchants, the main problem in the Canton trade was that the Chinese were self-sufficient and wanted nothing from America. The traders were reduced to loading ice from Boston's lakes and shipping ginseng root from New England or sea-otter pelts and furs from the northwest coast, or even sandalwood from the Sandwich (Hawaiian) Islands. Like the Europeans of the eighteenth century who traded at Canton, the Americans who turned up there after 1784 were from a relatively have-not region. It was they who took the initiative to go to China and seek profit from China's handicraft produce. During its first century the American China trade seemed to be a predominantly unilateral effort. But this impression was misleading. China's apparent passivity reflected the strength of its economy, not its weakness. China's tea and silk exports were an offshoot of the enormous growth of domestic production and commerce that had accompanied the doubling of China's already vast population in the eighteenth century. We must recognize that the growth of British and American trade around the globe, which dazzled all true believers in progress, was partly fueled by the growth of the Chinese domestic economy and the tea and silk exports that growth supported. After all, China's economy was expanding in a free trade area bigger and more populous than Europe. That this fact remained largely unnoticed in both China and the West makes it all the more interesting in retrospect. China was in on the ground floor of the modern world economy even though the statesmen of both sides only dimly perceived it.

Yet, because the inititative came from the West and because China's domestic economic growth is still mostly beyond our ken, our strategy in this volume is to focus first on the American trade and its role in China and America. It will be evident that our strategy is also opportunist, in a statesmanlike way, because American trade was only a part, sometimes indeed a small part, of the outside world's trade with China, yet it gives us a feasible target, a point of ingress into an otherwise impenetrable subject. We begin by looking at the tea trade, as Yen-p'ing Hao traces its course and suggests its influence in the United States. If later chapters concern mainly China, it is for the simple reason that the China trade in economic terms did not play a great role in America after the initial period.

Our studies naturally divide into three parts, the first of which concerns China's staple exports of tea and silk with which the American China trade began. Robert Gardella describes the great decades of tea export at Foochow, in which American enterprise played a part. Lillian Li analyzes the parallel rise of China's silk exports. In both cases, the Americans provided only a part of the foreign market. Chinese merchants met the occasion by applying their traditional skills of adaptability, organization, and enterprise, but they were woefully lacking in the capital necessary for introducing new technology, and they were badly let down by the Chinese government of the late imperial era. It failed to provide the planning, leadership, financial support, and quality control that the contemporary Meiji government was providing in Japan or the British regime in India. As a result, the tea trade was largely taken over by India and Japan, while Japanese silk largely supplanted Chinese in the world market. These two studies of what happened to China's tea and silk trades are stories of domestic failure. Foreign competition in Asia, not exploitation by the West, was China's nemesis, and American merchants played only secondary roles.

Studies in Part Two deal with American imports into China. Opium, however, though the best known of these imports, is not a special focus of our attention in this volume; the American opium trade in its heyday between roughly 1800 and 1860 was never more than about one-tenth the size of the Anglo-Indian opium import into China. To be sure, American enterprisers did what they could by bringing Turkey opium from Smyrna to Canton, but they were excluded from the Calcutta auctions of the British East India Company and could not compete with its standardized production for the China market. Some American fortunes were made in opium, no doubt, but the drug functioned as a minor means of laying down funds for teas and silks. The American government never derived essential revenues from the trade, which remains largely an aspect of British imperial history.

We therefore begin with American cotton cloth imported into China. Professor Chao shows how the heavier and coarser American cloth divided the China market with Lancashire, finding its main outlet in North China, until a combination of circumstances (mainly Japanese) led to a rapid collapse of American sales after 1905.

Bruce Reynolds then analyzes the fluctuations in sales of raw cotton, yarn, cloth, and textile machinery in East Asia during the modern century, in which Britain's overall dominance was supplanted by that of Japan. While the Americans had their day in meeting the Chinese demand for cotton, they were again only secondary figures in the general development of the trade.

Tobacco, however, was a different story. The British-American Tobacco Company (BAT), formed in 1902, was essentially the creation of James B. Duke, who shipped his first cigarettes to China in 1890. Sherman Cochran recounts the American success in monopolizing the Chinese market from 1890 to 1915, analyzing the methods used in developing Chinese production and sales. Though BAT's foreign salesmen saw themselves as "pioneers," it now seems that they were simply tapping into the indigenous Chinese commercial network. Yet, on balance, the evidence indicates that BAT's high-pressure tactics against Chinese competitors can be categorized as economic imperialism.

The American sale of kerosene is described by Chu-yuan Cheng. Where Britain's China trade had found an early motor in the Chinese demand for opium, the Americans of a later day seized upon a Chinese demand for cigarettes and for kerosene. The poverty of China dictated that foreign sales would be greatest in cheap goods for mass consumption. American supplies of cotton, tobacco, and petroleum products all shared in the growth and halting modernization of the Chinese economy.

Part Three of this volume puts forward two perspectives on

Chinese-American economic relations. Peter Schran looks at the American China trade in the context of the American and the Chinese foreign trades as a whole. His copious tables demonstrate that, for both countries, foreign trade was of minor importance, and within that framework trade with each other was, in the long run, even less significant. The chapter strikes a blow at sentimentality.

In perhaps the most interesting of all these contributions, Mira Wilkins examines the several ways in which American multinational corporations included China within their far-flung operations: Standard Oil in various forms, the Singer Sewing Machine Company, Western Electric, General Electric, Ford Motor Company, and others as well as the British-American Tobacco Company. She also considers the China trade corporations owned under American law by citizens resident in China, and takes note of American banks, the Shanghai Power Company, the China National Aviation Corporation (CNAC), an affiliate of Pan Am, and similar interests.

Much of the commerce discussed in these articles led to American investments in China, but the total American stake so accumulated did not bulk very large. A considerable element in the American trade with China was simply silver sent in various forms to lay down funds for purchases. No one staple product tied the two economies together; overall, it was neither a colonial nor an exploitative relationship.

How can historians of today best understand the record of American-Chinese economic relations? Surely the first conclusion to draw is that two countries of subcontinental size are not likely to become economically dependent one upon the other. Though the China market became a field for American enterprise, where some ventures found temporary success, no long-term umbilical connection was established. To be sure, American tobacco sales fostered a Chinese nicotine addiction that partly supplanted the opium addiction originally fostered by British India. But no great vested interests were built up in the American economy on the basis of exports to China or investments there. China did not assume the role for the United States that India did for the United Kingdom, nor did the American China trade play the fundamental fiscal role that Indian opium and

China teas played in the early growth of Britain's commercial empire.

A parallel conclusion follows—that the bouts of American enthusiasm for trade and investment in China originated in the American imagination, in a mind-set that believed in economic expansion, more than in concrete concerns and vested interests of business and industry. Study of Chinese-American economic relations thus suggests that those relations themselves have been inadequate to explain the course of American China policy (to say nothing of China's policy toward the United States). The student of policy who seeks a full picture of the Sino-American relationship must look to noneconomic factors as well as economic. Indeed, such an investigator may find it hard to discover a material substructure adequate to account for the superstructure of religious, cultural, and strategic interests that dominated the Chinese-American relationship. But such a conclusion can only emphasize the necessity of getting the economic relationships more fully into view in their precise size and quality. We cannot claim that the American approach to China was a phenomenon of the mind and spirit more than of the pocketbook, unless we realize how comparatively little of a material nature was ever at stake.

PART ONE

China's Major Export Trades

CHAPTER ONE

Chinese Teas to America—a Synopsis

YEN-P'ING HAO

It was symbolic of the Old China Trade that its main staple should be a handicraft product. After being picked by nimble fingers, tea leaves had to be skilfully sorted, pressed, rolled, fired (heated in iron pans as many as five times), and packed for shipment. When the American trade began in 1784, Indian production of tea was still negligible, Chinese tea was becoming the English national drink, and tea drinking was already a widespread mark of gentility in America.[1]

Until the Revolution, American traders had relied upon England for their tea. The East India Company, which enjoyed a monopoly on English trade at Canton, transshipped its tea imports from England to North American ports. Occasional smuggling from Holland failed to break the Company's tea import monopoly. In 1767, as America was fast becoming a country of tea drinkers, the notorious Townshend Acts imposed import duties on the popular commodity; the reaction was immediate. Political activists, merchants, and other citizens began a sustained boycott of tea that erupted in the "Boston Tea Party" of December 1773. Many patriots abstained from tea drinking throughout the Revolutionary War. Some ingenious substitutes were developed.

After the Revolution, the new United States had idle ships just in from privateering, experienced sailors, a domestic market for Chinese tea, and a market in China for at least one American product—ginseng. This was a roughly phallic-shaped root highly prized in China when steeped to make a supposedly restorative potion, the Geritol of its day. Ginseng root was found in New England. In December 1783, New England traders attempted to initiate direct trade with China by sending the *Harriet,* a Boston sloop of 55 tons, to Canton loaded with ginseng. At the Cape of Good Hope, the American vessel encountered some British traders who, "alarmed at this portent of Yankee competition . . . bought her cargo for double its weight in Hyson tea."[2] Though the American captain made handsome profits by the sale, he thereby lost his chance to go down in history.

DIRECT TRADE WITHOUT DIPLOMACY, 1784–1843

The first American ship to enter Chinese waters was the *Empress of China.* Fitted out by Robert Morris of Philadelphia and Daniel Parker & Co. of New York, it sailed for Canton on 22 February 1784, under the command of Captain John Green. Loaded with ginseng and other commodities, she reached Canton on 28 August after a voyage around the Cape of Good Hope. Carrying 3,000 piculs of Hyson and Bohea tea, she returned safely to New York the following year.

News of the successful voyage created intense interest among New England traders. Boston merchants soon laid plans to build and fit out a ship for another voyage. It was not long before Captain Steward Deane, an old privateersman, sailed for Canton in a small sloop of 84 tons. In June 1787, Robert Morris of Philadelphia sent out the *Alliance* with a cargo said to be worth half a million dollars. And from Providence John Brown's ship, the *General Washington*, sailed to Canton in December 1787, returning home in July 1789. Among other vessels making early voyages to Canton were the *Jenny* and the *Eleonora* of New York, the *Astrea* of Salem, and the *Massachusetts* of Boston. By 1790, the American tea trade at Canton had become regular.[3]

The Chinese-American tea trade steadily increased after 1785. Exports from Canton rose from 880,100 pounds in that year to 3,093,200 pounds in 1790 and 5,665,067 pounds in 1800 (see Table 1). No other nation except Britain had a larger number of ships in South China waters. For four years through 1807, an annual average of 36 American ships arrived in China.[4] Because the total volume of America's foreign trade was comparatively small during this period, the trade with China constituted a considerable part of it.

Compared with their British competitors, American traders enjoyed relative freedom from the restrictions of monopoly enterprise. During the early nineteenth century, ships of both nations purchased furs at the American northwest coast and sold them at Canton in exchange for tea. English vessels could go to the northwest coast only with special permission from the East India Company, and they were required to bring their cargoes back to China and exchange them, not for Chinese produce which could be taken to England and the Continent, but for specie which had to be deposited with the Company. For this specie the Company issued bills on London at twelve months' sight. The Americans, by contrast, bartered freely at Canton, underselling British pelts by about 20 percent, and carried their teas wherever they pleased.

The Sino-American tea trade grew enormously during the Napoleonic Wars. For several decades, the United States reaped commercial profits from its policy of political neutrality. As American ships became the common carriers of European goods, and large portions of the West Indies and the European Continent opened up to American commodities, the market for tea naturally expanded. The annual average of American ships visiting Canton grew from 7.4 in 1785–1800 to 23.6 in 1801–1811. Americans soon gained second place in Canton's foreign trade[5] (see Table 2).

TABLE 1   American Ships and Exports of Tea at Canton,
1785–1800 *(in pounds)*

Year[a]	Ships	Tea Exports to the United States
1785	2	880,100
1786	1	695,000
1787	5	1,181,860
1788	2	750,000
1789	4	1,188,800
1790	14	3,093,200
1791	3	743,100
1792	3	1,863,200
1793	6	1,538,400
1794	7	1,974,130
1795	7	1,438,270
1796	10	2,819,600
1797	13	3,450,400
1798	10	3,100,400
1799	13	5,674,000
1800	18	5,665,067

Source: Foster R. Dulles, *The Old China Trade,* p. 210.

Notes: [a]Based on season rather than on calendar year.

During the war years of 1809–1811, continental Europe's tea trade with China stopped completely. The Sino-American tea trade, however, was not so heavily affected by the war in Europe. The American people, more numerous and richer since the eighteenth century, demanded larger and larger quantities of tea. As Table 3 indicates, exports of tea from Canton to the United States increased steadily, rising from 6.6 million pounds in 1822 to 19 million in 1840.[6]

In the meantime, tea became more and more the dominant commodity. It was 36 percent of Chinese exports to the United States in 1822, 82 percent by 1840. This proportional increase was largely due to the insignificant amounts of other imported commodities. Silk had accounted for about one-third of the Sino-American trade during 1820–1835, but, possibly because of changing fashions, silk trade declined until, by 1841, it was

TABLE 2 American and European Continental Clearances
and Exportations of Tea at Canton, 1800–1811

| | Clearances | | Export of Tea | |
| | | | American | Continental |
Year[a]	American	Continental	(pounds)	
1801	23	7	4,762,866	3,968,207
1802	31	1	5,740,734	185,533
1803	20	12	2,612,436	5,812,266
1804	12	2	2,371,600	2,132,666
1805	31	3	8,546,800	3,318,799
1806	37	4	11,702,800	1,809,466
1807	27	2	8,464,133	1,534,267
1808	31	2	6,408,266	1,144,266
1809	6	0	1,082,400	0
1810	29	0	9,737,066	0
1811	12	0	2,884,400	0

Source: Tyler Dennett, Americans in Eastern Asia, p. 45.

Note: [a]Based on seasons rather than on calendar years.

scarcely 8 percent of the whole. A similar decline occurred in cotton cloths or nankeens, partly bcause the Americans had newly established a domestic cotton industry and were able to produce their own cottons. The American taste for tea, on the other hand, remained strong, and imports from Canton rose roughly in proportion to the increase in the American population.[7]

In the Anglo-Chinese struggle at Canton, the Chinese government attempted to use tea as a diplomatic weapon. Many scholar-officials firmly believed that the foreigners needed tea badly and that, if their supplies were cut off, the "barbarians" would become blind and would contract intestinal diseases. At least twenty citations from Chinese works of the period 1840–1860 express this belief. Surprisingly, among Chinese who subscribed to the concept were pragmatic statecraft (ching-shih) literati-officials such as Commissioner Lin Tse-hsu, Pao Shih-ch'en, and Hsiao Ling-yü. In answering an imperial inquiry, Commissioner Lin memorialized in 1840: "After careful investigation, we conclude that tea and rhubarb are necessities for the

TABLE 3 Tea Exports from Canton to the United States,
1822–1840
(in pounds)

Year	Amount	Percent of Tea to Total American Imports from Canton
1822	6,639,434	36
1828	7,707,427	45
1832	9,906,606	52
1837	16,581,467	65
1840	19,333,597	82

Sources: Timothy Pitkin, *A Statistical View of the Commerce of the United States of America,* pp. 246, 247, 301. *United States Senate Executive Documents 35,* 37th Congress, 3rd Session, p. 10.

foreigners. . . . If such exports are really suspended, it would bring about the end of their lives."[8]

TRADE UNDER THE TREATY SYSTEM, 1844–1895

A new phase in the Chinese-American tea trade began when the two countries signed the Treaty of Wanghia (Wang-hsia) in 1844. For one thing, a low Chinese conventional tariff, based on a uniform 5 percent ad valorem, was established, thus eliminating the complicated duties under the Canton system. A more important consequence of the treaty was the opening of other treaty ports, especially Foochow and Shanghai, as tea trade centers. Foreign trade at Foochow developed slowly at first. In 1850, its foreign population was 10, of whom 7 were missionaries. By 1855, it had 28 foreigners, of whom 17 were tea merchants, and, in the next five years, their five firms (three British, two American) shipped out of Foochow an annual average of 37.5 million pounds[9] (see Table 4 and Chapter 3 below).

Though many tea-producing areas were long distant from Canton, the Shanghai market was within easy reach. The Shanghai contribution to the total China export rapidly rose from one-seventh in 1846 to one-third in 1851 and to considerably over one-half in the years immediately following. Even after the shipments from Foochow came into the calculation, the Shanghai share in the trade was never much below one-half[10] (see Table 4).

TABLE 4 Tea Exports from Shanghai and Foochow,
        1855–1860
        (in pounds)

Year	Shanghai	Foochow	Total
1855	80,200,000	15,700,000	95,900,000
1856	59,300,000	41,000,000	100,300,000
1857	41,000,000	32,000,000	73,000,000
1858	51,000,000	28,000,000	79,000,000
1859	39,000,000	46,500,000	85,500,000
1860	53,500,000	40,000,000	93,500,000

Source: Hosea Ballou Morse, *The International Relations of the Chinese Empire* I, 466.

Favorable conditions similarly fostered the American end of the Chinese-American tea trade. In 1846, Congress passed a new tariff under which Chinese tea, formerly a revenue article, was admitted free of duty. With Britain's nullification of the old Navigation Acts as of 1850, American ships were permitted, for the first time since Independence, to engage in commerce of foreign origin destined for British possessions, on terms of equality with the British. American merchant tonnage grew quickly, and that in the China trade, never more than 10,000 tons prior to 1843, increased within a decade to more than 100,000 tons.[11]

In these circumstances, it is not surprising that the tea trade continued to thrive. Among American imports from China, tea retained its preeminent position, accounting for 60 to 80 percent of the total between 1844 and 1860. Table 5 shows that, although the relative proportion of tea to other imports from China fluctuated, the increase in the quantity of tea was fairly steady.

After 1860 the situation changed. The United States reinstated tariffs. The Civil War ruined the American merchant marine. Moreover, in Asia, Americans increasingly traded with Japan rather than China. While the annual dollar volume of America's China trade remained constant at around $22–23 million, that of the Japan trade rose from $193,365 in 1860 to $28,370,674 in 1894. Japanese tea eventually displaced Chinese tea in the American market. American purchases from China

TABLE 5 Tea Imports from China to the United States,
1821–1860
(in million pounds)

Year	Amount	% of Total American Imports from China
1821	5	42.5
1825	—	49.5
1830	9	62.5
1835	—	75.5
1840	20	82.0
1845	—	79.2
1850	30	71.5
1855	—	70.0
1860	26	65.5

Sources: Timothy Pitkin, *Statistical View,* pp. 246-247. I. Smith Homans, Jr., *A Historical and Statistical Account of the Foreign Commerce of the United States,* pp. 181-182. U.S. Department of the Treasury, Statistics Bureau, *Annual Reports, Commerce and Navigation* (1860), p. 269.

shifted from tea to what had previously been called the "muck and truck" trade—wool, vegetable oil, hides and skins, and other miscellaneous items. From 1865 to 1894, China's relative share in American tea imports declined from 77 percent to 51 percent; Japan's share steadily expanded from 19 percent to 44 percent. In the meantime, South Asia also came into the market. Of the tea imported into the United States in 1905, China supplied 40 percent, Japan 35, the remaining 25 coming mainly from India, Ceylon, and Java.[12]

TRADE MECHANICS

Purchasing

The early American purchase of tea at Canton was conducted by supercargoes, who traveled on the vessels. The next step in commercial organization involved the establishment of resident trading firms, which dealt on commission in their own right or represented American mercantile houses. For instance, Samuel Shaw, a supercargo on the *Ann and Hope* in 1795, established himself in about 1800 as a resident commission agent. Thomas

H. Perkins & Co. of Boston opened a branch at Canton in 1803, placing John P. Cushing in charge. Though primarily transacting Perkins business, this firm also engaged in a commission trade. B. C. Wilcocks of Philadelphia and Daniel Stansbury of Baltimore likewise became resident agents. Nicholas G. Ogden and Cornelius Sowle represented the legendary John Jacob Astor. And Samuel Russell, yet another former supercargo, also appeared as a resident agent at Canton.[13] These resident agents, together with mercantile houses founded at Canton, gradually replaced the supercargoes as the principal purchasers.

By the 1820s, a few large firms dominated American tea purchases at Canton. Perkins & Co., James Oakford & Co., Archer & Co., T. H. Smith & Co., Olyphant & Co., Russell & Co., and Wetmore & Co. ranked among the most noted establishments. The first four controlled about 80 percent of the trade in 1828. Philadelphia houses—representing the interests of Robert Morris, Stephen Girard, and Samuel Archer, among others—retained the commercial leadership for more than twenty years before yielding to New York-based firms. The American "factory" at Canton was said to be splendid, as befitted a nation whose commercial prowess was second only to that of Britain. ("Factories" were establishments of "factors," that is, merchants, not manufacturing plants.)[14]

Prior to 1842, the Americans purchased tea exclusively from the famous Canton hong merchants, who enjoyed a "monopoly" over China's foreign trade. Because a Western ship trading at Canton had to be "secured" by one of the hong merchants, who guaranteed the seamen's behavior and the payment of duties, it was important that American traders maintain good relations with their Chinese counterparts. When Samuel Shaw, the first American supercargo, arrived at Canton in 1784, he was warmly greeted by the hong merchants. Subsequent supercargoes and resident agents naturally cultivated their friendship. John P. Cushing and John M. Forbes of Russell & Co. developed an unusually cordial relationship with the dean of the hong merchants, the renowned Houqua (Wu Ping-chien).

The hong merchants themselves purchased the teas from other Chinese merchants. Some hong merchants, notably Houqua, also sent agents to the Bohea (Wu-i) tea districts to buy tea direct. While the hong merchants sold some of the tea to the Western traders, they occasionally shipped tea to the United States on their own account. In 1810, for example, an American ship carried a cargo of such tea valued at $38,310.[15]

The hong merchants lost their monopoly in 1842. Augustine Heard, Jr., has left us a detailed description of the new tea-purchasing procedures at Canton. When tea came in from the country, it went first to the warehouses along the river. "Canister samples, or muster, as they were called, were sent to all the foreign houses, and it was the business of the tea-taster to examine them and enter them, with description and valuation, in a book kept for the purpose." Each parcel of tea bore a name, called a "chop," usually the name of the countryman who had prepared it. The tea taster recorded the sale of every chop in his authoritative ledger. When purchases were decided upon and "there was substantial agreement as to price, very large settlements could be made in a short time."[16]

After the opening of new treaty ports in 1842, tea-purchasing became increasingly competitive. Merchants of Cantonese origin served as middlemen. Writing in the 1840s, Robert Fortune, the botanist-explorer who helped develop India's tea production, observed that, when tea was ready for market, the Cantonese merchants residing in the treaty ports would "go to the tea district and take up their quarters in all the little inns or eating houses. . . . As soon as the merchants are known to have arrived in the district, the tea growers bring their produce for inspection and sale. The little farmers or their labourers may now be seen hastening along the different roads, each with two baskets or chests slung across his shoulders on his bamboo pole." If the price was right, the bargain was struck. "But should the price offered appear too low," this traveler continued, "the baskets are immediately shouldered with great apparent independence, and carried away to some opposition merchants."[17]

After 1860, the three major treaty ports—Shanghai, Hankow, and Foochow—absorbed the upcountry teas. Shanghai dominated the tea districts of Kiangsu, Anhwei, and Chekiang; Hankow controlled the Middle Yangtze Valley areas of Hupeh,

Hunan, and northern Kiangsi; and Foochow drew from Fukien and southern Kiangsi.

American merchants resident in these ports could purchase tea in three ways. The easiest way, to buy on the open market, offered competitive prices but was often unreliable. Another method was to make cash advances to Chinese tea men, who would then proceed to the upcountry. This practice obtained frequently at Shanghai during the 1860s. A third method of tea-purchasing involved Chinese compradors, who were sent to the interior to buy tea directly from the tea grower. This procedure was often used at Foochow, the closest treaty port to the Bohea tea districts. The Taiping Rebellion made it difficult to export tea from Canton and Shanghai during the mid-1850s. In 1854, Russell & Co. sent its comprador from Foochow into the interior with large sums of money to make purchases directly from tea growers. The Russell firm's tea exports from Foochow expanded, and, in the following year, Augustine Heard & Co. made up-country purchases totaling $200,000.[18]

Financing

Financing the tea trade was a perennial problem for American merchants because, quite simply, they possessed few items that the Chinese really wanted to buy. In payment for tea the Americans exported various marginal commodities, making up the difference with silver dollars at first and London credit later on. Following British East India Company practice in colonial times, the first Americans sailing for China took ginseng with them. They also carried sandalwood.

When ginseng and sandalwood proved to be poor trading articles at Canton, American mechants turned to fur. John Ledyard of Connecticut was probably the first American to visualize a lucrative triangular trade linking New York, the northwest coast, and China. Having accompanied Captain James Cook on his expedition to the Pacific in 1776, Ledyard had visited the Nootka Sound area and was therefore acquainted with the immense fur resources of the northwest coast. He foresaw the sale of cheap ironware and other inexpensive items to the Indians in return for luxurious furs, which in turn would exchange at a handsome profit for Chinese tea. The idea, though not fully realized till 1790, caught on quickly at Boston and Salem. The fur trade enjoyed enormous initial success. From 1790 to the early 1830s, Americans sold furs to China totaling between $US15-20 million in value. After 1820, however, the Chinese desire for pelts diminished, and, by the early 1830s, the fur trade ended altogether.[19]

American traders desperately needed an attractive export commodity. The supply of Hawaiian sandalwood was soon exhausted, and the trade in ginseng and bêche-de-mer (the sea slug much prized by Chinese gourmets) was necessarily limited. There was little demand for American raw cotton since Chinese cotton was cheaper. To take up the slack, American traders continuously engaged in the opium trade during the 1820s and 1830s. Financed through London bankers and helped by their own permanent receiving vessels at the outer anchorage, they virtually monopolized the Turkish opium business. They also acted as agents at Canton for Indian opium that had been smuggled to China on ships of the "country trade." Overall, however, opium always played an insignificant economic role. For example, Americans sold $133,000 worth of opium in 1824 and $275,921 worth in 1836, but total American imports during those years amounted to around $7.5 million and $9 million, respectively. Furthermore, after 1830, American participation in this traffic began to fall off. Since American merchants had to get their opium from Smyrna or other ports in Turkey, their competition with the Anglo-Indian supply at its best gave them no more than 10 percent of the China market. Meanwhile, the American demand for Chinese tea continued to rise.[20]

In these circumstances, it was only natural that the American traders exported specie to Canton to make up the deficit. During the period 1805-1814, for example, the value of such specie was $22,719,000, about 70 percent of total exports. Between 1816 and 1844, the average annual export of specie to China was $3,181,000, and the average proportion of specie in total American exports to China was 65 percent (see Table 6).

During the early nineteenth century, the United States could ill afford to export specie, for the country then lacked adequate

TABLE 6 Bullion and Specie in American Exports to China,
1816–1844
($U.S. 1,000s)

Year ending September 30	Total value	Merchandise		Bullion and Specie	
		Value	%	Value	%
1816	4,220	2,298	54	1,922	46
1817	5,703	1,158	20	4,545	80
1818	6,777	1,176	17	5,601	83
1819	9,057	1,643	18	7,414	82
1820	8,173	1,876	23	6,297	77
1821	4,291	900	21	3,391	79
1822	5,935	860	14	5,075	86
1823	4,636	1,052	23	3,584	77
1824	5,301	837	16	4,464	84
1825	5,570	1,047	19	4,523	81
1826	2,567	915	36	1,652	64
1827	3,864	1,339	35	2,525	65
1828	4,481	4,025	90	456	10
1829	1,355	753	56	602	44
1830	742	662	89	80	11
1831	1,291	924	72	367	28
1832	1,261	809	64	452	36
1833	1,434	1,144	80	290	20
1834	1,010	631	62	379	38
1835	1,869	477	26	1,392	74
1836	1,194	780	65	414	35
1837	631	476	75	155	25
1838	1,517	788	52	729	48
1839	1,534	541	35	993	65
1840	1,010	533	53	477	47
1841	1,201	774	64	427	36
1842	1,444	837	58	607	42
1843	2,419	1,847	76	572	24
1844	1,757	1,190	68	567	32
Average	3,181	1,114	35	2,067	65

Sources: U.S. Senate *Executive Document 31*, 19th Congress, 1st Session. I. S. Homans, *Historical and Statistical Account*, passim. Calculations are the author's.

silver and gold mines. Therefore, Spanish dollars made up the bulk of the specie exports. To finance the purchase of tea from China, American merchants engaged in a triangular trade. They shipped American produce to Europe or South America. The proceeds in Spanish dollars were then transmitted to China to finance the trade of tea. Their ships could also earn Spanish dollars by carrying goods between European ports.[21] On the third leg of the triangle, tea was shipped from Canton to America. The actual specie had to be transported to China because of the absence of any banking facilities other than those provided by a merchant's own operations.

By 1850, the China trade was being financed by American domestic products rather than foreign specie. Following the gold and silver finds in California and elsewhere in the West, specie figured prominently among those domestic products. The annual average export was $0.8 million in the 1850s, but it increased to $7.95 million in the 1870s, then $8.77 million in the 1880s, and $7.47 million in the 1890s.[22]

The Chinese-American tea trade gradually turned to various kinds of more sophisticated credit arrangements. Bills on London, both convenient and safe, steadily gained popularity among American and Chinese merchants. From 1826 on, great London banking houses such as the Barings, the Browns, and the "three W's" (the firms of Wiggins, Wildes, and Wilson) issued credits and advanced them to American merchants. The merchants sent the credits to American commission houses in China for the purchase of Chinese goods. The goods were shipped to merchants in the United States who proceeded to sell them, and who then paid off the principal and interest due in London. By the 1830s, however, bills on London were largely in the hands of the hong merchants, who accepted them from the American commission houses in China as payment for tea and silk. (The hong merchants often used these bills to purchase opium, woolens, and cotton goods from the British merchants.) Because of the introduction of bills on London, American export of specie to China fell from $US2,525,000 in 1827 to $456,000 in 1828, and dropped further to $80,000 in 1830 (see Table 6).

American merchants made increasingly heavy use of bills on London. In the 1820s and 1830s, American commission houses began to receive bills on London directly on their own accounts. In 1828, the ship *Danube* of Perkins & Co. sailed from Boston to Canton carrying "a letter of credit on the Barings of London for sixty thousand pounds."[23] American commission houses advanced their American clients a substantial share of the funds that their purchases required. Merchants in the United States, no longer obliged to borrow from London, had only to place their orders and agree to pay the cost of the goods as well as interest and commission charges. Commission houses drew bills for their clients on terms that would allow clients enough time to sell the goods and recover proceeds. The clients then paid the London bankers principal and interest, and the commission house the balance of the charges. This credit system, though involving greater risk for the commission house, facilitated expansion of the tea trade.

When, in the 1830s, massive imports of British opium gave China an unfavorable balance of trade, American merchants found that it was cheaper to buy bills of exchange with American cargoes sent to England than to obtain specie from the Spanish. During the years 1827–1833, nearly 9 million dollars worth of English bills were used by the American merchants to pay off their debts at Canton. In 1833, specie accounted for only one-seventh the sum of the American bills on England, and merchandise for almost two-thirds.[24]

In subsequent years, American merchants continued to use bills on London to finance their Chinese purchases. In his letter to Donald Matheson dated 19 December 1844, David Jardine noted the following situation at Canton: "I find some of the Yankees, including your friend Mr. [Edward] King [of Russell & Co.], are offering to sell their bills to Chinese whom they have been buying teas from."[25] During the 1850s, London banking houses continued to work directly with American agency houses in China, extending credits to prominent American houses such as Russell & Co. and Augustine Heard & Co. These credit arrangements enabled the houses in China to draw bills for shipping to anyone they might choose. American business was heavily dependent upon British credit. In 1860, for example, the Heard firm obtained 75 percent of its purchases on credits from London. The situation eased somewhat in later years, due

to the appearance of American cotton textiles and other manufactured goods, but, during the period 1871–1894, British credit
still accounted for one-third of American payments to China.[26]

Meanwhile, Americans developed their own credit arrangements with Chinese tea merchants. In mid-century, Chinese
merchants began to receive credits for tea purchases in the interior. Tea in Canton warehouses served as security for these loans.
In an agreement between Augustine Heard & Co. and some Chinese tea merchants at Shanghai in 1847, the American firm
agreed "to advance to such teamen money sufficient for their
personal expenses to any amount under one thousand dollars."
The advance was repaid when the tea was sold, with interest
accruing at 1 percent per month. Some agreements specified
that the Chinese merchants would sell the tea to the American
firm at a fixed price or guarantee it the right of "first refusal"
to buy at the market price. Having thus received advances,
Chinese merchants went to the tea districts and made contracts
with the growers. The price was arranged and a portion was
usually paid in advance. Sometimes American traders financed
the tea transport from the upcountry to the treaty ports. After
the mid-1870s, the system of advances to Chinese for upcountry
tea purchases declined, owing to American unwillingness to
assume the risk.[27]

Chinese merchants also received credits from native banks,
which were instrumental in financing upcountry purchases of
tea. These urban institutions made loans to local tea merchants
in the form of native bank orders. A widespread practice during
the 1860s and 1870s, such loans became rarer in the 1880s, due
to an increasingly cautious investment climate.

Marketing

The marketing of Chinese tea began, of course, in the tea districts
of China. Tea generally came in two kinds, green and black, de-
pending on the way the leaves were processed. In the manufacture of green tea, the fresh leaves were steamed and fired.
For black tea, fermentation was also needed. Black tea, generally
cheaper, included grades such as Souchong, Orange, Bohea,
Congou, and Pekoe. Of the green teas, Hyson, Hyson-skin,

Young Hyson, and Gunpowder were the major kinds. Though both green and black teas were used by Americans during the first half of the eighteenth century, in the years immediately after 1784, Bohea, the cheapest grade, dominated American cargoes. Later Souchong, a better black tea, came to the fore. After 1800, the proportion of green teas—especially Hyson and Young Hyson—began to increase, and, by 1810, green and black teas were imported in nearly equal amounts. By 1837, the green teas made up four-fifths of the total. The steadily increasing demand for better grades of tea reflected a growing discrimination in American taste and increasing ability to buy.[28]

American traders in China used advanced marketing techniques. They always employed expert tea tasters, who selected teas for export on the basis of color, flavor, bouquet, and body. Merchants planned their purchases carefully. The tea was packed in moisture-free chests for shipment to the United States. American merchants used the largest and fastest vessels available for the long-distance trade. The great era of the tea clippers, a romantic chapter in maritime history, lasted from the early 1830s to the 1850s. When sail gave way to steam after mid-century, American merchants immediately adopted the new time-saving technology.[29]

Most of the tea was landed at ports along the northeast coast. Boston was, of course, an important tea market during colonial times, and, by 1790, many other ports—Salem, Providence, Baltimore, Philadelphia, and New York, for example—also engaged in the trade. But Providence was dropping out by 1812. By the 1820s Salem had lost its early significance, Boston and Philadelphia were soon to decline, and Baltimore had become no more active than Providence. By this time, New York stood out as the most important distribution center for Chinese tea.[30]

The marketing of tea involved a series of attempts to capitalize on the public's sense of novelty. For example, Augustine Heard & Co., in collaboration with its Chinese comprador, developed a "new style of Souchong" at Foochow in 1862. (The manager told his Cantonese underling "to spare no pains in making the chop.") Sometimes the classifications of tea were artificially changed to stimulate demand. At first, tea was graded rather simply; the name of the tea on the chest—for example, "Souchong" or "Congou"—indicated the general grade, and "super-ior," "fine," "extra-fine," or "curious" designated the precise quality. But, in 1849, an American supercargo, wishing to give variety and novelty to his purchases, devised a great number of labels, such as "English Breakfast Tea," "Old Company's Con-gou," and the like. "English Breakfast" struck the fancy of the American public, and it is still popular today.[31]

Much of the tea exported from China in American bottoms ended up in countries other than the United States. Part went direct to its final destination; part was reexported from America. During the Napoleonic Wars, the proportion reexported was large, usually a third of the year's imports. In the 1804–1807 period, for instance, the amount imported was 23.7 million pounds, and the amount exported 7.7 million pounds. In 1803, more than one-half of the tea imported to America was reex-ported to Europe. After the War of 1812, the proportion de-clined to one-fourth or even one-tenth, because much tea was carried directly to foreign countries by American ships. Ameri-cans dominated the tea markets of Holland and Canada, for example, until the 1820s. After Britain nullified the Navigation Acts in 1850, American traders began carrying large amounts of Chinese tea direct to the British overseas territories. Moreover, American clipper ships bearing Chinese tea appeared frequently in London. Anglo-American commercial competition was intense during the mid-nineteenth century.[32]

CONSEQUENCES FOR ECONOMIC DEVELOPMENT

The tea trade dominated Chinese-American commercial relations during the eighteenth and nineteenth centuries, but China never accounted for a very large percentage of American foreign trade, and the percentage generally declined over time. In the early nineteenth century, China was responsible for about 5 percent, but the figure decreased to 3 percent by 1860. Its share dropped to a mere 1.86 percent in 1880 and to 1.75 percent in 1894. During the 1860s, China ranked seventh among foreign suppliers of the United States, and was the sixth largest purchaser of American goods. By 1885, China had dropped to eighteenth place as supplier and to fourteenth as purchaser. America's share in total Chinese foreign trade was also generally declining. In 1872, the American share was 8.46 percent; in 1877, 6.33 percent; in 1881, 6.5 percent; in 1889, 5.2 percent; and, in 1893, 6.4 percent. In spite of the relatively unimpressive figures, the Chinese-American tea trade worked some important influences on both countries.

Despite occasional losses, Chinese and American tea merchants generally made money. Though the overall profit is not known, the evidence indicates that the tea trade was highly lucrative. For example, the net profit from the *Empress of China* in 1784–1785 was estimated at $30,727—25 percent of the original investment. The net proceeds of the *Betsy* in 1797–1798 exceeded $120,000, and the profits came to $53,118.[33]

During the era of the tea clippers, the rate of return was even higher, due to the speed of the ships. The *Oriental*, in a single voyage in 1850, made a profit of $48,000, a sum that equaled two-thirds the cost of the ship. Another clipper ship, the *Rainbow*, paid for her cost two times over in just one trip. Many tea merchants, reaping large and quick profits, rose "from rags to riches." Some made fortunes overnight. Many made and lost several fortunes in this lucrative but unstable trade. Chinese tea merchants were frequently referred to as the "quick-fortune-makers." (*k'uai fa-ts'ai*).[34]

Many of the American traders were essentially merchant-adventurers whose sole aim was to amass great wealth within the shortest possible time. John P. Cushing, for example, returned from Canton to Boston in 1828, at the age of forty-one, with over $600,000. Then he retired, entrusting William Sturgis with the management of his funds. Many American traders, including Robert B. Forbes and Augustine Heard, had pressing financial difficulties at the time they went to China in pursuit of quick profit. John Murray Forbes, of Russell & Co., made a handsome profit of $150,000 in two years. Other early Russell partners—Samuel Russell, Philip Ammidon, John C. Green, and Joseph Coolidge—shared in the firm's net profit of around $100,000 in 1834, a typical year. We do not know the exact rate of returns enjoyed by Augustine Heard & Co., but John Heard, III, wrote in his diary that he received an average annual profit of $50,000 during the period 1847–1852 and even more in subsequent years. "On the whole," he wrote in 1857, "It was very profitable, running from $180,000 to $200,000 a year."[35]

Chinese tea merchants also amassed fortunes rather quickly. Houqua built up a fortune of 26 million silver dollars (approximately $US52 million) by 1834 which was, according to H. B. Morse, the largest mercantile fortune on earth. Thanks to the tea trade, Kinqua (Liang Ching-kuo), another hong merchant, rose from poverty to fabulous wealth. Many other Chinese tea merchants, such as Hsu Jun and Tong King-sing, also became "quick-fortune-makers."[36]

How did the Chinese and American tea merchants invest their capital? Many American traders transferred their profits from the China trade to American domestic investments. John P. Cushing, for example, after his return to Boston, continued to trade with China, principally for tea. But, finding excellent opportunities for investment at home, he soon decided to withdraw his capital altogether from the Oriental trade. Cushing invested in railroads, textile mills, and other modern enterprises.[37]

John Murray Forbes followed a similar pattern. He returned in 1837 to Boston, where he established himself as a China trader and Russell & Co.'s agent. Seizing upon the opportunities for economic development in the United States, Forbes invested his capital and managerial ability in industrial enterprises such as ironworks, steamships, and, above all, railroads. Forbes began buying the stocks of New England railroads in 1838. By July 1840, he had invested $55,000, probably drawn from funds his brother forwarded him from Canton. In 1846, Forbes headed a group that purchased the Michigan Central Railroad, a line crucial to the economic development of the Middle West. By 1861, Forbes, now a wealthy entrepreneur, had created the important Chicago, Burlington, and Quincy system. It is interesting to note that some of the capital Forbes invested in Western rails came directly from Houqua's family. (Houqua himself, who died in 1843, had maintained a keen interest in American railroads.)[38]

As well as stimulating railroad construction, profits from the tea trade led to important developments in shipbuilding. The commerce in tea required larger oceangoing ships, and directly stimulated the development of the clipper ship.[39] On the China coast, both American and Chinese tea merchants invested in the new steamship companies. Edward Cunningham was instrumental in organizing the Shanghai Steam Navigation Company in 1862, and many Chinese merchants engaging in Sino-American tea trades, such as Hsu Jun and Koofunsing, subscribed shares in this and similar firms. During the next decade, Hsu Jun's capital played a decisive role in forming the China Merchants' Steam Navigation Company, the first steamship company owned and operated by Chinese.[40]

American participation in the old China tea trade at Canton until 1842 and then in the early treaty-port trade in teas left an aura of profit and romance to later generations. But, just as the Civil War reduced American activity in China's trade, so the growth of Japanese and then Anglo-Indian tea exports reduced the importance of China teas in America. After the 1880s, the two countries retained not much more than the memory of a mutually profitable interchange that might sometime come again.

CHAPTER TWO

The Boom Years of the Fukien Tea Trade, 1842-1888

ROBERT P. GARDELLA

The domestic consequences of nineteenth-century China's involvement in world trade have hitherto received little attention from Western historians. A notable exception is the work of scholars in the continental Marxist tradition, which generalizes about the commercialization and specialization of late Ch'ing agriculture in response to the emergence of a global capitalist economy.[1] There is need, however, to move beyond generalities and consider specific cases, in this instance, the history of the Fukien "tea boom" from the 1850s to the 1880s.

After a lull from 1842 to 1852, Fukien's major ports became tea-exporting centers. Speculative cash cropping increased throughout the province as peasants and merchants quickly responded to the growing foreign demand for tea. The dramatic upsurge in commercial activity, in turn, meant additional revenue for financially hard-pressed provincial and central governments. The tea boom revitalized Fukien's fiscal administration, and taxes derived from the trade supported provincial self-strengthening efforts during the T'ung-chih Restoration after 1861. The boom's influence was, nonetheless, short-lived. Within three decades, competition from colonial tea plantations in India and Ceylon disrupted the Fukien tea trade and ended China's traditional dominance in the international tea market.[2]

FUKIEN'S OPENING TO FOREIGN TRADE, 1842–1855

The Anglo-Chinese Treaty of Nanking in 1842 included Amoy and Foochow among the five treaty ports opened to foreign trade and residence. While a respectable commerce with Western merchants sprang up quickly at Amoy, a decade passed before Foochow became anything more than a depot for opium smugglers. The city's estimated population of 600,000 in the mid-1840s included numerous gentry hostile to any foreign presence whatsoever.[3] The Tao-kuang Emperor (r. 1821–1850) had personally opposed the opening of Foochow to Western commerce. Though much tea was grown in northwest Fukien, and much had been exported through Canton in the preceding century, there was a tacit understanding among local officials not to permit tea exports from Foochow.[4] The British attributed Peking's reluctance to foster trade there to the machinations of the "Canton interest," the merchants and officials of Kwangtung who sought to confine external trade as much as possible to their own province.[5]

By the late 1840s, however, a monetary crisis spreading through southern China impelled Ch'ing officials to abandon their efforts to restrict Fukien's foreign trade. On the eve of the Taiping Rebellion, central and southeastern China were in the grip of a severe price deflation. The drain of silver to pay for imported opium appears to have been at least partially responsible. Rice prices fell, while the price of silver rose spectacularly. Since the sale of rice brought less silver with which to pay land taxes, the deflation automatically increased the effective tax burden on peasants. Business activities, employment, and income contracted. Tax riots broke out in Fukien, Chekiang, Kiangsi, Hupeh, and Hunan.[6] A logical remedy seemed to lie in encouraging the export trade, for more silk and tea exports would bring more imported silver into circulation, thus decreasing the price of silver and the excessive land-tax burden.

Moreover the Taiping Rebellion and various local disorders disrupted the overland trade routes along which Fukien tea traveled and was taxed on its way to Canton and Shanghai. In 1853, the British Vice-Consul at Foochow reported that the Fukien Provincial Treasurer had urged his superiors to implore the Hsien-feng Emperor (r. 1851–1860) to suspend the tea export prohibition "temporarily."[7] The prohibition was, in fact, ignored after 1853, for the economic and fiscal arguments in favor of direct trade were too strong. By 1855, Lü Ch'uan-sun, the Fukien Governor (1854–1857), was seeking imperial approval for what was clearly current provincial practice:

Because the Kwangtung rebels have invaded Kiangsi and Hunan, the tea merchants have not arrived. I am deeply apprehensive that the local people who make a living from tea will lose their livelihood and cause trouble, so I memorialize for permission to relax the maritime prohibition. . . . Last year when coming to my post I entered Fukien from Hokow, Kiangsi, and took the road through Chungan. Along the whole route I investigated so that I would understand [the situation]. After reaching Fukien, when I talked with officials and local gentry, I always earnestly tried to sort out their opinions. They all said that, since [the arrival of foreign merchants on the coast], the profit from Fukien tea had increased several times. Given the convenience of water transportation within the province and [direct] shipment to the sea, the costs of transport and the transit taxes in silver were reduced. The merchants' profits have subsequently multiplied, but government revenues have begun to dwindle.[8]

Referring specifically to the diminution of customs duties at Chungan and other tea markets in the interior of Fukien, Lü proposed raising additional revenue by setting up new barriers to tax tea merchants bringing their wares to the coast. "There are many tea merchants," he wrote, "whose profits are so great that taking one-tenth [of them] will do no harm." The Governor justified the taxes by pointing out the military expenditure required to hold the province, threatened as it was by

Taiping armies.[9] Lü's appeal reflected the idea of "enriching [the state] and strengthening [the military]" (*fu-ch'iang*), a concept that gained currency during the self-strengthening efforts of the following decades. Peking authorities apparently raised no further objections to the maritime export of Fukien tea.

Western merchants organized the first tea shipments from Foochow. The credit for pioneering belongs to the American agency house of Russell & Co., whose commercial operations extended back to the days of the old Canton trade. At Shanghai, by the early 1850s, the firm had become accustomed to sending Chinese agents into the interior to purchase tea, under the supervision of a J. N. A. Griswold.[10] He was well acquainted with Wu Chien-chang (Samqua), the acting taotai at Shanghai since 1851. When Triad uprisings and the Taiping threat temporarily interrupted tea shipments to Shanghai in 1853, Wu urged Griswold to procure his firm's tea via Foochow.[11] Despite British predictions of failure, Griswold's Chinese comprador succeeded in buying and shipping a cargo of tea from northwest Fukien through agents sent into the hinterlands. The tea proved to be "the same chops which the English merchants were accustomed to buy at Shanghai, and which had been bought in the country, conveyed to Foochow at 2 to 4 taels per picul less cost of carriage, and arrived in London in better condition than any shipment of the year."[12]

Russell's success encouraged other American and British firms to follow its lead. During the 1853–1854 tea season, Fukien exported 1,355,000 lbs. of tea to the United States and 5,950,000 lbs. to Great Britain. A year later the corresponding figures were 5,500,000 lbs. and 20,490,000 lbs.[13] Even pessimistic observers such as Robert Fortune were forced to take note of the rapid increase in tea exports from northern Fukien.[14] Though navigation of the approaches to Foochow was rather difficult, and the Min River hinterland did not offer the large potential market for foreign imports or the diversified exports of Shanghai and the Yangtze basin, the American Consul at Foochow reported in 1855:

Foochow is destined to be the second port in China, both in its imports and exports, and in its tea trade will even rival Shanghai. The Chinese, having once discovered their teas can be shipped with as much greater [*sic*] ease from here than from Canton, will not return to the old system, which owing to the troubles at Canton is entirely broken up.[15]

The Fukien tea boom had begun.

ORGANIZING THE TEA TRADE

At first, Western firms dominated the tea trade. In northern Fukien and Taiwan during the 1850s and 1860s, Western traders provided the financial and commercial apparatus necessary for the initial organization of the trade. Once commercial channels had been established and stabilized, however, the profitable business (except for special Russian operations) quickly was taken over by Chinese merchants. Moreover, it is noteworthy that Fukien never became like India or Ceylon. None of the Western firms operating in Fukien, Taiwan, or elsewhere in China bought extensive tracts of land, hired workers to grow tea on them, and then supervised its processing, controlling every phase of tea production, in the manner of the plantations later established in India and Ceylon. The treaty system made no provision for foreign enterprise to undertake such activities. Even if plantations had been legally authorized, the typical mid-nineteenth century Western firm was unlikely to have developed them in China. The Western trading house was a conservative commercial institution staffed by merchants who performed their operations within the existing structure of the Chinese economy. Neither their purposes nor their profits required reshaping the organization of Chinese tea production. Western firms did control the export and sale of tea abroad, a business Chinese merchants were ill-equipped to handle. In this way they influenced the activities of Chinese growers, processors, and merchants who furnished their tea. They continued to be essential middlemen linking Chinese sellers and overseas buyers.[16]

During the 1850s and early 1860s, the Fukien tea trade was in the hands of several agency houses. Also known as commission houses or China houses, these were the chief Western business institutions in the treaty ports. All the best known firms in the China trade, such as the American firms of Russell & Co., Augustine Heard & Co., and their British competitor, Jardine, Matheson & Co., were agency houses. These were diversified trading firms which usually made their profits by providing their clients with market information and advice, offering facilities for transfer of funds, and acting as agents for the purchase, sale, and shipment of goods.[17]

When Russell & Co. began shipping tea from Foochow in 1853, in effect it was diverting to that port trade that normally would have gone to Shanghai and Canton. Western firms at first sought to insure that sufficient tea would arrive at Foochow during each trading season. This compelled them to organize and finance the procurement of tea in the interior of Fukien and to bring it down river either fully processed or in a semi-finished state. The Foochow agency houses located their go-downs (warehouses) and offices in Nant'ai, a commercial suburb on the Min River directly south of the city walls. From here, agents were sent into the interior, generally under the supervision of compradors, under an arrangement variously known as the "contract system" or "upcountry purchases."[18] Warehouses were established in tea-growing regions, buyers were sent out to the periodic markets in the countryside, and the leaf was collected, processed, and packed. These novel ventures were attended by great risk, for the agency houses had no right by treaty to purchase produce in the interior. Any financial losses they incurred between January, when money was first sent into the hinterland, and May, when the first tea shipments arrived at Foochow, were written off without the possibility of restitution.[19] Under the Canton system, the East India Company had also invested large amounts of money in the interior, but the local disposition of these funds had always been controlled by distant Chinese middlemen.[20] The novelty of upcountry purchases lay in the fact that Western firms, even if only for a short time, involved themselves directly in rechanneling tea production and distribution in the countryside.

Substantial sums were committed each season to obtain Congou and Oolong tea from northern Fukien. In March 1856, for example, Augustine Heard & Co. sent 48,400 taels in "chopped" (locally assayed) silver dollars by riverboat up the Min to

Chiehshou, Chungan hsien, for Congous, and 9,200 taels for Oolongs. Four chests of Malwa opium were included in the payments.[21] In 1860, the same firm sent almost a quarter million silver dollars inland, which bought about 50,000 half-chests of Pekoe, Oolong, and Souchong tea.[22] Other agency houses made much larger investments. In 1855, Jardine and another British firm, Dent & Co., each sent about $400,000 upcountry (Jardine was reputed to be the largest tea producer at Foochow from 1855 into the 1860s).[23] Three-fourths of these funds seem to have gone to defray the cost of fresh tea leaves. Of 124,324 taels expended in 1857 at Chiehshou by Heard's comprador, 100,396 taels were used to buy leaves. Of the remainder, 9,000 taels were paid as wages to processing workers and supervisors; 1,500 as rental for six buildings used as tea manufactories; 1,200 taels for iron pans, fireplaces, and processing tools; 2,820 for coolie porterage and transportation; 3,856 for tea boxes and lead lining; and 3,615 taels for inland taxes and bribes.[24]

The compradors were the key figures in the upcountry purchase system. In contrast to the variety of roles they played at other treaty ports such as Shanghai, the Foochow compradors' chief function was to obtain tea. Since much tea was purchased in a semi-processed state, they also supervised the refiring of tea in the premises of the Western hongs at Nant'ai. These men were invariably Cantonese, reflecting the long experience of Canton in the export trade.[25] Through building up a network of personal business connections, compradors could insure that their firms obtained their tea inventories. As Heard's 1866 report notes:

... the comprador has secured for one of his agents in the country a man who used to be with "Ahone" years ago, and who was one of the first who commenced tea business at Foochow. This man is so well known in the country that he will be able to influence teamen that we otherwise could not get at. He goes upcountry tomorrow or next day, and will go from place to place visiting teamen, in order to get together as large a connection as possible.

The same report also reveals that the comprador could expect support from one or two wealthy tea suppliers in the interior.[26]

The upcountry system of procuring tea, however, became out-moded in the early 1860s. By this time Foochow's development as the tea emporium for all of northern Fukien eliminated the risk and expense involved in carrying on business in the interior. Tea prices at Foochow were now generally lower than those in some of the most frequented upcountry districts, and ample supplies of tea were forthcoming through indigenous marketing channels during the trading season.[27] A group of Foochow tea brokers appeared and began to replace the compradors as inter-mediaries between tea-sellers and foreign exporters. Foreign firms continued to contract for tea consignments in advance through the brokers or compradors. Tea sellers became depen-dent on the agency houses for commercial credit and storage facilities, and were often required to give their foreign creditors the option of first purchase of the new crop.[28] Since they con-trolled the major source of capital for financing the trade, the China houses monopolized the Foochow tea market until the late 1860s, when alternative sources of credit began to be avail-able from newly established banks, such as the Foochow branch of the Hongkong and Shanghai Bank. This made it possible for smaller dealers to enter the tea market and stimulated competi-tion among tea buyers.[29]

Tea-purchasing was a highly competitive and somewhat spec-ulative enterprise. Although advances to Chinese tea merchants gave foreign buyers some control over their inventories, still much tea was bought on the open market. Firms had to esti-mate the quantity and quality of tea that would arrive during the spring and summer months. They had to determine when to "open the market," or close deals with Chinese brokers when the latter had arrived at some reasonable price.[30]

Like the old East India Company, Western firms in China still relied on skilled tea tasters (ch'a-shih) to evaluate potential purchases. The process worked as follows. Samples of tea ("musters") packed in lead-lined wooden chests were sent to the firms by brokers. If the tea taster declared that the tea "passed muster," an exchange rate was agreed upon, purchases were made final, and tea was shipped.[31]

Nevertheless, agency houses did not always buy wisely. Mar-ket information transmitted by mail was at best imperfect and dated; losses were unavoidable if the home market price for a certain type of tea fell below its selling price in China.[32] This problem persisted until the advent of the telegraph in the 1870s. Purchasing orders could then be sent directly to independent agents at Foochow, which diminished the need to deal through the old China houses.[33]

The development of the clipper ship in the mid-nineteenth century proved a great stimulus to the Foochow tea trade. Foochow was both the treaty port closest to a great tea-producing region and the one furthest south on the coastal shipping lanes. Tea could be shipped from Foochow some five or six weeks sooner than from Shanghai or Canton, and so the clippers could sail from the port with the new season's tea before the southwestern monsoons began.[34] During the 1850s, American and British clippers competed vigorously for the Foochow trade, but, by the following decade, British ships dominated the lucrative Foochow-to-London route, which placed a particular premium on speed.[35]

Foochow's tea market assumed a frenetic aspect in late spring as buyers and shippers sought to get their cargoes away as quickly as possible. When one firm "opened the market," its competitors immediately began to buy at the going market prices to avoid being out-maneuvered. In forty-eight hours the tea chests were weighed, labeled, and loaded onto lighters (small, well-caulked junks designed to keep the chests dry). These craft made the dozen-mile down-river voyage from Nant'ai to Pagoda Anchorage, where the clippers awaited them. Three or four clippers with the fastest passage records were chosen as the "going ships," the first ones to be loaded with chests.[36] Loading the vessels, a task performed entirely by Foochow stevedores, was a rapid and ingenious operation. After the ballast had been arranged (most ships arrived in ballast, there being little demand for imports at Foochow), a "ground chop" of low-quality tea was laid in to protect the more valuable teas from bilge water. Chests were then laid down in successive tiers, jammed so tightly together that, when loading was completed, they formed virtually a solid mass within the ship's hold.[37] The larger British clippers could load a million and a quarter pounds of tea, and their American counterparts could carry even more.[38]

There were obvious risks involved in a trade that placed such emphasis on speed. Much perfectly good tea that arrived tardily on the London market sometimes had to be sold at a loss. In October 1869, Matheson & Co., London, informed Jardine-Matheson & Co., Hong Kong, of the current poor market situation and suggested that purchases be reduced, as "experience has shown how difficult it is to get any attention paid to teas that are not of recent import, a fact which disposes merchants rather to accept a present loss than, by holding over their teas, to incur in nineteen cases out of twenty a still heavier."[39] As compared with the days of the East India Company, however, the quickened pace of the trade benefited the English consumer by increasing the turnover of goods.

The United Kingdom, of course, was the leading market for Fukien's (and China's) teas. Between 1840 and 1860, English per capita consumption of tea grew by 100 percent; from 1860 to 1880, it grew by 68 percent.[40] In addition to the commerce with England, a sizeable trade developed between Foochow and Australia. The rapid settlement of that continent by immigrants from the United Kingdom created a new market of tea drinkers. Per capita tea consumption in Australia was among the highest in the Anglo-Saxon world.[41] The third great consumer of Fukien tea was the United States, which imported mostly black tea from Foochow and Oolong from Amoy (and later from Taiwan). The volume of tea shipments from Foochow to these three markets during the period 1856–1866 is illustrated in Table 7.

Foochow's tea trade continued to expand during the 1870s. The value of tea shipments rose from 17,593,000 silver dollars in 1870–1871 to 29,533,000 dollars in 1878–1879. The Fukien capital now exported more tea than any other treaty port. While Shanghai's exports fell from 670,000 piculs in 1872 to 536,000 piculs in 1880, Foochow's climbed from 631,000 to 726,000 piculs.[42] From the late 1860s to the early 1880s, Foochow enjoyed its best years, as can be seen in Table 8, which compares black tea exports from Foochow to the total black tea and total tea exports of all China during the same period.[43]

Amoy tea exports lagged far behind Foochow's. The tea-growing hinterland of southeastern Fukien was much smaller

TABLE 7 Foochow Tea Exports, 1856–1866
(in pounds)

	United Kingdom	United States	Australia	Total[b]
1856–57	21,396,500	7,435,600	3,735,500	35,280,000
1857–58	21,813,300	6,259,300	2,684,200	32,050,300
1858–59	18,227,300	6,701,700	4,376,600	29,305,600
1859–60	26,472,500	8,615,400	5,363,700	41,348,600
1860–61	36,507,700	11,293,500	11,797,200	61,666,500
1861–62	35,417,650	7,215,010	8,094,944	55,713,433
1862–63	45,002,481	227,930	2,352,405	52,316,780
1863–64	46,152,936	6,966,702	8,037,750	63,468,298
1864–65	45,248,390	4,763,830	9,127,246	62,951,916
1865–66	44,000,000[a]	6,206,910	9,735,272	65,545,036

Sources: Great Britain, Parliament, *Sessional Papers, House of Commons*, Vol. LXVII (1867), Vol. LXVIII (1868), pp. 648, 654.

Notes: [a]United Kingdom figure is an estimate.
[b]Includes tea exports to all markets.

than that in the north, the climate was less suited to tea-growing, and, excepting the teas of Anch'i hsien, tea produced there was less popular overseas. Nevertheless, tea exports became important to the economy of the interior hill country (see Table 9). As the United States Consul at Amoy wrote in 1874 as he was visiting a region along the Chiulung River a week's distance from Amoy, "Although but a small proportion of the land is devoted to the culture of tea, it is by far the most important product of the district. The annual crop amounts to about 7,500,000 pounds, of which nine-tenths is sent to the United States."[44]

By the late 1870s, however, Amoy was relegated to the role of reexporting center for the rapidly developing tea industry of northern Taiwan, a frontier region whose humid uplands proved ideal for tea cultivation. The value of Taiwan tea shipments rose from 13,673 silver dollars in 1865 to 4,312,748 in 1885. The island became the second most important tea-exporting area in Fukien province (see Table 10 below). Oolong was virtually the only tea produced in Taiwan, and almost all of it was shipped to foreign markets, particularly the United States.[45]

Foreign enterprise played a catalytic role in the development

TABLE 8 Foochow and China Black Tea Exports, and Total
Tea Exports, 1866-1885
(in pounds)

	Foochow	All China Black	All China Total
1867	72,699,000	136,325,000	174,762,000
1868	80,031,000	156,408,000	191,653,000
1869	77,128,000	161,329,000	203,224,000
1870	64,472,000	143,374,000	182,476,000
1871	84,778,000	181,013,000	223,174,000
1872	83,923,000	188,860,000	236,075,000
1873	73,017,000	169,442,000	215,061,000
1874	86,982,000	192,052,000	230,755,000
1875	87,248,000	191,387,000	241,794,000
1876	73,150,000	188,195,000	234,479,000
1877	80,332,000	206,416,000	254,030,000
1878	86,317,000	201,894,000	251,237,000
1879	81,795,000	202,559,000	264,271,000
1880	96,558,000	220,913,000	278,901,000
1881	88,179,000	217,721,000	284,221,000
1882	97,230,000[a]	214,396,000	268,261,000
1883	84,173,000	208,943,000	264,271,000
1884	85,786,000	208,012,000	268,128,000
1885	92,843,000	215,194,000	283,157,000

Sources: All China black and total tea figures from Hsiao Liang-lin, *China's Foreign Trade Statistics, 1864-1949,* Table 3, p. 117; figures have been converted from piculs to pounds. Foochow figures from China, Imperial Maritime Customs, *Reports on Trade,* 1871-1872, p. 153; "A History of the External Trade of China, 1834-81," note 65, p. 142; U.S. Department of State, *Commercial Relations of the United States: Reports from the Consuls of the U.S.,* No. 94, 21 March 1884, No. 122, 17 March 1885, No. 152, 12 March 1886; Great Britain, Parliament, *Sessional Papers, House of Commons,* Vol. LXXXII (1882), p. 18; all rounded to the nearest thousand.

Note: [a]Foochow 1882 figure refers to 1881-1882 season.

of Taiwan's tea industry. Mid-Ch'ing immigrants from Fukien had transplanted tea shrubs from the Wuyi mountains to the Taipei basin, and, by the nineteenth century, Taiwan tea was being shipped by native craft to Foochow.[46] In 1861, Robert Swinhoe, British Consul at the newly opened port of Tansui, brought these shipments to the attention of his government, suggesting that foreigners should take initiatives to promote tea-growing on the island.[47] Four years later, a British merchant,

TABLE 9 Amoy Tea Exports, 1858–1879
        (in pounds)

1858–59	4,054,049	1870	9,487,050
1859–60	4,393,865	1871	7,659,163
1860–61	7,198,678	1872	8,906,427
1861–62	5,199,164	1873	11,287,885
1862–63	5,335,900	1874	9,096,709
1863–64	6,224,435	1875	8,834,392
1865	5,817,686	1876	8,246,665
1866	7,887,964	1877	12,156,732
1867–68	10,670,267	1878	9,305,611
1869	11,433,877	1879	8,597,918

Sources: China, Imperial Maritime Customs, *Reports on Trade,* 1864, p. 53; *Reports on Trade,* 1866, p. 35; *Returns of Trade,* 1867, p. 70; *Reports on Trade,* 1878, pp. xlviii–li, Table 45; *Reports on Trade,* 1879, pp. 48–49.

John Dodd, came across some wild tea plants while exploring the camphor trees in the hills near Tansui. The plants aroused his interest, and he relates:

On making inquiries I found that between Kelung [*sic*] and Banka [Wan-hua, now the western sector of Taipei], and to the southwest of the latter town, small patches of tea were cultivated in the gardens of farmers, but that it was grown principally for home consumption. All the tea I could get I bought up, and finding that it fetched a good price in Macao, I at once made loans to the farmers through my comprador for the purpose of extending the cultivation, and also imported slips of the tea plant from Amoy.

Dodd then began a small tea-firing business at Wan-hua and, as it prospered, moved to larger quarters at Tataoch'eng (now part of riverfront Taipei).[48] His comprador, Li Ch'un-sheng, an Amoyese from a poor family, encouraged local peasants and instructed them in how to cultivate and process their tea. Li eventually went into business on his own, becoming quite wealthy as a tea and camphor exporter.[49] Although other tea merchants from Amoy and Foochow at first regarded the development of tea cultivation on Taiwan with apprehension, it was not long before some of them (especially the Amoyese) came to the Taipei basin, buying property and erecting tea-

TABLE 10   Tea Exports from Taiwan (Tansui), 1865–1885[a]
(pounds)[b]

1865	180,859	1876	7,793,158
1866	179,423	1877	9,159,129
1867	268,693	1878	10,618,530
1868	448,704	1879	11,249,843
1869	441,999	1880	11,969,959
1870	1,394,457	1881	12,759,814
1871	1,967,045	1882	11,954,486
1872	2,581,638	1883	13,101,728
1873	2,065,194	1884	12,393,070
1874	3,255,963	1885	16,237,179
1875	5,500,181		

Source: Taiwan Tea Exporters' Association, The Historical Brevities of Taiwan Tea Export, 1865–1865, table facing p. 58.

Notes: [a]James W. Davidson, The Island of Formosa, p. 395, gives an alternate set of figures.
[b]Figures have been converted from kilograms to pounds.

firing houses, renting shops and warehouses, and bringing capital to finance tea production.[50]

Foreign firms dominated tea processing and the export trade at first. By 1873, branches of the British houses of Tait & Co., Boyd & Co., Brown & Co., and Ellis & Co., had joined the Dodd firm as Taiwan tea exporters.[51] The foreigners refired tea at their own premises in Tataoch'eng after purchasing it as crudely processed tea (mao-ch'a) from the growers. The firing rooms were adjacent to the tea hongs' godowns, and contained from 50 to 300 fireplaces. Oolong tea was placed in baskets above the fireplaces, then slowly roasted over charcoal, after which it was packed in lead-lined wooden chests. The critical need for lead and charcoal to prepare the island's tea shipments was illustrated during the Sino-French War of 1884–1885. Charcoal temporarily became scarce and costly because the Hakka hillmen, who ordinarily made a living as charcoal burners, were away fighting the French invasion of northern Taiwan. Meanwhile, lead was declared contraband of war by local authorities, and its importation was prohibited (lead was a major import at all of Fukien's tea ports).[52] The shortage of lead during the war was so serious that "every pound which had been used for less urgent purposes was requisitioned for tea. Chinese packers bought up leaden candlesticks and joss ornaments, and even the fishermen parted with the leaden weights attached to their nets."[53]

Chinese entrepreneurs soon gained control of the business of refiring and packing Taiwan tea, leaving only the actual export operations in foreign hands. In 1876, 39 Chinese firms were involved in preparing shipments for the buyer's market at Amoy. Nineteen of these were owned by Taiwanese, 14 by Amoyese, 5 by Cantonese, and 1 by natives of Swatow.[54]

Taiwan's tea trade was sustained by capital provided by foreign and native banks. Beginning in 1869, branches of foreign exchange banks—the Oriental Banking Corporation, the Chartered Mercantile Bank of London, India, and China, and the Hongkong and Shanghai Bank—were established at Foochow and Amoy.[55] The Hongkong and Shanghai Bank's Amoy branch was especially active in financing the expansion of Taiwan tea exports. Foreign export firms borrowed capital from this bank at 6 percent annual interest, half the normal rate of 12 percent. They then loaned these funds either directly or through their compradors to the Taiwan tea manufactories (*ch'a-kuan* or *ch'a-chuang*), giving them a claim on the latter's tea output during the next trading season. The exporters also utilized the services of *ma-chen-kuan* ("merchant firms," *ma-chen* being a transliteration of "merchant") as middlemen in these transactions.[56]

Ma-chen-kuan were small Chinese firms combining brokerage and lending activities. They were managed by men from Amoy, Canton, or Swatow, and they represented their clients by maintaining offices on Taiwan. Cantonese predominated, since many of them held property on the mainland and were good credit risks. The 20 *ma-chen-kuan* existing by the 1890s had assets ranging in value from $US 5,000 to $50,000. After they had borrowed money from foreign firms at 1 percent per month interest, they lent it to the tea manufactories. Eighty percent of the *ch'a-kuan*'s tea would be covered by the loan, the remaining 20 percent to be paid for when the consignment was sold on the Amoy market. The *ch'a-kuan* were obliged to sell only through the *ma-chen-kuan* from which they had borrowed. If the *ma-chen-kuan* managers required additional capital, they could obtain loans directly from the Hongkong and Shanghai Bank or local *ch'ien-chuang* (money banking shops). During a busy season, these managers could command $US 200,000 in working capital, or as much as a million dollars if they were willing to mortgage their own property.[57]

Whether borrowed from foreign firms, *ma-chen-kuan,* or independently from other native banks (called *hui-tui-kuan* or "remitting banks"), most funds obtained by the *ch'a-kuan* were subsequently readvanced to tea growers.[58] Peasant growers usually processed their raw leaves into *mao-ch'a,* which they sold to local tea-buying agents (*ch'a-fan* or *ch'a-k'o*). The latter either traded on their own account or acted on behalf of the *ch'a-kuan.* Transactions between the growers and buyers could proceed in several ways. Straight cash purchases involved no advances to the growers, who sold their tea at current market rates. Growers could also take partial payment for their tea at time of purchase, and receive the balance on the resale of their produce to the *ch'a-kuan.* If cash advances were given the growers, they were obliged to turn over their tea to the buyer at a discount of 10 percent less than the market price, plus interest of 1 percent per month on the borrowed capital.[59] The extension of such crop loans must have enabled growers of even small means to participate in tea production, though at obviously less advantageous terms than the open market afforded.

Still another institution developed at this time to facilitate tea marketing, the *ch'a-chan* or "tea godown." On Taiwan the *ch'a-chan* seems only to have bought and stored *mao-ch'a* for resale to the *ch'a-kuan,* but, in mainland Fukien and elsewhere, they became brokerage and warehousing agencies linking the tea manufactories to buyers for the domestic or foreign market. In the latter capacity they also became involved in financing the tea manufactories' operations.[60]

The organization of the tea industry and trade in mainland Fukien was similar to that on Taiwan, and functioned in much the same way. The major difference was that Fukien tea was distributed domestically as well as abroad, whereas Taiwan exported virtually all its tea. The channels for domestic tea marketing in Fukien roughly paralleled those of the export trade, but the process of financing the domestic trade was less complicated.[61]

Several Russian firms became involved in the Fukien tea trade during the 1870s and 1880s. Their production of brick tea gave them a unique role in the province's tea industry. For over half a century prior to 1850, increasing quantities of Fukien tea had been shipped overland to Russia. After the second treaty settlements (1858–1861), Russian merchants came directly to Hankow to buy tea for transport to Kiakhta on the Sino-Russian border. By 1868, Russian firms had already established three brick-tea factories in the vicinity of Hankow.[62] Brick tea, as the name indicates, consists of black or green tea ground into a powder (tea dust), and then formed by pressure molding into hard, portable, rectangular slabs. A few wealthy Russian firms controlled its manufacture and distribution. The opening of the Suez Canal in 1869 stimulated brick-tea production, for the Russian market could now be supplied more quickly by sea.[63] There were six Russian tea factories in the British concession at Hankow by 1878. Three of these employed steam-powered machinery. Russians were thus the first to introduce mechanized technology to the modern Chinese tea industry, though their innovations had no impact on the production of leaf tea.[64]

In the 1870s, Russian firms decided to set up branch factories in Fukien. The province was traditionally one of Russia's sources of fine tea, and Foochow was hundreds of miles closer than Hankow to the sea.[65] At this time Fukienese tea merchants had no use for the tea dust accumulated during leaf-tea manufacture. Dust often constituted part of the tea shipments from the interior, and was regarded by Western buyers as a nuisance. Large quantities of it were usually dumped into a stream near the city of Foochow.[66] In 1872, the firm of Ivanoff and Company set up Fukien's first brick-tea factory at Foochow, buying up the black tea dust and producing 800 baskets (about 100,000 pounds) of brick tea that year. The next year, the same firm established another factory at Chienning, in the very heart of the black-tea-producing region. This venture was prompted by the significant difference between the likin tax on brick tea and that on tea dust. Tea dust was taxed at the same rate as leaf tea (over 1 tael per picul), and brick tea at only 3 cash per picul. In addition, the export duty on tea dust was 2.5 taels per picul, but that on brick tea was only 8 cash per picul.[67] It obviously was cheaper for the Russians to manufacture and ship brick tea from the interior rather than concentrate all their factories at Foochow.

The number of tea factories rapidly increased, as did their output (see map, p. 51). In 1874, a third Russian factory was founded at Hsich'in near Yenping, and the next year another firm set up a factory at Nanyak'ou near Chienning. Chinese compradors now began to found their own manufactories to compete with the Russians (five in all were established in the 1870s). By 1875, the two Russian firms had operations at Hsich'in, Nanyak'ou, Chienning, and Foochow, and produced 36,403 baskets of brick tea (about 4,840,000 pounds), while 7,000 baskets were made by Chinese firms. Still a third Russian firm began operations at Foochow and T'aip'ing in Chienning prefecture in 1876.[68] These plants were smaller than the great Hankow establishments, which employed around 5,000 Chinese workers by the mid-1890s. Yet, up to 1,000 laborers were said to have been employed at the Russian factories in Fukien. Some of these plants used steam-powered machines to mold the tea bricks, but most of the work was apparently done by manual presses.[69]

Russian success in operating factories in the interior of the province contrasts with the inability of other foreigners to penetrate the countryside. British and American merchants now bought their tea on the Foochow market instead of preparing and shipping it from inland. Western missionaries (the only other foreigners actively interested in going upcountry) had experienced considerable trouble in propagating the Gospel in interior cities such as Yenping and Chienning.[70] In March 1876, a Foochow treaty-port journal, noting the toleration of Russian business activities inland, suggested that "it would be greatly to the advantage of both foreign merchants and the Chinese, if more of this direct intercourse with producers in the tea growing regions could be established. It would, no doubt, meet with strong opposition from Cantonese brokers, who are interested in keeping for themselves a lion's share of the profits." Cantonese brokers were allegedly opposed even to inland

FIGURE 1   Brick Tea Manufactories in Nineteenth-Century
Fukien

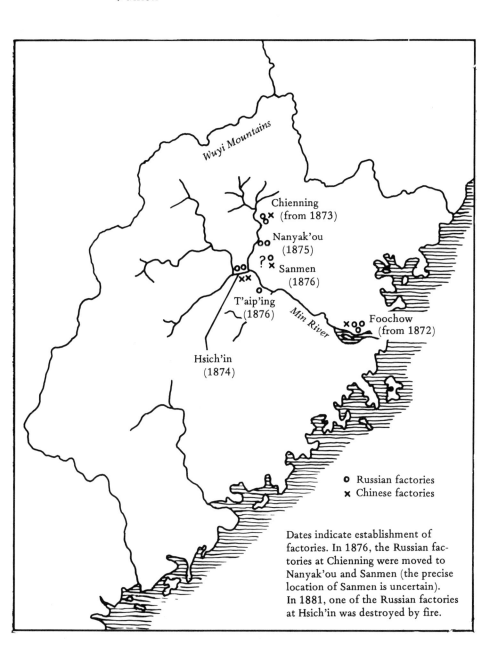

Dates indicate establishment of
factories. In 1876, the Russian factories at Chienning were moved to
Nanyak'ou and Sanmen (the precise
location of Sanmen is uncertain).
In 1881, one of the Russian factories
at Hsich'in was destroyed by fire.

evangelism for fear that, "if missionaries were established there, merchants would follow, and their [own] operations would be gone."[71]

The Chinese clearly showed favoritism to Russian firms. For example, Russian merchants often acquired inland property for factory sites, and their title papers received official verification.[72] The official rationale for this probably lay in the special nature of the brick-tea industry and trade itself. Both the market and technology for the business were exclusively Russian, and, in order to promote the trade, Chinese authorities permitted Russian entrepreneurs more latitude than they granted other foreigners under the treaty system. Russian involvement in the Fukien tea trade was compatible with local economic interests and Chinese sovereignty.[73]

In order to manage their factories, Russian merchants had to learn the Chinese language and how to operate without the services of native treaty-port middlemen.[74] However, local xenophobia sometimes made it hazardous for Russians to work in certain areas of the interior. Two factories at Chienning were shifted to Nanyak'ou and Sanmen in 1876 because of the opposition of Chienning's inhabitants, who threatened to burn them down. In 1881, a notorious incident took place at Hsich'in, where Piatkoff, Molchanoff & Co. had a factory employing 200 Chinese workers under the supervision of a foreign manager. In this case, the factory was destroyed by fire while local ruffians assaulted the workers and made away with several thousand dollars in cash.[75] But such isolated events had little impact on the development of the brick-tea trade in Fukien.

The volume of brick-tea exports from Foochow and the other treaty ports (Hankow and Kiukiang) where it was produced during the 1870s and early 1880s can be seen in Table 11 below. It is evident that Foochow's share of total brick-tea exports was declining. From 1876 to 1879, Fukien supplied at least one-third of the total, but less than one-sixth in 1885. In 1891, a number of large Russian firms closed several factories in Foochow and concentrated their businesses in Hankow and Kiukiang. The retreat from Fukien is noteworthy, for, before 1895,

TABLE 11 Brick Tea Exports from Foochow and All China,
1867–1885
(pounds)

	Foochow	All China
1867	–	8,645,000
1868	–	7,049,000
1869	–	9,842,000
1870	–	8,379,000
1871	–	11,172,000
1872	96,691	12,901,000
1873	475,209	14,231,000
1874	1,927,835	9,975,000
1875	6,244,882	22,211,000
1876	7,088,634	20,482,000
1877	6,924,911	19,684,000
1878	9,504,313	25,802,000
1879	13,634,362	36,708,000
1880	–	30,989,000
1881	6,689,501	32,851,000
1882	6,684,580	29,127,000
1883	4,423,116	29,127,000
1884	3,466,893	32,585,000
1885	5,768,891	37,240,000

Sources: Hisao Liang-lin, *China's Foreign Trade Statistics*, Table 3, p. 117, converted from piculs to pounds. For Foochow figures, see the following: China Imperial Maritime Customs, *Reports on Trade*, 1878, pp. xlviii–li; *Reports on Trade*, 1879, pp. 48–49; *Reports on Trade*, 1881, p. 13; Great Britain, Parliament, *Sessional Papers, House of Commons*, LXXII, 15; U.S. Department of State, *Commercial Relations of the U.S.*, No. 94, 21 March 1884, No. 122, 17 March 1885, No. 152, 12 March 1886.

the Russian brick-tea industry was second only to shipbuilding and repair among the most substantial foreign investments in China.[76] Fukien's loss of Russian investment is clearly attributable to competition from established centers of brick-tea production elsewhere in China. Fukien brick tea apparently lacked the strong flavor of the Hankow product, which appealed to Russian consumers.[77] Heavier likin duties in Fukien may also have contributed to the shift.

IMPACT OF THE TEA EXPORT BOOM
ON THE FUKIEN ECONOMY

The rapid growth of the tea trade had a pronounced effect upon Fukien's economy. Tea cultivation was intensified in the northwestern and southern regions of the province, where it had already been established, and it also spread into new areas such as northeastern Fukien and northern Taiwan. Good prices induced peasants to plant tea, and cash advances facilitated expanded production. Patterns of land use changed as areas other than the Wuyi mountains began to specialize in tea growing. This was particularly true in northern Taiwan. Labor flowed from one region of the province to another, and from neighboring provinces into Fukien, as additional manpower was drawn into the tea industry. As we have seen, Chinese merchants and native banks became involved in organizing and helping to finance the trade. In a surprisingly short time, land, men, and money were mobilized to support tea production at an unprecedented high level.

Increased tea cropping was possible with a change in land utilization. Either land previously planted to rice or other crops was replanted with tea, or waste or wooded land was newly planted to tea. Evidence of both practices exists for the mainland and Taiwan. In June 1859, the U.S. Consul at Foochow remarked that tea was being planted on land formerly reserved for rice.[78] There is little to indicate that the substitution of tea for rice cultivation persisted in the Foochow area, however. To keep it going would have depended not only upon the profitability of tea-growing but upon the regular availability of cheap rice imports to feed a densely populated region. Specialization in tea and dependence on imported rice were not unusual in the frontier setting of northern Taiwan, however. Surplus rice, grown elsewhere on the island or imported from the mainland, seems to have been readily obtainable, facilitating the extension of tea cultivation.[79]

In the T'aoyuan Plateau in northwest Taiwan (see map, p. 55), the conversion of rice land to tea cultivation was so extensive that such properties were given special tax consideration during the island-wide cadastral survey and land tax reassessment

FIGURE 2 Areas of Tea Production in Fukien and Taiwan, 1842–1888

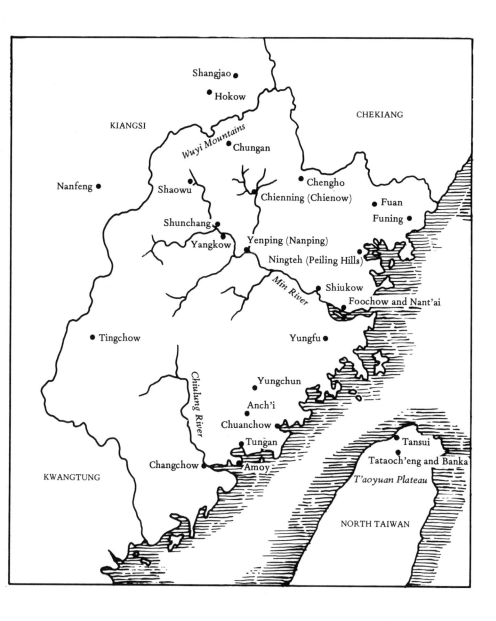

begun by Governor Liu Ming-ch'uan in 1886.[80] Over 80 percent of these contiguous tracts of upland had been planted to tea by the 1890s, many of them being tenant-farmed estates containing hundreds of hectares.[81] In the hilly region encompassing the rest of northern Taiwan, on the other hand, tea was usually grown in small terraced plots around peasant villages, with only 25 percent of the village land in tea (and 50 percent in rice).[82]

The degree of specialization in tea thus varied considerably from one region of northern Taiwan to another, but the rapid development of tea cultivation there is beyond doubt. Scrub land and wooded hill country that had hitherto been uncultivated were given over to tea gardens, which soon encircled the Taipei basin. Cleared slope land that had initially been planted to indigo and sweet potatoes was quickly converted to tea.[83] The process was not without its hazards, however. Fierce aboriginal tribesmen inhabiting the interior hills forcibly contested Chinese encroachments. The settlement of such areas required special arrangements to guarantee the security of cultivators.[84]

By the late 1880s, tea planting had increased in Fukien as well as on Taiwan. Pien Pao-ti, Governor General of Fukien and Chekiang (1888–1892), noted disapprovingly that, in the northwestern prefectures of Yenping, Chienning, and Shaowu, the gains from the tea trade induced rural people to "scrape off the soil and search for cliffs" on which to plant tea, leading to soil erosion in these areas.[85] Four decades earlier, the local scholar Chiang Heng voiced similar concern about the spread of tea cultivation in the mountains. Chiang worried that the influx of people to the tea-growing areas of northwest Fukien would exacerbate social tensions, as "bandits" and "unregistered vagrants" gathered to rob and disturb the peace. The increased population placed too great a burden on local rice supplies, leading to food shortages and high rice prices. Finally, Chiang alleged that erosion from improper tea-growing on slope lands further diminished rice production in the lowlands.[86] Pien and Chiang advocated curbing and eventually eliminating tea production in the northwest.

Specialization in tea, long a feature of the Wuyi mountains, now spread to other localities in northern and eastern Fukien.

In the 1880s, a survey sponsored by the Imperial Maritime Customs found that 9 out of 10 families in the village of Yangkow in Shunch'ang hsien, Yenping prefecture, grew tea on newly cleared mountain land. Twenty to 30 percent of the farm households in the same district were engaged in tea cultivation.[87] This situation was similar to what was happening in the hill country of northern Formosa.

In 1861, a foreign visitor to the Peiling hills, less than a day's journey northeast of Foochow, noticed the beginnings of tea-growing in that area.[88] By the 1880s, about 11,500 families were engaged in tea-farming in that region and the adjacent Tungling hills, producing around 28,400 piculs (3,777,200 pounds) per year. An 1888 survey taken in the Peiling area (Ningteh hsien) reveals that some peasants grew sweet potatoes, farmed paddy, or raised bamboo to supplement their earnings from tea, while others, lacking sufficient arable land for other crops, lived only upon tea cultivation. In Ningteh, four to four and one-half months were spent in growing and processing tea.[89]

The production of black tea for export also increased at this time in the Funing district of northeastern Fukien, as it did in neighboring Fuan hsien, as described in a local gazetteer of 1884:

With the abrogation of the maritime interdict, foreign vessels [arrived] and greedy merchants [came] to trade. Tea and opium [were planted] in the wastelands, in order to realize a threefold profit in the markets.[90]

In southeastern Fukien, forest cover was removed from hills to make way for tea bushes.[91] But tea there was clearly subordinate to paddy agriculture. An American visitor in 1874 was "astonished at the small proportion of land actually growing tea," for "the mountain tops are terraced and planted with rice as far up as water can be procured for irrigation, and only the steeper places and tops devoted to tea culture."[92]

Tenant farming of tea seems to have been rather common. Chiang Heng observed that, in northwestern Fukien, there were "those who rent mountain land to the 'guest households' (*k'o-hu*), who cultivate tea."[93] Accounts of the opening up of

mountain land for cultivation in Shunchang hsien and the Yenping area indicate that some other forms of joint proprietorship
and risk-sharing also existed in the northwest.[94]

Small-scale cultivation of mountain land was the rule in mainland Fukien. Mountain lands were by custom measured more
casually than paddy or lowland fields. Instead of the *mou,* a
vague unit called the *p'ien* ("piece") was commonly used to de-
marcate parcels of land planted to tea. The *p'ien* was so indefi-
nite and variable that it was impossible to calculate the exact
area under cultivation. Farmers simply reckoned their holdings
by the number of plants they grew. In the Peiling area and presumably elsewhere on the mainland, there was considerable
variation in the number of plants owned by individual proprietors. An 1888 survey calculated that in Ningteh there were
about 3,000 tea plots, ranging from 50 to 600 shrubs, held
by over 110 owners. In Yuanman, an adjoining district, 40,000
shrubs were distributed among 2,000 owners, some having
fewer than 50 plants and others 20 to 30 gardens. There were
numerous tenant cultivators in this part of the province raising
tea for their landlords. In return for the landlords' assumption
of local land tax obligations, tenants sold their tea to the landlords at fixed prices.[95]

More precise information exists regarding tenural arrangements in Taiwan. As we have seen, there were two types of
tea-growing environments, the small-scale tea- and rice-farming
village, and the large-scale tea estate. In the former, landholdings were small (rarely over 10 hectares), tenant cultivation was
more common on rice than on tea land (probably reflecting increased specialization in tea by owner-cultivators), three-fourths
of the land was tenanted, and about two-thirds of the land was
individually owned.[96]

An unusual situation obtained in the T'aoyuan region. Tea
was the predominant crop there, a few owners (some of whom
were wealthy absentees) usually held rights to extensive contiguous properties, and joint ownership accounted for up to 50
percent of the landholdings.[97] Some tea estates in T'aoyuan
were extremely large compared with anything on the mainland.
One of the greatest tea-land proprietors was the Lin family of

Panch'iao. The Lins were among the wealthiest families in late-nineteenth-century Taiwan. At the turn of the century, Lin Wei-yuan is said to have owned a total of 896,447 tea bushes.[98] Yet, there is no evidence that the Lins or any of the great landlords of northern Taiwan managed their estates as plantations. Their interest in tea was that of gentry rentiers, and the actual carrying out of production was delegated to their tenants.

A survey of tenancy contracts from the 1880s serves to clarify the terms under which tea land was cultivated in T'aoyuan. The landholder (who might himself be obliged to pay a fixed sum per year to an absentee patent-holder, or *ta-tsu*) and tenant would agree that the tenant was obligated to plant several tens of thousands of tea bushes on a certain piece of land.[99] After three years had passed, the tenant was to pay a stipulated rent (say 10 to 12 silver dollars) per every 10,000 bushes. If a number of the plants died or deteriorated, the tenant had to replant them or forfeit both land and bushes to the owner, who would engage another tenant. Tenants were frequently allowed to erect shacks called "tea huts" (*ch'a-liao*) on the property, where they could reside while engaged in cultivation. These contracts could be perpetual or limited in duration; in the latter case, the property would revert to the owner after a lapse of several decades.[100]

Such contractual agreements no doubt facilitated the rapid growth of tea farming in this section of Taiwan. Apparently tenants were not obliged to share either their output or the proceeds from actual tea sales with the landlords (there is no mention of this in the contracts). They therefore could realize the profits from their work after paying the annual rental fees. Landlords, of course, acquired a stable rental income.

Until the 1880s, tea growing was a profitable activity for Fukienese peasants. Over the period from 1850 to 1880 good prices for tea were reported from widely separated localities in eastern and northwestern Fukien. It was not uncommon for a grower to receive 20 to 30 taels for 100 *chin* (133 pounds) of top-quality first-crop tea.[101] Such windfall gains could produce visible improvement in the standard of living of mainland tea-growing areas, as witnessed by this 1875 report:

No more conclusive evidence could be adduced of the benefit which the Chinese have derived from the cultivation of the tea plant, than the reports which the teamen bring of the improvements in the social conditions of the inhabitants in the districts where it is grown. Whereas sweet potatoes used to form the staple of their diet, they are now able to afford the addition of rice and fish, while their dwelling-houses are much more substantial and kept in much better order than used to be the case.[102]

Although the testimony is not conclusive, the living standards of Taiwanese tea growers must also have improved. Taiwan tea prices increased during the first three decades after 1865. Since Taiwanese Oolong tea exports were not affected by foreign competition in the 1880s and 1890s, the island's growers fared better than those on the mainland. From 1866 to 1868, the average price of tea per picul at Tansui was $US9. This rose to $18 by 1876–1878, to $36.37 by 1886–1888, and to $42.94 by 1894–1898.[103] At the turn of the century, a small-scale producer of 1,000 chin (1,330 pounds) might realize an annual net profit of 48.5 silver dollars, while a large-scale grower could obtain 500 to 600 dollars from an output of 2,000 piculs (26,600 pounds) in a good market.[104]

The profitability of tea production stimulated population movements in Fukien and Taiwan. Migratory labor played an important role in the development of tea exports. Cultivators traveled from one area of the province to another to open up new tea lands, tea pickers came during the spring to harvest the crops, and skilled tea processors and merchants came to process and distribute them.

Northwestern Fukien was the destination of many migrant cultivators. These marginal farmers were disparagingly known as "shack people" (p'eng-min) from the rude style of their mountain huts. Their labor was welcomed by local landowners, however, as a saying from Nanping (Yenping) illustrates: "The shack people joined with the mountain landlords in the same industry" (P'eng-min yü shan-chu huo wei yeh).[105] During the tea boom, people from southwestern and southeastern Fukien descended upon Yenping to clear mountain land for tea. Those from Tingchow, Changchow, Chuanchow, and Yungchun were most numerous, but migrants came from as far away as Kwangtung.[106] In Chienou (Chienning) hsien, a local gazetteer notes that, "In the Hsien-feng and T'ung-chih eras, vagabonds (*k'o-mang*) again came to Chungshan to cultivate. They then spread out into other areas, and produced a great amount of tea. . . . Most of the planting and marketing were done by local people, who established themselves by enjoying the profits [of tea production]."[107]

In addition to the shack people, transient workers arrived in the northwest during the tea season. Tea production in the Wuyi region depended upon an influx of tea pickers from Shangjao and Nanfeng districts in neighboring Kiangsi.[108] In certain areas, the talents of itinerant tea processors were needed to fire the leaves after harvest. In Chienning, Oolong tea was usually fired by men hired from Chuanchow, while, in Shaowu, specialists from Nanfeng and Hokow in Kiangsi performed the work.[109]

Emigration from southeastern Fukien helped establish a flourishing tea industry in Taiwan. John Dodd's comprador was from Amoy, and other merchants came from Anch'i and Tung-an hsien to found export tea businesses in the Taipei area.[110] Migrating to Taiwan to make one's fortune in tea seems to have been common enough to inspire Taiwanese ballads, such as the tale of Chou from Anch'i. Chou is saved from a dissolute life in Tansui by his sworn-brother, Wang, whereupon the two establish a prosperous tea business.[111] Peasant cultivators as well as merchants brought their skills across the straits to the island and began growing tea, while other migrants came on a seasonal basis to work in the tea manufactories.[112]

As already noted, Cantonese tea brokers and compradors flocked to the new treaty ports, where they became established as middlemen in the tea trade. A sufficiently large community had grown up in Foochow during the T'ung-chih era to warrant the foundation of a Cantonese *hui-kuan* or fellow-provincials' association. One of the principal objects of this organization was to provide Cantonese tea dealers with security guarantors and a means of collectively resolving problems with local authorities.[113]

The tea boom had an immediate impact on the urban development of Taipei and Foochow. Concentration of foreign and Chinese tea firms at the riverside sites of Nant'ai and Tatao-ch'eng created new commercial suburbs near the older urban centers of Foochow and Banka, thus accelerating the economic diversification of these localities. Chinese tea processors, sorters, brokers, and merchants congregated in the new suburbs. At Tatao-ch'eng, for example, by 1896 there were 252 Chinese tea firms employing a total of 3,612 people and having a total capitalization of over a million silver dollars.[114] Tea firms often hired up to several hundred local women and children during the summer to sort tea.[115] Though no figures are extant for Nant'ai, one may assume that conditions there were similar. Foreign observers spoke of large numbers of people engaged in various tasks connected with the trade.[116] A surviving list of the occupational services required by one of the tea hongs includes several dozen positions, ranging from tea-box makers, godown keepers, and tea sifters to boatmen and transport coolies.[117] Many people in Nant'ai must have relied on the tea trade.

Finally, the monetary system of Foochow and its hinterland was affected by the growth of the export trade. Before the province was opened to foreign trade, Foochow had developed a relatively sophisticated system of traditional banks, which circulated their own paper bank notes in the city.[118] However, the large influx of foreign silver dollars to the port and the Min River valley to cover tea purchases overtaxed the system. There was too much bulky coinage in circulation, and urban currency-exchange transactions became unwieldy. This problem was resolved by the establishment of new native banks (ch'ien-chuang) at Foochow, which accepted many of the dollars and issued a new form of paper money backed by foreign silver. Called the Dai Fook dollar (Dai from Nan-t'ai, Fook being an abbreviation for fu-t'ou-chiao, the Hong Kong dollar), it was an essential part of the city's currency system until the late 1920s.[119]

Foreign silver dollars, colloquially known as ta-yang, continued in wide circulation in Foochow. They were in great demand in the interior of Fukien, where paper money was virtually unknown.[120] In the 1850s, provincial officials, heeding pleas from Chinese tea merchants and moneylenders, had sanctioned the circulation of the new types of foreign silver coins that Western traders were importing. Mexican and other dollars were approved along with traditional sycee silver for use in marketplace transactions and tax payments, "in order to make Sino-foreign trade convenient and benefit state taxation and people's livelihoods."[121] These imports of silver coinage expanded the province's money supply, alleviating the deflationary crisis of the 1840s. It is unlikely that this would have occurred in the absence of the tea export trade, for Fukien produced little else to attract foreign merchants.[122]

THE EFFECT UPON PROVINCIAL
GOVERNMENT FINANCE

The attitude of the Ch'ing government toward foreign trade is usually assumed to have been essentially negative. Chinese officials are said to have regarded foreign commerce and the revenue derived from it as insignificant until long after the T'ung-chih period.[123] While it is true that there was no national policy of promoting Chinese commerce until after 1900, it does not follow that central and provincial authorities ignored the fiscal potentialities of China's expanding trade after 1842. During the latter half of the nineteenth century, indirect taxation was given increasingly greater emphasis than direct taxation, which meant in practice that commercial taxes, being far more elastic sources of income than land taxes and surtaxes, became more important to the government.[124] The Chinese fiscal system thus began to shift from land taxation to taxes on commodities in transit, of which there were several distinct types, such as likin, miscellaneous associated local levies, and maritime customs import and export duties.[125] In Fukien, tea taxation became a major source of provincial government income from the 1850s to the 1880s.

Between 1853 and 1855, Fukien officials became aware of the potential revenue in the maritime tea trade. Fukien was the first province in China to levy a transit tax on tea (*ch'a-shui*), in April and May of 1853, five months before the origination of the likin tax in neighboring Kiangsi.[126] The Fukien tea tax was subsequently raised in 1855. The province initiated an opium likin tax in 1857 to raise money for military defense against the Taipings, and a tea likin levy (ch'a-yeh li-chin) was added in 1859. Between 1861 and 1865, still another tea surtax to cover military expenses was introduced.[127] What had begun in 1853 as a tax of 0.1485 taels per picul grew to 0.8877 taels in 1855, 1.6577 taels by 1859, and 2.3485 taels after 1865.[128] Tea taxes were calculated according to the weight of the tea, not its value. This method undoubtedly eliminated haggling over the actual worth of tea shipments, but it also meant that both inexpensive and costly teas were assessed at the same rate per picul (the standard taxable unit).[129] A few exceptions were made to this rule, notably for tea packed in special chests called 25-chin boxes, which were taxed at a uniform rate.[130]

Considerable official corruption and tea smuggling by foreign merchants accompanied the first decade of tea taxation in Fukien.[131] Under the governor-generalship of Tso Tsung-t'ang (1863–1866), these irregularities were largely eliminated, and the provincial likin collection system was centralized.[132] A network of likin bureaus, substations, and tea-tax barriers was established throughout the tea-producing regions along major arteries such as the Min River. By 1885, there were over 100 such octroi stations in existence. Eleven years later, there were 227, among which were 115 special tea-tax barriers (ch'a-shui chü-ch'ia). While likin stations operated year-round, the tea-tax barriers were staffed only during the tea season, from April to early November.[133]

The responsibility for payment of the tea tax and likin duties fell upon Chinese merchants, for tea destined for export was held to be in Chinese possession until purchased by Western merchants at the treaty ports. The government assisted native merchants by often delaying actual tax collections until the merchants were paid for their teas by the foreign exporters. But Fukien officials seldom granted transit passes for export tea, for these would have enabled Chinese dealers to convey tea to the coast without paying the full inland duty.[134]

Tea taxation revenue was dependent upon the seasonal fluctuations of tea markets in Fukien and elsewhere in China. As Tso Tsung-t'ang perceived in 1866:

Fukien produces much tea in out-of-the-way places, and foreign merchants purchase a great amount of it ... [but], in Chekiang, Kwangtung, Kiukiang, and Hankow, the foreign merchants have [also] established numerous tea godowns. News travels very fast by steamship, and sales are possible at various places. Thus, while Fukien tea must depend solely upon foreign merchants, foreign merchants do not only depend upon Fukien tea.[135]

Yet, although tea taxes were somewhat unpredictable sources of revenue, during the tea boom period income from both the tea tax and likin tended to increase. An average of over 40 percent of total Fukien likin income from 1853 to 1888 was generated by levies on tea (see Table 12 below).

Taiwan appears to have begun likin collection in 1861, when branch collectorates were first established on the island. Opium likin was the most important item of revenue, since each picul of the drug was assessed a tax of 60 taels. Tea likin collection apparently began in 1871. Tea was lightly taxed by comparison with the mainland, being assessed only 1 tael per picul. This may have been an additional factor encouraging the rapid expansion of tea production in northern Taiwan. For most of this period, tea likin records are not available, but in 1891 a total of 68,000 taels was reported, rising to 136,000 taels each year during 1892 and 1893.[136]

Besides the likin and tea taxes there was an export tariff collected by the Imperial Maritime Customs. Under the terms of Article 10 of the Nanking Treaty and Article 26 of the Tientsin Treaty, this tax had been fixed at the pre-1842 rate of 2.50 taels per picul, or 5 percent ad valorem of an average tea price of 50 taels per picul. Since the price of tea rarely reached this level thereafter, the maintainance of a 2.50-tael-per-picul export tax meant, in effect, that tea would be taxed at a rate higher than intended in the treaty stipulations.[137]

During the 1860s and 1870s, the Foochow export duties alone totaled over one million taels per year, or about one-fourth of the annual export duties collected by the Maritime Customs. Export taxes constituted more than half the Imperial Maritime Customs receipts until 1887.[138] Since tea and silk were China's principal exports during these years, it is safe to presume that taxes on these two commodities made up most of the total.

TABLE 12   Fukien's Tea Tax, Tea Likin, and Total Liken
Receipts, 1853-1888
(HKT)

	Tea Likin and Surtaxes	*Tea Tax*	*Total Likin*	*%*
1853	–	8,714	8,714	100
1854	–	14,098	14,098	100
1855	–	52,102	52,102	100
1856	–	160,717	160,717	100
1857	–	182,294	240,092	76
1858	–	118,778	269,268	44
1859	117,911	195,730	528,953	59
1860	159,108	255,779	797,269	52
1861	148,932	220,856	871,384	42
1862	290,996	253,002	1,288,507	42
1863	330,140	252,172	1,299,195	45
1864	231,298	240,604	1,115,229	42
1865	512,974	259,607	2,024,401	38
1866	519,266	259,345	2,163,645	36
1867	495,197	244,340	1,907,034	39
1868	605,094	307,704	2,120,200	43
1869	557,448	281,229	1,939,271	43
1870	515,402	255,454	1,858,891	41
1871	565,552	280,606	1,876,597	45
1872	614,793	304,364	1,945,796	47
1873	572,991	285,857	2,199,983	39
1874	632,372	310,726	2,155,688	44
1875	614,811	306,029	2,105,452	44
1876[a]	701,142	na	2,277,675	31
1877[a]	554,743	269,894	2,449,898	34
1878	628,760	311,226	2,455,034	38
1879	568,067	286,326	2,253,742	38
1880	681,835	341,851	2,222,053	46
1881	624,741	316,173	2,472,720	38
1882	569,735	293,305	2,221,844	39
1883	516,543	273,067	1,973,189	40
1884	529,225	274,512	1,926,455	42
1885	545,566	277,866	2,053,133	40
1886	614,592	318,585	2,189,143	43
1887	191,943	na	2,039,407	9
1888	475,303	246,370	1,889,671	38

Source: Lo Yü-tung, *Chung-kuo li-chin shih,* II, 562-563.

Note: [a]No figures given for tea tax in 1876 and 1887, and totals for these years
represent extrapolations from semiannual records.

The revenue was divided in a variety of ways between provincial and central authorities.

A portion of the proceeds from Fukien's tea likin and tea taxes was allocated to the central government. The largest annual disbursement to the Board of Revenue (Hu-pu) in the capital was for the "expenses of the capital" (*ching-hsiang*), and the funds to cover this depended heavily upon the tea tax. Out of an average 300,000 taels sent to Peking each year beginning in the mid-1860s, 200,000 came from the tea tax. A surtax varying from 30,000 to 100,000 taels per year was also collected on behalf of the Imperial Household Department (Nei-wu fu).[139] All in all, the Board of Revenue absorbed anywhere from 4 to 20 percent of Fukien's annual likin revenue. In addition, the province had to provide the central government with funds to defray the cost of military forces in Kansu and, to a much smaller extent, in Kweichow. (This item took between 2 and 36 percent of likin revenues between 1863 and 1884, after which such subsidies became nominal and infrequent.)[140]

Of the revenue retained by Fukien, by far the greatest amount was ordinarily devoted to military expenses. Military demands absorbed over 90 percent of total likin revenue prior to 1866. Although the figure dropped to between 40 and 45 percent between 1866 and 1886, no other item occupied a comparable place in the disbursement of Fukien likin funds.[141] In this respect the province was hardly unique, for Kiangsu, Anhwei, Kiangsi, and Hunan all depended heavily on likin receipts to finance their military establishments.[142] The subsidizing of provincial armies was one of the lasting consequences of the mid-nineteenth-century militarization of Chinese society described by Philip Kuhn.[143] Commercial taxes, such as those levied on tea and other important commodities, provided the resources to sustain local armed forces throughout southern China. The income from foreign-trade taxation thus contributed to provincial militarization in the late Ch'ing.

The maritime customs duties were employed by both central and provincial governments to support pacification and self-strengthening projects undertaken by various high provincial officials. After Tso Tsung-t'ang's departure from the post of governor general of Fukien and Chekiang in 1866, he began a series of extended campaigns to subdue Moslem rebellions in Shensi and Kansu. Espousing the principle of using "the resources of the southeast to support the army of the northwest," Tso requested that Fukien deliver 480,000 taels per year beginning in 1869 to feed and equip his forces. Although the province at first failed to deliver its full monthly quota, by 1871 Fukien's Governor and Governor-General had earned Tso's praise for their cooperation. The Foochow customs house and Kiangsu province were the only sources of financial assistance to deliver their entire quotas in that year.[144]

Foochow's dockyard and naval arsenal were the major self-strengthening projects undertaken in the province. Financing them out of maritime customs revenue became a persistent problem that set provincial officials against dockyard administrators. Begun under Tso Tsung-t'ang, the dockyard relied heavily upon the 60 percent of the customs revenue retained by the province, and occasionally upon whatever funds from the remaining 40 percent Peking agreed to part with.[145]

As a result of the tea boom, tea taxes assumed great importance in Fukien's fiscal administration. The province's largest single source of revenue in the Ch'ing period, the land tax, brought in 1,925,000 taels in 1753; by 1908 this had increased to 3,023,000 taels.[146] Land-tax estimates are lacking for the tea boom years, but it seems reasonable to assume a collection of around 2,500,000 taels per year during that period. From 1862 to 1886, tea likin and tea taxes totaled half a million to a million taels per year (see Table 12 above), or 20 to 40 percent of the estimated proceeds from land taxation. Assuming the additional collection of at least a million taels per year in export duties, total tea revenue would have approached 60 to 80 percent of that derived from land taxes.

Provincial authorities were aware of the significance of the tea trade to the fiscal and economic health of their jurisdiction. They therefore took pains to protect and encourage it. Some efforts were ill-advised, such as the attempt in 1876 by Hsia Hsien-lun, a Taiwan military taotai, to grow tea in the Tainan area. Hoping to extend tea cultivation from northern to southern Taiwan, Hsia procured 200,000 tea plants from Tansui, and from Chungan and Funing on the mainland, and had them transplanted. The drier, hotter climate of the south was ill-suited to tea, and the plants and Hsia's hopes quickly withered. [147]

Chinese tea merchants and tea boats venturing into and out of the interior were often preyed upon by the bandits who infested the banks of the Min River. To protect them, the provincial government stationed armed boats along the river, and took other precautions, as an 1883 account by a foreign traveler reveals:

All along the way from Foochow there were posted . . . frequent notices warning tea-dealers not to travel without an escort of braves, which the authorities would always detach free of charge. Certainly the government appears to take pains to foster the tea trade, which now embraces all Fukien north of Shui-k'ou. [148]

Aside from brigands, another potential and more insidious danger to the tea trade was the adulteration of tea by dishonest Chinese merchants. When foreign traders or consular officials acting in their interests complained of such practices, the result was generally a proclamation by provincial authorities threatening the offenders with punishment. For example, the Fukien Board of Trade (T'ung-shang tsung-chü) issued the following proclamation in April 1872, after a complaint by British and American merchants at Foochow:

Tea is the most important article of trade in this port, and from the time the commerce with foreign countries was established the number of warehouses has increased and the trade has prospered daily. Everyone should therefore make it the rule of his hong to trade honestly and equitably. . . . It is then hereby notified to the owners of Chinese mercantile establishments, teamen, and brokers . . . that in the future every kind of tea sold to foreign merchants must in accordance with the rule of the hongs be picked clean, and that in fixing the prices of the teas the chop and muster must correspond. If any dare to make up false tea, or mix up dust and fannings with the chops, the instant it is discovered, and a complaint preferred by the foreign merchant, strict measures will certainly be taken to arrest the culprits, who will on conviction be punished without fail. [149]

Fukien officials used the likin stations dotting the interior to combat such abuses. If the tea chests were properly inspected at these barriers, it was possible to detect practices such as filling the chests with tea dust as well as leaves.[150] Given the dispersed nature of tea production, and the large volume of exports passing through the hands of numerous middlemen before reaching the foreign buyer, it is remarkable that the tea trade maintained as high a level of commercial honesty as it did until the 1880s.

THE COMPETITION OF TEA PLANTATIONS ABROAD

From experimental beginnings in the late 1830s, the Indian tea industry required a full half-century before it surpassed China as the leading tea supplier to the United Kingdom. Since tea had never before been grown on the scale of tropical plantation crops such as sugar and coffee, the task of developing tea plantations understandably was difficult and prolonged.

Until its demise in 1858 as the governing agency for India, the East India Company utilized the services of men such as Robert Fortune to bring Chinese tea plants, cultivation and processing techniques, and a number of Chinese tea processors to northern India. By this means the company demonstrated that Chinese tea could in fact be grown and manufactured under Indian conditions. After 1858, private entrepreneurs proved that plantations owned by joint-stock companies could adapt tea production to those conditions.[151] The extension of Indian tea cultivation went hand in hand with the opening up of the rugged northeastern frontier region to British penetration and control. It was here in the early nineteenth century, that a species of tea native to India was found growing wild. The subsequent propagation of Assam tea and its crossing with imported Chinese plants in certain areas such as Darjeeling laid the botanical foundations of the Indian tea industry.[152] Assam became India's most important tea-growing region, but tea cultivation also began in other areas, notably the southern tip of the subcontinent.

The development of the plantation system depended upon an adequate supply of cheap virgin land, plentiful labor, and ready access to investment capital. Since the government of British India (and later, that of Ceylon) favored such colonial enterprises, the necessary factors of production were relatively abundant. Thousands of acres of sparsely populated wilderness were available in Assam at nominal cost to the companies, the seemingly limitless supply of Indian peasant labor could be tapped, and modern joint-stock corporate organization insured access to capital markets. Even the climate favored Indian tea, for the growing season was over a month longer in Assam than in southern China; in southern India and in Ceylon, tea could be grown throughout the year. As the tea plant produces new leaves, or "flushes," every few weeks, the longer tropical growing season naturally meant increased potential output.[153] Despite these advantages, it took time to develop the managerial and technical competence necessary for profitable operations.

Plantation operations were characterized by economies of scale. In 1880, there were an estimated 1,058 estates in Assam extending over 153,657 acres, an average of 145 acres each. Their total output was 34,013,583 pounds of black tea, an average of 32,150 pounds per plantation.[154] Processing could be done at a central location on the estates as soon as the tea was picked (this eliminated the need for a preliminary processing into *mao-ch'a*), and it was in this phase of production that substantial technological innovation occurred. The larger volume of output demanded greater standardization of processing techniques and greater attention to quality control. Under these conditions, tea processing became a capital-intensive activity. From the 1860s to 1900, British manufacturers and planters developed a series of intricate machines that could perform the various steps in black-tea manufacturing more efficiently. Large-scale production made this technology economically feasible, and the new methods of production in turn served to revolutionize the Indian tea industry.[155] In the 1880s, Ceylon borrowed Indian techniques to create another great center of tea production.[156]

The United Kingdom market was the prize for which the Indian and Ceylonese plantation owners and operators labored. Their hope was to oust Chinese tea from the British market, and eventually compete with it on a worldwide basis. Since it was the custom in Great Britain to blend different types of tea for sale to the consumer, India's black tea was introduced there in mixtures with the more delicate Chinese teas.[157] It was not long before the English mass market acquired a taste for the

strongly flavored, inexpensive Assam leaf, and Indian tea became accepted in preference to Chinese. In the late 1880s, imports of Indian tea began to displace the cheaper grades of
Chinese tea on the market. The rapid growth of Indian and
Ceylonese tea exports to Great Britain as compared with the
growth and decline of imports of Chinese tea is evident in
Table 13.

TABLE 13   United Kingdom Imports of India, Ceylon, and
China Teas, 1866–1889
(selected years, in pounds)

	India Tea	China Tea	Ceylon Tea
1866	4,584,000	97,681,000	–
1868	7,746,000	99,339,000	–
1870	13,500,000	104,051,000	–
1872	16,656,000	111,005,000	–
1874	18,528,000	118,751,000	–
1876	25,740,000	123,364,000	–
1877	27,852,000	132,263,000	–
1878	36,744,000	120,252,000	–
1880	43,836,000	114,485,000	–
1882	50,496,000	114,462,000	–
1883	58,000,000	111,780,000	1,000,000
1884	62,217,000	110,843,000	2,000,000
1886	68,420,000	104,226,000	6,245,000
1888	86,210,000	80,653,000	18,553,000
1889	96,000,000	61,100,000	28,500,000

Source: Adapted from Sir Percival Griffiths, *The History of the Indian Tea Industry*,
p. 125.

Indian tea began to undercut the market for cheaper grades
of Chinese tea such as Foochow Congous. The London price
per pound of plantation tea declined from 1S9.25p in 1878 to
1S in 1886. By 1890, it was estimated that Indian tea would
cost less than 6p per pound in London, where the average price
of Foochow Congou was at least one-third higher. South Asian
tea seemed destined to control the British market.[158] Planta-

tion tea exports also began to invade the American and Australian markets, once secure preserves for Chinese tea.[159]

By the late 1880s, the growth of foreign competition could no longer escape the attention of those involved in the Chinese tea trade. Government officials and foreign and Chinese tea merchants feared for the future of the tea export trade. Their concern found expression in Inspector General Robert Hart's report to the Tsungli Yamen in 1888. The lengthy document incorporated reports from Maritime Customs officers at every major tea port (including Foochow, Amoy, and Tansui).

In his introduction, Hart remarked that two reasons were generally adduced for the commercial success that South Asian black tea (and Japanese green tea) were enjoying in markets that once were China's. Foreign teas were now cheaper and better prepared. They were cheaper, not only because they were generally grown on large plantations, but because they were virtually untaxed—India, Ceylon, and Japan did not burden tea exports with the heavy transit and customs duties that the Chinese empire imposed.[160] They were better prepared because others had improved tea cultivation, processing, and marketing procedures while China had not. Western tea merchants now stigmatized Chinese tea as carelessly grown, sloppily prepared, subject to various forms of adulteration, and improperly packed for shipment.[161] They failed to agree upon measures to rehabilitate the Chinese tea industry, however. Some only proposed the reduction of tea taxation, while others urged that the Chinese government should promote the adoption of foreign techniques: "China should either open a tea school, or establish a model plantation, or place a given tea district under the supervision of properly appointed government experts, or charter a company to conduct the business of a tea plantation on the Indian plan."[162]

Some of the points raised in Hart's report were echoed by a few influential Chinese proponents of economic reform. As early as 1879, Hsueh Fu-ch'eng had warned that "India's tea is overcoming that of China. . . . In the future [China's tea exports will stagnate]. Two-thirds of the tea and silk used abroad will be from other countries, a source of profit snatched entirely from China. A solution must be found quickly." Hsueh urged that local officials take initiatives to promote the extension of tea-growing and advocated a ceiling on tea taxation.[163] In the 1880s and early 1890s, stronger pleas for reform were voiced by men such as the comprador Cheng Kuan-ying and the official Ma Chien-chung—so-called mercantile nationalists, to borrow Yen-p'ing Hao's term.[164] They castigated the Ch'ing government for having exploited China's commerce instead of promoting it. To Cheng and Ma, the self-strengthening policies of the preceding three decades had imposed crippling fiscal burdens on Chinese foreign trade. In order to survive in a world of intensified commercial rivalry, Cheng contended that China must learn to wage "commercial warfare" (shang-chan) rather than concentrate upon military preparedness. He called for the abolition of the likin tax, and criticized Ch'ing officials for not doing more to encourage tea and silk production and better processing methods.[165]

Ma entitled an 1890 essay "On Enriching the People" ("Fu-min shuo"), and it began with the phrase, "In governing a state, [one] considers wealth and strength as the basis, but, in seeking strength, [one] aims first for wealth." Since the true road to wealth and power lay in the development of domestic and for-eign trade, it followed that China's government must foster commerce as a matter of national policy. This would entail the end of export taxation, and state assistance for improving and promoting the tea and silk trades. (Ma was among the first to advocate the organization of large companies financially able to compete with foreigners in these businesses.)[166]

For tea growers and merchants in Fukien, however, the end of the tea boom was not a matter for policy debates but a ques-tion of livelihood. Since Great Britain, America, and Australia were among Fukien's prime markets, the province naturally severely felt competition from South Asian tea. Foochow's black-tea exports declined to about 38 million lbs. by 1900.[167] Amoy's tea trade also decreased sharply, owing to the decline in demand for tea grown in southern Fukien and the steady loss of the reexport trade in Oolong tea after the Japanese occupa-tion of Taiwan in 1895.[168] As prices fell to less than half what producers had obtained during the 1860s and 1870s, many growers allowed their tea fields to revert to wilderness.[169] The plight of those who had gambled on cash-crop production for a fickle world market and lost is vividly recounted in this 1888 recital from Yenping prefecture:

Those who relied on tea-farming for a living were not few in number: those who clear the mountains, the tea pickers, those who open *ch'a-chuang* to process and package tea, tea sellers, and tea experts and selectors. After 1881 tea prices were very low; first spring tea was only 7 to 9 taels for good and 3 to 5 taels for coarse. Those who opened *ch'a-chuang* and the tea-chest makers went broke, and many producers could no longer rely on tea [for income]. Those with fields recultivated them, and the ones without land cut brushwood for a living. How lamentable that people who labored to plant tea received so much bitterness from it! Only those cultivating land for food can continue to have tea gardens . . . People without food let the tea mountains return to wasteland—they cannot [afford] to look after them.[170]

Over the next half-century the number of tea growers and the amount of tea produced in Fukien continued to decline.[171] In the opinion of a Soviet scholar, the loss of foreign markets for tea resulted in the pauperization and "proletarianization" of the Fukienese peasantry and the gradual breakdown of the "closed character" of peasant villages.[172] One does not have to concur with this judgment to acknowledge that Fukien's economy proved highly responsive and highly vulnerable to the play of international market forces. If the history of the Fukien tea boom demonstrates that the traditional Chinese economy could capitalize upon the expansion of trade with the West, it also reveals its difficulty in coping with a rapidly changing world economy dominated by Western imperial enterprise.

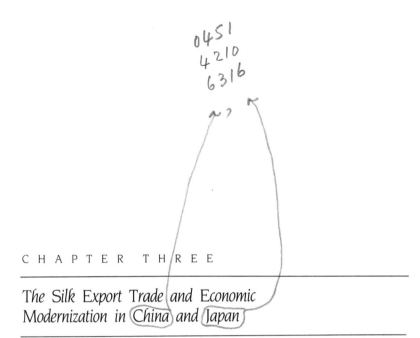

CHAPTER THREE

The Silk Export Trade and Economic Modernization in China and Japan

LILLIAN M. LI

In ancient times, China's silk trade with the West was conducted along the famous Silk Road, which traversed central Asia, bringing precious Chinese silks to the Roman Empire. Mention of Chinese silk usually evokes this memory. Yet, from at least the sixteenth century onward, China's silk exports to the West were carried primarily along maritime routes in Portuguese, Spanish, and other European vessels. And, from the mid-nineteenth century until the 1930s, both China and Japan exported silks to the West in quantities unknown in ancient times. Silkworm disease, which struck French sericulture in the 1850s, initiated the modern European demand for Chinese silk. But, even when that disease was brought under control, demand for Chinese and, later, Japanese raw silk expanded, since European sericulture

simply could not match the quality, quantity, or low cost of
East Asian silk. The French silk-weaving industry was especially
dependent on high-quality white raw silk from central China,
known as Tsatlee.

THE MODERN ROLE OF SILK EXPORTS

In the twentieth century, however, it was the new American
market, American tastes, and, ultimately, American technology
that shaped the international demand for raw silk. With an increasingly prosperous population, the United States became the
most important customer for raw silk in the world, and New
York replaced Lyon as the leading center of the silk trade. Silk
stockings became the standard of dress for both men and
women, making a virtual necessity of what had once been a
luxury.[1] The American silk-weaving industry, moreover, was
always alert to opportunities to parlay fads and fashions into
profits. Alice Roosevelt's wedding gown of American silk, or
Mrs. Woodrow Wilson's and her three daughters' inaugural
dresses in a new range of colors, were fashion news which made
silk manufacturers ecstatic. The revival of dancing in the United
States was hailed as a boon to the silk business.[2] Although
rayon was introduced into the American market after World
War I, silk remained competitive, particularly for stockings, and
it was not really until the invention of nylon by Du Pont in 1939
and World War II that the silk market effectively collapsed.[3]

Although limited in duration, the international silk boom
shaped the foreign trade of both China and Japan and played an
important role in their domestic economies. During the late
nineteenth and early twentieth centuries, silk was the most important commodity in the foreign trade of China and Japan. In
China, exports of raw silk steadily increased after the opening
of the treaty ports. Between 1868 and 1929, when silk exports
reached their peak, the volume more than tripled, rising from
3.42 million to 11.4 million kilograms.[4] As Table 14 shows, silk
surpassed tea as China's major export in the 1880s, and continued to be the leading export, although, as China's trade
became more diversified during its Republican period (1912–
1949), the proportion of silk exports declined. In 1880, silk

TABLE 14 Raw Silk and Tea in Chinese and Japanese Exports
(%)

	China		Japan	
	Raw Silk	*Tea*	*Raw Silk*	*Tea*
1870[a]	—	—	38	25
1880	38	46	35	22
1890	35	31	36	9
1900	31	16	28	4
1910	26	9	29	3
1920	19	2	28	0.9
1930	16	3	33	0.6

Source: For China, China Maritime Customs, *Decennial Reports, 1922–1931* I, 120, 190; for Japan, Miyohei Shinohara, "Economic Development and Foreign Trade in Pre-war Japan," p. 227.

Note: [a]The figures given are for 1868–1872, 1878–1882, 1888–1892, 1898–1902, 1908–1912, 1918–1922, 1928–1932.

exports represented 38 percent of Chinese exports by value, while, in 1930, they accounted for only 16 percent. In Japan, the expansion of silk exports was even more dramatic. Raw silk exports averaged about 656,000 kilograms per year in the 1868 to 1872 period, and soared to 34,275,000 kilograms in 1929.[5] Until the 1930s, raw silk was Japan's leading export commodity, outranking tea; it was not surpassed by cotton fabrics until after the Depression. Between 1870 and 1930, raw silk held a steady 28 to 38 percent of Japan's total exports, as Table 14 indicates. If silk fabric exports are added, total silk exports from China represented 16.6 percent of total exports by value, while total silk exports from Japan represented 43.3 percent of total Japanese exports in 1929.[6]

The most notable aspect of the world silk trade was Japan's stunning success in capturing the expanding market from China. Starting from a much lower base, by 1907 Japan had overtaken China as the world's largest silk exporter, and, according to one estimate, by the early 1920s Japan was supplying about 60 percent of the silk traded internationally, while China was providing only about 23 percent.[7] Table 15 shows the relatively steeper increase in Japanese silk exports compared with the gradual increase in Chinese exports.

TABLE 15 Chinese and Japanese Raw Silk Exports
(5-year averages in 1,000 kg[a])

	China	Japan
1871–1875	4,092	672
1876–1880	4,416	984
1881–1885	3,864	1,488
1886–1890	4,872	1,992
1891–1895	6,084	3,084
1896–1900	6,708	3,132
1901–1905	6,900	4,944
1906–1910	7,500	7,152
1911–1915	8,268	10,404
1916–1920	7,716	14,148
1921–1925	8,772	20,160
1926–1930	10,212	30,708
1931–1935	5,052	31,872

Source: Adapted from Table 16, Chapter 3 of Lillian M. Li, China's Silk Trade: Traditional Industry in the Modern World.

Note: [a]60 kg = 1 picul.

Japan's success in the world silk market rested in its ability to provide silk of consistent quality. The best Chinese silk was still superior, but Japanese raw silk was more reliable.[8] Standardization was critical for the American silk-weaving industry, which used power looms, whereas the French, who still used hand-looms for their high-quality luxury silks, continued to buy domestically reeled Tsatlees from China. Thus, the silk industry in Japan developed to satisfy the needs of American manufacturers. The portion of Japanese raw silk exports destined for American markets soared from less than 1 percent in the mid-1860s to 84.2 percent in 1920, and over 95 percent in 1925–1926.[9] Conversely, as the United States' raw silk imports mounted steadily, increasing more than tenfold between the 1890s and 1930s, Japan's share also expanded, until, by the early 1930s, it was supplying over 90 percent of American needs, while the Chinese portion dropped to below 5 percent (see Table 16). The American market never assumed such overwhelming importance for the Chinese silk industry. Around

TABLE 16   United States Raw Silk Imports, 1892–1935
(*5-year averages*)

		Japan		China	
	Total (1,000s kg.)	Amount (1,000s kg.)	% Total	Amount (1,000s kg.)	% Total
1892–1895	3,222	1,600	49.6	910	28.2
1896–1900	4,265	2,063	48.4	1,225	28.7
1901–1905	6,473	3,223	49.8	1,414	21.8
1906–1910	8,924	5,228	58.6	1,787	20.0
1911–1915	12,305	8,477	68.9	2,583	21.0
1916–1920	16,329	12,509	76.6	3,265	20.0
1921–1925	24,600	19,063	77.5	4,082	16.6
1926–1930	34,949	28,609	81.9	5,131	14.7
1931–1935	31,200	28,866	92.5	1,468	04.7

Source: Adapted from *Sen'i kōgyō (Chōki keizai tōkei,* Vol. XI), comp. Fujino Shō-zaburō et al., p. 309.

1920, for example, while 39.4 percent of silk exports from Shanghai were destined for France or Great Britain, only 32.9 percent were destined for the United States. At Canton, the American market was more important than the French until the late 1920s, when the proportions became about the same as at Shanghai.[10]

The success of Japan's silk export trade had profound significance for its overall economic development. In concrete terms, the development of a major export commodity enabled Japan to earn the foreign exchange to purchase machinery and raw materials necessary for industrialization. W. W. Lockwood has estimated that "probably the raw silk trade financed no less than 40 percent of Japan's entire imports of foreign machinery and raw materials used domestically" between 1870 and 1930.[11] Most other economists agree that foreign trade played a critical role in Japan's economic development.[12] Moreover, the silk-reeling industry ranked among the earliest modern enterprises in Japan, and in Kenzō Hemmi's words, "The silk industry was a training school for Japanese industrialization."[13] Silk and other export commodities gave Japanese entrepreneurs important opportunities for profitable investment, and manufacturing for foreign markets imposed a clear need for standardization of products and more efficient commercial organization.[14]

Although silk was also China's major export commodity, and modern filatures were among the earliest and most important modern industries, the development of the silk industry did not have the same long-term significance that it did in Japan. Foreign trade in general did not play a very large role in the Chinese economy, and it was barely tolerated by the Ch'ing government. The Chinese silk industry continued to be relatively more oriented toward its still substantial domestic market. Although estimates vary, the domestic market may have absorbed about 55–60 percent of total raw silk output during the early twentieth century. In Japan, however, from 1883 to 1937, between 58 and 78 percent of the raw silk output was exported, usually well over 65 percent in any given year.[15]

The differences in scale, however, are not sufficient to explain the contrasting reactions of the Chinese and Japanese economies to the same world-trade opportunities. To a significant extent, their different experiences with the silk trade typified their different experiences with economic modernization in general. During the 1950s and 1960s, East Asian historiography in the United States was largely organized around the notion of contrasting "responses" of China and Japan to the West, and the relatively greater success of the Japanese in achieving rapid "modernization."[16] Although concepts of "modernization" and "response to the West" have justifiably come under attack for reflecting a Western standard of judgment,[17] the amazingly rapid transformation of Japan from an isolated feudal agrarian society to an industrial superpower in little over a century has maintained—indeed increased—its fascination for Western scholars, especially in view of the apparently declining competitiveness of the American economy.[18] While it is the Japanese case that seems extraordinary for its speed, and not the Chinese for its slowness, the comparison between China and Japan still seems uniquely appropriate because of broad similarities in their cultural and economic backgrounds before the nineteenth century, and the clear similarity in their relationship to the West in the early nineteenth century.

Because the silk industry involved the same basic technology and the same world market for both China and Japan, it serves as an excellent case study through which we can systematically compare the process of economic change in these two countries. Although interpretations of China's and Japan's different responses to the West have tended to stress broad cultural and ideological explanations for the strength of Japan's political leadership and the vitality of its entrepreneurship—the two critical instruments of that country's economic development— this chapter will seek a more concrete level of explanation to show the methods by which government leadership and entrepreneurship helped develop the silk export trade.[19] Among Japanese historians of the Meiji Restoration there has been considerable debate about the relative emphasis that should be given to leadership from above and initiative from below,[20] but a comparison of the Japanese with the Chinese case highlights the extent to which both types of enterprise were essential. Government model factories, enlightened regulations, schools, inspection stations, banking, and other measures, constituted the principal institutions that facilitated change. However, government leadership could not have succeeded without a supporting social and economic infrastructure, which included entrepreneurial talent, institutional flexibility, and plentiful capital as its major elements.

CHARACTERISTICS OF SILK TECHNOLOGY

Silk manufacture is an excellent subject for the study of economic modernization, precisely because it had such deep roots as a traditional handicraft in China and Japan, and because it had both agricultural and industrial aspects. Sericulture had been known in China since prehistoric times; in Japan, also, its origins were ancient, although it did not become widespread until the early Tokugawa period (1600–1867). The manufacture of silk fabric involved four basic steps: the cultivation of mulberry trees, the raising of silkworms (sericulture), the reeling of silk from the cocoons, and the weaving of raw silk into fabric. Between the third and fourth steps occurred several intermediate processes such as dyeing, twisting to form warp or woof, and, in modern times, rereeling to produce a more even strand of silk. Although China's ancient silk export trade had consisted primarily of silk fabric, in the modern period it was raw silk that was demanded by European and American silk-weaving companies.

Many features of silk technology facilitated the industry's growth in response to the world market during the nineteenth century.[21] First, mulberry was not soil-specific, and, in fact, was often grown along the edges of fields or the banks of ponds, utilizing space that might otherwise have been wasted. Second, sericulture was an ideal rural side-occupation because it was well suited to small-scale domestic production. Traditionally, the sericultural season was completed in the early spring before rice was sown. Until relatively modern times, both Chinese and Japanese peasants raised only a spring crop of silkworms and thus were free to deal with other farming tasks later. Sericulture thus took advantage of seasonally under-employed labor. Moreover, although seasonal, sericulture required intensive concentration of labor; women and children engaged in round-the-clock feeding of mulberry leaves to the silkworms. A plentiful supply of rural female labor in both China and Japan thus favored the expansion of silk production. For a household to produce a few baskets of cocoons and then reel off the silk usually meant a good supplementary income for a relatively small investment of capital.

Other aspects of sericulture, however, limited the extent and rapidity with which silk production could expand. Above all, sericulture involved a high degree of natural risk. A substantial body of folklore had grown up in China concerning the likes and dislikes of silkworms. A slight change in the weather or other natural conditions could bring disaster. Indeed, the vulnerability of silkworms became apparent in the mid-nineteenth century in France and Italy, and later in China, when the problem of disease became acute. According to contemporary estimates, by the 1920s, 75 to 95 percent of the silkworm egg-sheets sold in China were diseased.[22]

In addition, sericulture involved a high degree of commercial risk. The peasant household was faced with an extremely volatile local market, which reflected an even more unstable international market, in which the whims of fashion, the constantly fluctuating exchange rate, and the uncertain supply each season all figured. The concentration of sericulture into one brief season further exacerbated the risks of the market, since most domestically reeled silk was sold at the same time each spring. Peasant producers were at the mercy of the prevailing market price. After steam filatures were established in China, peasant households that sold their cocoons rather than reeling them at home were even more vulnerable, for the cocoon business was more highly speculative than the raw silk market. Therefore, in the absence of institutional safeguards, the peasant household could not afford to commit very much of its financial resources to sericulture; in other words, it would not risk hiring outside help or devoting all its land to mulberry. The volume of cocoon or silk production was thus constrained by the amount of labor readily available in the household. In short, sericulture was an ideal secondary occupation for the peasant household, but it was often too risky to undertake as a major occupation.

"Modernization" of the silk industry, as narrowly conceived, involved the introduction of steam-powered reeling machines and factory organization. However, in many instances in both China and Japan, this technological step alone did not ensure commercial success. Modernization, as more broadly conceived, meant the introduction of a variety of technological and institutional changes that substantially reduced the natural and commercial risks inherent in the manufacture of silk and permitted the industry to expand. In Japan, silkworm disease was brought under control through mandatory inspection of silkworm eggs, standardized production, and eventually the licensing of egg producers. With the gradual introduction of summer and autumn crops of worms, sericulture became almost a year-round enterprise, and this helped reduce its speculative character. Constant scientific experimentation led to the development of better silkworm strains and higher yields for mulberry trees and cocoons as well as eggs.[23] On the commercial side, organization of rural cooperatives helped cushion the risk to individual peasants. At a later stage, better organization and vertical integration of production by steam-filature companies helped reduce the risk to enterpreneurs. In China, by contrast, even after steam filatures were introduced, commercial risks for entrepreneurs and peasants alike remained high in the absence of basic reform of financing. Sericultural schools and experimental stations were not widely established until the 1920s and 1930s, too late to be effective. In the meantime, not only had silkworm disease become rampant, but yields of mulberry and cocoons remained, at very best, stagnant.[24]

THE CHINESE PATTERN OF DEVELOPMENT

The deteriorating technological standards in Chinese silk manufacture, as well as the government's failure to assume greater responsibility in promoting the industry, seem remarkable in view of China's historical preeminence in silk products and the government's traditional vested interest in providing silks for its own needs. Since ancient times, demand generated by the Imperial Court, both for tribute purposes and its own consumption, had provided the main stimulus for the growth of the silk industry. Since the Southern Sung period (1127–1278), China's main silk-producing region had been the lower Yangtze Valley, particularly the northern prefectures of Chekiang province bordering Lake T'ai.[25] This was the most prosperous region of the country, and the concentration of Imperial Silk-Weaving Factories there during the Ming (1368–1644) and the Ch'ing (1644–1911) periods further stimulated production in the countryside. During the late Ming and early Ch'ing eras, sericultural technology reached unprecedented heights, and the silks from this area were highly prized. By the time treaty ports were opened to trade with the West in the mid-nineteenth century, however, technological improvement seems not to have continued, although the silk trade in the lower Yangtze, or Kiangnan, area was still flourishing. The sericultural manuals of this period were essentially based on those of the sixteenth and seventeenth centuries. Since the Imperial Factories were in a serious decline, raw silk was diverted to the export trade without causing serious domestic dislocation. After 1842, the locus of the export trade shifted quickly from Canton, where it had previously been relatively small in volume, to Shanghai, where it was closer to the main sericultural districts. However, the steady expansion of silk exports from Shanghai was interrupted by the Taiping Rebellion, which devastated many silk-growing localities.

After the Rebellion, there was rapid recovery in Kiangnan. Sericulture was introduced into many new localities in this region, particularly in the southern prefectures of Kiangsu province, north of Lake T'ai. The period from about 1870 to 1895 in the Kiangnan area could be described as a period of economic growth without technological change. Although attempts to establish steam filatures at Shanghai began as early as 1862, they were, with one or two exceptions, unsuccessful. Virtually all silk produced and exported continued to be reeled in simple hand or treadle machines in peasant homes. Not until the 1890s did mechanized reeling begin to play an important role at Shanghai. Thereafter steam-filature silk quickly assumed a leading role in the silk export picture. In 1895, steam-filature silk represented only about 12 percent of total silk exports from Shanghai, but in 1925 it represented about 99 percent.[26]

A kind of commercial dualism emerged in Kiangnan whereby the silk produced by the modernized sector of the industry supplied the export trade, while the silk produced by the traditional sector continued to supply the domestic market, which remained substantial. The domestic silk-weaving industry in Soochow, Nanking, and Hangchow recovered from the Taiping Rebellion, and even experienced a small boom during and after World War I. The economic dualism also expressed itself geographically. Since the modern sector was concentrated at Shanghai, and later Wusih, it was separated from its rural base and its source of cocoons. In Kiangnan, the old sericultural districts in northern Chekiang continued to produce domestically reeled silk, while the new districts in southern Kiangsu produced cocoons for the filatures to reel.[27]

In the Canton Delta, the second silk region to assume major importance in the export trade, a different pattern of growth emerged. The Kwangtung region was not as large a producer of silks for the domestic market before 1842 as Kiangnan was. With the expanded opportunities for foreign trade after 1842, sericulture spread rapidly in the delta region. Because it was largely oriented toward the foreign market, the silk industry in Kwangtung adopted steam filatures earlier than in Kiangnan.

Although the first few pioneering efforts met with local opposition, machine-reeled silk came to dominate the export picture in the 1880s. In 1882, filature silk was only 13.1 percent of all silk exports, but by 1895 it was close to 90 percent.[28] Thereafter virtually all silk exports were filature products.

The warmer climate of Kwangtung permitted the raising of seven crops of silkworms each year, thus eliminating the seasonal problems that existed in Kiangnan. Because the domestic market was less significant, the problem of economic dualism was avoided. Moreover, since filatures were located in the countryside, close to the source of cocoons, Kwangtung also escaped the problem of geographical dualism. Nevertheless, despite all the advantages Kwangtung possessed over the Kiangnan region, the Cantonese silk industry could hardly be called a success. Filatures were described by foreigners as dirty and inefficient, using backward machinery, and cocoons suffered from many defects.[29] Thus, while modernization in the narrow technological sense occurred earlier and more completely in the Canton Delta, modernization in the larger sense did not occur.

THE JAPANESE PATTERN OF DEVELOPMENT

The Japanese pattern of development differed from the Chinese in several respects. First, in Japan the opening of trade with the West coincided with a period of rapid growth and innovation in sericulture, whereas in China it coincided with a period of technological stagnation and decline of official demand. The expansion of sericulture in Japan during the Tokugawa period was directly related to political circumstances. During the seventeenth century, imports of raw silk from China had mounted, creating an imbalance of trade that greatly alarmed the Tokugawa Bakufu, which in 1685 imposed a quota reducing imports to about one-third the current level. Despite the official sumptuary regulations against the indiscriminate wearing of silks, the domestic demand for silk continued to grow, and the weaving industry centered at Nishijin in Kyoto needed new sources of raw materials. Consequently the Bakufu encouraged various *han* (domain) governments to promote sericulture, employing such measures as financial incentives, the distribution of mulberry seeds and silkworm eggs, and the publication of sericultural manuals.[30] By the late Tokugawa period, sericulture had been introduced to most parts of Japan, except the north.[31]

These efforts produced striking results. By the mid-nineteenth century, the Japanese had not only caught up with the Chinese in silk technology, but had begun to experiment with some techniques yet unknown in China.[32] The *zaguri,* or "sitting," type of reeling machine, already widespread in China, was introduced in Gumma and Fukushima, and marked a distinct advance over the hand-operated machines previously used in Japan.[33] Other technological improvements included the cold storage of eggs, and the development of summer and fall crops of worms.[34] Although Chinese techniques remained more advanced on the whole, there is no evidence of such a high level of innovative activity in China in the period just before the opening of the treaty ports. Moreover, in Japan these technological changes were accompanied by changes in the organization of production. For example, as early as the mid-eighteenth century, reeling was separated from sericulture in Gumma prefecture, where workshops were established outside the household.[35] In China, such separation of functions did not occur until the advent of steam filatures.

In the 1850s and 1860s, with the opening of the treaty ports, several new centers of sericulture emerged. Fukushima and Gumma prefectures, the traditional sources of the best raw silk, were now joined by Nagano, Gifu, and Yamanashi. The manufacture of egg-cards for export to Europe flourished in this period. Local entrepreneurs disseminated knowledge of sericultural techniques.[36] Fukushima and Gumma, among other places, further adopted the workshop form of production.[37] In this period, innovations took place within the framework of traditional technology, but, after the Meiji Restoration in 1868, a mixed pattern of traditional and modern production began to emerge. In the 1870s, several pioneering attempts at establishing steam filatures were made, the most important of which was the government model factory, the Tomioka, built in Gumma prefecture in 1872. This project was directed by a French expert working with 18 European assistants and the latest foreign machinery. Although ultimately a business failure, the Tomioka set an important example, and its staff were dispatched as instructors to other localities wanting to learn modern technology.[38]

The actual spread of steam filatures was, however, rather slow. Many enterprises classified as "factories" were in fact workshops having only 10 to 30 workers. The form of energy used in these early workshops was water power, not steam, which characterized the large-scale European filatures.[39] The adoption of Western technology was a complex process, and the various regions responded differently. In Gumma and Fukushima, for example, Western technology was accepted later and with greater difficulty than in the newer silk districts such as Nagano.[40] In Gumma especially, traditional technology was improved to produce kairyōzaguri ito, domestically reeled silk that was rereeled to produce a more even thread.[41] This type of silk was used in France and Italy as woof. The high-quality silk produced by modern steam filatures, necessary for warp-threads, did not have a large foreign demand until the growth of the American market became important in the 1890s.[42]

It was not until the turn of the century that machine-reeling assumed the dominant role in the production of silk. These modern filatures were larger in scale than the previous workshops or factories, and increasingly they used steam power.[43] After the 1910s, two giant companies, Katakura and Gunze, dominated the machine-reeling industry, spreading out from their respective bases in Nagano and Kansai to establish branch factories elsewhere.[44] In 1900, only 52 percent of Japan's total output of raw silk was machine-reeled; by 1925, over 87 percent was machine-reeled, including virtually all exported silk.[45] Though largely mechanized and factory-organized, the Japanese silk industry nevertheless retained its small-scale character. In 1926, for example, 36 percent of all filatures had fewer than 50 basins; 66 percent had fewer than 100 basins.[46]

In comparison with the Chinese pattern, the Japanese silk industry's development was smoother and more successful, but also more complex and diverse. Although some differences between old and new areas did exist in the early Meiji years, on the whole there was not the stark dualism between old and new, traditional and modern, rural and urban that tended to characterize the Chinese experience. The Japanese silk industry was geographically more extensive than the Chinese. By the Taishō period (1912–1925), some silk was produced by almost all the prefectures, and only Nagano and Aichi produced more than 10 percent of the total. In China, by contrast, the impact of the silk export trade was limited to a few regions, primarily the lower Yangtze Valley and the Canton Delta.[47] Furthermore, in Japan technological modernization was incremental and small-scale; the dramatic changes associated with big-factory production did not take place for several decades.

URBAN-RURAL INTEGRATION

In order to develop successfully, the modern silk-reeling industry had to be well integrated with its rural base. In Japan, sericulture not only became quite extensive across regions, but it also became a crucial source of income for many peasant families. Although it is estimated that, in the 1920s, at the height of its development, 32–40 percent or more of all Japanese farm families were engaged in sericulture, close to 90 percent of farm families in the more specialized areas such as Yamanashi engaged in sericulture, and as much as 56 percent of the total value of their crops came from sericulture, as opposed to rice or cash crops.[48] In China, by contrast, only in one exceptionally specialized sericultural district in the Canton Delta did silk income form as much as 80 percent of farm income. In the relatively specialized areas of Kiangnan, surveys show no more than 20–40 percent of farm income derived from sericulture, and, in the average nonspecialized area, income from sericulture could be considered only supplementary.[49]

Another distinctive characteristic of the Japanese silk industry was the extent to which it retained its rural character.[50] Rural entrepreneurs and laborers, as well as rural capital, played important roles in the development of the industry. In some areas, ex-samurai were the leading entrepreneurs.[51] In many areas, landlords ordered their tenants to plant mulberry and raise silkworms.[52] Moreover, filatures in the countryside drew on an abundant and cheap supply of labor—the daughters of peasant families. These girls provided extra income for their families, and yet they remained part of the rural context and could return to other pursuits during the slack season.[53] In areas where sericulture was older, silk-raising families were not really hurt by the loss of income from domestic reeling, for they could make it up through their daughters' wages.

Even with the increase in steam filatures, the rural and urban sectors of the silk industry remained solidly integrated. Filatures were relatively small, and they were well distributed through the rural silk districts and towns, which meant easier access to an adequate supply of cocoons. Cocoons represented about 80 percent of the operating costs of a filature, and their quality was the single most important factor in determining the success of an enterprise.[54] For example, a key reason for the failure of the model filature established in 1871 in Tsukiji, a district of Tokyo, was its inability to secure good cocoons.[55] With the advent of the large-scale filature companies, it became increasingly common for filatures to distribute silkworm eggs to peasants—an even more effective way of insuring the quality of the cocoon supply.[56]

The strength of the rural sector was an inheritance from the Tokugawa period, which persisted into the modern period. The rural-centered commercial growth of the early modern period— which had no parallel in Ch'ing China—reflected the waning control of the bakufu over the countryside and the decline of the economic leadership of the cities. In Thomas C. Smith's view, the modern textile industry was derived from this formative premodern experience. "The modern textile industry," he wrote, "grew mainly in districts of traditional manufacture; much of the growth occurred in villages and former 'country-places'; entrepreneurs, plant managers, buyers, shippers and labour contractors came from these same districts; and labour came overwhelmingly from farm families."[57]

The formation of various types of rural cooperatives helped silk producers overcome the disadvantages of small-scale and atomized production. As early as the 1870s and 1880s, silk-reelers' cooperatives undertook the weighing, packing, and shipping of silk to Yokohama.[58] Although the Gumma prefecture "improved" silk-reelers' attempts at forming a federation of such cooperatives in 1880 was unsuccessful, later attempts did succeed.[59] By the end of the Meiji period, small filatures with relatively little leverage in negotiating loans for the purchase of cocoons joined together in *kumi,* or unions, to obtain financing from Yokohama wholesalers. By the Taishō period, peasant producers of cocoons organized themselves into village-wide unions in order to deal with the filatures more effectively. With government support, the cocoon unions formed federations within each prefecture, and a nationwide federation appeared in the early Showa period (1926-).[60]

Cooperatives were an especially effective form of organization for silk production because they provided some economic centralization of a technologically decentralized productive process, and they gave the vulnerable peasant producers some leverage. As G. C. Allen and Audrey G. Donnithorne have observed, "The silk trade for its successful organization, needed a high degree of centralization at some points and wide dispersion at others. . . . This trade which in most branches is necessarily a small scale industry depends for its success on central supervision and government intervention at a few key points."[61] The marketing of cocoons was one key point. In China, cooperatives were not even the subject of experiments until the 1930s—when the world silk trade was already in decline.[62]

In the Kiangnan region of China, the problem of rural-urban integration was particularly pronounced. Steam filatures, being concentrated first at Shanghai and later at Wusih, were institutionally, as well as geographically, remote from the rural sector. Moreover, the urban filatures tended to be large-scale enterprises, which made them greater risks to operate.[63] Without any base in the rural areas, the filatures depended on rural cocoon hongs to provide their cocoon supply. The hongs bought cocoons from local peasants, dried them, and shipped them to warehouses or filatures at Shanghai. They were usually financed by local businessmen and contracted to a filature or cocoon broker.[64] Although the price of cocoons soared when filatures were established, their quality deteriorated, since the peasants no longer had a stake in the reeling process. The peasant households could not defend themselves against commercial fluctuations by withholding their cocoons from the annual spring market, since the moths would break through the cocoons within ten days unless the cocoons were dried. In addition, the location of the filatures in the cities meant that peasants were denied the potential income their daughters might have earned if the factories were nearby.

There were two major reasons for the rural-urban split in the Kiangnan area. First, the silk-weaving industry strongly opposed the growth of the raw-silk export trade, and particularly the modern filatures associated with the trade. Fearing a further rise in the price of raw silk, the weaving interests prevailed upon the Chekiang and Kiangsu provincial governments to limit the number of cocoon hongs in each locality. Such legislation, although sometimes ignored, was not repealed until the late 1920s.[65] In Japan, the traditional weaving centers, at Nishijin in Kyoto, and Kiryū in Gumma, also experienced great difficulty, but they did not have the political strength to resist the trend toward foreign trade.[66] Second, the weakness of the Ch'ing government permitted Shanghai and the other treaty ports to dominate the development of modern enterprises. Shanghai, in particular, had all the advantages of extraterritorial protection, access to financing and shipping, and immunity from arbitrary taxation. Wusih's emergence as a subsidiary center of steam filatures in the Kiangnan area did not begin until after World War I, when political unrest at Shanghai caused concern and the advantages of Wusih's location in a major sericultural district became apparent.

In the Canton Delta, urban-rural integration was not such a problem, since the filatures were located in the countryside, and factory workers were local peasant girls and women. The potential advantages of Canton as a treaty port were outweighed by the convenience of a rural location. "Native," as opposed to foreign, capital also played a larger role in the early Canton filatures, although in fact the silk industry at Shanghai too was largely a Chinese business except in the early years. Nevertheless, the Canton filatures also had no direct control over their cocoon supply, and depended on cocoon markets and cocoon merchants.[67] This suggests that, while they were not geographically separated from rural sericulture, Canton filatures were almost as institutionally separated as their Shanghai counterparts. Better urban-rural integration was not enough to compensate for another critical weakness.

COMMERCIAL INSTITUTIONS AND PRACTICES

This weakness, which was felt by all segments of the Chinese silk industry, was a pervasive scarcity of capital[68] and was reflected in the way the silk trade was organized. The silk export trade operated within the framework of preexisting commercial practices. The traditional organization of internal silk commerce was highly specialized in function but very decentralized. Each stage in silk manufacturing—from the marketing of mulberry saplings to the embroidering of brocades—was controlled by a series of middlemen or brokers, whose function was exchange, not production.[69] With the opening of trade with the West, this chain of middlemen was simply lengthened by one or two links. Peasants in the silk districts sold their reeled silk to the local silk hong, which in turn sold the silk to a Shanghai raw-silk broker with whom it generally had some long-term working relationship.[70] The Shanghai brokers then sold the silk to the Western export firms.[71]

The export trade itself was entirely in the hands of Western firms, but they did not, indeed could not, interfere with the internal commercial network, which remained firmly under Chinese control. The Shanghai silk-brokers formed the crucial link between Western merchants and Chinese producers. Numbering about 50 in the 1920s, these brokers were extremely powerful, often serving in dual roles as compradors to Western firms and as independent businessmen.[72] They were the masters of the silk trade. Each brokerage had its own "chop" and reputation to maintain.

This system worked satisfactorily until the advent of filatures, when traditional business procedures were extended to the new institutions, but not successfully. The Shanghai filatures were frequently undercapitalized, and numerous ventures failed. The shortage of capital accentuated the decentralized organization of the silk business. First, the filature companies did not own their own physical plants. Instead, they rented plants from real-estate owners when the season looked promising. Some filatures did not operate in bad seasons. Thus, the companies had no fixed capital and little long-term risk.[73] The cocoon hongs in Kiangnan, too, operated on a seasonal basis and did not have their own fixed plants. At Canton, clans or families frequently built filatures to rent out.[74] The cocoon markets were owned by one set of local landlords or merchants and operated by another.[75] The effect of these practices on the quality of the equipment and the final product was, needless to say, not beneficial, and exacerbated the speculative aspects of the silk business.

While the need for fixed capital was thus minimized, a substantial amount of operating capital was needed each spring to purchase cocoons—an estimated 75 million dollars per season at Shanghai.[76] The *ch'ien-chuang,* or "native" banks, became the chief financial backers of the cocoon hongs, as well as of the filatures. After the contract was made with a cocoon hong, a *ch'ien-chuang* would send a man to the silk district to pay the money and supervise the shipment of cocoons to Shanghai, where they were stored in a designated warehouse. Foreign exporters were also directly and indirectly involved in the financing of cocoon purchases and filatures, but for the most part the silk industry remained in Chinese hands.[77]

In Japan, by contrast, silk export development coincided with a period of transformation of economic institutions. Some changes—such as the gradual abolition of the *kabu-nakama,* or trade associations—had been initiated during the Tokugawa period.[78] In the silk trade, this cleared the way for different social groups to emerge as rural entrepreneurs.[79] Recent studies claim that social structure was an important factor in determining the receptivity of a locality to innovations. Nagano, for example, was quicker to accept foreign technology than Gumma, in part because merchants and peasants were more influential in the former, while officials exercised stronger influence in the latter.[80] Like the Wusih area of Kiangnan, Nagano possessed the advantages of newness with respect to silk production. By contrast, Fukushima, which had been the major supplier of raw silk to Nishijin in the Tokugawa period, did not flourish in the export trade precisely because of the presence of old commercial groups with vested interests.[81] Later, the large-scale filatures tended to cluster in new sericultural areas such as Yamagata, Aichi, Mie, and Kyoto.[82] Unlike the comparable areas in China, the old sericultural areas in Japan did not pose an obstacle to the general development and spread of sericulture to the rest of the country.

The most important new institution associated with the silk industry was that of the Yokohama wholesaler, or *urikomi-tonya*. During the Meiji period there were 20 to 30 of these *tonya*, 4 of whom together accounted for about 75 percent of the business transacted by the brokerages.[83] The basic function of the Yokohama wholesaler was to mediate between the rural silk producers and the silk exporters at Yokohama. Starting in the late 1880s, the wholesalers also began to finance the operations of small filatures, mostly of a semi-modernized type. They extended to these filatures working capital to purchase cocoons.[84] They also worked with these enterprises to organize group purchases of cocoons and other cooperative ventures designed to lower costs.[85] The Yokohama brokers were extremely powerful, and they became extremely wealthy, earning profits both from their consignment fees and from financing loans.[86]

Unlike the compradors of Shanghai, whose strongest ties were to the treaty port itself, the Yokohama wholesalers often came from the rural areas; for example, Maebashi and other Gumma merchants became Yokohama dealers.[87] Although there were superficial similarities between the Shanghai brokers and Yokohama wholesalers, the Japanese silk merchants played a more dynamic—some would say more oppressive—role in developing the silk trade.[88] They were much more active agents of change than the Shanghai brokers. The Yokohama dealers themselves spearheaded the movement toward standardized inspection of silk exports, for example.

However, in the long run, the movement toward direct export led to the decline of the Yokohama brokers' influence.[89] Eventually Japanese companies began to take the lead over foreign firms in the export trade. In 1888, for example, Japanese firms handled only about 8 percent of silk exports, while by 1912 they handled over 53 percent.[90] The large filature companies also engaged in direct exporting to their Western customers, and their financial resources exceeded those of the wholesalers.[91] Katakura, for example, owned 9 egg-manufacturing stations, 54 filatures, testing laboratories in Yokohama and the rural districts, and had a branch office in New York after World War I.[92] Thus, these large firms engaged in the vertical integration of the silk industry, while rural cooperatives, where they existed, provided a form of horizontal integration.

The growing role of local and city banks in financing silk transactions also contributed to the decline of the Yokohama wholesalers. Since the establishment of the Yokohama Specie Bank in 1880 and the Bank of Japan in 1882, commercial banks were able to assist the wholesalers in extending credit to silk-reelers.[93] Generally, local banks lent money only when the Yokohama wholesalers did so.[94] By the first decade of the twentieth century, bank loans represented about 75 percent of silk financing, and wholesalers' loans about 25 percent.[95] The growth of the banking system was a critical factor in encouraging the flow of capital into the silk business, but the silk trade also contributed to the development of Japanese banking.[96] Certainly the development of a modern banking system at an early date distinguished the Japanese modern experience from the Chinese. Behind the banking system stood the Japanese government, which was directly responsible for a substantial portion of the financing of the silk trade.[97]

Why the Japanese government promoted the development of banking far earlier than the Chinese; why Japanese companies took direct control of exporting, while Chinese companies left the exporting side to foreign firms; and why Japanese firms directly controlled shipping, while Chinese companies permitted foreign firms to dominate shipping along the China coast—these are all basic questions that must be addressed in the larger context of Chinese and Japanese economic history and lie beyond the scope of this inquiry. The experience of the silk industry, however, highlights certain aspects of economic development that have received relatively little attention. The growth of the Japanese silk industry and its preeminence in the international market by the early twentieth century may appear to be quite dramatic, but some of the factors behind that growth are less than dramatic. It was not merely a story of strong government, big business, and rapid technological change, but also a story of significant early modern momentum, steady incremental growth on a small scale, and the continued strength of the rural sector and its integration with the industrialized sector. From an historian's point of view, the degree to which fundamental changes in technology and economic organization had already been set into motion in Japan before the opening of the treaty ports and the degree to which "modernization" rested on traditional forces and institutions are most impressive.

Although this chapter has focused on the more successful performance of the Japanese silk industry in the world market, and in so doing has emphasized the differences between Chinese and Japanese economic performances, it must be said that the Chinese industry did not perform poorly. It was not unresponsive to market opportunities. The industry did expand and change. It is simply that the extent of the change was not sufficient to have a structural impact. From a longer historical perspective, however, as the nineteenth century recedes farther into the past, the similarities between Chinese and Japanese institutions and practices will indeed appear more striking than their differences, and their common strengths more important than their weaknesses. Shorter-term historical and economic factors will play a larger role in explaining short-term phenomena. It is only when we view the Chinese experience in juxtaposition with the Japanese, and in the context of the international market, during this relatively limited period of time, that the Chinese industry seems backward or unsuccessful.

PART TWO

American Imports into China

CHAPTER FOUR

The Chinese-American Cotton-Textile Trade, 1830-1930

KANG CHAO

The United States was one of China's major trading partners during the century prior to the outbreak of the Sino-Japanese War in 1937. The volume of trade between the two countries was below that for Britain or India during the years 1871–1900, but the United States rose to second place during the first three decades of the twentieth century (and Japan replaced Britain as China's trade partner.)[1]

Unlike trade with Britain and Japan, however, China's trade with America developed along a natural course, in the sense that the American government did not apply military or political pressure, or any other artificial device, to promote trade with China. The volume and composition of Sino-American trade were generally determined by the comparative advantages of the two economies, plus some accidental factors. This is apparent in the persistent trade deficits on the American side until the turn of the century.[2] Even from 1901 to 1918, America still experienced alternating favorable and unfavorable balances. It was only after 1918 that the United States enjoyed consistent surpluses.

The American exportation of cotton cloth offers a typical case illustrating the natural development of commercial relations between the two nations. Following a few explorative attempts by the East India Company to sell cotton goods to China at the beginning of the nineteenth century, cotton goods became a key Chinese import (only opium outranked them). After the middle of the nineteenth century, cotton goods reached first place, accounting for about one-third of China's annual imports.[3] At the outset, the Chinese market for foreign textiles was dominated by Britain and India, but the U.S. quickly joined them as a major supplier. Table 17 shows the amount of cotton cloth exported by America to China during the period 1826–1930. As can be seen, this item was dominant until its virtual collapse during the 1910s. Between the initial rise and the final demise, several short-term fluctuations occurred that were readily explainable by events in those years. The opening of the treaty ports in 1842 caused a sudden spurt in exports to China in the ensuing years. The Taiping Rebellion, which devastated the economy of China's coastal provinces, led to a drastic decline in foreign trade after 1853. As a result of the opening of more treaty ports along the northern coast, the Chinese importation of cotton goods jumped in 1859. This was followed by a slump during the period of the American Civil War, which seriously curtailed the supply of raw cotton from southern states to American cotton mills and interrupted American shipping.

Our chief concern here, however, is not those short-term fluctuations but the basic factors underlying the development of Sino-American trade in cotton goods. In the following pages, we shall attempt to analyze the success of American cotton cloth in the Chinese market during the nineteenth century, and the reasons that America lost that market in the early twentieth century.

TABLE 17   American Exports of Cotton Cloth to China,
          1826–1930

	Exports of Cotton Cloth to China ($1,000)	*Percent of Total American Exports to China*
1826	14	5.8
1830	52	33.3
1835	172	51.2
1840	361	77.0
1845	1,413	68.0
1850	1,203	81.0
1855	586	68.3
1860	3,897	69.3
1870	314	8.3
1875	548	37.4
1880	334	30.3
1885	3,405	53.2
1890	1,223	41.5
1895	1,703	44.3
1900	8,783	57.6
1905	27,760	52.0
1910	5,763	35.3
1915	1,381	7.9
1920	7,651	5.3
1925	1,083	1.2
1930	71	0

Source: U.S. Department of Commerce: *Foreign Commerce and Navigation of the United States,* various years.

CHARACTERISTICS OF THE AMERICAN COTTON-TEXTILE INDUSTRY

In order to appreciate the potential of American cotton-textile export to China, and the nature of the international competition during the period between 1830 and 1930, it is necessary to understand the unique features of the cotton-textile industry in the United States (see Table 17). It was from that uniqueness that the American products derived their appeal to Chinese consumers.

The modern cotton textile industry in the United States can be traced to 1790, when a young Englishman, Samuel Slater, helped some people in Rhode Island construct a mill equipped with a water frame and other machines. The infant industry gradually spread throughout New England. The pace of development was moderate at first, the spindleage reaching only 130,000 in 1815.[4] But total capacity increased rapidly thereafter, reaching 2.3 million spindles by 1840 and 5.2 million by 1860.[5] The ante-bellum tariff policy restricting foreign textiles, especially those from Britain, and the increased production of raw cotton in the south, undoubtedly contributed to the expansion. Most important, however, was the ingenuity of American entrepreneurs, who invented new machines and organizational techniques to suit the local factor endowment.

There were significant differences between the cotton industries in the United States and in England. English textile machines were invented to suit a labor force that had been trained for generations in the spinning and weaving processes. Labor conditions in the United States were very different during the early stage of the industry. The United States was sparsely populated and seriously short of skilled workers. The labor cost per unit of output was comparatively high; more important, many English textile machines were too complicated for American workers. Under the circumstances, mill owners were anxious to acquire machines that unskilled workers could operate at high speeds. A variety of such devices soon appeared; new mills benefited from the inventions, and older mills immediately replaced their equipment with new machines. As one federal government official observed in 1832, the garrets and outhouses of most textile mills were crowded with discarded machinery. A Rhode Island cotton mill built in 1813 had replaced every original machine by 1827.[6]

The important nineteenth-century inventions included the self-acting temple, automatic loom, automatic roving machine, self-acting mule, ring spindle, fly frame, bale-breaker, and automatic distributor. In addition, significant modifications were made on the existing equipment in order to raise the speed of operation. One example is the driving belt, invented by Paul Moody and first used in 1828, when the Appleton Mill was built. The operation speed of American belt-driven machines was considerably higher than gear-driven machines of the English type.

The high wage level in the United States led mill owners to adopt sophisticated organizational techniques, in particular a high degree of specialization and vertical integration. Unlike Lancashire mills, where spinning, weaving, bleaching, printing, dyeing, and packing were done separately by small, independent firms, most New England cotton mills were large in size and vertically integrated in structure.[7] Such practices meant substantial cost savings.

While the early innovations raised the speed of machine operation and reduced the skill requirement of workers, American mills could not manufacture high-grade products. The mills were able to make only a narrow range of coarse and medium-grade products. It was a mass-production industry in which the minimum acceptable order is said to have been about 6,000 to 10,000 yards of a single pattern.[8] In England, cotton mills were quite willing to cater to small orders from diverse sources, and, as a result, British mills produced a wider variety of goods.

The American innovations undoubtedly enhanced productivity. Although there are no accurate statistics for the early years of the industry, the rough estimates establish this point beyond any doubt.[9]

The first half of the nineteenth century witnessed a rapid expansion of cotton planting in the south, chiefly because of the invention of the cotton gin by Eli Whitney. It is no surprise, therefore, to note astonishing decreases in the prices of both raw cotton and cotton cloth in the years before 1850.[10] The American cotton industry retained its early characteristics even after its center moved from New England to the South. Though wage levels in the South were generally lower than in the North, labor skills also were less developed. The lower cost of raw cotton in the South provided an additional incentive for mills to concentrate on the more material-consuming coarse yarn and cloth.

The ante-bellum tariff policy insured a well-protected domestic market for American cotton manufacturers. As a result, American production was basically intended to satisfy domestic demand. The English, by contrast, produced mainly for foreign markets. It has been estimated that no more than 5 or 6 percent of total output left the United States in any year before 1840; the percentage rose slowly to 7.8 in 1850 and 9.5 in 1860.[11] The tendency not to export was even stronger in the case of cotton yarn, which was produced by integrated mills for their own internal consumption. Because they were a vent for domestic surpluses, American textile exports tended to fluctuate in the opposite direction from the movement of domestic sales.[12] American consular officials and import-export firms frequently complained that their cotton manufacturers at home refused to produce goods according to the specifications preferred in foreign markets.[13] Cancellations of overseas sales were also frequently reported. This happened when a mill had accepted foreign orders during a period of a slackened domestic demand, and then decided to cancel the orders as soon as business revived at home.[14] It was not until the end of the nineteenth century that a few large mills were established in the South that produced exclusively for the export trade.[15]

QUALITY AND PRICE OF AMERICAN COTTON CLOTH

When Western merchants first introduced power-loom cloth into China, they discovered a special preference pattern among Chinese consumers. Wealthy people in cities tended to prefer fine, light-weight cotton fabrics as substitutes for silk products. But peasants and low-income urban dwellers preferred heavy, coarse cloth. The preference of the latter groups, which constituted by far the great majority of the population, stemmed from several centuries' use of handicraft cloth in the country. Since hand-spinning could produce only coarse yarn equivalent to the range of 6 to 14 count, cloth woven with native yarn was naturally much heavier per unit of area in comparison with imported fabrics woven with machine-spun yarn. Heavy cloth was believed to be more durable and warmer. But that was not always true; some cloth woven with thinner machine-spun yarn could be as durable, or even more durable compared with the heavier native cloth. It took some time for Chinese consumers to recognize this fact and to change their preference. However, heavy cloth was definitely warmer because the yarn was thicker. Added warmth was appreciated especially by users in the northern provinces, and there the preference pattern remained unchanged.

When British merchants tried to promote sales during the first half of the nineteenth century, they encountered a serious problem. Though Lancashire had an abundance of skilled workers who could produce high-grade fabrics, it lacked an adequate domestic supply of raw cotton. Cotton prices were high. If a mill put sufficient cotton in the cloth to make it heavy enough for the Chinese, the price of cloth would be exorbitant. Nevertheless, English mills tried hard to imitate native Chinese cloth by producing the so-called T-cloth. Closely resembling Chinese handloom cloth in construction, except the doubled width, T-cloth soon became one of the most popular items among imported fabrics in the Chinese market.[16] It was imported in the grey form and was sold to native dyers, who could tincture it according to Chinese tastes.

In the early records of American external trade, the term *nankeens,* a popular type of Chinese handicraft cotton cloth, appeared on the export side. These goods were reexported nankeens that some American merchants had just imported from China.[17] It was unnecessary for American mills to imitate Chinese handicraft cloth. The cloth manufactured by New England mills was quite compatible with the Chinese preference.

The structural features of the American cotton-textile industry and the types of equipment used by it dictated, in a general sense, the type and quality of its products. Most of the automatic devices invented before the Civil War were suitable only to the production of low-count yarn and cloth. On the early ring frame, for instance, yarn was continually dragged around the traveler; hence the yarn was subject to greater strain than that spun by the mule. Because of the strain, the ring frame could not be employed to spin high-count yarns. But, the yarn produced on the ring frame was harder, stronger, and more tightly twisted, in comparison with the mule-spun yarn, which was soft and gave what was called a "clothy" feeling.

Moreover, the low price of raw cotton in the country was another great advantage for American mills in the manufacture of the highly material-consuming types of fabrics. Thus, American mills adopted mass-production techniques to turn out heavy and coarse cloth in large quantities; very few of the more elaborate cloths such as checks and plaids were manufactured until some later time. Since American producers were not export-oriented and had no incentives to tailor their production to any special needs of foreign consumers, heavy cloth was the main type of cotton fabric available for exporting in that period.

American cloth did not resemble the native handloom cloth in appearance, but merchants could easily demonstrate the product's heavy weight to Chinese consumers.[18] Consequently, sales of American cloth in China quickly rose in value from $899,400 in 1826 to more than $8 million in 1853. It threatened the English-made T-cloth, whose share in the Chinese market dwindled during the nineteenth century.[19] As a result, some British exporters were tempted to place American trademarks on British products;[20] this was possible because at certain Chinese ports the customs offices did not make any distinction between manufactures of American and British origin.[21]

The crisis of the Lancashire mills deepened after the American Civil War broke out. The wartime blockade of shipping practically shut England off from the American supply. British producers reacted by reducing the amount of raw cotton used per unit area of cloth and increasing the amount of sizing material in order to maintain the same total weight. The fact that English mills employed mules instead of ring spindles made it possible for them to apply heavy size, because the yarn spun by mules was not twisted as hard as on the ring frame, which left more surface area for the size to adhere to. It did not take long for the practice of heavy sizing to spoil the reputation of English cloth in the Chinese market. Users quickly realized that much of the weight disappeared after washing. Still worse, after absorbing moisture, some sizing materials induced mildew. Chinese merchants soon concluded that American cloth was preferable to British cloth. As time passed, moreover, it became clear to the Chinese that light-weight fabrics were not necessarily less durable. More and more people, especially in the cities, learned to appreciate the softness, smooth surface, and brighter colors of the finer fabrics,[22] and boosted the demand for those goods. Since English mills commanded inherent advantages over other countries in producing finer fabrics, they finally secured a firm hold on the market in south China and the coastal cities. American mills refused to follow suggestions made by many American consuls that they manufacture lighter goods for the Chinese market.[23]

Even then, American cotton textiles were by no means losing ground. On the contrary, they continued to make inroads in regions where light-weight products from England could not penetrate. American piece goods became popular in inland areas where people had not shaken off their habitual attachment to heavy cloth.[24] More important, North China and Manchuria developed into a rich market for the heavy grey plain texture goods from American mills.[25] The preference of people in those chilly provinces for heavy cloth was based on genuine physical need.

By the 1870s, there was a clear division in the Chinese market for imported fabrics: The British dominated the fine-cloth segment of the market, and the Americans kept a firm hold on the trade in coarse cloth. Taking the five-year averages for 1886–1890, the proportions of British and American products were as follows:[26]

Sheetings
British goods	31.5%
American goods	68.5%

Coarse drills
British goods	36.3%
American goods	60.3%

Fine drills
British goods	75.6%
American goods	14.1%

Around the turn of the century, the proportion of American products in total Chinese imports of coarse cloth reached 80 to 90 percent.[27]

An equally clear pattern of geographical distribution in China was also established by the 1870s. It is plain from Table 18 that more than two-thirds of the American goods arrived at ports in North China and Manchuria. It should be pointed out that the

TABLE 18 Net Imports[a] of American Cotton Fabrics at
All Treaty Ports, 1876 and 1879
(values in 1,000 HKT)

| | 1876 | | 1879 | |
	Value	Percent of Total	Value	Percent of Total
North China				
Newchwang	252	33.5	352	10.5
Tientsin	292	38.8	1,788	53.1
Chefoo	72	9.6	445	13.2
Central China				
Ichang	—	—	—	—
Hankow	7	0.9	211	6.3
Kiukiang	—	—	11	0.3
East China				
Wuhu	—	—	20	0.6
Chinkiang	4	0.5	75	2.2
Shanghai	70	9.4	402	11.9
Ningpo	9	1.2	32	1.0
Wenchow	—	—	3	0.1
South China				
Foochow	21	2.8	13	0.4
Tansui	6	0.8	—	—
Takow	—	—	—	—
Amoy	10	1.3	10	0.3
Swatow	—	—	—	—
Canton	6	0.8	2	0.1
Kiungchow	3	0.4	1	—
Pakhoi	—	—	—	—
Total	752	100.0	3,365	100.0

Source: China, Imperial Maritime Customs Service, Report on Trade, 1879, p. 28.

Note: [a]Net imports means imports minus reexports.

bulk of American piece goods landed first in Shanghai and
then were transshipped to the northern ports by Chinese
dealers. Shown in the table are the figures for net imports,
or the gross imports at each port minus the reexports from
there to other ports, a category that best represents the geographical distribution of final sales. When the port of Newchwang

TABLE 19 Chinese Imports of Drills and Sheetings
at the Port of Newchwang from America and
England, 1882–1901
(values in 1,000 HKT)

	Drills		Sheetings	
	English	*American*	*English*	*American*
1882	34	226	44	136
1883	44	267	28	177
1884	12	325	49	362
1885	16	229	33	424
1886	40	380	48	459
1887	78	215	115	549
1888	70	219	70	423
1889	74	258	30	388
1890	182	334	102	851
1891	55	572	62	1,198
1892	46	401	93	980
1893	224	303	196	770
1894	119	489	44	1,004
1895	131	265	89	411
1896	30	856	83	1,319
1897	–	1,186	34	1,939
1898	5	1,270	52	2,154
1899	12	2,024	41	3,911
1900	–	419	10	1,534
1901	2	1,967	11	3,528

Source: China, Imperial Maritime Customs Service, *Decennial Reports,* 1892–1901,
p. 40.

is singled out, some breakdown data on imported cloth by type
are available (Table 19). The American dominance in drills and
sheetings is unmistakable.

The structural characteristics of the cotton-textile industries
in America and Britain were reflected in the prices of their
products in the Chinese market. The Customs Office in Newchwang published figures on quantities and values of drills and
sheetings imported from the two countries, respectively, for the

years between 1882 and 1901. These data allow calculation of the "unit values" of the two items from the two sources, as shown in Table 20. The HKT prices, shown in the left half of the table, display certain rising trends over the twenty-year period. The increase stemmed primarily from the continuous decline in the exchange rate between the Chinese silver tael and foreign currencies.

It would be more revealing to examine dollar prices of the imported fabrics, as presented in the right half of Table 20. A number of points stand out. First, dollar prices of English fabrics were relatively stable throughout the period, probably because British mills were more export-oriented and it was in their interest to maintain stable selling prices in external markets. In contrast, dollar prices of American drills and sheetings were subject to frequent fluctuations. In disposing of surplus products abroad during domestic recessions, American mills were quite willing to lower their export prices.[28] Second, the selling prices of British drills and sheetings during the 1870s and 1880s were substantially lower than those of American products, yet Americans in fact outsold British exporters. Obviously, Chinese customers were quite quality-conscious, willing to pay a substantial premium for the "honest cloth" rather than the cheaper but adulterated product. Third, dollar prices of English drills and sheetings remained roughly constant over the two decades, whereas the dollar prices of American goods displayed a generally downward trend. Prices of drills and sheetings from the two origins became about equal toward the end of the nineteenth century. By then, the superior quality of American goods had driven English drills and sheetings out of the markets in Manchuria and North China, as shown by the statistics in Table 19.

TRADE ORGANIZATIONS
AND MARKETING TECHNIQUES

Unlike most other Western powers, the United States had neither concessions of her own in the treaty ports nor a sphere of influence in any part of China. Americans in China were overshadowed by the British politically as well as commercially. The

TABLE 20 Chinese Prices of Drills and Sheetings Imported from England and America, 1882–1901

| | HKT per Piece | | | | Dollars per Piece | | | |
| | Drills | | Sheetings | | Drills | | Sheetings | |
	English	*American*	*English*	*American*	*English*	*American*	*English*	*American*
1882	1.55	2.50	1.78	2.45	2.14	3.45	2.46	3.38
1883	1.76	2.38	1.81	2.45	2.38	3.22	2.45	3.32
1884	1.81	2.35	1.83	2.36	2.44	3.17	2.47	3.19
1885	1.77	2.25	1.60	2.27	2.27	2.88	2.05	2.91
1886	1.90	2.17	1.95	2.14	2.32	2.65	2.38	2.61
1887	1.94	2.14	2.04	2.13	2.33	2.57	2.45	2.56
1888	2.01	2.12	1.93	2.22	2.31	2.44	2.22	2.55
1889	2.04	2.07	1.93	1.99	2.35	2.38	2.22	2.29
1890	1.97	2.07	1.90	2.05	2.50	2.63	2.41	2.60
1891	2.11	2.59	2.23	2.63	2.53	3.11	2.68	3.16
1892	2.42	2.61	2.26	2.65	2.59	2.79	2.42	2.84
1893	2.79	3.00	2.75	3.06	2.68	2.88	2.64	2.94
1894	3.25	3.46	3.31	3.46	2.50	2.66	2.55	2.66
1895	3.40	3.65	3.55	3.00	2.72	2.92	2.84	2.40
1896	3.04	3.46	3.04	3.51	2.46	2.80	2.46	2.84
1897	–	3.40	3.40	3.42	–	2.45	2.45	2.46
1898	3.10	3.45	3.40	3.44	2.17	2.42	2.38	2.41
1899	3.15	3.46	3.44	3.55	2.30	2.52	2.51	2.59
1900	–	3.60	3.60	3.60	–	2.70	2.70	2.70
1901	3.50	3.60	3.50	3.60	2.52	2.59	2.52	2.59

Sources: Quantities and HKT values: From the trade returns at Newchwang, in *Decennial Reports, 1892–1901,* p. 40. Exchange rates: Hsiao Liang-lin, *China's Foreign Trade Statistics,* pp. 190–191.

oriental market was unimportant to American exports; U.S. exports to China and Hong Kong constituted only a negligible portion of total exports throughout the nineteenth century.[29] Except for a few American trading houses that specialized in the China trade, most American merchants regarded the Chinese market as peripheral. Consequently, the mechanisms of American trade in China remained relatively underdeveloped.

During the first half of the nineteenth century, except for East India Company shipments, foreign trade in China was generally carried on through so-called commission houses run by Western merchants. Instead of confining themselves to the agency business and commission incomes, the large trading houses engaged in a variety of activities. They maintained their own commercial fleets, bought merchandise with their own capital, kept sizeable stocks of goods, and operated foreign exchange banks, insurance companies, and warehouses. Their multifarious activities were important, for otherwise there would be no such modern institutions in China to facilitate foreign trade. As a rule, trading houses hired compradors to deal with local problems.

The prominent American trading houses in China included Augustine Heard & Co., Olyphant & Co., Russell & Co., King & Co., and Wetmore & Co. Generally, the risk factors for the American trading houses were somewhat greater than for the British firms, for a number of reasons. Since American manufacturers, especially cotton-mill owners, were not export-oriented, there were fewer consignment transactions. American trading houses had to take the initiative by themselves and bought the goods on their own account, which naturally required heavier capital investment. Furthermore, as noted earlier, most of the imported British fabrics were destined for consumers in big cities along the Yangtze River and the southern coast, whereas the American cloth had to be transported over longer distances to the inland areas and the northern provinces. The frequent internal disturbances in China often disrupted marketing of the American goods. This was another important reason for the comparatively greater fluctuations in both quantity and price of imported American cloth. In other words, local disturbances created a greater risk to American trading houses than to their British counterparts. It is not surprising, therefore, to note a higher rate of failure—or what was called "bursted" in contemporary jargon—among American trading firms.[30]

Significant institutional changes took place gradually after 1860 in China. Modern banks, insurance companies, and other complementary services were established one by one. New trading firms no longer needed to diversify their activities. The availability of telegraphic communication, and the faster shipping time made possible by steamships and the opening of the Suez Canal made it unnecessary to hold large stocks of goods on hand. New firms were inclined to concentrate on commission transactions rather than to buy on their own account. Since doing business in the new way entailed less capital and involved less risk, small new trading firms mushroomed. Other important developments inducing organizational change included the opening of new ports along the Yangtze River and in the north, and the increasing involvement of Chinese merchants in external trade, especially the import business. Having extended their financial resources and manpower to so many activities and so many localities, the old trading houses now found themselves in a precarious position. The keen competition compelled them to close down their branches in small ports and retreat to the major cities. Foreign trade in small ports was left largely to Chinese merchants, who purchased from trading houses in the major centers.

Chinese merchants had mastered the operations of foreign trade by the 1860s. Chinese dealers usually had lower distribution costs, moreover, and were contented with smaller profit margins. As reported by the Customs Office in Foochow in July 1966:[31]

Native consumers of foreign produce naturally prefer dealing with Chinese merchants, as the latter generally procure remnants of goods in Hong Kong, which they can afford to dispose of here at lower prices than those demanded by foreign merchants.

There are indications that local dealers, even those operating inland, were well informed regarding commodity supplies.[32] The role of these merchants was particularly important in the northern ports. For instance, the Customs Office at Tientsin remarked in 1866: [33]

Imports have been very large, but nearly all consigned to Chinese. . . . It may be remarked, in proof of how entirely the foreign trade of piece goods is now in the hands of the Chinese merchants, that out of the 146,000 pieces of grey shirtings imported during last month, no one piece has been consigned to a foreign Hong on foreign account.

By 1891, no foreign traders in piece goods remained at Foochow or Chefoo, as the trade had been entirely taken over by Chinese. [34]

Importing American cotton goods typically necessitated the following procedures. A Chinese cloth merchant went to an American trading agency in his own locality or in a large trading center such as Shanghai or Hong Kong. The agency then placed an order with an American cotton manufacturer or an exporter in New York. In addition to the basic cost (including f.o.b. price, freight, and insurance), the agency charged a commission. The agency or the consignee then had to make credit arrangements with a bank.

In addition to the usual problems faced by foreign merchants in China, American firms were handicapped by a number of special burdens. One complaint often heard among American merchants was that no American bank existed in China to meet their credit needs. Edward C. Lord, U.S. Consul at Ningpo, wrote in September 1878: [35]

That our banking facilities here should be inadequate may seem a little strange in view of the number of banks and bank agencies located at the Chinese ports; but these banks are all, in character and connection, European, and they do not afford us what we greatly need, a simple and easy communication with our own country. We can, of course, make remittances and effect exchange through these banks and their European connections, but in doing it we are liable to needless inconvenience and needless loss.

The situation remained unimproved until the 1910s. [36]

Many American merchants in China experienced annoyance at the attitudes of American producers. The latter were interested in selling standardized goods in large quantities and special patterns. More serious was the problem of cancellation of sales by manufacturers. Should the domestic market turn out to be stronger than originally expected, manufacturers did not hesitate to cancel foreign orders they had previously accepted. Even if the orders were not canceled, actual delivery was often considerably delayed.

A more common and immediate headache was the poor packaging of American cotton goods. This was noted in numerous consular dispatches. The problem was twofold: Bales of American cloth were fastened with narrow metal strips which cut into the bales and damaged the merchandise, and there was no waterproofing. In sum, American cotton manufacturers demonstrated no great concern about overseas sales.

HOW THE MARKET WAS LOST

Sales of American cloth in China boomed during the years 1890–1905, almost doubling every five years, until reaching their peak in 1905 (at a total value of 42.1 million HKT). Sales then began to decline at a surprisingly high speed. The precipitation was attributed to intensified competition from several sources.

First of all—and contrary to what has been commonly assumed—China's closer economic contact with the West during the late nineteenth century actually stimulated its handweaving industry. For one thing, since imported machine-spun yarn was now available, handweavers no longer had to depend upon the traditional hand-spun yarn. Second, by imitating the fly shuttle and other devices on foreign looms, the Chinese were now able to build wider and better handlooms for native weavers.[37] As a result, hand weavers were able to produce wider and smoother cloth, thereby enhancing their power to compete with imported cotton cloth, especially the coarse types. The rising trend in imported cotton yarn and threads from 1870 to 1915 may be seen in the following statistics (1,000 piculs):[38]

1870	52	1895	1,134
1875	91	1900	1,491
1880	152	1905	2,570
1885	388	1910	2,298
1890	1,083	1915	2,701

Virtually all imported yarn was consumed by handweavers, and the bulk of it was under 20 count. Although there is no way to ascertain the output of handloom cloth during the nineteenth century, some estimates for later years can be obtained. The average annual output is estimated to have been 1,876 million square yards in 1905–1909; an all-time high of 2,845 million square yards was reached in 1924–1927.[39] Since much hand-woven cloth was of the heavy type, it must have displaced some of the American cloth in the Chinese market.

The second contending force came from modern textile mills operating in China. The first modern cotton mill, a public-private joint enterprise, was established in Shanghai in 1890 with 35,000 spindles and 530 power looms. The industry developed remarkably quickly thereafter, and, by 1930, it was able to turn out 2.4 million bales of cotton yarn and 679 million square yards of cloth.[40] Due to the relatively low level of Chinese textile technology, most fabrics from domestic mills were coarse. To a significant extent their products directly competed with American piece goods.

Perhaps the greatest threat came from Japan. The rapidity with which the Japanese cotton-textile industry developed and entered the international arena was an amazing phenomenon in modern commercial history. As shown in Table 21, the market share of Japanese fabrics in China soared from 2.7 percent in 1902 to 60.8 percent in 1919, reaching a second peak of 72.2 percent in 1930. The immediate victim of Japanese cotton trade expansion in China was the United States, whose market share of cotton cloth dropped from 35.5 percent in 1905, to 1.4 percent in 1922. American fabrics practically disappeared from the Chinese market thereafter. Fabrics woven by Japanese mills in the early years were comparable to American products in quality. Sales of the finer British cloth were less affected at first, but eventually Japan manufactured high-grade yarn and cloth as well.

TABLE 21 Shares of Imported Cotton Cloths, by Origin,
1902–1930
(% of total cotton cloth imports)

	British	American	Japanese	Others
1902	55.3	26.8	2.7	15.2
1905	49.2	35.5	2.5	12.8
1907	72.2	5.7	4.7	17.4
1909	54.7	18.1	8.3	18.9
1911	61.3	9.5	13.8	15.4
1913	53.3	7.9	20.2	18.6
1916	43.3	2.4	39.7	14.6
1917	32.6	0.4	55.0	12.0
1918	32.0	0.6	56.0	11.4
1919	25.6	1.4	60.8	12.2
1920	43.1	1.2	45.3	10.4
1921	43.1	2.1	42.6	12.2
1922	40.2	1.4	46.0	12.4
1923	34.8	0.2	51.7	13.3
1924	34.7	0.1	50.0	15.2
1925	23.9	0.7	65.5	9.9
1926	23.6	0.2	67.3	8.9
1927	16.6	0.2	68.1	15.1
1928	21.5	0.2	66.6	11.7
1929	22.1	0.3	65.4	12.2
1930	13.2	0.1	72.2	14.5

Sources: 1092–1913: Ralph M. Odell, *Cotton Goods in China*, p. 33. 1916–1930: Yen Chung-ping, *Chung-kuo mien-fang-chih shih-kao*, pp. 358–361.

One reason that Japanese textile producers gained the upper hand, even though their products were no better than the American, was that their production costs were considerably lower and their promotional activities much more aggressive. In addition, the Japanese government was highly instrumental in expanding overseas markets.

From the outset, Japanese cotton mills decided to imitate the structural features of the American rather than the British model. Most of them were equipped exclusively with ring spindles.[41] They also emphasized specialization and standardization. When a British textile expert visited Japan in 1926 and was invited to inspect a large cotton mill in Osaka, he was greatly surprised to discover that the mill was making only six types of fabrics.[42] Its machines were operated at constant tempo, and its workers were engaged in the same type of work day in and day out. In fact, a high degree of specialization was more feasible among Japanese than American mills. Since a majority of the Japanese mills were owned or controlled by a few giant companies, division of labor was possible among all the mills affiliated with the same parent company.

Wage levels were considerably lower in Japan than in most Western countries. Moreover, Japanese mills employed relatively more women and juvenile workers, who received even lower wages than the male adults. Yet there is no evidence that the productivity of Japanese textile workers was substantially lower than their Western counterparts.[43] It naturally follows that the labor cost per unit of output must have been lower in Japan. The economies arising from low labor costs were more pronounced, however, in weaving than in spinning, because weaving was more labor-intensive.

With regard to the cost of materials, Japanese mills suffered from an inherent weakness when compared with American textile manufacturers. Japan grew very little cotton; virtually all the cotton consumed by modern mills had to be imported. Fortunately, this drawback was largely overcome by certain ingenious devices. First, Japanese mills developed some unique cotton-blending techniques, mixing different varieties of raw cotton in making yarn. This enabled mills to use cheaper varieties of cotton without affecting the quality of yarn. It was an important cost-saving technique.

Equally significant was the method of importing raw cotton. The Japanese organization called Bōseki Rengōkai (Cotton Mills Association) was not only a cartel of cotton mills but also an enterprise that vertically integrated the operations of procuring raw cotton and distributing the finished products, especially in overseas markets. On behalf of its member mills, Bōseki Rengōkai entrusted three major cotton importers—the Tōyō Menka (Toyo Cotton Trading Co.), the Nihon Menka (Japan Cotton and General Trading Co.), and the Gōshō (Gosho Co.) to buy raw cotton from India and China.[44] Large-scale procurement provided considerable cost savings. The three big cotton importers dispatched their procurement agents to the interior areas of India and China to buy directly from cotton farmers or local cotton merchants.[45] In North China, the three Japanese firms often extended credit to Chinese cotton growers in the spring so that the farmers became bound by contract to deliver cotton at harvest time at prices lower than those prevailing in the market. In addition, Bōseki Rengōkai had an agreement with Japanese steamship companies whereby member mills enjoyed freight rebates of 30 percent on cotton shipments from India.[46]

Savings accrued not only on production costs but also on distribution costs. The proximity to the Chinese market entailed lower shipping costs and smaller inventory requirements on the part of Japanese exporters. This was particularly true in the case of Manchuria. In addition to the shorter distance, Japanese textile exporters enjoyed certain discounts on freight rates. In 1892, the Bōseki Rengōkai reached an agreement with Japanese steamship companies to reduce the freight rate by 40 percent.

In this connection, the contribution of the Japanese government should not be ignored. In 1899, the Bank of Japan gave the Yokohama Specie Bank 3 million yen to finance exports of cotton goods at low interest rates. A few years later, this scheme of financial assistance was transformed into an arrangement whereby Japanese mills exporting yarn and coarse cloth would receive certain premiums from the government.[47] In selling goods to Manchuria, Japanese firms enjoyed yet another special advantage. Beginning in June 1913, all goods entering Manchuria via Antung, a city bordering Japanese-occupied Korea, were entitled to a one-third reduction in customs tariff.[48] Although this privilege was granted by the Chinese government to all nations, Japan alone could benefit from it because of her geographical location. If Western firms had used this shipping route, their tariff savings would have been largely offset by additional freight costs.

According to a 1914 study conducted by an American cotton expert, W. A. Graham Clark, the price differentials between American and Japanese piece goods landing in Dairen (before customs) were as follows (with the Japanese price as 100):[49]

Grey Sheetings	128.0%
Grey Drill	115.6%
Grey Shirtings	116.2%
Grey Jeans	109.1%
White Sheetings	114.0%

The differential was greater for coarse cloth than for fine cloth. Another study comparing prices of American and Japanese sheetings, in April 1915, placed one differential at 136 percent.[50]

It should be remembered that the above comparisons refer to goods just landed in Chinese ports. The differences tend to widen when selling costs within China are taken into consideration. By virtue of an agreement between the Chinese government and the Japanese-controlled South Manchuria Railway, Japanese goods shipped to the so-called railway zone were tax-exempt. When the goods left the railway zone for interior areas, they were supposed to be subject to local taxes. In reality, most Japanese goods going to the Manchurian market via the South Manchuria Railway escaped local taxation.

The most important factor creating a sizeable difference in selling costs was the superior marketing techniques of Japanese exporters. In April 1906, the major Japanese cotton mills formed the Japan Cotton Export Guild, with Mitsui Bussan Kaisha as its trustee, for the purpose of conducting unified selling activities abroad. Mitsui Bussan maintained branch offices or retained representatives in a large number of Chinese inland cities. Japanese textiles reached almost every corner of the country. Commissions to middlemen were largely avoided by delivering goods directly to retailers. Because of their large-scale operations, Japanese exporters were able to take a smaller profit margin.

As mentioned earlier, American merchants stayed only in the big cities, especially in Shanghai, and depended on the services of compradors and Chinese distributors. While most Western traders were quite satisfied with the performances of those groups, it was by no means a cheap marketing method. As one British textile expert observed in the late 1920s, Japanese trading companies were content with a 1-percent profit mark-up on greys and delivered the goods directly to the retailers, whereas Western traders asked for at least 3 percent on the same type of greys.[51] In addition, Western merchants had to pay a standard commission of 1.5 percent to their compradors, and further mark-ups were charged by the distributing dealers. The total cost incurred in the distribution process was estimated to range from 8.5 percent to 17 percent, not counting transportation costs.[52] One of the largest exporters of cotton goods once attemped to establish a direct-selling mechanism in Manchuria by sending its own representatives to local markets. But the endeavor turned out to be unsuccessful, in part because the firm had to pay its field representatives American salaries, which were much higher than Japanese.[53]

Another crucial factor was the credit made available to Chinese retailers by Japanese firms. This was particularly important in promoting sales in Manchuria. In other parts of China, the bulk of imported piece goods were sold primarily to urban people, while rural households wove their own cotton cloth. Natural conditions in Manchuria did not permit widespread handicraft weaving, and so a large quantity of imported cloth was sold to farmers in that region. Very often the retailing stores could collect payments from buyers only after harvest time. Thus, the availability of credits from the exporters was extremely appealing to the local retailers. As a rule, American exporters insisted on cash—partly because they had no way to evaluate the credit standing of local dealers. By contrast, Mitsui Bussan and its affiliated firms were financially strong enough to extend credits to customers. In fact, being an importer-exporter, Mitsui Bussan was able to authorize its sales representatives to accept Chinese native products, such as soybeans and beancakes, in payment. Once the Japanese producers became firmly intrenched in the Chinese market, they dissolved the Japan Cotton Export Guild and began to sell their own chops independently. But they continued to follow the direct-selling technique.

A review of the early history of the cotton goods trade between America and China reveals that it was largely guided by the economic force of comparative advantage. In a dynamic world, however, the structure of comparative advantage among the trading nations may change over time. Today, although cotton-textile production is generally regarded as a labor-intensive industry, that was by no means true in the early stage of the industry. The fact that textile production was the first industry mechanized in the Industrial Revolution proves that it was capital-intensive and technology-intensive in the early years. It was only after other industries had subsequently developed, entailing more capital and more sophisticated technology, that cotton-textile production began to appear as relatively labor-intensive.

Cotton textiles may be further divided into different categories showing different characteristics in production. Production of yarn is more capital-intensive than production of cloth; fine yarn and cloth are more technology-intensive (requiring higher skill), whereas coarse yarn and cloth are more resource-intensive (requiring more material per unit of output). Moreover, in the nineteenth century, American mills were more capital-intensive than British mills. Throughout the period under study, the Lancashire manufacturers had a substantial advantage in producing fine cotton goods that required higher skill on the part of workers and consumed less raw material per unit of output. However, the comparative advantage in producing coarse products shifted from American mills to Japanese and Chinese mills during the early twentieth century.

In addition to the economic force of comparative advantage, the marketing techniques of trading firms also played an important role. Generally, three patterns of behavior have been observed. The first was that of American exporters, who followed a natural course independent of any artificial devices. American merchants shipped whatever was available at home to wherever there was a demand. The rapid rise in cotton-cloth exports to China during the nineteenth century was not facilitated by any artificial measures imposed by either the American producers or the American government. In fact, trade expansion was so natural and so effortless that the 1905 U.S. Census of Manufactures could make the following remark: [54]

The export trade—that with China as well as with other countries—may be described as an accident rather than a business. Up to a certain point it grew rather than was created.

Shortly after 1905, American exports of cotton cloth to China began to decline drastically. The fall was so precipitous that an American textile expert, Ralph M. Odell, warned his government in 1915 about the imminent disappearance of American piece goods from the Chinese market unless some drastic changes were made by American mills in production and by American exporters in marketing techniques. Yet, instead of making special efforts to reverse the tide, the Americans chose to let things take their natural course. American exporters shifted to petroleum products and machinery as new exportable items for the Chinese market.[55] These new fields became comparatively advantageous in the United States during the early twentieth century, and their products were naturally chosen as new exportable items.

The second behavioral pattern was seen among British textile merchants during the nineteenth century. They attempted to employ some artificial measures, such as oversizing cotton cloth, to offset their inherent disadvantages. Such devices could hardly succeed in the long run. The behavior of Japanese firms represented the third pattern—using artificial measures to reinforce their natural advantages in production.

The East Asian "Textile Cluster" Trade, 1868-1973: A Comparative-Advantage Interpretation

BRUCE L. REYNOLDS

Trade in the "cotton textile cluster"—raw cotton, yarn, cloth, and textile machinery—dominated international economic relations during much of the modern era. This commodity grouping fueled the industrial revolution in Europe and transmitted it to the rest of the world, including East Asia. It was the most important import (raw cotton) and the leading export (cloth and yarn) of the growing Japanese economy after World War I. Cotton textiles represented 32 percent of Japanese industrial production in 1930-1934.[1] An authority on Japanese industry maintains that "the modernization of the entire Japanese industrial structure evolved from foundations laid in the textile industry."[2] In China's nine most highly industrialized provinces in 1937, textile factories accounted for about 26 percent of the industrial labor force of 1.2 million.[3]

In the first half of the nineteenth century, American vessels carried Indian (and later American) cotton to Britain, and Lancashire goods to Asia.[4] In the latter half of the nineteenth century, American cotton cloth competed actively in China, temporarily dominating the market in North China and Manchuria.[5] As the quality of yarn and cloth manufactured in Japan and China rose during the first decades of the twentieth century, demand grew for American cotton, which displaced the shorter-staple Indian fiber. Particularly after World War I, when Japan developed techniques for blending American and coarser cottons, American cotton came to dominate the Asian cotton trade. The United States was also active in exporting textile machinery.

The United States eventually became the major supplier to China and Japan of raw cotton and hosiery machinery. But the bulk of the textile-cluster trade was dominated by Britain and Japan. Thus, it seems appropriate to deal first with East Asia generally in the context of the world textile industry during the nineteenth and twentieth centuries. Then, narrowing our focus, we shall examine the U.S.–East Asia trade.

The world textile industry of the nineteenth century possessed two notable characteristics: first, a decline in the percentage of output entering the world market; and, second, a "passing of the torch" from Britain to Japan. Even during the latter half of the nineteenth century, nearly one-half of all manufactured yarn and cloth still entered into world trade, whereas by 1953–1955 only one-tenth did so.

At the height of its dominance, in 1880–1884, Britain supplied 87 percent of world exports of cotton cloth.[6] In the years up to World War I, Britain's position began to erode as textile industries grew up in Europe, the Americas, and Asia. After World War I, Japan rapidly eliminated British goods from East Asian markets. In 1933, Japanese cloth exports exceeded British exports for the first time.[7] Until the oubreak of World War II, Japan was the world's leading cotton-cloth exporter.[8] By 1951, it had recovered that position and was also a leading producer of artificial fibers.[9] Today, although Japan is still a leader in the textile trade, its position in cotton textiles is being eroded by less-developed East Asian countries.

TWO APPROACHES

What caused these two trends? The decline in the percentage of textile production entering the world market derived from the textile industry's becoming more widely distributed geographically. And this, in turn, reflected increasing standardization of the technology of spinning and weaving. As the sophistication involved in manufacturing spindles and looms declined, and as the skill required to spin and weave decreased (or, to put it differently, as the general skill levels of world labor forces rose), there was a decline in value added; that is, the percentage rise in the price of cotton subsequent to its transformation into yarn and cloth became smaller and smaller. Transportation costs therefore represented an increasingly large percentage of value added. Table 22 shows this decline for yarn. A comparable decline in the importance of value added obtained for cloth.

TABLE 22 Value Added in Yarn Manufacturing as a Percent
of Yarn Price, 1779–1936

Year	No. 40 Yarn	No. 60 Yarn	No. 100 Yarn
1779	87		
1786			89
1812	40		55
1882	32		56
1883–1885		47.5	
1909–1911		37.4	
1934–1936		29.7	

Sources: Nos. 40, 100: S. Shapiro, *Capital and the Cotton Industry,* p. 266; No. 60:
R. Robson, *The Cotton Industry in Britain,* p. 366.

It was this decline that made it less and less profitable, and eventually impossible, to ship American or Indian or Chinese raw cotton to Britain or to Japan, manufacture it into yarn or cloth, and then return it to its place of origin for sale. Countries developed their own domestic textile manufactures, thereby reducing the amount on the world market.

What of the second characteristic, the decline of Britain, and the rise of Japan? Many authorities have argued that Britain's decline was due to "entrepreneurial failure."[10] According to this view, British businessmen in the late nineteenth century failed to adopt the best available production techniques, neglected research and development, invested in overly conventional directions, failed to establish international cartels, and were, in addition, bad salesmen.[11] These charges are difficult to refute. Superficially, it seems baffling that Japan, a net cotton-cloth importer as late as 1908,[12] within twenty-five years displaced Britain as the world's leading cloth exporter. The "decline and fall" theory is seductive.

Recently, however, a few economic historians, notably Lars Sandberg, have argued that this second characteristic of the textile trade may have resulted from economic forces over which British businessmen had little or no control.[13] For convenience, I shall call this new interpretation the "comparative-advantage" approach, and call the first viewpoint the "eclectic" approach.

The comparative-advantage approach argues that two factors determined the places where yarn and cloth were produced: the factor endowments of the countries involved (in particular, the ratio of capital to labor in their economies), and the factor-intensity (or skill-intensity) of the product relative to other products entering world trade. Sandberg argues that, when cotton yarn and cloth manufactures first began in Britain, they constituted the most technically complex and mechanized industry in the country. Textiles employed relatively large amounts of physical capital and human capital (skilled labor). Since capital was relatively abundant and thus relatively cheap, textiles were Britain's natural export goods. But, during the course of the nineteenth century, new products entered the British and the world economy, most of them more capital-intensive and more technologically complex than textiles; and textile machinery, meanwhile, was increasingly standardized and less demanding of its labor force. From this view, it was inevitable that Britain's ability to export these goods would decline, and that leadership in textiles would pass to a country with a lower ratio of capital to labor in its factor endowment.

The eclectic approach rests its case on a greater variety of causal factors: entrepreneurial and managerial ability; the adaptability of the labor force to factory conditions; subsidies and other forms of government intervention; tariff wars and military aggression; and infrastructure such as banking and railroads. In contrast with the comparative-advantage approach, many of these factors were affected by national governments. Thus, the eclectic approach tends toward the conclusion that Britain's fate was in its own hands, that it could have done better by doing differently.

The transfer of textile production from the West to the East was, in fact, a far more complex process than this simplified review suggests. This paper proposes to examine the process in detail, with particular attention to China and Japan, and to ask: Broadly speaking, do we find the economic forces of comparative advantage to be actively and persistently at work? Or does the eclectic approach best explain what we see? In the process, we shall learn more about the details of textile cluster production and trade.

To lay the groundwork, first we shall explore the nature of yarn, cloth, and cotton. Next we shall examine the way cotton, yarn, and cloth production and trade moved to China and Japan during the nineteenth and twentieth centuries. Finally, we shall analyze the international competition in Asian markets for cotton, yarn, cloth, and textile machinery.

SOME CHARACTERISTICS OF TEXTILES

Cotton cloth divides into high quality and low quality. Cotton yarn divides into high count and low count. Cotton fiber divides into long staple and short staple. Long-staple cotton is used to make high-count yarn, which is used to make high-quality cloth—and conversely for short-staple cotton, low-count yarn, and low-quality cloth. High-quality cloth requires a thin, light yarn. "Count" is a measure of lightness: n-count yarn is yarn one pound of which is n hanks long (1 hank = 840 yards). But, in seeking lighter weight, one cannot afford to sacrifice tensile strength, since this might make it impossible to weave the yarn into cloth. The longer-staple cottons (those with longer fiber length) can be attenuated and spun more finely than short staples without losing their tensile strength.

Another distinction between high- and low-quality yarn and

cotton, and a very impotant one for our argument, is that higher
qualities require a higher capital-labor ratio in production. They
require more human capital—greater skill. As Robson puts it:

A higher degree of skill is required [in producing fine goods because] it
becomes necessary to avoid or remove faults and imperfections . . . [and]
it requires more care on the part of the operative, since the yarn will not
stand rough handling. . . . Similarly, it requires more precision and a closer
adjustment of machines . . . a higher standard of maintenance . . . and a
higher standard of performance from the operatives.[14]

For yarn, a higher ratio of spindles to workers is also inevitable,
because, to spin a higher count, one spins the yarn for a longer
time, leaving it on the spindle longer.[15] In Chinese mills in
1932, for example, we find in Table 23 the following variation
of capital-labor ratio by count of yarn:

TABLE 23   Spindles per Worker in Chinese-Owned Mills in 1932
            (by count)

Average Count Spun	Spindles per Worker
24	776
18	722
16	538
13	399

Source: Wang Tzu-chien, Ch'i-sheng hua-shang sha-ch'ang tiao-ch'a pao-kao, Appendix, Table XXV.

In addition to these technological or "supply-side" considerations, demand also plays a role in the distinction between high-
and low-quality textiles. High-quality cloth is likely to be less
durable; or, if more durable, substantially more expensive. People are more likely to trade off durability and cheapness for
smoothness and light weight if their incomes are high.

Handicraft yarn proved much more vulnerable than handicraft cloth to competition from the manufactured equivalent.
Even though manufactured cloth was much smoother and
lighter, handwoven cloth was more durable, and thus continued
to find a market in the low-income part of the population, in
both India and China, well into the twentieth century.

TABLE 24 Yarn and Cloth Supply in China, 1875–1931

	1875	%	1905	%	1919	%	1931	%
			Sources of Cloth Supply					
			(million square yards)					
Manufactures	—	—	27	1.1	158	5.8	831	28.2
Imports	457	21.8	509	20.2	787	28.7	300	10.2
Handicrafts	1637	78.2	1981	78.7	1798	65.5	1815	61.6
Total	2094	100.0	2517	100.0	2743	100.0	2946	100.0
			Sources of Yarn Supply					
			(million pounds)					
Manufactures	—	—	90.2	11.5	297.6	36.8	966.9	90.9
Imports	12.4	1.9	304.3	38.6	178.5	22.0	-76.0	-7.1
Handicrafts	632.3	98.1	393.2	49.9	333.6	41.2	173.3	16.3
Total	644.7	100.0	787.7	100.0	809.7	100.0	1064.2	100.0

Source: Bruce L. Reynolds, "The Impact of Trade and Foreign Investment on Industrialization: Chinese Textiles, 1875–1931," p. 64.

Handspun *yarn,* however, disappeared rapidly after the advent of mechanization. Spinning is a rotary motion. High-tolerance metal spindles are therefore an efficient user of mechanical power—far more efficient than power looms, and capable of extremely high rpm's. Hand-spinning, therefore, disappeared quickly—well before handweaving.[16] Table 24 shows the pattern of decline for hand yarn and handwoven cloth in China. In India as well, even in 1931–1932, handwoven cloth constituted 30 percent of total cloth consumption.[17]

As hand-spun yarn disappeared, handwoven cloth became a major user of machine-made yarn, splitting the yarn market into yarn for handloom cloth and yarn for power-loom cloth. The former was low count, the latter high count, for reasons both of taste and technology. Low-count yarn was rough, durable, adequate for low-income users; low-count yarn was weak, appropriate for use on handlooms, but too weak for power looms, where greater tension was applied to the warp threads.[18]

Finally, with regard to raw cotton, we should note that cotton grown in China was generally short staple. Indian cotton was somewhat longer, though still considered short staple. American cotton was longest. Therefore, as the pattern of demand for cloth and yarn moved into higher qualities, demand for raw cotton moved toward Indian and then American strains.

TRADE DATA: PRELIMINARY OBSERVATIONS

Tables 25–27 display a number of patterns in the textile cluster trade of Japan and China with the rest of the world. These patterns can be conveniently subdivided into patterns common to both countries, and patterns of contrast between the two countries.

Common Patterns

CLOTH. Imports of machine cloth appeared earlier than yarn imports. They peaked rapidly, but at a modest level, never occupying more than one-third of the domestic market for cotton cloth. They remained at this approximate level for as long as fifty years.[19] Meanwhile, cloth exports began, and eventually

TABLE 25   Cotton Textile Trade in Japan and China,
1868–1932
(net imports, 5-year averages, million pounds)

Years	Japan			China		
	Cotton	Yarn	Cloth	Cotton	Yarn	Cloth
1868–1872	24	11	13	30	10	185[a]
1873–1877	51	17	21	14	13	163
1878–1882	3	37	24	15	20	200
1883–1887	6	34	13	14	49	215
1888–1892	59	47	17	-33	132	213
1893–1897	202	7	14	-73	172	163
1898–1902	381	-84	4	-33	290	198
1903–1907	469	-103	-9	-111	329	270
1908–1912	601	-114	-37	-92	284	223
1913–1917	948	-210	-131	-66	333	268
1918–1922	1051	-129	-246	10	169	235
1923–1927	1311	-90	-357	123	48	219
1928–1932[b]	1360	-12	-490	250	-30	212
1932–1941[c]				263	113	

Sources: Japan: Keizō Seki, *The Cotton Industry of Japan,* pp. 302–307. Cloth converted at 1 square yard = 0.30 pounds. China: Reynolds, "The Impact of Trade," pp. 231–232. Cotton and yarn converted at 1 picul = 133 pounds. Cloth converted at 1 piece = 11 pounds. 1933–1941 from Hsiao Liang-lin, *China's Foreign Trade Statistics,* p. 39.

Notes: [a]1872 only.
[b]For China, 1928–1931 only.
[c]Gross imports, not net of exports. Net yarn imports are negative in this period.

both countries became net cloth exporters. The lag between the peak year for imports of cloth and the point at which exports exceeded imports was twenty-five to fifty years.

YARN. Compared with cloth, yarn was a much more volatile good. Yarn imports grew rapidly, soon outstripping cloth. Yarn imports came to occupy 50 percent or more of the Chinese yarn market. Then an equally rapid decline and reversal occurred. Japan was a net yarn exporter only ten years after imports peaked; China, after fifteen years.

RAW COTTON. The quantity of cotton that a country consumes depends on its population and per capita cotton cloth consumption. Both these quantities were changing only slowly in Japan

TABLE 26   Cotton Textile Trade in China, 1955–1973
          (*$US million*)

Year	Cotton (net imports)	Yarn (net exports)	Cloth (net exports)
1955	56	21	na
1956	35	na	na
1957	54	na	na
1958	50	70	na
1959	31[a]	29	93
1960	70	26	122
1961	34	19	90
1962	28	20	78
1963	81	16	78
1964	87	20	108
1965	120	24	97
1966	72	23	125
1967	49	15	107
1968	35	27	110
1969	42	32	121
1970	60	36	108
1971	84	32	100
1972	147	53	126
1973	280	118	259
Annual Averages, 1955–1973			
Exports	2.6	36.4	114.8
Imports	77.0	2.7	0.4

Source: Data bank on Chinese trade, maintained by the Project on Chinese Economic Studies, University of Michigan.

Note: [a]Cotton exports as recorded in the source jump from $US 3M to $US 56M, 1958 to 1959. I assume that the 1959 entry should read $US 5.6M.

and China. The domestic supply of cotton also changed slowly, relative to the rates of change in foreign trade. Given a relatively unchanging demand for cloth, and a relatively unchanging domestic supply of cotton, the inflow of cotton from abroad was perforce also relatively constant.

The flow was in three forms: cloth, yarn, and raw cotton. As imports of the first two grew, raw cotton imports necessarily

TABLE 27 Chinese Textile Machinery Trade, 1910–1973
(*1910-1932 in HKT, 1933-1941 in Chinese dollars,
1956-1973 in $US; all figures in 1,000s*)

Year	Imports	Year	Exports	Imports
1910-1913	408	1956	37	4,704
1914-1918	1,649	1957	387	3,312
1919	3,744	1958	1,117	4,468
1920	6,904	1959	na[a]	4,402
1921	26,723	1960	na[a]	1,187
1922	30,480	1961	na[a]	2,834
1923	12,316	1962	na[a]	802
1924	5,710	1963	579	862
1925	3,611	1964	548	6,852
1926	4,467	1965	2,358	9,040
1927	4,138	1966	2,210	12,487
1928	4,352	1967	922	4,593
1929	9,239	1968	1,963	2,016
1930	14,452	1969	2,075	1,660
1931	14,332	1970	3,133	509
1932	10,337	1971	3,789	432
1933	9,081	1972	3,152	908
1934	14,206	1973	11,731	6,603
1935	14,301			
1936	13,939			
1937	20,986			
1938	24,946			
1939	20,582			
1940	12,934			
1941	6,955			

Sources: 1910-1941: Hsiao Liang-lin, *China's Foreign Trade Statistics*, p. 47. 1910-1913 and 1914-1918 are annual averages. 1956-1973: Data bank on Chinese trade, University of Michigan.

Note: [a]Data not available. Imports in these years of "textile and sewing machinery" were 4,584, 3,918, 4,709, 4,950 respectively. This broader category was three times as large as textile machinery proper in 1958, and twice as large in 1963.

declined; in fact, China became a cotton exporter. Then, as yarn and cloth imports declined and exports grew, raw cotton exports declined, and imports grew. Both countries remain net cotton importers today.

MACHINERY. Domestic manufactures of yarn and cloth began within twenty years after the first substantial imports. Increasing domestic output led to imports of spindles and looms, and eventually to domestic manufacture of spindles and looms. These grew, displacing imports, until both countries eventually became net exporters of textile machinery. In China, machinery imports swelled during the early 1920s and remained high up to World War II. Domestic machinery production began during World War I, domestic machinery exports began in the 1950s, and China became a net textile machinery exporter in the early 1970s. In Japan, all of this occurred somewhat earlier and faster. During World War I, Japanese mills were forced to depend on domestic machinery producers, which led to domestic manufacture of every kind of textile machinery. Machinery imports after World War I were minimal, and, by the late 1920s, Japan was "able to compete in export markets" with Britain and the United States.[20] In 1933–1934, Japan was a principal supplier of textile machinery to China, providing 39 percent of China's imports.[21]

Contrasting Patterns

Yarn illustrates the major difference between Japan and China. In Japan, the "reaction time" to foreign yarn was far shorter— both the reaction of domestic yarn consumers and, later, the reaction of Japanese manufacturers of machine yarn. Manufactured yarn reached both countries at roughly the same time, during the 1860s, but foreign yarn penetrated Japan much more rapidly. The peak of Japanese net imports occurred in 1878–1882, while the peak in China came twenty-five years later. Yet, for all its speed, penetration by foreign yarn into the Japanese yarn market was roughly as extensive as in China. At the time of the Chinese peak, around 1905, the Chinese handicraft industry provided 50 percent of the yarn consumed in China.[22] For Japan, in 1878–1882, the figure is probably also close to 50 percent.[23] In both countries, then, domestic purchasers of hand-spun yarn switched to foreign yarn, but more quickly in Japan. In both countries, as the falling market share of hand-spun yarn approached 50 percent, a domestic machine-yarn industry grew up, progressively displacing both foreign yarn and the last of the domestic hand-spun yarn. But the process was slower in China, where it took perhaps sixty years (1870–1930) before the market share of hand-spun yarn dropped below 15 percent. In Japan, this appears to have occurred in fifteen or twenty years (1870–1892).[24]

Summary

What is the significance of these developments, in light of the international rivalries described below? With regard to the trade in cotton cloth, during the nineteenth century first Britain, then the U.S., and then India, entered the East Asia market. Japan entered the trade in the twentieth century. Japan drove foreign cloth from the home market and captured the Chinese and Manchurian markets. China stopped importing cloth only after 1949. By the 1960s, cloth was a major Chinese export. In general, imported cloth occupied less than 30 percent of the markets in question.

In cotton yarn, India and Britain exported large amounts to China and Japan during the nineteenth century. The yarn supplied handlooms, occupying perhaps half the domestic yarn market at its peak. Japan in the 1890s and China in the 1920s rapidly developed their own yarn-manufacturing industries. Both countries eventually eliminated imported yarn and domestic hand-spun yarn. Until the 1920s, Japan exported some yarn to China. But, by 1931, the yarn markets in India, China, and Japan were supplied almost exclusively from home production.

Flows of raw cotton adjusted to these movements in the location of yarn and cloth production. In the case of Japan, domestic cotton disappeared by 1896. After that date, any increase in exports of cotton goods implied an increase in raw cotton imports. In China, the large domestic raw cotton supplies meant that imports and exports simply fulfilled a residual need. But the flow was still very substantial. At the peak of cotton-goods imports (1903–1907), there was a cotton outflow of over a hundred million pounds annually. During the 1920s, domestic yarn production rose threefold, resulting in a very large cotton inflow that reached 250 million pounds by the end of the decade. These flows reflected the Chinese farmer's inability to react as quickly as foreign suppliers. In addition, one-third of the imports in the late 1920s represented American cotton, which may have been filling a need for long-staple cotton that Chinese farmers could not meet.[25]

Regarding textile machinery, the same import-substitution cycle occurred in both countries. By the time of World War I, Japan's textile-machinery industry was advanced enough to substitute for blockaded foreign supplies, and it successfully defended the home market after the end of the war. By the end of the 1920s, the industry was challenging British exports of textile machinery to China. China went through the comparable stages after 1949, becoming a net textile-machinery exporter in the 1970s.

INTERNATIONAL COMPETITION IN TEXTILE CLUSTER TRADE

The Market for Yarn in China and Japan

Five nations competed for this market: Britain, India, the United States, Japan, and China. Table 28 shows details on the Chinese yarn market.

Reviewing the competition,[26] we find that at the outset, in 1885, Britain was supplying 36 million pounds to China and 22 million pounds to Japan, while India supplied 5 million pounds to China and 22 million to Japan. By 1898, Japan was selling yarn in China, India had left the Japanese market, and Britain had almost left the Chinese market. In 1902, Britain sold almost no yarn in China, and had left the Japanese market as well. By 1913, Japan and India were splitting the Chinese market evenly. By the 1920s, Japan's share in the dwindling Chinese market moved toward 100 percent.

This is a confusing picture. It becomes much clearer when we examine the quality of the yarns sold by each country.[27] English yarns were all of much higher quality than Indian yarns. It is interesting to note that, when Japan entered the Chinese market in the late nineteenth century, she did so with "counts" intermediate between those sold by Britain and those sold by India.

TABLE 28 Chinese Yarn Imports by Country, 1885–1924
(% and million pounds)

Year	UK %	India %	Japan %	US %	Total million pounds
1885	89	11	–	–	41
1891	52	48	–	–	161
1898	5	71	24	–	261
1906	–	77	23	–	339
1913	–	50	50	–	358
1926	–	24	75	–	77
1927	2	9	89	0.4	60
1928	–	2	98	–	38

Sources: 1885, 1891: China, Imperial Maritime Customs, *Decennial Reports, 1882–1891*, Appendix, pp. xxii–xxiii (in value terms). 1898: Hatano Yoshihiro, cited in Sung-jae Koh, *Stages of Industrial Development in Asia: A Comparative History of the Cotton Industry in Japan, China, and Korea*, p. 142. 1906. 1924: Koh, p. 148. 1913: Charles F. Remer, *The Foreign Trade of China*, p. 152, says that "at the end of this period (1908–1913) imports from Japan and India were about equal." 1926, 1928: Yang Tuan-liu, et al., *Liu-shih-wu nien lai Chung-kuo kuo-chi mao-i t'ung-chi*, p. 68.

That is, Japan competed with Britain first in the lower range of the British count spread, and then rapidly moved to eliminate the highest of the counts sold by Britain in the Far East.[28]

The Indians, meanwhile, were selling 16s and 20s in China. It took Japan much longer to move into that range—at least fifteen years, from 1898 to 1912. Even so, India was selling nearly as much yarn in China in 1913 as in 1898. The evidence suggests that Japan may never have successfully competed with India in these low counts, and that it was Chinese domestic machine yarn, developed after 1900, that eliminated Indian yarn.

It was shown earlier that higher counts of yarn require a higher capital-labor ratio in production. A country with relatively abundant capital therefore enjoys a comparative advantage in producing them. Comparative advantage clearly determined the order in which countries fell to yarn competitors. The fact that Japan eliminated British yarn first suggests that its capital-labor ratio was intermediate between Britain's and India's. The fact that Chinese domestic machine yarn eliminated Indian yarn first, and Japanese yarn only in the 1920s, suggests that Chinese capital was relatively less plentiful in that period than Indian.

Japan's ability to drive Indian yarn from the Japanese market might seem to suggest that its capital-labor ratio lay below India's. But this was not true, nor was it true that a high capital-labor ratio enabled China to eliminate Japanese yarn in the 1920s. In both these cases, *domestic* industry drove out *foreign* goods, and the change reflected the sensitivity of yarn trade to transportation costs.[29] Comparative-advantage effects in yarn can be inferred only in the case of competition between two countries in the yarn market of a third country.

Did "eclectic" factors play an important role in yarn competition? Failure to remove the Japanese yarn export tariff in 1894, for example, might have preserved Britain's position in the Chinese yarn market for a bit longer. But the tariff *was* removed. And one wonders whether earlier removal would have led to an earlier surge of exports—whether it is correct to argue that only the 1894 removal allowed Japan to "break into the . . . Chinese market."[30] Japan's own yarn market at this time consumed about 100 million pounds.[31] Domestic output in 1893 was 89 million, and broke 100 million in 1894 for the first time. It seems likely that the pressure to export led to the decision to remove the tariff, rather than vice-versa.

It has also been argued that the substantial Japanese investment in Chinese spinning mills in the 1920s reflected fear on the part of the Japanese that Chinese tariff barriers would one day exclude Japanese yarn exports. But we have seen that before World War I the Japanese had difficulty selling yarn to China. Thus, it seems likely that Japan built textile mills in China, not because tariffs might soon make it impossible to produce yarn in Japan and sell it profitably in China, but because it was *already* unprofitable (for comparative advantage reasons) to do so.

Competition in the Market for Cloth in China

During the nineteenth and twentieth centuries, Britain, India, the United States, and Japan competed in China and Manchuria. British, American, and Indian goods were established first. After 1905, Japanese cloth eliminated American and Indian cloth, but

British cloth remained in China until after World War I, when it, too, was eliminated.[32]

Once again, an analysis based on "quality" is instructive. British cloth exports were "usually quality goods."[33] The United States, on the other hand, "exported the cheap grades of cotton cloth . . . such as came to be the chief products of the Japanese mills."[34] Again, the Japanese evidently entered the market producing a quality of goods below that of Britain, comparable to that of the (southern) United States mills, and above that of India, and then expanded toward both ends of the quality spectrum.

Raw Cotton in China and Japan

China has traditionally been a cotton-importing country. It imported Indian cotton at least as early as 1774.[35] The cotton trade grew during the nineteenth century, as American cotton displaced Indian cotton on the British market. American cotton averaged 50 million pounds annually in 1821–1830,[36] which must have represented over 20 percent of China's domestic consumption of cotton.[37] Imports declined for perhaps fifty years, 1860–1910, as foreign yarn and cloth entered China, and then bounded back in the 1920s and after.

At the time when the penetration of China by foreign yarn and cloth was at its peak, around 1905, China was exporting approximately 15 percent of its cotton crop.[38] During the following twenty-five years, as domestic yarn production displaced imports, and to a smaller extent domestic cloth as well, the cotton trade shifted direction.[39] By 1929–1932, China was importing 250 million pounds of cotton a year.[40] During the 1920s, cotton imports represented perhaps 16 percent of China's total cotton consumption.[41] Large imports continued through World War II and the Civil War, and through the postwar period. China remains today a major cotton importer.

In Japan, the picture is less complex, since domestic cotton production was negligible after 1892.[42] Imports fed the domestic yarn and cloth industries, which generated a very large demand for cotton in the twentieth century.

Where did China get its cotton? In the nineteenth century, virtually all of it came from India. When imports rose again after 1900, Indian cotton was still important, but American cotton gradually assumed equal importance.[43] The shift in the source of supply toward the United States was relative, not absolute, in that the absolute amount of cotton arriving from India remained large. The shift was nonetheless striking. It reflected changes in yarn and cloth tastes and technology. During the nineteenth century, India supplied raw cotton to Chinese hand-spinners resident in southern cotton-deficit areas. Some of the cotton imported from India in the twentieth century doubtless continued to fill this need. But the large increase in imported cotton during the 1920s, most of which came from the United States, was destined for machine-spinning factories. The difference between cotton for hand-spun yarn and cotton for machine yarn is principally that the latter must be stronger and longer. The longer-staple length of American raw cotton must have had much to do with the pattern of change in the 1920s.

A similar pattern obtained in cotton imports to Japan. When cotton imports began, Japan bought much of its cotton from China. From 1888 to 1895, Japan was China's chief purchaser of cotton.[44] After 1895, as the need for cotton grew, Japan turned increasingly to India. A contemporary observer explained:

The Japanese mills had found that they could neither hold their home market in cotton yarns nor increase their export while continuing to use as harsh and low-grade a raw material as Chinese cotton. In comparison with Chinese cotton, Indian cotton was much better suited to the needs of the Japanese mills, and was essential if they wished to make yarns of somewhat higher count and better quality, so they became anxious to displace Chinese cotton with Indian.[45]

Thus, the move from Chinese to Indian cotton coincided with a move toward higher counts of yarn. American cotton also entered the scene. In 1898, 31 percent of Japan's cotton imports came from the United States.[46]

Again, yarn count apparently explains a good deal. A "count-based analysis" would argue that early Indian cotton went to Japan to make yarn for the Japanese domestic market. Then,

Japanese yarn made with high-quality American cotton entered China (starting in 1896) and displaced high-quality British yarn there, and India continued to send Japan just enough Indian cotton to supply the domestic Japanese yarn market. During the first decade of the twentieth century, Indian cotton going to Japan represented only slightly more than the domestic market could absorb; some of this cotton probably went to China as Japanese yarn, displacing Indian yarn there.

Beginning with World War I, Japanese cotton cloth displaced British and U.S. cloth in East Asia. Japanese cloth used yarns with counts even higher than those of the British yarn which had already been displaced by Japanese. The raw cotton for the Japanese cloth was long-staple American cotton. American cotton exports to Japan boomed. They constituted 18 percent of total Japanese imports in 1906–1910, and 35–40 percent of a much greater volume of imports in the 1920s. From 1931 to World War II, Japan was America's largest purchaser of cotton.[47]

The Chinese Market for Machinery

Table 29 shows the shares enjoyed by major suppliers of machinery to the Chinese market after World War I. There is a clear trend away from British and American products and toward Japanese. A similar trend appears in textile machinery alone. Up to the end of World War I, British machinery predominated in Chinese textile mills and in imports of new machinery.[48] But, by 1932, Japan had become the largest supplier of textile machinery.[49] After 1935, this tendency was even more pronounced, as Table 30 shows.

Three somewhat different explanations for this pattern could be adduced. First, one could argue that textile-machinery manufacturing reaches its lowest-cost scale of production only at a high level of output, and that consequently a country (such as Japan) will be able to export machinery only when its domestic market is large. Second, one could argue that textile-machinery production is technologically complex, and that therefore production costs will fall (and exports become possible) only after domestic production has gone on for a substantial period of time—long enough for expertise to build up. Third, one could

TABLE 29   Chinese Machinery Imports, 1919–1931
            (% and million HKT)

Year	US %	UK %	Japan %	Germany %	Total M HKT
1919	33	na	25	na	15
1922	20	49	18	13	51
1924–1925[a]	20	47	20	13	20
1926–1928	22	38	25	15	20
1929–1931	17	31	22	14	43

Sources: 1919–1926: Ch'en Chen et al., comps., *Chung-kuo chin-tai kung-yeh shih tzu-liao, ti-ssu-chi,* p. 823. 1927–1931: Ts'ai Cheng-ya, *Chung-jih mao-i t'ung-chi,* p. 163.

Note: [a]Figures for 1924–1931 are annual averages.

TABLE 30   Textile Machinery Imports to China by Country
            (includes Manchuria), 1935–1937

Supplier	%
Japan	71
United Kingdom	19
Germany	3
United States	2

Source: Chih Tsang, *China's Postwar Markets,* p. 19.

argue specifically that a country's share of the textile machinery market in China hinged not so much on production costs of machinery as on ownership of the Chinese mills: British-owned mills in China bought British machinery, Japanese-owned mills bought Japanese machinery, and so forth.

The facts of the Chinese case are consistent with all three of these explanations, although perhaps most completely with the third. In 1919, most Chinese mills were British-owned. By 1932, Britain owned less than 4 percent of total spindles, and Japan owned 40 percent.[50]

The United States provided 26 percent of the 3 million new spindles installed between 1919 and 1931.[51] But almost all these sales came before 1924, in an atypical postwar market. U.S. exporters were able to dominate the Chinese (and world) market for hosiery machinery, but it was much smaller than the market for cotton-textile machinery.[52]

Our review of the competition in raw cotton, yarn, cloth, and machinery establishes that a central element of that competition was the quality of the yarn and cloth and the staple of the raw cotton. We have demonstrated that the technology employed in producing high-quality textile products was relatively capital-intensive. When coupled with the traditional theory of international trade—that a country enjoys a comparative advantage in the export of those commodities whose production employs intensively the productive factor with which that country is relatively well-endowed—this characteristic of textiles would lead us to predict that the highest grades of yarn and cloth would be the grades in which British trade dominance would continue the longest. We have shown that this was in fact the case in the East Asian trade in textiles. Furthermore, we have traced other changes in East Asian trade, in particular shifts in the trade in raw cotton, to this distinctive comparative-advantage pattern in yarn and cloth trade.

Other scholars have noted the tendency of low-quality textile goods to emerge first in the infant industries of less developed countries, as in the cases of the United States, Italy, Brazil, Russia, and continental Europe.[53] But the usual argument given is that tariffs, because they were a constant ad valorem percentage, offered more protection to low-quality than to high-quality goods.[54] That is correct.[55] But the textile industries of India, China, and Japan grew up in the absence of any significant tariff protection, at least until the 1930s. That being true, the comparative-advantage element stands out as the most likely explanation for their rapid growth.

Some trade goods show less evidence of comparative advantage effects than of other determinants. But the competition in yarn—first in Japan in the period 1890–1900, and later in China in the period 1895–1925—and the competition in cloth after World War I give evidence which seems strong and compelling.

Lars Sandberg has pioneered the comparative-advantage thesis in the case of Great Britain. "Great Britain," he writes, "lost the comparative advantage she had obtained from her early start in cotton textiles, principally because she began to accumulate capital and develop other industries."[56] Ironically, after presenting convincing evidence for "Lancashire's decline," thereby refuting the eclectic "entrepreneurial decay" argument, Sandberg uses a variant on the argument he has just rejected in order to explain why Japan, rather than India or China, led the way in East Asian textile exports. He attributes Japan's success to "the supply of entrepreneurship and management skill together with the adaptability of the work force to factory conditions."[57] But comparative advantage was just as active in the East as in the West, and was just as important in the Japan-China-India competition as in the Japan-Great Britain competition.

CHAPTER SIX

Commercial Penetration and Economic Imperialism in China: An American Cigarette Company's Entrance into the Market

SHERMAN COCHRAN

Historians of Sino-American relations have generally maintained that American businessmen who attacked the market for
industrial goods in China between 1890 and 1915 found it
impenetrable. According to the "myth of the China market," a
generalization accepted by many historians, Americans expected
an almost inexhaustible demand for their goods to develop in
China but had to settle for a very small volume of trade—so
small, compared to the Americans' high expectations, that it
made the market seem like a myth. Preoccupied with this myth,
historians have paid little attention to the activities of American
companies within China and have left the impression that American economic penetration of China was so insignificant between
1890 and 1915 as to be unworthy of attention.[1] And yet, some

American-owned companies succeeded before World War I in penetrating the China market and making it pay. If historians are to analyze the full impact of American trade in China—not only on its economy but also its politics and society—these commercially successful companies need to be taken into account, for they, not the failed American companies, had the greater impact.

Like other American businessmen supposedly imbued with the "myth of the China market," American cigarette manufacturers spoke of China as though it would provide an endless demand for their product simply by virtue of its large population, but in their case the market proved to be no myth. James B. Duke (1865–1925), an American tobacco tycoon from North Carolina, for example, had had China's population figures on his mind since the invention of the cigarette machine in 1881—a time when cigarettes were still new and unfamiliar in America, much less China. According to a story told by executives in his company, Duke's first words upon learning of the invention were:

"Bring me the atlas." When they brought it he turned over the leaves looking not at the maps but at the bottom, until he came to the legend, "Pop.: 430,000,000." "That," he said, "is where we are going to sell cigarettes."[2]

And "that" was China. Duke never visited China, but Americans he sent there also were excited by the prospect of tapping such a large market. James A. Thomas (1862–1940), a representative of Duke's company overseas as early as 1888 and its managing director in China from 1905 to 1922, originally calculated possible sales by imagining that each of "China's population of 450,000,000 . . . in the future . . . might average a cigarette a day."[3]

These were high estimates of China's potential as a market for cigarettes, but Duke, Thomas, and other Americans involved in the trade with China were not disappointed. Exporting the first cigarettes to China in 1890, their sales at first grew gradually and then rose meteorically in the early twentieth century, increasing from 1.25 billion cigarettes in 1902 to 9.75 billion in 1912 and to 12 billion in 1916—ten times as many as in 1902.

By 1915 (and every year thereafter in the 1910s and 1920s, with only one exception), more cigarettes were exported annually from the United States to China than to all other nations of the world combined. And, as early as 1916, China consumed at least four-fifths as many cigarettes as the United States (where 15.75 billion were consumed in 1916).[4]

As the premier firm in this booming market, Duke's company enjoyed sales in 1916 valued at $20.75 million with a net profit of $3.75 million. Such high sales and handsome profits delighted Duke. "We have made big progress in China," he reported to the press at the time. "The possibilities . . . there can hardly be overestimated."[5]

If other American businessmen and traders failed in their pursuit of a "mythical" China market between 1890 and 1915, why did Duke's company succeed in finding a real market and extracting profits that fully satisfied its American management? How did it penetrate the China market? Did its commercial penetration make it an economic imperialist? These questions are explored here with respect to three aspects of the American cigarette trade in China: the investments of Duke's multinational corporation, the dependence of the company on Chinese, and the company's dealings with East Asian opposition to it.

AN AMERICAN MULTINATIONAL
CORPORATION IN CHINA

Part of the explanation for the commercial success of Duke's company in China lies in its transfer of cigarettes, tobacco leaf, capital, technology, and managerial techniques from the West to China. Of these, little reached China prior to the founding of the British-American Tobacco Company (BAT) in 1902, but, between 1902 and 1915, the branch of this company in China invested on a large scale.[6] BAT, which became a multinational corporation with worldwide operations, originated in an Anglo-American alliance between Duke's American Tobacco Company and the Imperial Tobacco Company of England after a "tobacco war" between the two companies in 1902. The war had been fought largely over international markets, and, in the truce that followed, BAT was formed to serve, in effect, as the two former rivals' international division—making it one of the first organizational units ever created by an American multinational corporation to administer international business.[7] Duke and his American Tobacco Company and its American affiliates, as winners of the war, took as spoils 12 of the 18 positions on BAT's board of directors and two-thirds of the $24 million (6 million British pounds sterling) worth of stock at which BAT was initially capitalized. In this arrangement, Duke remarked to a friend, he made "a great deal with British manufacturers covering the world."[8]

Like many American-owned businesses abroad at the time, including other American multinational corporations in China, BAT was registered in England and legally based in London, but it had a distinctly American identity. The American Tobacco Company held controlling interest until the dissolution of Duke's "tobacco trust" in 1911, stockholders in the United States (not necessarily in the American Tobacco Company) owned the majority of BAT shares at least until 1915, and an American (Duke) was chairman of BAT's board until 1923.[9] Americans were made managing directors of BAT's branches in parts of the world where the American Tobacco Company had been well established before 1902, and English directors managed branches where Imperial had held stronger positions. In China, site of the largest of BAT's overseas operations, the first managing directors were both Americans, C. E. Fiske from 1902 to 1905, and James A. Thomas from 1905 to 1922.

Immediately after the founding of BAT, James Duke began to extend its reach deep into China, using an approach that earlier had been the key to his swift rise to the top of the cigarette industry in the United States. According to Alfred Chandler's incisive analysis, Duke had succeeded in the United States because he had recognized the commercial possibilities for continuous-process cigarette machinery, which had been invented by James Bonsack in 1881—especially the possibility of creating mass markets to absorb the greater quantities of cigarettes made available by mass production. In Chandler's words, Duke's "success resulted from his realization that the marketing of the output of the Bonsack machine required a global selling and distributing system . . . Duke became the most powerful entrepreneur in the cigarette industry because he was the first to build an integrated enterprise."[10] After building up this enterprise in the United States during the 1880s and 1890s, Duke sent salaried American executives to extend it to China in the early twentieth century. They had the responsibility for integrating mass cigarette production with mass cigarette distribution there, following the example he had set in the United States.

Duke's determination to integrate mass production with mass distribution in China was reflected in BAT's decision to manufacture cigarettes there. Duke probably made this decision himself, for he took a keen interest in BAT's China branch. As one of Duke's first managing directors in China later recalled:

> Mr. Duke kept in close touch with what was going on. Not only did he have long talks with the men who had been in the Far East, but he regularly read the reports that were sent in. . . . In discussing a proposition in far-away China or India, the question would always come up as to whether Mr. Duke would approve of the policy chosen. If the project were submitted to him, even after it had been put into effect, his advice and counsel were always helpful.[11]

As the final sentence implies, Duke did not originate all policies for BAT's China branch, but a decision to manufacture on a large scale abroad was too significant to have been made without his approval, and, in this case, he gave his wholehearted approval, urging that the company's factories in China be built and expanded even faster than his American managing director there had anticipated.[12]

With Duke's support, the first two managing directors of BAT's branch headquarters in Shanghai carried out an investment policy in China almost identical to the one Duke had used earlier during his rise to the top of the cigarette industry in the United States. Even as Duke had first bought and consolidated existing cigarette firms and then introduced machinery capable of mass production in America in the 1880s, so BAT went through the same two-phase sequence in expanding its industrial base in China. In 1902 and 1903, BAT completed the first phase, consolidation, by bringing under one management the two Western factories that had produced almost all of the small number of cigarettes previously manufactured in China. One had been operated since 1891 by Duke's agent in China, an import-export house registered in England called Mustard and Company, and the other, the American Cigarette Company, had been founded in 1890 and purchased by the Imperial Tobacco Company of England in 1901. In 1902, under the terms of the agreement between Duke and Imperial, both came under the management of BAT.[13]

In 1905, with the old factories in hand, James Duke selected a new managing director to supervise the company's policy of large-scale investment and expansion in China. For this major undertaking he chose one of his most trusted subordinates, James Thomas. Duke had several reasons for trusting Thomas. First of all, the two men talked easily together, perhaps because they came from similar backgrounds. Like Duke, Thomas was the son of a tobacco-belt farmer; in fact, he was born in the same county of North Carolina as Duke was.[14] Second, Thomas had a personality that undoubtedly appealed to Duke as it did to others in BAT. On the one hand, he was gracious—"an impressive, soft-spoken North Carolinian," as one American BAT representative described him, "with the natural directness and good manners some topnotch people have."[15] On the other hand, he was tough—"as tough as a hickory nut and as square as a dye" in the words of one of his fellow North Carolinians in China.[16]

Besides possessing personal qualities Duke could appreciate, Thomas had experience as a businessman that qualified him for the position of managing director. Forty-three in 1905, Thomas had been selling cigarettes since the age of nineteen.[17] Still more important, he had begun selling cigarettes across the Pacific as early as 1888. His explanation for taking his first assignment overseas, which sent him to Australia and New Zealand, reflected an attitude that surely appealed to Duke:

It was the chance, the life that drew me. . . . As a missionary of this new American industry I went out to the East . . . I knew not a soul. I used to walk the streets alone at night, possessed about equally with the longing for a friend and with the idea of how to market cigarettes. In the end I made a life-long friend of my idea. I married it.[18]

Although Thomas's omission of any reference to the profit motive may cause cynics to smile, this passage shows a determination to seek out and take advantage of unexploited commercial opportunities that undoubtedly contributed to his success. Once Thomas began to work for Duke's company in 1899, he rose rapidly from one post to the next. He managed its branch in Singapore from 1900 until 1903 and then its branch in India from 1903 to 1904 before accepting the job as managing director in China in 1905. Perhaps the first sign that Thomas had Duke's complete confidence came in 1902 when Duke chose him to act as the company's courier during the trans-Atlantic negotiations that led to the founding of BAT. Thereafter, as Thomas was promoted to higher positions, his salary rose too. As managing director in China, he became the best-paid foreign businessman in Asia, reportedly receiving between $60,000 and $100,000 per year.[19]

Thus, before BAT made its first large investments in China, James Duke appointed an American managing director whom he knew and trusted to form the managerial link between his own headquarters in New York and the headquarters of BAT's branch in Shanghai. Serving in this capacity, James Thomas reported to Duke and George G. Allen (Duke's closest associate), took orders from them and secured their approval for any changes in the China branch's major policies. Subordinate to them, Thomas, in turn, had an administrative staff subordinate to himself. In 1906, within one year of being appointed managing director in China, he had 33 American and British executives under him at the headquarters for BAT's China branch in Shanghai.[20] Like Thomas, they were all salaried BAT employees sent by the company to Shanghai, but, unlike Thomas, they worked within specialized departments, concentrating on manufacturing, marketing, or purchasing.

Once the administrative linkages between New York and Shanghai had been established, BAT entered the second phase in its plan for achieving mass production in China by making large investments there between 1905 and 1915. Initially capitalized at $2.5 million, the company's branch in China was valued at $16.6 million by 1915.[21] According to an estimate by one historian, Wang Hsi, BAT's reinvestment rate in China was especially high between 1902 and 1912; unfortunately, Wang does not quote a figure, but if high, it was perhaps at least 30 percent, the median figure for a majority of foreign firms in China between 1872 and 1936, according to the estimates of another historian, Hou Chi-ming.[22] If the $16.6 million at which the company valued its China branch in 1915 was all direct investment, then BAT was responsible for no less than 15 percent of the total direct investment ($110.6 million) made by all foreign manufacturers in China at the time.[23] And even if the $16.6 million was not all direct investment (for it might have included the cost of inventories), BAT was unquestionably one of the leading foreign investors in early twentieth-century China.

A large share of the capital BAT invested in this period was used to expand its production capabilities in China. In 1906 and 1907, the company built huge new plants in Shanghai and Hankow: The one in Shanghai—part of a BAT complex at Pootung (across the Whangpoo River from the International Settlement) that included 160 buildings on 200 *mou* of land—had the capacity to make 8 million cigarettes per day; the one at Hankow could produce at an even faster rate, turning out as many as 10 million per day. Soon BAT added factories in two Manchurian cities, building one in Mukden in 1909 with a capacity of 2 million cigarettes per day, and buying another from Russian tobacco men in Harbin in 1914 with a capacity of about 250,000 per day. These factories employed more workers—13,000 by 1915—than any other industrial enterprise in China except Kawasaki, the Japanese textiles company in Dairen.[24] By 1916, BAT relied as much or more on these factories to produce cigarettes for China as it did on its factories in the United States and England, manufacturing in China between one-half and two-thirds of the 12 billion cigarettes it marketed annually there.[25]

Along with Western capital and technology that BAT exported to manufacture cigarettes in China, it sent Western salesmen to distribute them there. Again following Duke's example (and presumably Duke's orders), Thomas set out to create an organization of Western sales representatives that would give the company mass distribution in China of the kind Duke had achieved in the United States. Since 1885, Duke had transformed the cigarette industry in America by setting up branch sales offices and hiring salaried managers to supervise each one.[26] Beginning in 1905, Thomas sought to do the same in China by creating an administrative hierarchy staffed by young, salaried Westerners. Thomas recruited and trained only bachelors under age twenty-five perhaps, as one of the recruits observed in retrospect, because Thomas and the other directors "believed that only inexperienced and adventurous young men would be fools enough to risk what they proposed."[27] Men of various nationalities and backgrounds were hired, but, according to Thomas, the majority were from the American South. As he later recalled:

Most of the Far Eastern representatives of the company in the early days were recruited from North Carolina and Virginia. From infancy [they] had cultivated, cured, and manufactured tobacco, so that it was second nature to them. In addition, these farm-bred boys were healthy, well-reared, and had a background of good character and good habits.[28]

Representatives were hired at a salary of $1,200 per year plus living expenses for a four-year term—during which they were not permitted to marry—and were then granted a one-year leave of absence. Only two out of five remained after their first year, and many returned home complaining that China was incomprehensible and that their lives there had been unbearably lonely.[29] Those who stayed were urged to overcome barriers between themselves and Chinese merchants by learning to speak colloquial Chinese and were given an incentive to learn it well, a $500 bonus awarded to anyone who passed BAT language examinations which were held once every six months. Representatives were expected to become familiar with the dialect of the region to which they were assigned, and, by 1915, a number of BAT representatives achieved a degree of fluency in the spoken language uncommon among Westerners in China.[30]

This corps of young sales representatives took up assignments in all parts of the country. They were based, according to the recollection of one North Carolinian, in "divisional and territorial offices" which numbered between 20 and 25 when he started to work for BAT in 1916.[31] Within these offices, the representatives were responsible for the company's warehouses, which were so extensive by 1912, according to the British minister to China, Sir John Jordan, that there was "probably not a city of any size in the eighteen provinces where such warehouses have not been established by the British-American Tobacco Company."[32]

Besides their work in these urban-based offices, some BAT representatives "roughed it" (in their words) outside China's cities. They went on caravans into China's "interior," slept in Chinese country inns, and rode boats up the Yangtze, mules in the mountains of Yunnan, horses outside the Great Wall, and camels across the Gobi Desert.[33] They may have romanticized the tales of their exploits, but the fact remains that they contributed to a BAT marketing system that developed the capability to distribute cigarettes on an enormous scale.

Regular shipments of BAT cigarettes reached all parts of China. Aware of the obstacles to empirewide or nationwide distribution, BAT management adopted a regional approach. Through its territorial sales "divisions" it established centers for distributing cigarettes, not only around its factories at Shanghai, Hankow, Mukden, and Harbin, but in all China's regional marketing systems: Northeast, North, Northwest, Lower Yangtze, Middle Yangtze, Upper Yangtze, Southeast, South, and Southwest.

BAT entered most regions by using railroads or foreign-owned steamers, which, unlike foreign carriers in sovereign nations, enjoyed the privilege of access to inland waterways in China.[34] Cigarettes were first transported to BAT's division centers in the metropolitan cities, which lay at the core of each of China's regional marketing systems, and were then disseminated from the cities to the suburbs and ultimately to the periphery of each region.[35] In North China, BAT cigarettes were shipped up the Grand Canal from Shanghai to division centers at Tientsin, Peking, and Paoting. For Northwest China, the company's division centers were Chengting and Taiyuan, and, for markets in Mongolia, Sinkiang, Ili, and elsewhere beyond the Great Wall, BAT representatives dispatched monthly camel caravans from two border cities, Kalgan and Tatung. Along the Yangtze, BAT cigarettes traveled by steamer to river ports and then overland to inland cities with major division centers in the Lower Yangtze area at Shanghai, Hangchow, Chinkiang, Nanking, and Anking;

in the Middle Yangtze at Chiukiang, Sha-shih, Nanchang, Wuhan, and Changsha; and in the Upper Yangtze at Chungking and Chengtu. Along the Southeast Coast, the division center was Foochow. In South China (Lingnan), BAT goods were sent from the Canton Delta east to Swatow and west up the West River to Wuchow in Kwangsi province. In Southwest China (Yun-Kwei), BAT reached Kunming from three different angles by 1901. From the east, steamers carried its cigarettes as far up the West River as possible, at which point they were loaded onto mules and packed through the mountains; from the west, BAT goods were brought overland via Bhamo in Burma; from the south, they came as far as Mengtzu on the newly completed French railroad that originated in Indochina and the rest of the way by mule. And, in the northeast, the one area where BAT faced much Japanese and Russian competition, it used trains, carts, wheelbarrows, and men's backs to reach from Mukden and Harbin throughout the region—even to the Amur River along the Russian border—and captured 70 percent of the Manchurian market.[36]

To support this vast distributing system and attract attention to its product, BAT produced advertising that was disseminated as widely as its cigarettes. In this as in other areas of business, James Thomas emulated his mentor, James Duke. *Collier's* magazine had reported early in the century that Duke "was an aggressive advertiser, devising new and startling methods which dismayed his competitors; and he was always willing to spend a proportion of his profits which seemed appalling to more conservative manufacturers."[37] Encouraged by Duke to use similar methods in China,[38] Thomas invested heavily in advertising. In 1905, as new BAT factories were constructed in Shanghai, the company built beside them new print shops equipped with imported printing presses that provided some of China's most sophisticated printing facilities.[39] Between 1905 and 1915, these presses turned out an enormous quantity of advertising matter.

BAT's advertising system left no region of China untouched. In 1905 in Manchuria, for example, BAT put up 2,000 large paper placards and 200 large wooden or iron signboards in the city of Yingkow, creating an effect that reminded an American journalist of the sensational billing the Barnum and Bailey circus arranged in advance of its arrival in American cities.[40] In North China, a newspaper correspondent in Kaifeng reported in 1907 that "the whole city has been placarded with thousands of staring [BAT] advertisements," and another correspondent in Sian writing in 1911 described "huge [BAT] posters on the city gates, city walls, on every vacant piece of wall or board in the street, on the brick stands supporting the masts in front of the yamens, in fact anywhere and everywhere."[41] In South China an observer commented in 1908 that "the walls of Canton City and the delta towns are literally covered with the brightly coloured [BAT] advertisement posters."[42] And, west of Canton, a Western diplomatic official noted in 1904 that BAT agents had canvassed the area along the West River "in a houseboat gaily decorated with flags and other emblems [from which they distributed] picture placards and samples of their wares, with the result that their cigarettes are now on sale in every town and village along the river."[43] In the southeast, according to a report from the British consul at Foochow in 1909, BAT agents drummed up business by

... preaching the cult of the cigarette and distributing millions gratis so as to introduce a taste for tobacco in this particular form into regions where it was as yet unknown. ... The streets of Foochow are brilliant with [BAT's] ingenious pictorial posters, which are so designed to readily catch the eye by their gorgeous coloring and attractive lettering, both in English and Chinese.[44]

In the southwest (Yun-Kwei) the British Consulate General in Kunming observed in 1910 that there was "hardly a bare wall in the town that is not brightened by the [BAT's] flaming posters," and a journalist making a tour across Szechwan, Yunnan, and Burma in the same year found that he was "rarely out of sight of the flaring posters in Chinese characters advertising the [BAT] cigarette."[45] Along the Lower, Middle, and Upper Yangtze, BAT inundated every city from Shanghai to Chungking with advertising, crowning its campaigns with a large billboard placed prominently in the river gorge. (Although directors had expressed pride in the sign, they removed it in 1914 in response to complaints that it defaced the gorge.)[46]

By 1915, BAT's advertising had so impressed Julean Arnold, U.S. Commercial Attaché in China, that he urged all American companies interested in advertising to contact and learn from BAT. While he praised BAT's advertising publicly, he teased James Thomas about it privately. "You have gotten so accustomed to the advertising game that you seem unable to pull off anything without it from one end of China to the other," he wrote to Thomas in 1915. "Yes, when it comes to advertising you have them all skinned."[47]

As BAT's manufacturing, distributing, and advertising systems grew, its management showed an interest in growing tobacco in China. The great bulk of its tobacco continued to come from the American South, which exported over 11 million pounds to China in 1916, more than to any other non-Western country. But, as early as 1906, Duke sent American agricultural specialists from North Carolina to conduct experiments with American tobacco seed in China. By 1913, BAT procured the first Chinese-grown harvest of a type of American tobacco commonly used in cigarettes, bright tobacco, a mild and fragrant leaf characterized by a bright golden color and a low nicotine content, which had been developed in Virginia and North Carolina just prior to the American Civil War.[48]

American BAT agricultural specialists induced Chinese peasants to plant bright tobacco by giving away free tobacco seed imported from Virginia and North Carolina, lending curing equipment such as thermometers and iron pipes, promising to pay cash for the entire first harvest regardless of its quality, and even assuring peasants that they would be reimbursed for any damages or losses they might suffer from planting American seed. In Hupeh province, where peasants were still wary, the Americans also agreed to hand over after the harvest, free of charge, four curing barns used in the initial BAT experiment. After two years of building up its operations in this way at two locations, Weihsien in Shantung province and Laohokow in Hupeh, in 1915, BAT procured over 2 million pounds of bright tobacco grown from American seed, 435,00 pounds of flue-cured, almost all from Weihsien, and 1,750,000 of sun-cured, most of it from Laohokow. This tobacco was good enough to be used in the most expensive brand of cigarettes made by BAT

in China, and a study by the United States government of efforts
to plant bright tobacco in many parts of the world showed that
the Chinese variety came closest of all to duplicating the color
and texture if not the aroma of the American original. Though
the total yield supplied no more than 10 percent of the bright
tobacco used by BAT in China during 1915, BAT's management was pleased with the savings on taxes, labor, and transportation costs arising from this agricultural operation, and
production of bright tobacco expanded rapidly after 1915.[49]

By introducing bright tobacco, BAT started a purchasing system to integrate backwards and achieve vertical integration of
its operations in China. That is, by linking tobacco purchasing
with cigarette manufacturing, distributing, and advertising, BAT
management intended to form a chain reaching from the tobacco
fields of Shantung and other provinces to factories in Shanghai
and Hankow, and ultimately to customers all over China. Again
following the example of Duke, who had vertically integrated
the American tobacco industry with remarkable speed in the
1880s,[50] the American-led management of BAT sought to
achieve vertical integration of the Chinese tobacco industry
by 1915.

These findings suggest one explanation for BAT's commercial penetration in China. BAT successfully exploited the Chinese market because it did not merely dump surplus goods on
China to relieve a glut in Western markets (although Duke, like
many American manufacturers, may initially have turned to
foreign markets in the early 1890s because of overproduction in
the United States). Instead, BAT invested heavily in China in
order to create an efficient, well-organized, vertically integrated
operation in the image of James Duke's American Tobacco
Company. It created economies of scale, cut costs, and effectively utilized Chinese resources to manufacture goods within China for sale to Chinese consumers.

Such an interpretation is helpful in that it highlights Western
features of BAT's operation, but it is at best only a partial explanation for the company's commercial success. Was BAT
manufacturing efficient because of superior capital-intensive
technology or because of low labor costs? Was BAT marketing
effective because of its American organizational techniques or

because of its relations with Chinese intermediaries? Was bright tobacco successfully grown because of American agricultural expertise or because of BAT's reliance on Chinese cultivators? Before judging the efficiency and organizational strength of BAT and the extent of its vertical integration, it is necessary to explore these questions by taking into account the role that Chinese played in the company.

THE ROLE OF CHINESE IN BAT

Impressed by BAT's American business practices, Western officials, journalists, and other observers in China tended to maximize the importance of Americans and minimize the importance of Chinese in the company. James Thomas was dubbed "the most brilliant American taipan" and was personally credited with bringing "American cigarettes within reach of China's ragged millions."[51] The sophistication of BAT technology was lauded, particularly the Hankow factory, said to be "second to none of its kind."[52] BAT was praised for initiating the "scientific cultivation of tobacco [which] has been one of the greatest blessings that ever happened to Shantung."[53] And BAT's young American "pioneers" and other Western representatives were applauded for breaking away from "the old, established method of conducting business through import houses and compradors [and for putting in] their own elaborate dealer system throughout the interior, supervised directly by foreigners in branch offices located at strategic points."[54] BAT, it was said, "had no compradore—just a few young Chinamen to take care of the money."[55]

Such accounts leave the impression that Chinese contributed nothing more to BAT than a market of consumers—a land of "400 Million Customers." But this impression is misleading, for BAT depended on Chinese workers, peasants, compradors, and merchants in every phase of its operation.

Chinese industrial workers, for example, gave BAT a large, efficient, and comparatively inexpensive labor force. According to Thomas, James Duke found the prospect of manufacturing in China "particularly interesting" precisely because labor was cheaper there than in the United States.[56] In America, Duke had relied heavily upon capital-intensive technology; in fact, a study of the American Tobacco Company indicates that he led the industry from labor-intensive to capital-intensive technology in the United States and concludes that "Duke's introduction of machine production was clearly the most significant innovation he made in the industry."[57] But in China the company hired large numbers of unskilled laborers—13,000 by 1915—to perform simple tasks such as preparation of tobacco leaves and packaging of cigarettes by hand.

The company relied on a chain of Chinese intermediaries to recruit workers who, like their counterparts in other Chinese industries, were women. A Chinese comprador (employed by the company) contacted a Chinese labor contractor (not employed by the company) who retained the women on a daily basis. The women received their wages—as little as 0.20 to 0.50 yuan per day—through the Chinese comprador and contractor rather than directly from BAT and had little if any job security.[58] Although the cost of employing the Chinese women (including the shares of their wages taken by compradors and labor contractors) was much lower than labor costs in the United States and Great Britain, the quality of the women's work fully satisfied BAT's management. "We have an abundance of good, cheap and efficient labor which works eighteen hours a day without the assistance of labor unions," Thomas enthusiastically reported in 1915.[59] Pleased with the low cost and high performance of Chinese workers, he urged his friend Willard Straight, formerly a China specialist in the U.S. diplomatic corps who had joined the banking firm of J. P. Morgan & Co. in 1915, to encourage other American businessmen to take advantage of the Chinese labor force as BAT had.[60]

In growing tobacco as in manufacturing cigarettes, BAT relied on Chinese workers and used Chinese middlemen as recruiters. Duke approved this investment in a China-based tobacco-purchasing system for the same reason that he approved investing in BAT's China-based manufacturing system: to lower production costs on goods made for distribution within the country. According to Thomas, "Mr. Duke maintained that if Chinese could produce [bright tobacco] cheaper than we could over here [in the United States], we ought to buy it from them, thus enabling them to buy more cigarettes"—and thus enabling BAT to expand sales, lower costs, and raise profits.[61]

The key to low production costs was cheap agricultural labor at appropriate locations in the Chinese countryside, and BAT gained access to this labor through Chinese intermediaries. Despite the American tobacco specialists' vaunted expertise, they had to rely on Chinese to guide them to the sites best suited for tobacco. It was Chinese middlemen like Jen Po-yen, later BAT's purchasing agent at Hsuchang, not Americans, who selected locations for BAT's experiments. American "experts" merely confirmed the choices made by Jen and other Chinese familiar with agricultural conditions. Moreover, it was the Chinese middlemen who bought land for BAT experimental stations and compounds because, under the treaties, a foreign company did not have the right to own land in the interior. Americans also relied on Chinese middlemen to act as bilingual liaisons with the local community, especially peasants.[62]

To appreciate the role peasants played in BAT's agricultural system, it is important to recognize that they did not by any means learn their first lessons in tobacco growing from Americans. By the time BAT "experts" arrived, Chinese had been raising tobacco for more than two centuries. It was introduced in the late Ming period, probably from the Philippines, and, by the eighteenth and nineteenth centuries, this valuable cash crop was grown in virtually all China's provinces, despite numerous imperial decrees prohibiting cultivation of it to prevent it from supplanting needed food crops. By the late nineteenth century, Chinese local gazetteers had already recorded tobacco growing on a large scale in the very provinces where BAT American agricultural specialists later conducted their experiments. Moreover, a study done by a Chinese scholar at the end of the nineteenth century confirms that Chinese peasants were already using sophisticated techniques for growing and drying tobacco prior to the arrival of BAT.[63] In fact, Ameican agricultural advisers could not improve upon many of the Chinese techniques and technology. Chinese fertilizer, for example, proved to be as effective as fertilizer used in the West. The company imported

10 tons of chemical fertilizer from the United States and tested it in the fields side by side with Chinese beancake fertilizer (*tou-ping*) for a season in 1912 before deciding not to import any more. It is true that BAT distributed new seeds and curing equipment, but even these seem to have been used by Chinese peasants with a minimum of guidance from the Americans. In private correspondence, the North Carolinian in charge of BAT's collection station in Shantung expressed amazement at the speed with which Chinese mastered the "new" American techniques. They learned, he observed, "even quicker than the average farmer at home."[64]

These reports suggest that BAT benefited from agricultural labor in the Chinese countryside that was not only cheap but highly skilled at tobacco growing and well organized for the purpose of tobacco production. Members of local society in tobacco-growing areas did not need to make many adjustments to supply BAT's needs. They were already accustomed to marketing indigenous tobacco as a commercial crop, and they sold American tobacco to Chinese BAT agents in the same manner that they had sold indigenous tobacco to middlemen who had represented Chinese tobacco merchants in the years before 1913. Peasants planted new imported American seed but otherwise accommodated BAT without changing their agricultural techniques or departing from established patterns of intensive farming in small plots. Making adjustments as slight as these, peasants produced high-quality bright tobacco, and middlemen sold it to BAT at a far lower price than the company paid for imported tobacco.[65]

In cigarette marketing even more than in cigarette manufacturing and tobacco purchasing, BAT depended on Chinese intermediaries and workers. Despite all of the Americans' boasting about the independence of BAT's daring young American "pioneers," they and other Western BAT representatives, like Western merchants throughout the nineteenth century, were dependent on (salaried) Chinese compradors and (nonsalaried) Chinese agents. To understand the significance of the contributions that Chinese made to BAT's marketing, it is necessary to question the assumption—commonly held by American observers at the time—that American pioneers enabled BAT to create its own distributing system for a new product. It is true that BAT representatives were among the first Western merchants to travel inland from the coastal treaty ports and deal directly with major Chinese agents, but only in this very limited sense do they deserve to be called "pioneers."

The true pioneers of tobacco products in China long antedated BAT. They were Chinese who had introduced tobacco as early as the seventeenth century and had widely distributed it and opium—often mixing the two—by the end of the nineteenth century. These Chinese paved the way for BAT's later introduction of cigarettes by distributing tobacco through an elaborate marketing system and persuading Chinese to smoke pipes on a gigantic scale.[66] During the first decade of the twentieth century, this market became particularly receptive to alternate forms of smoking because anti-opium campaigns cut many consumers off from some of the most popular smoking mixtures, creating a void in the smoking market at the very time BAT began distributing cigarettes in China.[67] Evidence of Chinese switching from opium to cigarette smoking in 1910 was noted, for example, by a Western journalist in southwestern China:

In Yun-nan, especially since the exit of opium, this common cigarette is smoked by high and low, rich and poor. I have been offered them at small feasts, and when calling upon high officials at the capital [Kunming] have been offered a packet of cigarettes instead of a whiff of opium, as would have been done formerly.[68]

The number of people who substituted cigarettes for opium is difficult to estimate, but observers at the time were struck, as one put it in 1915, by the "astonishingly rapid" spread of cigarette smoking among men and women "of all classes and ages, from ten years up."[69] As evidence that it had penetrated the lower classes and become commonplace among the poor as early as 1911, another noted that bearers and carters and other haulers of heavy loads gauged the distance between two points not by miles but by the number of cigarettes smoked en route.[70] The earlier history of pipe smoking does not fully explain the speed with which cigarette smoking spread in China, but it is a partial explanation for this phenomenon, and it serves as a reminder that BAT did not introduce a new social habit so much as it offered a variation on the already popular habit of pipe-smoking.

The term *pioneer* was a misnomer for Western BAT representatives not only compared to Chinese distributors of previous tobacco products but also compared to Chinese within BAT's own sales organization, for Western BAT representatives did not generally introduce cigarettes into China's regional markets. Instead, they left the job of penetrating new markets to Chinese compradors and agents who took responsibility for distribution at local, regional, and eventually national levels. By 1907, before BAT had begun to employ many Western representatives in China, its Chinese compradors and agents had already established numerous agencies for the company in all of China's major population centers—12 Yangtze River ports, 12 towns in the south and southwest, 8 in the southeast, 35 in the north, and 6 in Manchuria. [71]

The kind of man who served as a liaison between Westerners in BAT and Chinese markets is evident in the career of Wu T'ing-sheng. First hired by James Thomas at the age of twenty, Wu was destined to become BAT's leading comprador. He was from Chekiang—the home province of many Chinese compradors and financiers at the time—and he had grown up in close proximity to English-speaking Westerners because his father had been a Chinese Christian minister and because his father had arranged for him to be educated at the Anglo-Chinese College in Shanghai. [72] Thomas recollected that he was attracted to Wu because Wu was "ambitious . . . and was of good address and pleasing personality. He understood also how to approach a Chinese merchant and gentleman." [73] Other Westerners were impressed by the range of his Chinese connections and the aggressiveness of his manner. Wu acted as a troubleshooter and mediator, representing BAT in disputes and negotiating agreements with people from various strata of Chinese society, not only "merchants and gentlemen" but officials, militarists, businessmen, and peasants. He served BAT for more than twenty years and remained in the tobacco industry until murdered by a competitor in 1935. [74]

Wu and other Chinese salaried employees of BAT (generally called "interpreters" rather than compradors in BAT's terminology), not Westerners, performed the crucial task of recruiting Chinese merchants to serve as (nonsalaried) BAT agents and distributors. To get Thomas started, for example, Wu attracted potential Chinese distributing agents by acting as cofounder of the Shanghai Tobacco Trade Guild in 1898. At first it had only 10 members, but between 1898 and 1909, the period in which BAT's distributing network took shape, its membership rose to 300, all of whom, according to a Western observer, were "leading merchants doing a large business with all the principal towns in China." [75] Even if BAT "induced the formation" of this guild, as a British official suggested in 1906, it was still a traditional form of Chinese organization, adapted to serve BAT's purpose. [76]

Wu seems to have worked mainly within his home region, the Lower Yangtze River Valley, but BAT hired compradors in other regions as well. Li Wen-chung, for example, a graduate of a Methodist missionary school in Peking and an experienced bilingual interpreter, was a leading BAT comprador in North China. Within that region he persuaded Chinese merchants to become BAT dealers in 19 new locations during a single year, 1905. He recruited Chinese merchants to accept BAT dealerships in Paotow and Suiyuan and was said in his career to have "traveled into ice and snow even as far north as the Russian frontier and as far west as the vicinity of Tibet." Still other BAT compradors led mule trains over rugged mountains in Yunnan and plied rivers in Fukien. When Western BAT representatives finally began to go on such expeditions, Chinese compradors always accompanied and guided them. [77] In performing all these tasks, BAT's Chinese compradors were more like pioneers than were any of its Western representatives.

Even more essential to BAT's distributing network than Chinese compradors were Chinese merchants whom compradors recruited to act as agents for the company. These were pioneers in the sense that they made the critical decision whether to permit cigarettes to enter China's markets at the regional and local levels. But they were by no means pioneers in the sense of outsiders breaking into new or unfamiliar markets. Instead, they were established merchants who operated through well-worn and often complex channels of distribution. Ma Yü-ch'ing, for example, who agreed to act as a BAT agent in Tientsin in 1903, was general manager of the Yü-sheng-ho house, a firm that had existed for more than fifty years and that had branches in Tientsin, Kalgan, and other towns in Chihli and Shantung provinces. He succeeded as a regional distributor not because he "pioneered" or deviated from common Chinese commercial patterns but because he operated through an established business house and traded on its reputation. In similar fashion, other leading merchants represented the company at the core of each region— H. H. Kung (later Minister of Finance under Chiang Kai-shek) in the northwest at Taiyuan; Yu Shao-tseng in the Peking-Tientsin area and Ts'ui Tsun-san around Paoting in North China; Liu Chin-sheng in southern Manchuria and Hsu Lo-t'ing in the northern part; Ch'in Sung-k'uan in the southeast at Foochow; and numerous merchants in ports along the Lower, Middle, and Upper Yangtze. All these Chinese BAT agents came from merchant families that had been in business for generations in their respective locales, and they were therefore well connected within regional and local merchant associations and guilds that were based on vocations and native-place ties and that had served commercial purposes in China since at least the sixteenth century. They received no salary from BAT, and, after becoming BAT agents, they continued to deal in a variety of products besides cigarettes, including other foreign products such as Standard Oil's paraffin candles and coal.[78]

In moments of candor, American BAT representatives admitted that Chinese compradors and Chinese agents were the key to the company's sales organization. One Chinese-speaking American recollected after serving as a BAT representative in north and northwest China between 1911 and 1914:

We [Western BAT representatives] were called salesmen. But actually we did no selling. The large majority of foreigners in the company spoke no Chinese; [Chinese] interpreters and dealers took care of that end. The foreigners were really inspectors, overseers, advisers. More than anything else, it seemed to me, our job reduced itself to advertising.[79]

Another American who was a BAT representative in northeast China during the 1910s made the point even more strongly. "I was simply window dressing for our Company," he conceded.

In public his Chinese comprador left the impression that the foreigner managed the market, for, "being a good Chinese, he always kept the Foreigner puffed up and believing himself [to be] a man of great affairs." But the American recognized that it was the Chinese who actually supervised all the "business affairs" in his division of BAT's selling organization.[80]

With this Chinese sales network in mind, it is possible to evaluate critically James Thomas's and other Westerners' claims for the originality of BAT's distributing system. For example, Thomas spoke of having spent fifteen months in Hong Kong in 1903 "getting my goods established in the maritime provinces of South China," but what he did was hand the goods over to Chinese compradors and regional agents who, in turn, arranged for Chinese merchants from Macao, Canton, Swatow, and Kunming to act as local agents. The Chinese, not Thomas, actually managed the market.[81]

In addition to working through Chinese regional agents, BAT also distributed cigarettes through two Chinese nationwide distributing agents, the Yung-t'ai-ho (Wing Tai Vo) Company and the Mao-i Company. Like most of BAT's other leading agents, Cheng Po-chao (Cheang Park Chew), the President of the Yung-t'ai-ho Company, was a well-established merchant before becoming affiliated with BAT; his company had been in existence for thirty years, and its management was mostly in the hands of his family before he began to act as a BAT agent in Hangchow in 1912. Unlike other BAT agents, Cheng was given exclusive rights to handle one or two brands throughout China. According to his agreement with BAT, the foreign company designated the prices of his cigarettes, took all returns from his sales, and then paid him a commission—literally "handling charges" (*shou-hsu fei*)—according to the volume of his business.[82]

The strategy employed by Yung-t'ai-ho and Mao-i in Manchuria in 1914 illustrates the selling techniques these distributors used. Upon entering the market in 1915, the Mao-i Company added 1.5 million to the 35 million cigarettes distributed by BAT every month in Mukden, and Yung-t'ai-ho immediately added another 3 million. They marketed goods by spreading their network of Chinese representatives throughout Manchuria

and by supplying local Chinese agents. The local agents, in return, submitted inventory reports on their stock and paid up
their accounts every three months. According to a spy for one
of their competitors, these local agents also led advertising campaigns through "wine shops, tea houses, schools, yamen, military administrative centers . . . down every street and alley,
sticking up posters everywhere."[83]

BAT heralded its delegation of authority for nationwide distribution to the Chinese distributing companies, Yung-t'ai-ho
and Mao-i, as a grand "experiment,"[84] but the Japanese historian, Ōi Senzō, has offered a more plausible interpretation.
Rather than a new experiment, Ōi has argued, BAT's arrangement with Cheng Po-chao represented a successive phase in the
evolution of the nineteenth-century comprador system. Cheng
differed from nineteenth-century compradors, according to
Ōi, only in that he was a "capitalist comprador"—a capitalist
in the sense that he retained the majority of stock in his business and a comprador in the sense that he represented the
interests of a foreign firm in Chinese markets. Ōi's characterization is more apt than BAT's, but it has its limitations, for it
makes no distinction between salaried employees of a foreign
firm (which I have designed as compradors) and nonsalaried
participants in a foreign firm's distributing system (which I
have designated as agents); according to this distinction, Cheng
was an agent, not a comprador, of BAT. Moreover, Ōi has failed
to note the related point that Cheng, like other leading Chinese
BAT agents, differed from compradors in that he was an established, independent merchant long before he agreed to represent
BAT or any other foreign firm, and, therefore, that he need not
have been as dependent on foreigners for initial capital as compradors were. This degree of financial independence gave him
more power and leverage vis-à-vis BAT than compradors had
with their foreign employers.[85] For this reason, Cheng was perhaps more of a capitalist than a comprador.

However he is labeled, Cheng—and for that matter all of the
leading BAT agents—bore a resemblance to nineteenth-century
compradors insofar as they provided a bridge between a foreign
firm and China's complex commercial system. Over this bridge
BAT hoped its cigarettes would flow into China unimpeded by

obstacles that had previously stymied Western businessmen—obstacles such as the variations in regional marketing structures, differences in spoken dialects, and idiosyncracies in local currencies and standards of weights and measures.[86] As one BAT pamphlet expressed BAT's premise, for Chinese people "to disturb [Cheng Po-chao's and other Chinese BAT agents'] markets, to place difficulties in the way of the cigarettes they sell, is to destroy the business of Chinese companies and merchants."[87] But the business of Chinese distributors was not destroyed. Most of the Chinese BAT agents continued to represent BAT for two decades or longer and distributed huge numbers of cigarettes.[88]

Thus, BAT's marketing system had as its foundation a solid and substantial Chinese sales organization, and, once this sales organization delivered the goods to the core of a regional market, Chinese agents and merchants, not Westerners, invariably managed local distribution. Even in Shanghai, the site of BAT's headquarters in China, the company relied on an established Chinese distributing system rather than attempting to "modernize" it or institute close Western supervision over it. A Chinese company that was planning to enter the Shanghai market discovered how this system excluded newcomers. In 1915, one of its representatives tried the shops on every one of the commercial streets of Shanghai, but no merchant would agree to accept his goods, even when he offered them on consignment. Through this frustrating experience, he learned that BAT had formed restrictive agreements with Shanghai's 20 largest mercantile houses (*hang*) to distribute BAT tobacco products and no other brands. The 20 leading *hang,* in turn, controlled 170 smaller *hang* in the city. Together these *hang* formed an intricate network through which BAT utterly dominated the cigarette market in Shanghai. According to a study by one of BAT's potential competitors in January 1915, BAT sold over 100 million cigarettes per month, more than 50 times as many as its combined Shanghai competitors, giving it monthly sales valued at 400,000 yuan.[89]

In other cities, the Westerners' role in marketing was even less significant. Generally the foreigners dealt with no one lower in the marketing hierarchy than a "division dealer," a Chinese regional distributor like Ma, Kung, Yu, Ts'ui, and others mentioned earlier, each of whom was responsible for a territory usually as large as, but not necessarily coterminous with, a whole province. The division dealers distributed the cigarettes among subdealers. Upon receiving the merchandise, division dealers put up cash security generally in silver dollars amounting to at least half the value. Credit was granted for the remainder on consignment, the balance being secured by written guaranty bond or "shop guaranty" for thirty, sixty, or ninety days. Division dealers were held financially responsible for subdealers and received a rebate ranging from 5 to 10 percent. On retail sales, the subdealers made a profit ranging from 10 to 20 percent.[90] The tendency for BAT agents to rely on established Chinese merchants to market goods in this manner may be documented for cities in several regions: Peking, Tientsin, Chinwangtao, and Changli in North China; Mukden in Manchuria; Chungking on the Upper Yangtze; Shanghai and Hangchow in the Lower Yangtze; Foochow in the southeast; Canton in the south; Kunming in the southwest.[91]

How far outside the treaty port cities did BAT's distributing system reach? The question is an important one because of its possible relevance to the larger issue of whether imported Western industrial goods competed with native goods and crushed native handicraft industries. Albert Feuerwerker, for example, has argued that foreign industrial goods—including BAT cigarettes—did not reach rural markets and therefore did not significantly affect Chinese handicraft industries. In his words:

The simplistic indictment of "foreign capitalism" by some contemporary Chinese historians for having progressively "crushed" and "exploited" domestic handicraft industry from the mid-nineteenth century onward is belied by the actual state of the Chinese economy as late as the 1930s . . . Anyone who would claim that the Hunan or Szechwan peasant in the 1930s . . . smoked BAT cigarettes . . . has a big case to prove.[92]

The available statistical evidence on the tobacco industry tends to support Feuerwerker's thesis concerning the staying power of China's traditional handicraft industries, for it shows that the gross value of hand-made tobacco products (mostly shredded tobacco smoked in pipes) rose from 38.5 million yuan in 1914 to 115.6 million yuan in 1916; declined to about 70 million yuan per year in 1917–1918; fell to less than 30 million yuan per year in 1919–1920; but then recovered and surpassed previous levels, reaching between 128.9 and 171.8 million yuan by 1933.[93] Nonetheless, while acknowledging, in light of this evidence, that the distribution of BAT cigarettes seems not to have crushed the handicraft industry for tobacco products, I believe that a case can be made that Chinese peasants smoked BAT cigarettes before the 1930s. The case is based primarily on evidence from a BAT house organ published in Chinese for Chinese compradors, dealers, and agents that described the work of Chinese BAT agents in rural markets.[94]

According to the BAT publication, Hsieh I-ch'u, based in Chinwangtao in northeastern Chihli, proved himself to be an exemplary BAT agent by doing outstanding work for the company in rural markets. He kept informed of activities in the countryside and set up a mobile cigarette concession when villagers gathered for plays, feasts, festivals, and fairs. Accompanying him were attendants who displayed brightly colored posters, played a gramophone, distributed lottery tickets, and gave away prizes. He and his team, it is said, went "everywhere" in the region.[95] Jonathan Spence has pointed out that itinerant vendors were able to widen the market for opium by making cheap sales during such festivities, at which time people from the countryside "in high spirits with loose cash in their pockets (for probably the only time in the year) might well contract a habit that would last a lifetime."[96] Hsieh I-ch'u tried to attract customers from rural areas in the same manner, and, according to reports from Maritime Customs officials, he was successful. In 1909, BAT's business in his territory around Chinwangtao grew, they reported, because in "the surrounding rural areas . . . the demand for cigarettes was exceptionally great."[97]

Other Chinese BAT agents used similar techniques to penetrate rural markets elsewhere in China. In Shantung and Anhwei provinces, Wu K'o-chai circulated cigarettes in small market towns along the Tientsin-Pukow railroad. Around Kalgan, just south of the Great Wall, Yang Teh-fu, another Chinese agent, extended BAT's reach into rural areas by hiring carter-hawkers to pull mule carts full of cigarettes into outlying towns and villages. In southern Manchuria, Liu Chin-sheng hired children to do hawking in the streets of Mukden and sent vendors into rural marketing areas around the city. And other Chinese BAT agents in South as well as North China conducted sales campaigns in rural markets.[98]

The results of the Chinese BAT agents' work outside the treaty ports deeply impressed Chinese businessmen. In 1914, a spy for a Chinese cigarette firm reported that BAT cigarettes were selling in small market towns (ch'eng-chen) all over Manchuria.[99] In 1916 and 1917 a Chinese businessman took trips up the Yangtze and overland in North China to study BAT's operation and was awed by what he found. He confided to his Chinese business associates that BAT had canvassed not only treaty ports and market towns but even villages (hsiang) that were "extremely poor." Moreover, in inland areas where "the land is vast and the people are few," shopkeepers had pledged to carry only BAT cigarettes and customers had already become loyal to BAT brands.[100] This report gains credence from an American BAT representative's recollection that he and Chinese BAT agents regularly visited small market towns (chen) in the early 1910s where "the average population was about 1,000 of which at least two-thirds were children and babies."[101]

This evidence is not statistically grounded, but it indicates that BAT cigarettes were reaching rural markets in many parts of early twentieth-century China. If complete statistics were available, they would probably show that the farther markets were from treaty ports, the fewer BAT cigarettes appeared in them. Nonetheless, whatever the magnitude of this trade,[102] the point is that Chinese agents were able to reach outside the treaty ports and widen the market for their product in rural as well as urban areas.

To enhance the appeal of BAT cigarettes, the company also relied on Chinese to design and disseminate its advertising. Chinese artists and calligraphers were hired to draft advertisements, and they showed a talent for adapting BAT's message to the Chinese cultural setting. Westerners in BAT were inclined to advertise through newspapers, sign boards, wall paintings, posters, and cigarette cards (the latter introduced in the 1880s in America by James Duke) as they had in the West. BAT advertised extensively in these, but, on the basis of recommendations by Chinese employees, it also used scrolls, handbills, calendars, wall hangings, window displays, attractive and strong cigarette packing cases (whose wood and nails were reused by the Chinese), cotton canvas covers for the tops of carts, and small rugs to serve as footrests in riskshas—all bearing BAT's trademark. Of the 1.8 million yuan BAT allocated annually for publicity and sales promotion by the late 1910s, only 10 percent was spent on newspapers and publications. The remaining 90 percent was invested in Chinese-style advertisements.[103]

Within both Western- and Chinese-style advertising, Chinese artists presented portraits of legendary and semi-legendary figures familiar to almost any Chinese. Subjects included, for example, Yang Kuei-fei, an artful concubine supposedly responsible for the decline of the T'ang dynasty; Yueh Fei, a patriotic general of the Southern Sung; the White Snake (*Pai-she*), an immortal serpent transformed into a beautiful woman; and whole series of characters from Peking operas and popular novels such as *Water Margin* (*Shui-hu chuan*), *Monkey* (*Hsi-yu chi*), and the "Twenty-four Stories of Filial Piety" ("Erh-shih-ssu hsiao"). Occasionally BAT artists portrayed figures from their own day, but, rather than show contemporary celebrities endorsing BAT products (as advertising has tended to do in the West), they pictured nameless representatives of broad social groups: women (represented by "beauties" from Shanghai's *filles de joie,* and, beginning in 1914, by the "new women" in roles as social activists); children at play (based on the "Hundred Children Pictures" [*Pai-tzu t'u*]); and working people engaged in the "360 Trades" (*San-pai liu-shih hang,* an expression used to mean all trades and professions). Sensitive to China's "Little Traditions" as well as its "Great Tradition," BAT artists screened all the company's advertising proposals and adjusted any details in Western advertisements which, because of cultural differences, might have been considered offensive in China (for example, a green hat was taboo, for it signified cuckoldry in the Chinese vernacular). And they kept advertising up to date by dropping symbols that became unfashionable; the dragon, for example, was not used after the monarchy, which it had symbolized, was overthrown by the Revolution of 1911.[104]

As time passed, less and less language was used in BAT's advertisements. Pictographic advertising was believed to be more effective because it helped BAT reach potential customers who were illiterate and because it made posters less subject to embarrassing and damaging puns. The latter was a problem because the Chinese language is rich in opportunities for punning, and the opportunities are even greater as one moves from one dialect to another. Carl Crow, a veteran journalist in China, remarked in the 1920s, "An advertising phrase which is quite suitable and effective in Shanghai is turned into a vulgar or ludicrous pun in Canton."[105] To prevent punning, some posters had no words at all—except BAT's trademark, a bat (a symbol of happiness in China)[106] and the roman letters "B.A.T." with their Chinese equivalent, *Ying-Mei yen-ts'ao kung-ssu*.

To design appealing advertisements, BAT quickly learned to rely on Chinese who had a knowledge of Chinese traditions, an awareness of local customs, and a sensitivity to the popular imagination—cultural sensibilities that Americans and other Westerners on the staff did not possess. At first the company had entrusted Westerners with the responsibility for advertising, but they chose pictures (for example, from German fairy tales) and introduced slogans (for example, "Beauty has a short life") that made no sense in the Chinese context and became objects of derision and sources of amusement among Chinese customers.[107] Embarrassed, BAT's management began to rely on Chinese artists and to protect itself against future mistakes by arranging for its Chinese distributing agents to check the advertising staff's work. To prepare its annual calendar, for example, the company paid retaining fees to several leading Chinese artists to submit sketches, and they circulated these sketches in rough draft among all Chinese BAT agents throughout the country, who evaluated them, checked to see that the characters in them carried no potentially damaging local double meanings, and cast votes for their favorites. The winning entry was reproduced in full-color calendars in time for Chinese New Year. In the words of an American BAT representative who later returned from China to become a successful copywriter with the American advertising agency, J. Walter Thompson & Co. in New York, BAT's calendar became its "big advertising smash every year" and was distributed "in every nook and corner of the nation."[108]

Chinese in BAT's marketing system not only distributed advertising matter but also adjusted cigarette packaging and initiated promotional campaigns appropriate to their own locales. To make the product accessible to the poor, for example, hawkers broke down packages of the cheapest BAT brands, which were priced at $0.02 for a pack of twenty cigarettes, and sold as little as one cigarette at a time. To attract crowds, Chinese BAT distributors organized parades in which BAT banners waved, held lotteries in which first prize was a gold watch, and paid itinerant storytellers to weave into their tales appealing references to brands of BAT cigarettes. BAT's management supplied prizes and rewarded anyone showing initiative in promotional work.[109] In this way, the company encouraged Chinese distributors and dealers to supervise their subdealers and hawkers more closely and penetrate into local markets more deeply.

Thus, in all aspects of its business—manufacturing, distributing, purchasing, and advertising—BAT's success depended on Chinese. Without the work they did and the links to Chinese society they provided, BAT would not have been able to manufacture its product so cheaply, distribute it so widely, and profit from the trade so handsomely.

These findings require modification of earlier conclusions concerning the efficiency, organizational strength, and vertical integration of BAT. First, the role of workers and peasants in BAT shows that the company's "efficiency" derived not merely from its transferral of a superior capital-intensive technology to China but also from its reliance on cheap labor. Second, the prominence of Chinese compradors and agents in BAT's marketing system suggests that the company's "organizational strength" derived more from the established Chinese network into which Duke and Thomas injected their product than from changes in marketing patterns introduced by American "pioneers." BAT pioneered in the sense that it (along with the Standard Oil Company) was one of the first businesses ever to distribute a trademarked product on a national scale in China (that is, in all of the country's regional markets), but it did so by relying heavily on Chinese compradors and agents who, in turn, operated through their connections within the existing marketing structure. And third, if we attribute BAT's success to "vertical integration," it must be understood that only the Americans and other Westerners in its organization were tightly centralized and departmentalized; the Chinese who actually controlled labor, purchasing, and distributing were generalists, and—except for their incorporation of new advertising—they continued to rely on business practices that were not radically different from the ones used in the past.

Americans and other Westerners in the company depended so heavily on Chinese compradors that the foreigners seem to have been only dimly aware of the commercial processes beneath the highest levels of the operation. Looking back on his career, James Thomas admitted that he had not been able to impose his own authority and that he had accepted Chinese commercial practices as they were because he had felt powerless to change them. "When I landed in China," he recalled in the early 1920s after retiring from BAT,

I felt that someone had taken me by the heels and thrown me into the Pacific Ocean. I had to swim out. The thing was overwhelming. Here was a huge country of four hundred million people extraordinarily true to their civilization . . . Their ways, unlike though they were to mine, were worthy of my respect.

My conviction, therefore, was that I ought to trade with these people as nearly as possible according to their ideas. . . . I knew that not in my lifetime could I educate a handful to my ways; I must adapt myself to theirs.

That is the word in either cigarettes or civilization—adaptability.[110]

Overwhelmed by Chinese "civilization" (by which he seems to have meant China's traditional commercial system), Thomas sought to accommodate Chinese marketing conditions by delegating a large measure of authority to Chinese compradors. The compradors were salaried employees who recruited Chinese nonsalaried agents, who, in turn, worked through other Chinese networks that enabled BAT to reach deeply into Chinese economic life. These Chinese intermediaries—compradors, agents, and others—not Westerners, were between BAT's Western management, capital, and technology on the one hand, and Chinese labor, agriculture, and marketing structure on the other. The chains of Chinese intermediaries that linked the company with Chinese commercial institutions were held together by distinctive Chinese social and commercial relationships that were neither directly controlled by BAT's Western management nor formally integrated into the company's organizational structure.

Thus summarized, the complex process by which BAT penetrated markets in China may appear to have been completed more simply or more smoothly than it was. Even if, as I have suggested, BAT succeeded in gaining access to Chinese markets in these ways, it nonetheless aroused hostility among many Chinese. To evaluate the full consequences of BAT's commercial penetration, it is necessary to consider the sources of this hostility, analyze the resistance that the company faced, and explain why, despite resistance to it as a foreign intruder, its operations expanded and its sales and profits rose in these years.

EAST ASIAN OPPOSITION TO BAT

In assessing opposition to BAT in China, it is helpful to consider earlier opposition to the company in Japan, for the comparison between the two is illuminating. In Japan, in contrast to China, the strongest opposition to James Duke's company in the late nineteenth and early twentieth centuries came directly from the national government. The Japanese government mounted opposition to Duke's company as part of an effort to revise the unequal treaties, and it achieved success along these lines much earlier than governments did in China. Whereas Chinese governments did not recover tariff autonomy until 1929 and did not abolish extraterritoriality until 1943, the Japanese government began negotiating agreements with the Western powers as early as 1894 and eventually eradicated extraterritoriality by 1899 and regained tariff autonomy by 1911. In the late 1890s and early 1900s, the Japanese government followed up on these diplomatic initiatives by passing laws to limit commercial penetration by foreign companies, including Duke's.

The Japanese government first acted against Duke in 1897, promulgating a higher tariff on cigarettes that was scheduled to go into effect in 1899. The significance of the proposed tariff did not escape Duke, who responded by more than doubling exports of cigarettes to Japan in 1898, an increase that brought his company's total sales in Japan for the years 1894–1898 to 985 million cigarettes. After the higher tariff went into effect in 1899, he then adopted the same strategy that other American exporters had used to overcome high tariffs at the time in continental Europe, jumping the new barrier by investing in local factories.[111] Duke made his investment in Murai Brothers Company, largest of the many private Japanese cigarette firms founded in the 1890s. He initially paid $2 million in cash for stock in Murai Brothers and subsequently secured controlling interest by buying 60 percent of the $5 million worth of stock that Murai Brothers issued. This investment, the largest by any foreign company in late Meiji Japan, gave Murai a total capitalization of 10 million yen—a huge sum compared with the financial backing of its Japanese rivals.[112] By the beginning of the twentieth century, Murai Brothers, with Murai Kichibei as President and American Tobacco's Edward J. Parrish as Vice-President, produced on a large scale, advertised widely and extravagantly, and enjoyed high and rising profits in Japan— 772,641 yen in 1900; 1,408,623 yen in 1901; and 1,687,691 yen in 1902—which, during the last year alone, added almost $500,000 to the treasury of Duke's company in the United States. Early in 1903, just after Murai Brothers had become a subsidiary of the newly founded BAT, Parrish reported to Duke that within a few months Murai's most popular brand would be selling at the rate of 100 million cigarettes per month, and Duke calculated that Murai's net income would reach 2 million yen for the year but, contrary to these expectations, the life of this Japanese-American venture was cut short.[113]

Murai Brothers was undone by Japanese opponents who demanded governmental action against it on patriotic grounds. Japanese cigarette firms carried out nationalistic advertising campaigns in newspapers attacking Murai Kichibei for his capitulation to foreigners and accusing him of permitting his foreign backers to drain revenue out of Japan. Although these native competitors remained tiny by comparison with Murai and posed little threat to it, the message in their advertising appealed to political leaders who had never been enthusiastic about direct foreign investment in Japanese industry and who had taken pride in the nation's independence, especially since the victory over China in the war of 1894–1895. Japanese political leaders accused Duke of being "the capitalist [who] is intending to monopolize the whole world," and, on these grounds, they ended American involvement in the Japanese cigarette industry in 1904 by expropriating every existing private cigarette firm, including Murai Brothers. In thus nationalizing the industry, the government compensated Duke for his investment but forced him to dissolve his interests in Japan.[114] Thereafter the Japanese Imperial Tobacco Monopoly, capitalized at 10 million yen (5.8 million paid), imported tobacco directly from the United States and controlled the cigarette industry not only in Japan but also in Korea (annexed by Japan in 1910). Forced to withdraw from Japan and Korea, Duke shifted his attention and his capital investments to China.[115]

While strong action by the Japanese government decisively ended American penetration of the cigarette market in Japan and Korea, the absence of direct governmental opposition to Duke's company in China encouraged him to invest there. In contrast to his experience in Japan, for example, Duke was virtually unhindered by tariffs in China. Prior to 1902, tobacco and tobacco products entered China duty free. Under the Treaty of Tientsin in 1858, the tariff on almost all goods had been 5 percent ad valorem with an additional duty of 2.5 percent on goods reshipped to a second port (the maximum rates under the treaties).[116] But the cigarette had been exempted from these low duties on the grounds that it was for the personal use of foreigners in China. In the list of duty-free items, the treaty did not actually specify cigarettes, a product unimportant in the West and nonexistent in China when the treaty was signed. It did, however, specify "tobacco (foreign), cigars (foreign)" in the English text and "foreign prepared tobacco and tobacco leaf" in the Chinese text. These items were construed to include cigarettes until 1902.[117]

In 1902, the Chinese government, still lacking tariff autonomy, attempted to begin taxing BAT at the maximum rate under the treaties of 5 percent ad valorem upon arrival in a Chinese port and 2.5 percent ad valorem for reshipment, but the attempt was only partially successful. Despite the fact that the new tax was clearly intended to apply to all of the Western company's goods and any other machine-made cigarettes sold in China, BAT argued that all its cigarettes manufactured in China were subject not to this tax but only to a tax on "native prepared tobacco." The latter tax was designed to cover pipe tobacco that was shredded or pulverized by hand, and it was payable at the much lower rate of 0.675 taels per picul on goods when first marketed in a city and 0.3375 taels per picul for transshipment, or a total of 1.0125 per picul, the equivalent of no more than 1 or 2 percent ad valorem. Though BAT's cigarettes were all machine-made, its management insisted that this tax be applied to all the goods that it manufactured in China because these deserved to be considered "native" products. In 1904, Prince Ch'ing (I-k'uang), the highest ranking official in foreign affairs in Peking, challenged BAT's contention and proposed that cigarettes be taxed at the higher rate. But BAT, with the support of the American and British ministers in China, convinced him to accept the company's position on the condition that foreign cigarettes not be exempted from transit duties (which were paid at the rate of half the basic tax, that is, 0.3375 taels per picul), likin, and other local taxes outside ports. In January 1905 (six months after BAT's ouster from Japan), BAT obtained formal assurance from the Ch'ing central government that the company would be considered a "native" manufacturer and that cigarettes it made in China were taxable at the lower rate.[118]

With this favorable tax arrangement in hand, BAT made its first substantial direct investments in China, inaugurating construction of its largest factories at Shanghai and Hankow in 1906 and 1907, but, as its building program continued with the addition of a plant in Mukden in 1909, the company encountered stronger opposition from officials at the provincial level in Manchuria than it had faced from the Ch'ing central government in Peking. BAT had expected cigarettes made in Mukden to be taxed at the same low rates as in Shanghai and Hankow. The company's proposal to this effect was approved by the Chinese Foreign Ministry (Wai-wu pu) in Peking on 1 August 1909, but, to BAT's surprise, it was rejected by Chinese provincial officials in Mukden. Hsu Shih-ch'ang, the Governor General of Manchuria who was experienced at dealing with Americans, proposed that BAT pay taxes at Mukden at 5 percent ad valorem. One of Hsu's subordinates in Mukden pointed out that a rate of 1 or 2 percent ad valorem was "ridiculously small" and the rate of 5 percent ad valorem was "reasonable and generous" in light of the taxation imposed on cigarettes in other countries.[119] Hsu's successor, Hsi-liang, who resolutely resisted foreign encroachment here as he had in other provinces, continued the campaign and finally convinced the Ch'ing Foreign Ministry to reverse its position. One month after approving BAT's proposal for lower taxes, the Foreign Ministry endorsed Hsi-liang's demands for a tax of 5 percent ad valorem. BAT loudly complained, claimed the company had been led to build the factory under false pretenses, and curtailed production there. It paid the tax between 1909 and 1911 but finally threatened to close the factory if taxes were not reduced.[120]

In 1911, rather than lose tobacco revenue in the region altogether, officials in Mukden and the Foreign Ministry in Peking accepted a compromise. On its side, BAT agreed to pay 1 tael per picul at the factory in Mukden (as compared with 0.675 tael per picul in Shanghai and Hankow), 0.45 tael per picul in Manchuria on cigarettes exported to China proper, and 0.225 tael per picul at the point of entry in China proper; the cigarettes were declared exempt from likin and other local taxes in Manchuria but not in China proper. And, on its side, the Foreign Ministry agreed not to use this as a precedent for changing the 1904 agreement concerning taxation of BAT's factories in Shanghai and Hankow. Although this arrangement was less favorable for BAT than the one in Shanghai and Hankow, the rate of taxation was still very low by comparison with tobacco tariffs and taxes in other countries, and the exemption from local taxes gave BAT advantages over its Chinese competitors in Manchuria.[121]

After thus keeping the Ch'ing government at bay, BAT sought still greater political and fiscal concessions after the fall of the dynasty in 1911. Within months after a Republican government replaced the Ch'ing, the company "voluntarily" (in James Thomas's words) sent "two experts to Peking to study the question of taxation on tobacco and cigarettes."[122] By 1914, these "experts" and Chinese officials worked out a scheme whereby the young Republican government would obtain a new source of revenue and BAT cigarettes would be exempted from likin or any other taxes beyond the import tariff. According to BAT's version of the scheme, the Chinese government would create a bureau in which two Chinese government officials, two BAT representatives, and one "independent party" would preside jointly over tobacco taxation. The function of this board would be to organize tobacco taxation and, "without hurting the tobacco industry," gradually increase revenue. The board would be responsible for regulating the industry and issuing excise stamps indicating that cigarettes so marked should be taxed no further. The Chinese government in Peking was to benefit from the increased revenue from loans BAT would help it negotiate with other Westerners and from a loan BAT agreed to make directly to the government. The arrangement would have given BAT a long-term monopoly over the cigarette industry in China because it granted the company power to determine which cigarette firms were to be licensed and which cigarettes taxed. In addition, BAT proposed that it be given a fixed fee (the amount to be negotiated) plus 10 percent of the revenue accruing to the bureau in return for the company's "experience and services in this matter." BAT executives anticipated that they and the Chinese government would preside jointly over tobacco taxation for twenty-five years.[123]

BAT's scheme aroused opposition from both government officials and businessmen. Western governments protested that such a bureau would violate the Treaty of Tientsin, which forbade the creation of any new monopolies in China after 1858; the Japanese government objected to BAT control over a market where the Japanese Imperial Tobacco Monopoly was involved; and the Association for the Protection of Chinese Tobacco Interests published letters and circulars complaining that such an arrangement would ruin Chinese tobacco businesses.[124]

BAT replied that the proposed agreement would result not in a monopoly but in a stamp tax that would provide an alternative to likin and other inland taxes. This was the line of argument taken by Wu T'ing-sheng, a BAT comprador who put himself in a position to further BAT's interests by securing an appointment from the Peking government as Special Commissioner for the Investigation of the Tobacco Tariff in the Ministry of Finance in 1913. But, even working within the Peking government and as a member of it, Wu was not able to make a case for BAT's monopoly scheme that was acceptable to the government's representatives with whom he held talks, Chou Tzu-ch'i, Minister of Finance, and Liang Shih-i, Director of the Tax Administration and personal secretary to President Yuan Shih-k'ai. A year after Wu's appointment as Special Commissioner, he still had not persuaded Chou and Liang to approve the monopoly, and, in June 1914, his talks with them stopped. In 1915, BAT and the government resumed their discussions briefly, but the company's monopoly scheme was never put into practice.[125]

Failing to secure a tax monopoly, BAT continued to resist the government's attempts to impose new taxes. In 1915, when the Peking government instituted a new tax on tobacco products made in China's "native industry" (*t'u-yeh*), some bureaus in the provinces levied it on BAT goods. Despite BAT's earlier eagerness to secure tax privileges as a "native" company, its management in this instance protested that it deserved to be exempted from the tax because it was Western and was protected from the tax by China's treaties with the West. The company seems to have had no legal grounds for invoking the treaties, but it never did pay the tax.[126]

In this series of negotiations over taxes prior to 1915, Chinese governments clearly failed to offer Duke's company any direct opposition comparable to that which Japan had given it. Within this period, the late Ch'ing and early Republican Chinese governments did not nationalize the cigarette industry and oust Duke's company as the Japanese government did in 1904, nor did they regain tariff autonomy as the Japanese government did in 1911. Lacking tariff autonomy, each Chinese government had a legal limit on the tariffs it could impose on BAT; and, failing to overcome BAT's legal arguments, financial strength, and diplomatic support, Chinese officials yielded to the company's demands for taxes that were even lower than the legal limit. Insofar as the Ch'ing government checked BAT's commercial penetration at all, it did so not directly (as the Japanese government did) but only indirectly by inspiring or tolerating popular movements that threatened BAT. Of these movements, by far the strongest before 1915 was the anti-American boycott of 1905 and 1906.

The Ch'ing government indirectly encouraged this boycott by refusing in 1904 to renew an American treaty excluding Chinese laborers from the United States. The Ch'ing leadership made this decision as part of a reform program designed to promote nationalistic opposition against foreign aggression and save the dynasty. As part of the same program, between 1901 and 1904 the Ch'ing had approved the opening of new schools and military academies to give Chinese youth the expertise to cope with foreigners and had authorized the creation of chambers of commerce to enable merchants to resist foreign commercial penetration. Patriotic merchants and students who joined chambers of commerce and attended the schools were determined to bring an end to a period of national humiliation which they traced from the Opium War of the early 1840s to the Boxer Uprising of 1900.[127] After the negotiations over the treaty dragged on first in Washington and then in Peking for several months in 1904 and 1905, these merchants and students lost patience with the slow-moving processes of diplomacy and decided to take direct action against the Americans. Organizing within their new government-approved chambers of commerce and schools, they urged the Chinese people to show their support for a more equitable treaty by boycotting American goods.

Chinese merchants in the Shanghai Chamber of Commerce inaugurated the boycott on 20 July 1905, and BAT immediately became its prime target. At the meeting called to announce the boycott, two Chinese spokesmen for BAT, the comprador Wu T'ing-sheng and the tobacco merchant Hao Chung-sheng, rose to defend the company, but, according to reports circulated by boycott leaders, Wu and Hao "had not said more than a few words when they were removed by unanimous consent of their angry hearers."[128] In the months that followed, participants in the boycott identified BAT as an American firm and demonstrated against it more widely and spectacularly than against any other company. Boycott leaders placed the names of its brands at the top of blacklists and singled out its product in one of the movement's most popular slogans, "Don't use American goods, don't smoke American cigarettes."[129] Merchants in the Lower Yangtze River Valley and in South China responded to this plea, especially in Shanghai and Canton. Ironically, leaders of the boycott in these cities beat BAT at a game in which the Western company believed itself supreme—advertising.

In Shanghai, red posters appeared with messages written in big, black characters. The signs all urged patriotic Chinese not to buy American goods, and many specified BAT cigarettes as contraband. In one poster, a dog—an animal that Chinese disesteemed—was pictured smoking a cigarette labeled "Pinhead" (one of BAT's most popular brands). "Those who smoke American cigarettes," read the caption, "are of my species." The poster was signed by "The Fraternity of Chinese Merchants." Another poster purported to be an edict issued by the "God of Thunder." It congratulated "virtuous men and women" for refusing to buy the Standard Oil Company's kerosene, the American Trading Company's soaps, and BAT cigarettes (naming the three most popular BAT brands). It also warned that any person violating the boycott should "beware of my thunderbolt." Another poster named seven BAT brands of cigarettes and one BAT brand of plug tobacco to be boycotted "to maintain the dignity of our 400,000,000." In yet another, Buddhist priests declared several BAT brands contraband.[130]

In South China, boycott leaders attacked BAT in a variety of ways. They persuaded Chinese newspaper publishers in Canton not to carry BAT advertisements. They circulated, according to BAT, "divers pamphlets . . . throughout the entire provinces" of Kwangtung and Kwangsi. They issued handbills, one of which, in the words of a BAT complainant, pictured "one of our Canton dealers as a disgusting reptile or animal, thereby intimidating him against continuing the sale of our goods."[131] They made persuasive posters such as one that showed a hearty common laborer accosting a blasé young scholar. Snatching a Western cigarette from the lips of the "idle young man" and replacing it with a Chinese cigarette, the laborer demanded, "Sir, you must have more pride!" The poster's caption exhorted the people of Canton to be sincere like the worker and not an enemy of the people like the young scholar.[132]

Cantonese also sang anti-American songs. Composed in the form of Cantonese love songs, their distinctive idiom, rhyme, and form surely enhanced their appeal.[133] One satirical song in this genre might have been the most influential anti-BAT boycott device of all. Called "Elegy to Cigarette," its lyrics playfully mourned the decline of BAT's popularity in 1905:

> You are really down and out,
> American cigarette.
> Look at you down and out.
> I think back to the way you used to be
> In those days when you were flying high.
> Who would have rejected you?
> Everyone loved you
> Saying you were better than silver dollars
> Because your taste overwhelms people
> And is even better than opium.
> Inhaling it makes people's mouths water.
> We've had a relationship
> In which up to now there has been no problem.
> I thought our love affair would remain
> Unchanged until earth and sky collapsed.
> Who would have expected that the Way of Heaven would not be as
> always.
> That human things might change.
> Then this movement against the treaty got underway
> And spread everywhere
> Because America mistreated our Overseas Chinese
> Degrading us like lowly oxen and workhorses.
> Therefore everyone has united to boycott America,
> And that means opposing Americans.
> What is the most ideal way?
> People say it is best not to sell American goods
> And to this end we must all unite into a collective body.
>
> Ah cigarette,
> You have the word American in your trademark for everyone to see
> So I must give you up along with my bicycle.[134]
> Our love affairs (*chiao-ch'ing*)
> Today must end.

Ai,
Cigarette please don't harbor resentment.
Perhaps a time might come when we meet again,
But it must be after Americans abrogate the treaty.
Then as before I shall be able to fondle (*ch'an-mien*) you.[135]

How many smokers sang or heard this song is impossible to say. Shortly before the boycott, a student of Chinese music said of Cantonese love songs, "Today they are known to high and low, rich and poor: they are sung alike by 'toys of paint and powder' [prostitutes] on board the gilt and scarlet flower boats, by blind minstrel-girls in the houses of wealthy men, and by the dirty beggar in the suburban slum."[136] Spread widely over this popular network, "Elegy to Cigarette" might well have reached a huge Cantonese audience. (If Arthur Waley is justified in saying that Po Chu-i's ninth-century ballads which were sung in the streets and aroused popular interest in political questions became "the T'ang equivalent of a letter to the *Times*," then it is possible to say with equal validity that this song was a late Ch'ing Cantonese equivalent of a letter to the *Daily News*.)[137] Behind this propaganda were organizations formed by students and merchants. While student leaders denounced BAT in public speeches, merchant leaders persuaded shopkeepers to throw their stock of BAT cigarettes onto bonfires at boycott rallies and to make pledges not to place new orders.[138]

The campaigns brought results, and BAT immediately felt the effects. Within a week after the boycott began, BAT's management in Shanghai complained that the company's posters had been damaged, that Chinese clients had been intimidated, and that business was suffering. An eye-witness report by Julean Arnold, interpreter for the American Consulate, lends credence to the last of these complaints. After translating posters and observing consumers' behavior in the streets of Shanghai, Arnold concluded in early August that the boycott against American goods was 90 percent effective. Maritime Customs officials in the Lower and Middle Yangtze regions reported that BAT sales declined outside Shanghai as well. In Chia-hsing and Wuhu, BAT cigarettes completely disappeared from the market, and, in Hankow, BAT and Standard Oil were the main targets of the boycott.[139]

In South China, BAT's business also suffered. According to newspaper reports, smokers from every social class in cities throughout the region gave up BAT brands. BAT representatives fell victim to the spirit of the boycott in rural as well as urban areas. One was attacked near Wuchow across the western border of Kwangtung province, and another was stoned and beaten near Swatow in eastern Kwangtung. According to a representative in the South China region, within the first month the boycott caused a 90-percent decrease in the company's sales, an immediate loss of over $200,000 to the company, and a "stupendous" change in the company's future prospects in the region. He probably exaggerated the company's losses, since other sources estimated that BAT sales fell off 50 percent rather than 90 percent in South China, but the company clearly suffered substantial losses.[140]

BAT representatives and other foreign businessmen made every effort to end the boycott, including appeals to American diplomats. Partly in response to these complaints, the American Minister, W. W. Rockhill, with the backing of President Theodore Roosevelt, ordered his consuls in China to exert maximum pressure on local officials. Nonetheless, many Americans—businessmen, journalists, politicians—grew impatient when the boycott continued throughout the summer of 1905. At the end of August, Senator George C. Perkins of California requested that President Roosevelt take advantage of Secretary of War William Howard Taft's presence in East Asia. He urged the President to instruct Taft to take time out from his "good will" tour of China for a visit to Canton, the "backbone of the boycott." Roosevelt denied this request and rebuked Perkins for meddling in the affair.[141]

At this point, BAT approached Roosevelt. Within a few days of the President's riposte to Perkins, a BAT representative made virtually the same proposal, requesting that Taft be sent to Canton to "call officially on the viceroy . . . with a view to settling [the] boycott."[142] On the same day, the Standard Oil Company also urged Roosevelt to send Taft to Canton. Judging from Roosevelt's previous pronouncements, one would have assumed that these messages had little hope of success, for he had frequently expressed low opinions of the parent companies of

BAT and Standard Oil, specifically citing them as examples of evil trusts in America.[143] But, this time, the combination of demands from politicians, diplomatic officials, and businessmen, culminating in the telegrams from BAT and Standard Oil, persuaded him to act as they wished. The very day, 2 September, that Roosevelt received the requests from BAT and Standard Oil he cabled Taft to meet with officials in the Canton area.

Taft's visit to South China on 3 September did not calm Canton. All through the city, he was greeted by anti-American posters, some of which insulted Alice Roosevelt, the President's daughter, who was accompanying Taft. After Taft failed to stop the boycott, BAT representatives and other foreign businessmen contravened directions from the American Consul General in Canton, went directly to the leaders of the boycott, and pledged to support Chinese demands for changes in United States immigration laws. But still the boycott continued in South China.[144]

In the meantime, an imperial edict, issued on 31 August, ended the boycott against most American goods outside South China but not against cigarettes. By mid-September, customers in Shanghai and the Lower Yangtze region, for example, ceased to boycott American goods but continued their campaign against BAT products into the spring of 1906. In the Middle Yangtze region at Hankow and Wuchang, as late as December 1905 and January 1906, weekly meetings were held at which the chief denunciations were directed at BAT. Placards charged that BAT masqueraded as a British firm when it was in fact American, that it gave away free cigarettes out of "bestial motives," and that BAT cigarettes contained poison. In Canton, the boycott against BAT cigarettes persisted longest of all. Students continued to draw crowds near the waterfront and exhorted people to continue or revive the boycott of American cigarettes and other goods. When local police tried to silence them, they claimed to be agents for European cigarette companies concerned only with making sales at the expense of their American rivals, not political activists promoting the boycott. This ruse was apparently effective until 1 March 1906, when the Canton municipal police headquarters issued an order to arrest anyone posing as an agent for a Western cigarette company and calling for a boycott of American goods. Revived repeatedly, the boycott did not finally run its course in Canton until the end of 1906.[145]

Why were BAT cigarettes boycotted for so long and with such intensity? Part of the answer lies in BAT's lack of experience with Chinese antiforeign movements. Later, BAT's management learned to shunt aside Chinese antiforeign sentiment or even turn it against the company's rivals. Part of the answer lies in the nature of BAT's product. As clearly labeled consumer goods, cigarettes (like American kerosene, flour, soap, and textiles) were more tempting targets than industrial goods (such as American coal, cement, paper, or machinery) because a large segment of the Chinese population could learn to recognize and reject such a commodity. And part of the answer lies in the availability of local substitutes. In the early stages of the boycott, there were only 4 small Chinese cigarette companies, but, by the end, more than 20 had come into existence.[146]

The boycott stimulated Chinese to enter the cigarette industry (and mining, textiles, shipping, railroading, banking, and other Western-style businesses) because it temporarily freed them from foreign competition. All the Chinese cigarette companies were small—indeed tiny by comparison with BAT. One had a capital base of 300,000 yuan, four had between 100,000 and 140,000 yuan, and the others had less than 100,000 yuan. (Capitalized at $2.5 million [approximately 5,250,000 yuan], the financial resources of BAT's Shanghai headquarters were then over 17 times greater than the largest of these.) Almost all were managed exclusively by merchants (shang-pan). The only exceptions among the largest companies were the Peiyang Tobacco Company and the San Hsing Tobacco Company, which were jointly managed by merchants and officials (kuan-shang ho-pan).[147]

The Chinese entrepreneurs who opened these businesses did not originate, organize, or lead the boycott, but, once the boycott was underway, they actively tried to capitalize on the nationalistic sentiment it had generated. Several of them identified their products with the movement to "recover economic rights" from foreigners; some emphasized that they used Chinese rather than imported American tobacco leaf; and one of the most successful, the San Hsing Company, advertised in newspapers and posters in several Lower Yangtze cities using the slogan, "All enthusiastically supporting the nation should smoke Chinese cigarettes." In their advertising, naturally none mentioned that several of them relied on foreign advisers and imported foreign supplies, particularly Japanese technicians and technology and American-grown tobacco.[148]

While BAT was beleaguered in 1905 and 1906, some of these small companies grew rapidly, but, as soon as the boycott ended, BAT drove almost all of the 20 existing Chinese cigarette firms out of business or out of the market. According to Sheng Hsuan-huai, a leading Chinese official and industrialist and a stockholder in the San Hsing Tobacco Company, the Western company resorted to unethical (though not illegal) tactics to force these companies to close. Lodging a protest in 1909 with Tsai-tse, President of the Ch'ing Ministry of Finance, Sheng complained that BAT had, for example, drastically reduced prices, starting price wars that its smaller Chinese competitors could not hope to win; it had intimidated Chinese officials into banning many Chinese cigarettes for allegedly imitating BAT brands; and it had formed exclusive dealing arrangements which, in Sheng's words, bound "every single retailer in the interior as well as the coastal ports" not to carry any cigarettes except those of BAT.[149] Sheng's charges gain credence in light of the past record of BAT's owners, for Duke and his American associates had relied on similar tactics to pound their rivals into submission in the West, forcing other companies in the American cigarette market to merge with Duke's company in the 1890s, coercing the Imperial Tobacco Company of England into forming BAT in 1902, and subverting a rival American cigarette company's plans to enter the China market in 1903.[150] With these precedents to follow, Duke's BAT subsidiary in China probably behaved as ruthlessly toward young Chinese cigarette firms in the aftermath of the boycott as Sheng claimed. Victimized by BAT's aggressive methods, the Chinese cigarette industry could not withstand BAT's return to the market. Although the boycott had protected the Chinese firms briefly (almost as a higher tariff might have), it did not last long enough to give them time to experiment, overcome financial problems, and develop economies of mass production and technological efficiency that might have enabled them to continue to compete with their better financed and more experienced foreign rival.

After BAT disposed of the new Chinese firms between 1906 and 1908, it periodically faced additional boycotts and anti-smoking campaigns but encountered no serious competition from rival companies before 1915.[151] Following the boycott, as earlier noted, BAT built its largest factories at Shanghai and Hankow, completing them in 1906 and 1907. These factories gave BAT economies of scale that also discouraged new firms from entering the market because the Western company's cost advantages over potential Chinese rivals grew still larger.

By 1915, BAT's monopoly in China seemed unstoppable. As early as 1904, the American executive at Duke's subsidiary in Japan had predicted that the company would overcome any obstacle it might face in China. As he had prepared to return to the United States after his company's ouster from Japan in 1904, he had written to his counterpart in Shanghai:

You have a great field and untold possibilities are in your reach. The situation in China, with prospective business, makes it an inviting field, requiring large views and gigantic movements . . . I shall expect to hear that your Sales in China alone have passed the *One Thousand Million Cigarettes per Month mark* . . . As I see it . . . your ball of snow [is rolling] and it will not be long before it is so large as to crush everything in its pathway.[152]

In 1915, little more than a decade later, his prediction came true: BAT cigarettes were selling at the rate of a billion per month. Its manufacturing system, which employed 13,000 workers at factories in Shanghai, Hankow, Mukden, and Harbin, produced between half and two-thirds of these cigarettes within China. Its marketing system distributed cigarettes and advertising in every region of the country. Its purchasing system in China procured less than 10 percent of the bright tobacco it used there in 1915 (importing the remainder from the United States), and, with reception stations recently built in Shantung and Honan provinces, it was prepared to take advantage of the much larger harvests of Chinese-grown bright tobacco that were soon to come. With these systems all in place and functioning effectively, BAT did indeed "crush everything in its pathway." [Not until after 1915 was BAT given serious competition by a Chinese-owned firm, Nanyang Brothers Tobacco Company; but that is another story.]

COMMERCIAL PENETRATION
AND ECONOMIC IMPERIALISM

The process of commercial penetration has been analyzed here to explain how an American firm made high sales and profits in China, exploiting a market which, far from a "myth," turned out to be a large and lucrative reality. But the findings presented here also raise a broader question: Was this American-owned firm an economic imperialist in China? Since the answer depends on how imperialist exploitation is defined, let us consider five major definitions of this term and determine whether they apply to BAT's record in China.

According to one definition of imperialist exploitation that has been used by mercantilists in the West since the seventeenth century and by Chinese historians and social commentators at least since the late nineteenth century, it is the process whereby foreign capitalists drain (*lou-chih*) wealth from the economies of poor countries for use in the imperialists' home countries.[154] BAT had the opportunity to transfer capital from China to the West in this way, for its business generated large amounts of sales revenue in China (for example, a net profit of $3.75 million annually by 1916), but available records do not show what fraction of BAT's net profits went to foreigners in the West, what fraction was paid to foreigners in China, what fraction was paid to Chinese in China, and what fraction was reinvested in China. According to Wang Hsi, a Chinese historian who has assessed BAT's performance on the basis of records in China, the company plowed a "comparatively high" share of these profits back into BAT's operations in China during the first decade in the market (1902–1912) but maintained a very low reinvestment ratio of 7.2 percent between 1912 and 1941. Assuming that Wang has defined reinvestment ratio (which he renders *li-jun tsai-t'ou-tzu lü*) as Western economists generally do—the ratio of a business's undistributed profit to its total profit—then BAT's reinvestment ratio fell far below the median figure for other foreign firms that have been studied by Hou Chi-ming. So, assuming that BAT distributed no larger share of its profits in China than other foreign firms did, its reinvestment policies appear to have made it more imperialistic in this sense of the term than other firms were.[155]

Another definition of imperialist exploitation has been advanced by David Landes to serve as a basis for evaluating foreign management's relations with local labor. According to Landes, to show imperialist exploitation of labor, it is not enough to demonstrate that a foreign firm paid local workers wages that were low in relation to wages in other countries or in other industries within the local economy. He insists that "this kind of imprecision simply will not do" and asserts that the only significant definition of imperialist exploitation is "the employment of labor at wages lower than would obtain in a free bargaining situation; or in the appropriation of goods at prices lower than in a free market."[156]

So defined, imperialist exploitation of BAT's factory workers is impossible to document. Wang Hsi has shown that the income of most BAT workers was so low that they were barely able to buy enough rice to survive day by day in the 1910s and 1920s. And John Gittings has noted that, because of wide wage differentials, "a minority of trusted [BAT] workers was comparatively well paid while the majority was not much better off" than other Chinese cigarette workers in the 1920s.[157] But there is no evidence that BAT workers received less than the "going wage" for comparable work in China's other cigarette factories at any time in the company's history. In fact, as Gittings' comment implies, BAT workers were slightly better paid than workers in Chinese-owned cigarette factories. Moreover, there is no evidence that BAT exploited Chinese compradors, distributors, and other BAT commercial agents, for BAT's wages, commissions, and mercantile credit proved more than lucrative enough to persuade them to cooperate with the company.

A third definition of imperialist exploitation has been used to analyze the consequences of foreigners' procuring raw materials in agrarian economies. According to this usage of the term,

imperialists have distorted the development of agrarian economies by introducing extractive industries (plantations, mines,
oil wells) and exporting raw materials for processing in Western factories; or, as a variation on this pattern, raw materials
have sometimes been processed in foreign-built factories within
agrarian countries, after which the finished product is then exported for sale abroad. In either case, according to Ernest Mandel's formulation, the agrarian countries' economies have tended
to become monocultures which abandon various food crops in
favor of the one cash crop demanded by the imperialists, and,
as a result, the agrarian economies are made dependent on the
vicissitudes of foreign markets, for "the capital exported to the
under-developed countries specializes in production *for the
world market.*"[158]

This definition is applicable to BAT to the extent that it (perhaps more than any other foreign company in China) induced
peasants to plant imported seed for the purpose of growing a
commercial crop after 1915, and it led more and more peasants
in certain localities (Weihsien in Shantung, Hsuchang in Honan,
and Fengyang in Anhwei) to abandon food crops in favor of
this cash crop in the 1920s and 1930s. But BAT never did significantly alter the overall structure of China's agricultural markets, for bright tobacco at its most widespread in the first third
of the twentieth century occupied no more than one million
mou, which was less than 9 percent of China's total tobacco
land and a mere 0.007 percent of China's total cultivated acreage
at the time.[159] Within the comparatively small area where bright
tobacco was introduced, BAT did not set up plantations, trans-
form the landscape, or "modernize" tobacco growing and marketing. Instead, it capitalized on existing Chinese agricultural
expertise, which had been developed while growing a different
type of tobacco, and it procured bright tobacco leaf through
Chinese middlemen in the existing market structure. Moreover,
at no time in its history did BAT extract tobacco leaf from
agrarian China for use in the industrialized West. In fact, from
1905 until the 1940s, it did the reverse, exporting substantial
amounts of tobacco from the United States for use in its factories in China. And its Chinese-made cigarettes, like its Chinese-
grown tobacco, were distributed and consumed within China.

Like many American multinational corporations in the early twentieth century, BAT thus showed more concern for exporting goods, capital, and technology abroad than for importing raw materials into its home country.[160]

A fourth definition of imperialist exploitation has been used to characterize foreign businesses' relations with governments. According to this definition, foreign businesses used the support of their own governments against weaker local governments to protect or further foreign businesses' material interests. Stephen Endicott implied his acceptance of this definition in his study of British foreign relations with China in the 1930s, which concluded, "The pioneers of British enterprise in the Far East [among whom Endicott includes managers of BAT, Asiatic Petroleum Corporation, Imperial Chemical Industries, and other firms] had always been able to count upon effective military-diplomatic support [from the British government] to back their claims."[161]

In its dealings with Chinese governments, BAT engaged in this kind of exploitation in that it consistently benefited from Western treaties with China that maintained a low ceiling on tariffs. In addition, sometimes BAT received American or (more often) British diplomatic support for its campaigns to reduce Chinese tariffs or taxes to levels still lower than the limit set in the treaties. But BAT was not always able to count on this kind of support from its home governments. In promoting its cherished and potentially lucrative scheme for a cigarette monopoly in 1915, for example, BAT was not able to win support from Western governments and was forced to abandon its proposals.

A fifth definition of imperialist exploitation has been used by Chinese since 1895 to evaluate the impact of a foreign company on its local rivals. According to this definition, a foreign industrial trust maintains a monopoly of the market that exploits customers as well as competitors in the local economy. Customers suffer because the foreign monopolist charges high prices and earns excess profits, and local producers suffer because the foreign monopolist has better access to capital markets and uses superior technology and aggressive competitive tactics to crush local handicraft industries and bar the entry of local industrial rivals into the market.[162]

Of all these definitions of imperialist exploitation, this one most aptly characterizes BAT's behavior in China. Though BAT had little effect on Chinese handicraft industries, it made every effort to secure a monopoly of China's cigarette market. Driving its new Chinese rivals to the wall after the boycott of 1905 and 1906, it blocked the development of any significant competitor within China's industrial sector prior to 1915. Using its monopoly control over the market, it set prices that yielded high profits—18.75 percent on net sales in 1916, for example, a profit rate higher than that of most foreign manufacturing firms in China, and 6.65 percent higher than James Duke's American Tobacco Company earned on the average in the United States at the time.[163]

Thus, BAT's behavior in China meets the specifications of some of these definitions of imperialist exploitation and does not meet the specifications of others. And yet, after acknowledging that BAT's behavior did not conform perfectly to all these definitions, I think it is important to note that the company's presence in China had adverse consequences for Chinese industrialists that were economic as well as political and psychological.[164] Some of BAT's Chinese critics might have underestimated its financial investments in China or exaggerated its unfavorable economic effects on China because they resented its political privileges and its Western managers' arrogance, but they did not exaggerate when they accused BAT of crushing or absorbing potential competitors in China's industrial sector. Whatever redeeming features BAT may have had, its use of coercive tactics to destroy or buy out Chinese cigarette companies or block their entrance into the market clearly had adverse economic effects on the development of Chinese-owned industry. Accordingly, no matter how one may choose to characterize the other consequences of BAT's commercial penetration, it is impossible to escape the conclusion that the American company's campaigns against its Chinese competition were acts of economic imperialism.[165]

CHAPTER SEVEN

The United States Petroleum Trade with China, 1876-1949

CHU-YUAN CHENG

From 1876 to the 1920s, petroleum products dominated American exports to China. Starting from the negligible amount of 30,000 gallons in 1876, the inflow of American kerosene grew to an annual volume of 12 million gallons in 1887 and 200 million gallons by the eve of World War I. Between 1912 and 1935, kerosene ranked first among American exports to China for seventeen years, second for three years, and third for the remaining three years. Among China's imports, kerosene generally ranked third or fourth during 1930-1937, and constituted 5 to 6 percent of China's total imports.

In recent decades, economists have contended that the flow of new industrial products from industrially advanced to less developed countries produces negative effects on the traditional economies.[1] Scholars and government officials of the Manchu Court held much the same opinion. Chinese Communists also agree. In particular, Chinese Communist authorities have attributed the retardation of the Chinese petroleum industry in the pre-1949 era to the flood of petroleum products from America.[2]

However, the importation of petroleum products from the West, particularly from the United States, in fact made significant contributions to China's economic modernization. The influx of gasoline and liquid fuel facilitated the mechanization of handicrafts. The substitution of kerosene for vegetable oil as a household illuminant released millions of tons of vegetable oils for export.

TRENDS IN CHINA'S PETROLEUM IMPORTS

During the eighty years under review, China's petroleum imports fell into three time periods with respect to growth rate and composition of products. Kerosene represented the vast bulk of petroleum imports during the first period, 1876 to 1912, maintaining an impressive 18-percent annual rate of growth. The rapid rate was not maintained, however, during the second period, 1912 to 1928, when gasoline, lubricants, and liquid fuels became important. Indeed, kerosene imports averaged only 180 million gallons per year, and kerosene's share of petroleum imports declined from 99 to 72 percent. In the third period, 1929–1947, kerosene imports suffered a relative and absolute decline. They never exceeded 120 million gallons per year after 1934. In 1947, among the three major petroleum products imported to China, liquid fuel ranked first, followed by gasoline and kerosene. In that year, kerosene represented only 16 percent of total petroleum imports (see Table 31).

An examination of the kerosene trade between the United States and China after 1890 reveals a negative relationship between price changes and quantity imported. In 1894, when the Standard Oil Company intended to forestall the introduction of Russian oil into world markets, Standard deliberately lowered the price of kerosene to 5.19 cents per gallon, despite a 30-cent rise in the per barrel price of crude oil.[3] The lower price largely accounted for the 39-percent increase in kerosene imports that year. In 1904, as Sumatran kerosene flooded into China and threatened the virtual American monopoly, Standard Oil sold its products in the Orient at a price lower than the cost of the crude oil from which they were made.[4] The cut in price does much to explain the 85-percent surge of kerosene imports to China in that year.

In 1911, when Standard Oil was in the throes of an all-out price war with Royal Dutch-Shell, the importation of kerosene to China escalated 47 percent in response to the sharply lower prices. In 1933, as a consequence of an intensive price war between the Soviet Union and three Western oil companies, kerosene imports rose 28 percent, again attesting to the relatively high elasticity of demand for kerosene in China.[5]

China's petroleum imports peaked in 1938. This early peaking was contrary to the experience of other developing countries. For example, consumption of petroleum products showed a prodigious increase in Western Europe and Japan as their industrialization progressed. The Chinese case can be partially explained by the rise in kerosene prices after 1930, and by the disruptive impact of the Sino-Japanese War, which sharply curtailed China's quest for industrialization.

Prior to 1938, kerosene was the mainstay of the Chinese petroleum trade. It accounted for 90 percent of total petroleum imports in 1920 and 72 percent as late as 1938. The importation of increasingly large quantities of kerosene into a poverty-stricken country in the late nineteenth century was due primarily to its lower price relative to that of substitutes. Maritime Customs reports show that, when American kerosene was first offered to Chinese consumers, its retail price was substantially lower than that of the vegetable oils which Chinese had used for illuminating purposes for several thousands years. In 1879, for instance, when one picul (weighing 133.3 pounds) of tea oil sold at 5.6 taels in Hankow, the same quantity of American kerosene cost only 2.8 taels.[6] By 1884, the retail price of kerosene in Ningpo dropped to approximately 40 percent of the going price for bean oils.[7] It was the low price of kerosene that led Chinese consumers to abandon the time-honored vegetable oils.

At the turn of the century, however, the price of kerosene

TABLE 31 Imports of Petroleum Products from Various
Countries, 1885–1948
(in 1,000 American Gallons)

Year	(1) Kerosene	(2) Gasoline	(3) Liquid Fuel	(1)+(2)+(3)	(4) Lubricant	Total[a]
1885	14,000	0	0		0	14,000
1886	23,038	0	0		0	23,038
1887	12,015	0	0		0	12,015
1888	16,613	0	0		0	16,613
1889	20,655	0	0		0	20,655
1890	30,829	0	0		0	30,829
1891	49,349	0	0		0	49,349
1892	40,533	0	0		0	40,533
1893	50,007	0	0		0	50,007
1894	60,705	0	0		0	60,705
1895	52,018	0	0		0	52,018
1896	66,958	0	0		0	66,958
1897	99,349	0	0		0	99,349
1898	96,882	0	0		0	96,882
1899	88,413	0	0		0	88,413
1900	83,580	0	0		0	83,580
1901	131,119	0	0		0	131,119
1902	89,934	0	0		0	89,934
1903	84,998	0	0		0	84,998
1904	156,891	0	0		0	156,891
1905	153,472	47	762	154,281	negligible	154,281
1906	128,688	127	254	129,069	negligible	129,069
1907	161,284	144	254	161,682	negligible	161,682
1908	186,085	196	508	186,789	negligible	186,789
1909	145,720	164	1,016	146,900	negligible	146,900
1910	161,390	225	1,016	162,631	negligible	162,631
1911	235,898	280	1,524	237,702	negligible	237,702
1912	197,902	400	1,270	199,572	negligible	199,572
1913	183,984	466	3,048	187,498	negligible	187,498
1914	230,201	820	2,286	233,307	negligible	233,307
1915	185,070	693	2,286	188,049	442	188,491
1916	147,390	686	1,270	149,346	437	149,783
1917	157,911	1,184	4,572	163,667	330	163,997
1918	110,443	1,194	4,572	116,209	438	116,747
1919	199,399	2,175	9,398	210,972	5,915	216,887
1920	189,589	2,605	19,050	211,244	5,776	217,020
1921	175,110	4,664	10,414	190,188	4,349	194,537
1922	209,192	4,818	16,002	230,012	6,307	236,319
1923	214,836	6,308	14,478	235,622	7,500	243,122
1924	223,207	7,265	26,416	256,888	9,129	266,017
1925	258,571	8,824	24,384	291,779	7,080	298,859
1926	232,992	12,797	34,036	279,825	9,026	288,851
1927	163,969	13,203	39,878	217,050	8,099	225,149

TABLE 31 (continued)

Year	(1) Kerosene	(2) Gasoline	(3) Liquid Fuel	(1)+(2)+(3)	(4) Lubricant	Total [a]
1928	262,793	20,042	56,388	339,223	12,384	351,607
1929	239,263	28,644	51,816	319,723	13,767	333,490
1930	185,609	29,725	51,562	266,896	13,029	279,925
1931	171,140	29,755	57,658	258,553	10,394	268,947
1932	145,919	24,115	59,690	229,724	8,227	237,951
1933	187,261	31,282	85,364	303,907	11,149	315,056
1934	119,022	39,661	102,073	260,756	11,168	271,924
1935	102,180	40,997	99,542	242,719	10,377	253,096
1936	104,427	45,510	78,370	228,307	13,114	241,421
1937	118,346	54,787	64,770	237,903	12,012	249,915
1938	66,736	31,904	41,402	140,042	not available	
1939	61,941	35,893	42,164	139,998	not available	
1940	69,798	34,106	51,816	155,720	not available	
1941	38,598	28,816	39,878	107,292	not available	
1946	77,380	93,982	82,550	253,912	not available	
1947	100,338	143,348	301,752	545,438	15,690	561,128
1948	33,641	89,488	248,158	371,287	not available	

Sources: Data for kerosene, gasoline, and liquid fuel: Hsiao Liang-lin, *China's Foreign Trade Statistics,* pp. 42–46. The ton figures are from the same source. The gallon figures: Chang Chia-yu, "Fei-ch'ang shih-ch'i ying-ch'ü chih shih-yu cheng-t'se," pp. 23–24. For lubricants, the figures for 1915–1930 are from Wu Pan-nung, *T'ieh mei ho shih-yu,* p. 64; 1931–1932: Wei Ching-chuan, "Ying-Mei-Ngo chih shih-yu-chan yü wo-kuo chih kuo-chi-min-sheng," p. 135; 1933–1936: Chang Chia-yu; 1937: Helen Smyth, "China's Petroleum Industry," p. 187; 1947: *Ta Kung Pao* (Tientsin), 2 March 1948.

Note: [a]The original figures for liquid fuel were expressed in tons. In order to arrive at an aggregate figure for all petroleum products, the ton figures are here converted into gallons at 1 ton = 254 gallons. The ratio is derived by comparing two sets of figures for the same years (one expressed in tons and the other in gallons) from 1933–1936.

began to rise. Between 1912 and 1918, the importing price of kerosene was raised from 0.13 to 0.26 Haikwan taels per gallon. In 1930, the market price of a gallon of kerosene was 0.48 Haikwan taels, almost 4 times the 1912 price. The upward movement of prices was a significant factor in the decline of kerosene demand after 1929.[8] The upward trend of kerosene prices in China was a consequence of two factors: the increase of import duties and the decline of the silver exchange rate.

During the pre-World War II years, the Chinese import tariff duties constituted the major source of tax revenue to the government. In 1929, the Chinese government resumed the right to set customs duties. The rates were continuously revised upward from 3–4 percent in 1926–1928, to 10.9 percent in 1929, 16.3

percent in 1931, and 34.3 percent in 1934.[9] In short, import tariffs on kerosene underwent a 20-fold rise in less than twenty years. In 1919, import tariffs for one case of kerosene (10 gallons) amounted to 0.08 Haikwan taels. The rate was raised to 0.847 in 1929, to 1.69 in 1931, and to 2.18 in 1934.[10] The tariff increases accounted for 40 percent of the price increase for kerosene during the 1919-to-1934 period.

The second factor was the sharp fall of silver prices in international markets and the concomitant decline in China's foreign exchange rate. Until November 1935, China was the only commercially important country in the world still on the silver standard. Fluctuations in world silver prices were reflected in China's foreign exchange rate. The drastic decline of world silver prices during the late 1930s severely depreciated the Chinese silver exchange rate, thereby causing a sharp rise in import prices. Between 1926 and 1931, the Chinese foreign exchange rate dropped by 55 percent,[11] and import prices moved up accordingly. In the 1880s, it was the cheaper American oil that drove the vegetable and tea oils out of the market. Fifty years later, the relatively less expensive vegetable oils came back to replace the higher-priced imports.

In contrast to kerosene, the demand for gasoline, although subject to the same high tariffs and depreciated silver exchange rate, showed no sign of subsiding. As China undertook programs to modernize highway transportation in the late 1920s, there was a steady increase in automotive vehicles and concomitant increases in the demand for gasoline.[12] Since there was no real substitute for gasoline, high prices had little impact on demand. Of course, consumers of gasoline differed greatly from kerosene consumers, the latter being primarily peasants and other poor people, while the former usually were the country's wealthy, the military and governing classes.

Demand for liquid fuel and lubricants was also very strong in the 1930s as a consequence of the expansion of modern industry. During the 1922 to 1936 period, the textile industry, China's most advanced industry, more than doubled the number of spindles. There was also widespread adoption of more advanced methods of production in coal mining, iron-ore extraction, and pig-iron production.[13] Industrial development was accompanied by a drive to expand the railroad system, which, in turn, led to steady increases in consumption of lubricating and diesel oil.

During the wartime period (1937–1945), most of China's coastal areas fell under Japanese domination, and imports of petroleum products (mainly from Hong Kong before 1941) dropped to 50 percent of the prewar level. Following the war, there was a strong resumption of demand for foreign petroleum products. In 1946, imports of kerosene, gasoline, and liquid fuel attained the 1934 level. In 1947, the total value of petroleum products imported reached a new high, more than doubling the 1930 level.

THE CHANGING ROLE OF AMERICAN OIL COMPANIES

Prior to 1880, the Chinese kerosene market was virtually monopolized by the Standard Oil Company. Russian oil did not enter China until 1889. Imports from the Dutch East Indies and Borneo did not begin until 1894 and 1901, respectively. During the 1867–1912 period, American kerosene made up 50–60 percent of China's annual kerosene imports (Table 32). The relative shares in the 1912–1935 period were 65 percent for the United States, 12.4 percent for Hong Kong, 11.2 percent for the Dutch East Indies, and 14.5 percent for other countries.[14]

The dominant position held by American firms was not an historical accident. The United States was the first country in the world to process petroleum products on a large scale. In the 1860s, more than half the petroleum products refined in the United States were for export. After the establishment of the Standard Oil Company in 1870, strenuous efforts were made to expand foreign markets. By 1882, American petroleum products practically monopolized world exports of illuminating oils.[15]

In 1882, American and European demand for kerosene commenced to decline, due to the development of electric lighting. American refiners suddenly found themselves with a huge surplus of kerosene. The need for seeking new overseas markets was obvious. Given its huge population and its limited prospects for electrification, China appeared to be an ideal outlet. The Standard Oil Company therefore set out to capture the Chinese

TABLE 32 U.S. Share in China's Total Imports of Kerosene, 1912–1935

| | In Million American Gallons | | | In Million HKT | | | Place in U.S. |
Year	Total Volume	U.S. Supplies	U.S. as % of Total	Total Volume	U.S. Supplies	U.S. as % of Total	Total Imports to China
1912	198	110	55.6	24.8	12.2	49.2	First
1913	184	97	52.7	25.4	11.6	45.7	First
1914	230	136	59.1	35.1	19.0	54.1	First
1915	185	108	58.4	28.0	14.6	52.1	First
1916	148	94	63.5	31.8	18.2	57.2	First
1917	158	92	58.2	33.3	19.8	59.5	First
1918	113	39	34.5	28.3	10.1	35.7	First
1919	203	140	69.0	46.7	31.3	67.0	First
1920	191	125	65.4	54.3	33.8	62.2	First
1921	177	117	66.1	58.1	37.5	64.5	First
1922	217	160	73.7	63.4	46.9	74.0	First
1923	218	160	73.7	58.3	42.2	72.4	First
1924	223	157	70.4	57.8	40.4	69.9	Second
1925	259	201	77.6	66.1	50.6	76.6	First
1926	235	199	84.7	56.6	47.3	83.6	First
1927	168	128	76.2	43.3	33.0	76.2	First
1928	263	204	77.6	62.4	46.9	75.2	First
1929	247	168	68.0	55.2	37.9	68.7	First
1930	186	123	66.1	54.9	33.3	60.7	Third
1931	171	107	62.6	64.5	38.5	59.7	Second
1932	146	82	56.2	60.4	34.2	56.6	Second
1933[a]	187	93	49.7	56.7	32.8	57.8	Second
1934[a]	119	62	52.1	25.5	13.7	53.7	Third
1935	102	47	46.1	24.1	n.a.		

Sources: Total Volume and U.S. Supplies: Po-chuang Ch'en and Y. L. Huang, Statistics of Commodity Flow of Chinese Maritime Customs and Railways, 1912–1936, p. 98. U.S. Supplies (value): Ho Ping-hsien. Chung-kuo ti-kuo-chi mao-i, pp. 77–78. Total Value: Hsiao Liang-lin, China's Foreign Trade Statistics.

Note: [a]1933–1934 values are converted into HKT.

market. The venture proved very successful. By 1898, American kerosene was widely accepted by the Chinese masses and was consumed throughout the country.

The key to Standard Oil's success was its ability to market kerosene in rural areas. Market penetration was accomplished by giving away millions of small tin lamps to potential customers, and by keeping the retail price of kerosene stable for many years. Standard Oil's virtual monopoly was, however, soon challenged by two rising forces in the petroleum industry: the Russian and the British-Dutch interests. Russian oil first entered the Chinese market in 1889. Its market share, however, was insignificant. In 1912, when the United States supplied 55 percent of China's kerosene, Russia supplied only 2 percent, and Russia's share dropped to less than 1 percent after the Bolshevik Revolution.

The real menace to Standard Oil's dominance during the early twentieth century came from the Royal Dutch-Shell group. In 1904, Royal Dutch-Shell sought to negotiate an agreement with Standard Oil for the division of the Chinese kerosene market. When the negotiations failed, a fierce price war ensued.[16] Taking advantage of its geographic proximity to China, the Royal Dutch-Shell combine was able to sell kerosene at a price substantially lower than the production costs of the American company. At first, Standard Oil attempted to crush its competitor by resorting to the proven tactic of the past—a dramatic price reduction. For a time, Standard Oil sold kerosene in China 50 percent cheaper than in Western Europe, despite the fact that transport costs were much lower in Europe than in East Asia.[17]

Although suffering heavy financial loss, Royal Dutch stood its ground. Standard Oil, however, fought back by again cutting prices drastically, but Royal Dutch-Shell refused to yield. Moreover, 1911 found Standard Oil fighting for its very existence in the U.S. Supreme Court because of antitrust charges. Consequently, it decided that the time had come to share the Chinese market with Royal Dutch. In the autumn of 1911, an agreement was reached whereby Standard Oil yielded 50 percent of the East Asian market.[18] Standard Oil having lost its monopoly, another major American oil firm ventured into China. In 1913, Texaco employed a Far Eastern Representative at Shanghai, and in the following year, the company shipped 7.1 million gallons of kerosene to China in one month. In 1921, Texaco's sales accounted for only 5 percent of U.S. kerosene exports to China. However, Texaco's market share advanced to 17.6 percent by 1927 and 54 percent by 1935.[19]

During the late 1920s and early 1930s, competition in the Chinese market developed into a triangular struggle among

Standard Oil, Royal Dutch-Shell, and the Soviet Oil Trust. In early 1931, a Soviet oil firm, the United Petroleum Trust of the U.S.S.R. (Soyuzneft) established branch offices in Shanghai. After several months' planning and negotiations, arrangements were completed whereby the Soyuzneft would provide 1.5 million gallons of oil to the Kwang Hwa Petroleum Company, Ltd., a leading Chinese oil firm.[20] The Soviet office warned the Western oil interests that Soyuzneft was in the market to stay. Competition from the Soviet Union resulted in a gasoline price war in 1932. Between April and August 1933, the retail price of gasoline in Shanghai declined 32 percent. The cutthroat competition climaxed in October 1933 when the per gallon price of Soviet gasoline dropped from 1.05 dollars (Chinese standard dollars) to 0.20 dollars—an 80 percent decrease. Shortly thereafter, the Soviet Union decreased kerosene prices from 11.5 dollars to 5.2 dollars per 10-gallon case. After several months of a protracted price war, the four companies in China finally reached agreement. The Chinese market was divided, with 30 percent for Asiatic Petroleum, 25 percent each for Standard Oil and Kwang Hwa (representing the Soviet Union), and 20 percent for Texaco.[21]

Obviously, the 1932 price war significantly reduced the market share enjoyed by American oil interests. Between 1930 and 1935, the U.S. share declined from 66.4 to 46.1 percent of the kerosene market, and from 50.8 to 37.6 percent of the gasoline market. Russian and Dutch oil were now much cheaper than the American product. Despite the relative decline, American influence on the Chinese petroleum business remained profound. As the Sino-Japanese War continued, the United States emerged as the closest ally of China. In 1946–1947, American oil companies again resumed their dominant role. The U.S. share rose to 65.3 percent in 1946 and 50.5 percent in 1947.[22]

MARKETING AND DISTRIBUTING SYSTEMS

The hegemony of Standard Oil in the Chinese petroleum market for half a century derived from its advantages as pioneer and from its unique marketing and distributing efforts. Kerosene marketing in China required the distribution of minute quantities to the poverty-stricken masses. To penetrate the Chinese market, Standard Oil assiduously pursued a policy of reducing the costs for refining, transporting, and marketing. The economies effected in these areas helped Standard to price kerosene at half the cost of native vegetable oils. However, this low price was still well below actual cost. The low Chinese price was subsidized by Standard Oil's above-normal profits in other markets. The company did this in order to acquire an opening wedge in the fabled Chinese market.

Penetration of the Market

The key to penetrating the Chinese rural market, however, was free distribution of millions of small tin lamps. Previously, kerosene was considered very hazardous. Without a safe lamp, the use of kerosene for lighting would have been limited. So Standard Oil developed a reliable tin lamp equipped with a small chimney, bowl, and wick. The lamps won immediate acceptance by the peasants, and, in the 1890s, Standard Oil distributed some 8 million lamps.[23] Lamp distribution served as an indirect advertisement for kerosene, directly stimulating demand. The lamps were well designed; they were embossed with Chinese characters which read, "Burn Standard Oil kerosene" and bore the SOCONY emblem on their base.[24] The lamps brought Standard Oil's trademark "Mei-foo" into millions of Chinese homes (the characters *mei-fu* mean literally "beautiful and trustworthy" but *mei* also can mean "American").

The penetration of the Chinese market was the outcome of much study and planning. From the very beginning, the oil companies considered the exploitation of the Chinese market as a long-term project. They established schools in New York to train carefully screened personnel. Indeed, Standard Oil's selection process was far more rigorous than that of the U.S. Foreign Service.[25]

Standard innovated in other ways as well, notably in its refusal to employ compradors. By opening agencies in the interior in 1910, the company thereby circumvented the need for compradors, and, by appointing its own agents, Standard Oil greatly expanded its sales network into the Chinese interior. Moreover,

Standard adopted many ingenious marketing techniques. In 1904, when confronted with cheaper oil from Russia, Standard Oil introduced a cheap, low-grade kerosene, called "petrolite." This new kerosene, made from low-priced California crude oil, enabled Standard to withstand the Russian competition.[26] Prior to 1908, kerosene shipped to China was contained in cases, two tin cans packaged in one box. Later, as tin cans became more expensive, Standard resorted to bulk tanker shipments to large importing centers, where the oil was stored in tanks. Near the tanks, the kerosene was tinned and cased for transshipment to the interior. These container factories required a substantial investment by Standard Oil.[27]

This distribution network for kerosene provided the base for the marketing of gasoline, lubricating oils, bunker fuel oils, heating oils, aviation products, and other petroleum products. During the 1930s, the growing demand for gasoline required additional investment in service stations and roads. By 1949, there were 366 gasoline filling stations in the major cities of China, more than half of them belonging to the American oil companies.[28]

Expansion of Sales Networks

Standard Oil opened its first office in Shanghai in 1885. Eight years later, in August 1894, another office was established in Hong Kong. In 1903, Standard Oil further expanded its operations, and by 1908 it had erected branches at Foochow, Amoy, Swatow, and Canton.[29]

Initially, the Shanghai and Hong Kong offices worked independently of each other. The former marketed petroleum products in Central and North China, while the latter covered districts as far east and north as Foochow and included Taiwan, the Philippines, Indochina and Siam (Thailand). In 1914, to further expand kerosene sales, Standard Oil set up a distribution network under its own direct control. In addition to the head office in Shanghai, and the sub-head office in Hong Kong, district offices were opened in Tientsin (North China), Hankow (Central China), and in Manchuria. Branches were opened in all important treaty ports. By 1919, Standard Oil had 6 district offices,

20 branch offices, and some 500 agents throughout China.[30] Widely scattered sources suggest that Standard Oil's branches and sub-branches included the following cities by the 1930s:[31]

Manchuria	Dairen (Liaoning)
	Newchwang (Liaoning)
	Chinwangtao (Liaoning)
North China	Tientsin (Hopeh)
	Peking (Hopeh)
	Shichiachuang (Hopeh)
	Paoting (Hopeh)
	Chengteh (Jehol)
	Taiyuan (Shansi)
	Chefoo (Shantung)
East China	Foochow (Fukien)
	Amoy (Fukien)
	Canton (Kwangtung)
	Swatow (Kwangtung)
	Kongmoon (Kwangtung)
	Kiungchow (Kwangtung)
	Wuchow (Kwangsi)
	Nanning (Kwangsi)
	Kweilin (Kwangsi)
	Changsha (Hunan)
Central China	Hankow (Hupeh)
	Kiukiang (Kiangsi)
West China	Chungking (Szechwan)
	Mengtze (Yunnan)
	Kunming (Yunnan)

Below the sub-branches, the oil companies used local merchants as their agents. Agents were usually located in large cities. For example, in 1932 there were 15 agents in Hangchow for the three American and British oil companies.[32] In more sparsely populated regions, company products were placed in the hands of the local wholesalers. The sales network of the Standard Oil Company is shown in Figure 2. Parallel networks were established by the other two companies, the Texaco

FIGURE 3   Sales Network of Standard Oil Company in China in the 1930s

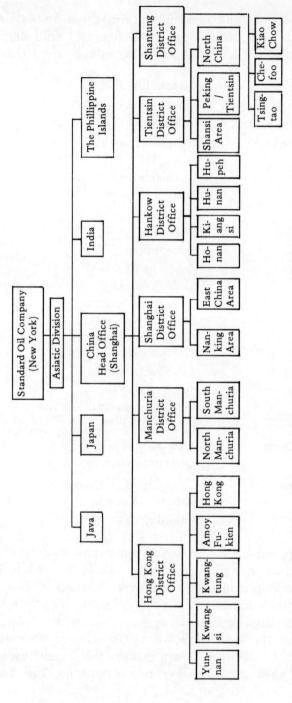

Sources: Arnold Wright, ed., *Twentieth Century Impressions of Hong Kong, Shanghai, and other Treaty Ports of China III,* 213–214, *Commercial Intelligence Journal* (Ottawa) No. 1380, 12 July 1930, pp. 62–63. Carroll Lunt, *Some Builders of Treaty Port China,* pp. 30–37.

Company and the Asiatic Petroleum of the Royal Dutch-Shell. Texaco opened its head office in Shanghai in 1913. By 1929, the company had offices in Hong Kong, Shanghai, Amoy, Swatow, Dairen, and Canton. In 1936, when the California Texas Company acquired a share of Texaco (China) Ltd., there was a headquarters office in Shanghai and a sub-head office in Hong Kong. The Shanghai office also had a district office. Other district offices were located in Canton, Hankow, Tientsin, Tsingtao, and Nanking. Sales volume was generated by 600 consignment agents located throughout China.[33] Texaco's Tientsin district alone had 220 consignment agents.[34]

Relations with Local Agents

Through circumventing the comprador system, American oil companies in China relied primarily on Chinese agents to do the actual selling. The role of Chinese agents was similar to that of traveling salesmen in America. Success was largely contingent upon the agent's connections with local consumers and his sales abilities. Each branch office appointed selling agents to cover its territory. These agents were local Chinese merchants; some were specialists in oil; others were engaged in general business.[35] The specialists were concentrated in the larger cities, and their oil products included soaps and candles imported from the United States and Britain. The generalists were found in small cities.

Agents worked on commission. A Chinese consignment agent had to deposit $20,000 to $30,000 with the American company. The value of the petroleum products he could draw from the company was limited to the amount of his deposit.[36] In essence, this meant that Standard Oil shifted the risk to the agent. Commissions received by consignment agents amounted to 0.1 to 0.2 percent of their sales. When the agents ordered kerosene from the company, a 10-percent discount was granted. Similarly, customers who purchased 5 cases (10 tins) or more of kerosene in a single order also received a 10-percent discount. Those who bought 5 tins or more in one order obtained a 5-percent discount.[37] In most cities where the agents of different oil companies operated, trade guilds were formed. The main function of the guild was to set retail prices in order to avoid price wars.[38]

The oil consigned to the agents remained the company's property until sold, and the agent was officially required to remit the proceeds within two weeks. In practice, a longer period was allowed. Due to the logistic problems of distributing petroleum products in China, stocks equivalent to four to five months' consumption were frequently inventoried. The companies employed a large number of itinerant stock-checkers and inspectors to supervise the agents and to promote sales. At first these inspectors were foreigners. In later years, Chinese were employed in these posts, although periodic tours of the agencies were still made by foreigners.[39]

Compared with the old comprador system, the appointment of consignment agents was a superior method of marketing. It was also more profitable. The profits received by agents were lower than those received by compradors. Whereas the compradors received commissions varying from 0.25 percent to 1 percent, the agents derived but 0.1 to 0.2 percent. During the 1890s, some of the compradors of Standard Oil in China were able to amass sizeable fortunes. For example, in 1890, the wealth of a long-time comprador of Standard Oil in Shanghai, Yeh Ch'eng-chung, was estimated to be more than 8,000,000 taels.[40] In the post-1910 period, few if any of the agents became millionaires. In fact, during periods of rapid price fluctuation (such as 1910 and 1930–1932), many agents who ordered kerosene from the company when prices were high suffered severe inventory losses. Moreover, under the old system it was the compradors who in fact controlled the local oil business. The new system put the oil company directly in command. The company could discharge any consignment agent whenever it saw fit.

Price Formation and Competition

Until 1910, Standard Oil established petroleum prices in China by a rather complicated procedure. As a rule, the head office in New York set the price limits for the various foreign markets. The limits generally served as a floor rather than as a ceiling price, and they varied from country to country. Two factors explain the different price levels. First, different grades of kerosene were shipped to meet the specific flash-test requirements of different countries. These were higher in Europe and Japan and lower in China and India. Quality variations also accounted for some of the difference in prices.[41] Second, transportation costs and tariffs also varied among markets. In 1939, retail prices and taxes on kerosene and gasoline exhibited wide variations in the several districts in East Asia (see Table 33). In the case of kerosene, duties plus taxes ranged from a low of only 9 percent of retail price in Singapore and Adelaide to a high of 34.8 percent in Saigon, and 32.8 percent in Shanghai. Limits set in New York, however, did not determine the exact selling prices. General managers in the respective districts were free to sell above the minimum if they could hold their market share.

During the 1919–1927 period, Standard Oil maintained a two-tier export prices schedule: a published and an "inside price." The published price formed the basis for pricing most of the business with nonaffiliated companies, while the lower "inside prices" were quoted principally to affiliates. In principle, a differential of around 0.25 cent per gallon was maintained between the two schedules; in practice, the gap was sometimes much wider than that. Most of the foreign affiliates were not informed of the prices quoted by Standard Oil to the others, and the parent company sometimes gave preferential quotations in order to allow a particularly hard-pressed affiliate to meet a competitive local situation.[42] For years, Standard maintained relatively lower prices in China in order to undersell its rivals. For example, on 13 August 1904, the New York export price was set at 4.8 cents per gallon or $2.02 per barrel for Standard-white kerosene in bulk. Crude sold at the well for $1.50 for a 42-gallon barrel, and it cost 60 cents to get it to the seaboard by pipeline. Thus, the dollar outlay for 42 gallons of crude oil to the seaport was $2.10, or 8 cents more per barrel than its selling price. The low export price was intended to meet the competition of the low-priced Oriental and Russian oil in the East Asian market.[43]

Competition among the major oil companies also influenced prices. The sometimes erratic price behavior of petroleum products in China during the 1908–1938 period provided a relatively typical example of oligopolistic competition. Whenever one company cut prices, its rivals tended to follow suit, thus triggering

TABLE 33 Retail Prices of Gasoline and Kerosene in China and the Twelve other East Asian Areas in 1939
(in U.S. cents per gallon)

Areas	Gasoline			Kerosene		
	Retail Price	Duty and Taxes	As % of Price	Retail Price	Duty and Taxes	As % of Price
India, Delhi	40.8	13.6	33.3	22.6	6.8	30.1
Malaya, Singapore	29.3	13.7	46.8	21.5	2.0	9.3
Burma, Rangoon	36.0	19.5	54.2	27.5	4.5	16.4
Ceylon, Colombo	32.0	18.0	56.3	26.5	5.0	18.9
China, Shanghai	21.4	7.1	33.2	18.6	6.1	32.8
Dutch East Indies	44.5	26.0	58.4	24.5	8.0	32.7
Indochina, Saigon	28.0	7.1	25.4	20.7	7.2	34.8
Hong Kong	22.7	6.2	27.3	–	–	–
Japan, Yokohama	18.0	5.8	32.2	17.0	2.9	17.1
Philippines, Manila	30.3	10.2	33.7	27.0	3.6	13.3
Thailand, Bangkok	34.1	14.6	42.8	21.0	7.0	33.3
Australia, Adelaide	28.4	12.2	43.0	20.0	1.8	9.0
New Zealand, Wellington	30.0	16.0	53.3	15.0	0.4	2.7

Source: Leonard E. Fanning, American Oil Operations Abroad, pp. 222–223.

a price war. The price war was then followed by some collusive agreement to divide the market and stabilize the price. As long as the market-share agreements were adhered to, there was a tendency for the companies to agree on price increases in order to recover the losses sustained during the price war. Most of the erratic price fluctuations during the 1908–1938 period can be attributed primarily to the oligopolistic structure of the market.

MAJOR ECONOMIC EFFECTS

The impact of foreign petroleum imports on the Chinese economy had substitutional and retarding, as well as modernization, effects, but the net effect is difficult to ascertain.

Substitution

Kerosene was a substitute for native vegetable oils and candles. Although illumination expenditures accounted for only 3–4 percent of the average Chinese household budget,[44] vegetable oil pressing ranked among the nation's most important handicraft industries. The importation of kerosene had an impact upon peanut and bean plantations, and it also affected beancake manufacturing. Maritime Customs records reported wide substitution of kerosene for bean oil, tea oil, and wood oils. In 1886, a report from Yan-tai (Chefoo), in Shantung province, revealed that "kerosene is in the process of replacing local bean oils because it generates better light and costs less."[45] Another report, from Hankow, revealed that "the trade in kerosene oil has developed with astonishing rapidity into one of the most important articles of import, demonstrating the eagerness of the Chinese to adopt useful and cheap foreign articles."[46] Similar data can be obtained for almost every treaty port. A report from Chinkiang in Kiangsu indicated that "kerosene oil, in spite of adverse exchange rate, has experienced wonderful sales progress, and finds ready favor with the natives everywhere who adopt it because of its extreme brilliancy as compared with the native oils."[47]

The widespread substitution of kerosene for vegetable oils caused alarm among Chinese officials. Fearing that the native oil-pressing industry would be destroyed, Chang Chih-tung, Governor General of Kwangtung and Kwangsi, wrote the Imperial Court:

... since the wide circulation of kerosene in China, the market for peanut oil has been deeply depressed, the acreage allocated to peanut plantations decreased, the handicraft oil-pressing industry damaged, and businessmen are suffering from deprivation from the decline in oil trade. Given the damages from kerosene imports, further importation should be banned without delay.[48]

Chang's assessment was wrong. In fact, the vegetable-oil industry prospered in the late nineteenth and early twentieth centuries. In Yingkow in Manchuria, the number of oil-pressing mills increased from 2 in 1866 to more than 30 by 1895.[49] In Shantung, one of the major peanut-producing centers in China, the oil-pressing industry expanded during the 1910–1920 period.[50] The same was true for Hunan, Shansi, Kiangsu, and most parts of Manchuria. The vegetable-oil-pressing industry expanded for the following reasons: (1) many new uses for bean and wood oil were discovered in Western industrial countries, and (2) the use of foreign machinery increased productivity. Bean oil was used for making soaps, glycerine, cooking oil, oleoresins, and stearin. Wood oil came to be used for making paints, waterproof materials, and a wide variety of industrial items. Foreign demand for Chinese bean oil and wood oil increased dramatically between 1910 and 1930. Exports of bean oil rose from 570,000 piculs in 1910 to 2.67 million piculs in 1925, a 4-fold increase. Exports of peanut oil surged from 246,000 piculs in 1910 to more than 1.2 million piculs in 1919, and the export of wood oils rose from 582,000 piculs in 1912 to 1.2 million piculs in 1920. The combined export value of bean oil, peanut oil, and wood oil registered a continuous advance from 74,284 Haikwan taels in 1882 to 1 million in 1894, to 2.2 million in 1896, and 13.2 million in 1910. By 1930, the total export value of vegetable oils reached 67.9 million taels (Table 34).

The differential between the import value of kerosene and the export value of vegetable oils rapidly diminished. In the 1890–1894 period, the import value of kerosene stood at 10 times the export value of vegetable oils. The ratio dropped to 6 to 1 in 1895–1900, then 4 to 1 in 1901–1909, to 2 to 1 in 1910–1915, and almost 1 to 1 in 1917. During the years 1918–1919, the export value of vegetable oils exceeded the import value of kerosene. In the last decade of the period, the aggregate value of these two categories was about equal. In short, the substitution of kerosene for vegetable oils did not generate a "backwash" effect. Instead, the release of millions of tons of vegetable oils from domestic consumption enabled China to expand its foreign exports, thereby helping to finance the importation of petroleum products.

Whether the substitution effect constitutes a gain or a loss to an economy depends in part on the terms of trade between these two commodities, that is, the ratio of export prices to import prices. A favorable change in the terms of trade allows a given quantity of exports to purchase a greater quantity of imports, thereby releasing additional resources for development. The terms of trade between kerosene and vegetable oils are found in Table 35.

In the period between 1912 and 1935, for which statistics for import prices of kerosene and export prices of vegetable oils are available, the terms of trade appear to be unfavorable to China. In 1912, one picul of peanut oil exchanged for 64.5 gallons of kerosene, whereas in 1921 it exchanged for 30 gallons. The evidence suggests long-run deterioration in the terms of trade between kerosene and vegetable oils.

Retardation

China was the first nation to discover petroleum. It was first recorded eighteen centuries ago by the famous historian Pan Ku in his *History of the Han Dynasty*.[51] The Chinese also appear to rank as the ancient world's most accomplished well-drillers. They invented bits to penetrate different types of rock strata, and developed casing methods to protect the well against cave-ins and water.[52] However, these ancient beginnings have mainly antiquarian interest, for, until the early 1960s, China was heavily dependent upon foreign supplies of petroleum, first from the Anglo-American oil trusts, and, after 1949, from the Soviet

TABLE 34 Import Value of Kerosene and Export Value
of Vegetable Oils, 1890–1931

Year	Import Value of Kerosene (1,000 HKT)	As % of Total Imports	Export Value of Vegetable Oil (1,000 HKT)	As % of Total Exports
1890	4,093	3.22	283	
1891	5,267	3.93	248	
1892	4,203	3.11	256	
1893	5,571	3.68	802	
1894	8,005	4.94	1,003	
1895	6,615	3.85	1,018	
1896	9,083	4.48	1,422	
1897	13,299	6.56	2,212	
1898	11,915	5.68	2,462	
1899	13,002	4.91	2,046	
1900	13,956	6.61	2,291	
1901	17,293	6.45	2,797	
1902	11,564	3.67	3,500	1.63
1903	15,724	4.81	3,257	1.52
1904	27,908	8.11	4,295	1.79
1905	20,287	4.54	3,638	1.59
1906	12,579	3.07	4,865	2.06
1907	19,999	4.80	4,226	1.60
1908	27,326	6.93	5,489	1.96
1909	23,628	5.51	6,102	1.80
1910	21,743	4.70	13,213	3.47
1911	34,812	7.38	13,774	3.65
1912	24,846	5.25	14,145	3.82
1913	25,403	4.46	11,414	2.83
1914	35,094	6.16	12,895	3.62
1915	28,031	6.17	15,624	3.73
1916	31,816	6.16	25,378	5.27
1917	33,355	6.07	29,722	6.42
1918	28,323	5.10	41,020	8.44
1919	46,713	7.22	46,876	7.45
1920	54,318	7.13	32,401	5.98
1921	58,077	6.41	20,289	3.37
1922	63,442	6.71	28,007	4.28
1923	58,292	6.31	42,049	5.59
1924	57,811	5.68	47,521	6.16
1925	66,117	6.97	46,454	5.98
1926	56,595	5.03	57,422	6.64
1927	43,293	4.27	59,865	6.52
1928	62,386	5.22	39,937	4.03
1929	55,178	4.36	42,691	4.20
1930	54,865	4.19	67,904	7.59
1931	64,549	4.50	51,896	5.71

TABLE 34 (continued)

Sources: Kerosene Value: Hsiao Liang-lin, *China's Foreign Trade Statistics,* pp. 43–44. Kerosene Percentage: China, Maritime Customs, *Synopsis of External Trade,* 1882–1931, Import statistics, p. 181. Vegetable Oil Value: Ibid., p. 190. Vegetable Oil Percentage: Ibid., p. 188.

Union. This large-scale influx of foreign petroleum products may well have impeded the development of China's petroleum industry.

At the turn of this century, the Manchu government ventured to exploit Chinese petroleum resources because kerosene imports resulted in the outflow of some 70 million taels annually. The first wells were drilled by Japanese engineers at Yenchang in Shensi in 1903, but only two were productive. Owing to mismanagement, these wells were flooded and the whole enterprise failed. A few years later, the operation of these wells was resumed and several new wells were drilled, yielding a total of 1,440 metric tons of crude oil per year.[53] In 1914, an agreement was signed in Peking between the Chinese government and the Standard Oil Company of New York, in which Standard Oil agreed to supply geological experts to survey Shensi and Chihli. The agreement provided that, should an adequate quantity of oil with commercial value be found, an American-Chinese corporation would then be formed with 55 percent of the capital being supplied by Standard Oil, and 37.5 percent by the Chinese government, which would retain the option to purchase the remaining 7.5 percent at par within two years.[54] This agreement represented the first major effort by the Chinese government to seek American assistance.

Accordingly, Standard Oil sent two geologists, M. D. Fuller and F. G. Clapp. The two worked in the Yenchang oil field during 1913–1915, but the project was abandoned in 1917. According to the experts, the deposit was too shallow. Seven wells were sunk in succession, and, although oil was observed, no gushers were tapped.[55] The Standard Oil experts concluded that "a large part of the Chinese Republic consists of rocks of types and ages in which there is no possibility that commercial oil deposits exist."[56] Other American geologists expressed the same assessment. Eliot Blackwelder of Stanford University asserted that "China will never produce large quantities of

TABLE 35 Import Prices of Kerosene and Export Prices of
Vegetable Oils, 1912–1935

Year	Import Prices of Kerosene (gallon/HKT)	Export Prices (piculs/HKT)		Price Indexes (1912=100)	
		Bean Oil	Peanut Oil	Kerosene	Peanut Oil
1912	0.13	7.51	8.39	100	100
1913	0.14	7.50	11.02	108	131
1914	0.15	8.18	10.89	115	130
1915	0.15	7.35	9.75	115	116
1916	0.22	7.56	10.68	169	127
1917	0.21	9.62	11.19	162	133
1918	0.26	10.97	12.12	200	144
1919	0.23	8.92	11.40	177	136
1920	0.29	8.63	11.28	223	134
1921	0.33	8.48	9.77	254	116
1922	0.30	8.31	11.31	231	135
1923	0.27	8.32	13.22	208	158
1924	0.26	9.66	12.58	200	150
1925	0.26	10.25	12.98	200	155
1926	0.24	11.25	13.08	185	156
1927	0.26	11.21	14.53	200	173
1928	0.24	11.01	15.87	185	189
1929	0.23	10.98	16.00	177	191
1930	0.30	11.86	16.43	231	196
1931	0.38	11.61	15.64	292	186
1932	0.41	9.92	13.47	315	161
1933	0.30		11.74	231	140
1934	0.21		8.33	162	99
1935	0.24		10.72	185	128

Source: Ch'en and Huang, Statistics of Commodity Flow, pp. 395, 398.

oil."[57] Given the preeminent influence of the American geologists, spurious conclusions may have exercised a retarding effect on exploration for petroleum in China.

Some Chinese experts and a few foreign geologists regarded their conclusions as a plot designed by the American oil trust to discourage the Chinese from developing their own petroleum production.[58]

Their reasoning was generally based on two basic arguments.

First, oil seepages of a permanent character had been known for hundreds of years in Shensi and Szechwan. In 1929, according to Isaac Mason, Vice-President of the Shanghai branch of the Royal Asiatic Society, a Swiss expert declared that the Red Basin of Szechwan, including the Tzeliutsing, Pangchi, and She-hung fields, is "possibly the fourth largest in the world."[59] In 1934, estimates made by the Chinese National Geological Survey put China's petroleum reserves at the large figure of 4,337 million barrels, and the American Geological Survey estimated China's petroleum reserves at 3,274 million barrels. Both surveys included only Manchuria and the provinces of Shensi and Szech-wan, and were considered by some experts to be "far too conservative." In a 1934 survey by the Chinese National Geological Society, new oil deposits were found at the Kansu corridor and in Sinkiang, Kweichow, Chinghai, and Sikang.[60]

Second, the optimists reasoned that the Western oil trusts had billions of dollars invested in their own domestic oil fields and in areas subject to their direct control, and that their own wells were capable of meeting world demand. The oil companies, went the argument, were therefore reluctant to develop new oil fields in other countries.[61]

But these objections were without foundation in fact. H. Foster Bain, former special assistant to the U.S. Secretary of the Interior assigned to the Bureau of Mines, and technical adviser on mines to the President of the Philippines in the 1930s, offered an explanation for Standard Oil's withdrawal from the oil exploration in Shensi in 1915. According to Bain, the decision was made not because of lack of oil but because of the distance from the markets. "The wells were small and the potential reserves much too low to warrant investment in the necessary facilities for production, transportation, and refining the oil."[62] It was a business decision, pure and simple. But it was bad for China.

In 1931, when the price of petroleum products escalated, Chinese industrialists in Kwangtung and Chekiang constructed refineries. Through relatively simple distillation procedures, they successfully extracted kerosene from diesel oil. Since the tariff duty for diesel oil was but a small fraction of that for kerosene, locally refined kerosene undersold the imported kerosene, gradually extending its market share. In 1932, several hundred small refineries were built in Canton. Fearing the loss of sales, the major oil firms—Standard, Asiatic, and Texaco—raised the import price of diesel oil and supplied low-quality kerosene at a price lower than that of the local product. Within six months, almost all the local refineries were out of business.[63]

Another example of the conflict between foreign oligopolistic profits and Chinese development happened in 1945. At the end of the Sino-Japanese War, the China Petroleum Corporation, a government enterprise, planned to build a 500,000-ton-per-year refinery in Shanghai, which would use U.S. equipment and Iranian crude oil. The plan failed because of protests from Standard Oil and Texaco.[64]

In sum, though it remains unlikely that American geologists conspired with the foreign oil companies to prevent exploration of China's oil reserves, there is evidence that foreign oligopolistic price collusion was employed in ways detrimental to the growth of the Chinese petroleum industry.

Modernization

Nevertheless, the importation of large quantities of petroleum products helped produce important changes in China that might well be grouped under the "modernization" rubric. The importation of petroleum produced such modernizing changes as: (1) facilitating the mechanization of traditional handicrafts by providing a more efficient liquid fuel; and (2) stimulating the demand for highway systems by providing fuel for automotive vehicles.

China's first major industrialization drive was initiated between World Wars I and II. Shortages of many foreign products during World War I provided the impetus. In the period immediately following the war (1919–1921), imports of electrical apparatus and machinery for textile and flour mills increased dramatically. Those years witnessed the erection of more mechanized factories than had been known during the entire previous history of the country. The Chinese government estimated that by the end of 1921 there were 70 modern cotton mills in China, with a total of 14,000 looms and 2 million spindles, 125 flour mills, and around 2,000 other modern factories.[65] Most of the imported machinery was powered by engines and consumed either crude oil, gasoline, or kerosene.

The installation of modern machines meant ever-greater reliance upon the importation of liquid fuels and lubricants. For example, in 1929, following a hefty 150-percent increase in machinery imports, the demand for foreign liquid fuel doubled and the demand for lubricants increased 9-fold. Again, in the 1929–1931 period, a 12-percent rise in machinery imports was accompanied by a 10-percent increase in the importation of liquid fuel (Table 36). As one Communist Chinese historian has commented:

Owing to the adoption of steam engines and kerosene engines, Chinese handicrafts were gradually mechanized. By 1910, at Yingkow, one of the major vegetable-oil-producing centers in North China, almost all the original oil-pressing mills were transformed into mechanically powered operations. The benefits of mechanization became so evident that other handicraft industries in the fields of food-processing, textiles, soap, candles, and matches soon followed suit. Diesel engines won high popularity in all parts of the country. The character of Chinese handicrafts underwent a fundamental transformation.[66]

The contribution of foreign petroleum supplies to the development of the Chinese highway system was also significant. China began to import motor cars and buses in large quantity in 1924. Between 1924 and 1931, some 42,000 foreign motor vehicles were purchased. As motor vehicles required road beds, a highway construction movement was launched in 1927. By 1931, highway mileage totaled 39,114.[67] By 1937, some 50,000 miles had been opened. These figures, when compared with the 3.7 million miles in the United States and the 575,000 miles in Japan, may appear insignificant, but the highways were of critical importance during the Sino-Japanese War. Relentless Japanese bombing of the railways that formed the main arteries of the Chinese transportation system made truck transport of military supplies and personnel a necessity. When the Chinese army was forced to retreat from the coastal cities in the latter part of 1937, it was apparent that continued resistance to Japan would have to depend upon motor vehicles.[68] The increased use

TABLE 36   Imports of Liquid Fuel, Lubricants, and Machinery
and Equipment, 1917–1931

Year	Imports of Liquid Fuel (in 1,000 gallons)	Index	Imports of Lubricants (in 1,000 gallons)	Index	Imports of Machinery & Equipment (in 1,000 HKT)	Index	Imports of Electrical Equipment (in 1,000 HKT)	Index
1917	4,572	100	330	100	14,274	100	4,027	100
1918	4,572	100	538	163	14,594	102	4,133	103
1919	9,398	206	5,915	1,792	36,827	258	4,992	124
1920	19,050	417	5,776	1,750	41,120	288	6,295	156
1921	10,414	228	4,349	1,318	89,528	627	13,204	328
1922	16,002	350	6,307	1,911	76,389	535	9,403	253
1923	14,478	317	7,500	2,272	38,530	270	8,103	201
1924	26,416	578	9,129	2,766	36,584	256	8,195	204
1925	24,384	533	7,080	2,145	28,442	199	6,890	171
1926	34,036	744	9,026	2,735	35,128	246	8,941	222
1927	39,878	872	8,099	2,454	36,616	257	9,868	245
1928	56,388	1,233	12,384	3,753	38,986	273	11,307	281
1929	51,816	1,133	13,767	4,172	59,822	419	13,279	330
1930	51,562	1,128	13,029	3,948	71,268	499	17,299	430
1931	57,658	1,261	10,394	3,150	69,267	485	18,411	457

Sources: Liquid Fuel and Lubricants: Table 31; Machinery and Equipment: China,
Maritime Customs, Synopsis of External Trade 1882–1931.

of motor vehicles was accompanied by a parallel increase in
gasoline imports. In 1927, China imported only 358,000 barrels of gasoline. By 1937, the figure had risen to 1,524,000 barrels—a 4-fold increase.

In conclusion, an assessment of China's net gain or loss from
the foreign petroleum trade involves many subjective judgments.
Indeed, to explore the psychological, social, and political aspects
of the subject would be fruitful, but beyond the limits of this
chapter. Several points are clear, however. The assertion that
the importation of relatively cheap products from more industrially advanced nations necessarily results in a "backwash"
effect on traditional handicraft industries does not pertain to
the Chinese vegetable-oil-pressing industry. On the contrary,
kerosene not only served as a superior substitute for vegetable
oils used as an illuminant, but also provided the source of power
for the vegetable-oil-pressing industry. The vegetable-oil industry
experienced a sustained period of rapid growth. Moreover,

motor vehicles have made important contributions to the economic and social life of modern nations, and their introduction to China as a concomitant of petroleum imports was a necessary effect of industrialization. In statistical terms, the number of motor vehicles imported and road mileage constructed seems minuscule, but the contribution of modern highway transportation during the Sino-Japanese War was significant.

It is true that foreign oligopolistic pricing collusion impeded the development of the domestic petroleum industry in China. However, there is no evidence that American geological surveys were consciously designed to seal off China's petroleum resources from the rest of the world.

PART THREE

Perspectives on Trade and Investment

CHAPTER EIGHT

The Minor Significance of Commercial Relations
between the United States and China, 1850-1931

PETER SCHRAN

Commercial intercourse between the United States and China did not live up to American expectations. The China trade remained a marginal affair in United States perspective, and the U.S. trade did not amount to much more from the Chinese point of view. The reasons are not hard to find. Size of country, level and speed of development, and distance explain quite well why the opportunities for mutually beneficial exchange remained limited.

THE RELATIVE IMPORTANCE OF FOREIGN TRADE

It has often been observed that the larger the size of a country, the more limited tends to be its external trade relative to its internal trade—*ceteris paribus*. Needless to say, all other things were far from equal in the cases of China and the United States. Nevertheless, the proportions of exports and imports in their total commercial activity were similarly small, and much more limited than in the case of Japan, China's major East Asian competitor.

Comparative commercial involvement with the rest of the world may be measured by the shares of all exports and imports in each country's gross national product (GNP). Table 37 shows that the United States usually experienced shares in excess of 5 percent. It indicates further that the share of imports as well as the share of exports in GNP tended to fall after 1869–1873, which is the earliest period for which GNP data have been reconstructed. Such declines, which appear to be unusual by comparison with the experiences of most other countries, probably reflected the increasing settlement and development of the United States. The nation's development not only redirected the commercial activities of the initially more foreign-trade-oriented coastal regions toward the interior but also raised the proportion of total GNP contributed by this less foreign-trade-oriented part of the country.

Comparable data for China are lacking. But two related attempts at estimating its GNP deserve mention. On the basis of T. C. Liu's exploratory study, *China's National Income, 1931–1936*,[1] Chang Chung-li calculated for the 1880s a GNP of 2,781 million HKT.[2] Albert Feuerwerker considered this estimate too low and raised it to 3,339 million HKT.[3] China's average annual exports and imports during the 1880s accounted for 2.8 percent and 3.3 percent of the initial GNP estimate and for 2.3 percent and 2.7 percent of its revised version.[4] In addition, T. C. Liu and K. C. Yeh have refined Liu's previous estimate for 1933.[5] China's exports and imports in that year accounted for 2.0 percent and 4.5 percent, respectively, of the gross domestic product (GDP) estimate of 29.88 billion yuan.[6] Since China's GDP seems to have changed relatively little while its foreign trade, especially its exports, fell drastically during the early 1930s,[7] one may surmise that the share of trade was somewhat larger during the late 1920s. The growth in the share of imports relative to exports during the interval from the 1880s to the 1930s was made possible by foreign investment, which seems to have grown similarly to the cumulative balance-of-trade deficit.[8]

TABLE 37 United States Trade with China and Japan, 1821–1931

	Share of U.S. Foreign Trade in U.S. GNP (%)		Share of Total U.S. Exports[a] (%)		Share of Total U.S. Imports (%)		Average Annual Balance of Trade (million U.S. $)	
	Exports[a]	Imports	China	Japan	China	Japan	China	Japan
1821–1825[b]	n.a.	n.a.	7.6	n.a.	7.9	n.a.	–1	n.a.
1826–1830	n.a.	n.a.	2.9	n.a.	6.9	n.a.	–3	n.a.
1831–1835	n.a.	n.a.	1.3	n.a.	5.6	n.a.	–5	n.a.
1836–1840	n.a.	n.a.	1.2	n.a.	4.9	n.a.	–5	n.a.
1841–1845	n.a.	n.a.	1.6	n.a.	5.2	n.a.	–3	n.a.
1846–1850	n.a.	n.a.	1.3	n.a.	4.8	n.a.	–5	n.a.
1851–1855	n.a.	n.a.	1.2	n.a.	4.1	n.a.	–8	n.a.
1856–1860	n.a.	n.a.	2.0	n.a.	3.4	n.a.	–5	n.a.
1861–1865	n.a.	n.a.	2.5	n.a.	3.4	n.a.	–3	n.a.
1869–1873[c]	6.2	7.9	0.6	0.2	3.8	1.0	–17	–4
1872–1876	6.9	7.5	0.2	0.2	3.4	1.6	–18	–8
1877–1881	8.2	5.8	0.4	0.3	3.3	2.3	–14	–10
1882–1886	6.6	5.9	0.8	0.4	2.7	2.0	–12	–10
1887–1891	6.3	6.2	0.8	0.6	2.3	2.5	–11	–14
1889–1893	6.7	6.2	0.7	0.5	2.3	2.7	–12	–17
1889–1893[d]	6.5	6.0	0.7	0.5	2.3	2.7	–12	–17
1892–1896	6.6	5.7	0.6	0.5	2.6	3.1	–15	–19
1897–1901	7.4	4.3	1.0	1.5	2.8	3.7	–9	–8

TABLE 37 (continued)

	Share of U.S. Foreign Trade in U.S. GNP (%)		Share of Total U.S. Exports[a] (%)		Share of Total U.S. Imports (%)		Average Annual Balance of Trade (million U.S. $)	
	Exports[a]	Imports	China	Japan	China	Japan	China	Japan
1902–1906	5.3	4.4	2.0	2.1	2.5	4.4	+4	−15
1907–1911	5.8	4.4	1.1	1.8	2.2	5.0	−10	−37
1911–1915	6.0	4.4	0.9	2.0	2.1	5.3	−15	−44
1916–1920	10.1	5.1	1.1	3.9	3.8	8.9	−57	−50
1921–1925	5.3	4.2	2.4	5.5	4.1	9.7	−38	−93
1926–1930	4.9	4.1	2.3	5.2	3.5	9.4	−31	−133
1931	3.2	2.7	4.0	6.4	3.2	9.9	31	−50

Source: Derived from U.S. Bureau of the Census, *Historical Statistics of the United States, Colonial Times to 1957*, pp. 139, 542, 550–553.

Notes: [a]Including reexports.
[b]Figures for 1821–1865: U.S. trade with China including gold and silver.
[c]Figures for 1869–1893: GNP according to Kuznets concept.
[d]Figures for 1889–1930: GNP according to Department of Commerce concept.

TABLE 38 Share of Japan's Foreign Trade in Japan's National
Income, 1876–1931

	% of National Income according to Yūzō Yamada		% of National Income according to Kazushi Ohkawa	
	Exports	Imports	Exports	Imports
1876–1880	4.2	4.9		
1881–1885	4.5	3.9	5.3	4.6
1886–1890	5.6	5.7	7.8	8.0
1891–1895	6.9	6.5	9.9	9.3
1896–1900	8.0	11.1	9.9	13.7
1901–1905	11.2	13.3	13.3	15.7
1906–1910	12.9	13.5	14.1	14.8
1911–1915	13.6	14.0	14.7	15.1
1916–1920	18.6	16.9	19.1	17.5
1921–1925	13.1	16.4	13.9	17.3
1926–1930	14.8	16.1	14.9	16.3
1931	10.7	11.6	10.8	11.7

Source: Bank of Japan, Statistics Department, *Hundred-Year Statistics of the Japanese Economy,* pp. 28–29, 32, 290–293.

The GNP shares of exports and imports in both countries are small not only per se—in the case of China literally "marginal" in the sense of being concentrated in the coastal treaty-port region—but also by comparison with Japan. Table 38, which relates official Japanese trade data to two series of national income estimates, shows that the shares of exports and imports rose from small beginnings during the late 1870s to 3 times that level during the 1920s, with a spurt during the decade between the Sino-Japanese War of 1895 and the Russo-Japanese War. Japan's greater involvement with the rest of the world entailed a greater dependence on outside events. Table 38 makes the windfalls of World War I and the setbacks of the Depression apparent.

THE RELATIVE IMPORTANCE OF BILATERAL TRADE

Trade relations between pairs of countries vary not only with size but also with a host of other factors, such as level and speed of development, structure of economic activities, and distance, to name the most important.

All those elements combined to make commercial relations between the United States and China relatively unimportant to the former. The share of the China trade in total U.S. trade approached 8 percent in the early 1820s according to Table 37— thereby perhaps providing some foundation in fact for its allure in later years. Yet, the relative shares of exports to and imports from China fell immediately thereafter and did not rise again until the turn of the century. The share of exports, which consisted largely of reexports at first, declined drastically, giving rise to a balance-of-trade deficit that persisted until the Great Depression and was met in large part by specie exports.[9]

The volume *Historical Statistics of the United States* fails to distinguish trade with Hong Kong, which served as an entrepot for South China throughout the period. Until 1874, the Hong Kong data are included in the China data. During subsequent years, U.S. trade with Hong Kong usually accounted for less than 0.5 percent of total U.S. trade. However, exports to Hong Kong tended to exceed imports from there, and this balance-of-trade surplus offset a substantial part of the deficit in the trade with China.[10]

The development of commercial relations with Japan differed drastically from this pattern. Until the mid-1860s, U.S. trade with Japan was so limited that it was not accounted for separately in the published statistics. In the late 1860s, U.S. exports to and imports from Japan were one-third or less of the corresponding China values. Well before the turn of the century, however, the shares of the two countries were equal, even with Hong Kong added to China. By the 1920s, Japan's shares of U.S. exports and imports were more than twice as large as those of China. Like China, Japan exported more to the United States than it imported from that country.

A comparison of tables 37 and 39 indicates that trade with the United States was substantially more important for China than trade with China was for the United States. Table 39 also shows that the United States was usually the second or third ranking partner, at first way behind Britain and eventually well behind Japan. The share of Chinese exports to the United States in total Chinese exports remained fairly stable, above 10 percent, until World War I, when it rose to a new level near 15

TABLE 39 China's Trade with Great Britain, Japan, and the United States, 1868–1931

	Share of Total Chinese Exports (%)			Share of Total Chinese Imports[a] (%)			Average Annual Balance of Trade (million HKT)		
	U.S.	Japan	GB[b]	U.S.	Japan	GB[b]	U.S.	Japan	GB[b]
1868–1870	12.2	2.5	55.9	1.3	2.8	35.5	+6	-0.4	+9
1871–1875	12.7	2.1	50.3	0.7	3.7	32.9	+8	-1	+12
1876–1880	10.9	2.7	39.6	2.0	4.5	25.3	+6	-2	+9
1881–1885	12.5	2.4	32.6	3.6	5.1	24.4	+6	-3	+2
1886–1890	9.7	4.1	18.6	3.3	5.5	22.0	+5	-3	-8
1891–1895	10.7	8.0	9.8	4.3	6.0	19.5	+6	+0.1	-19
1896–1900	9.6	9.7	7.2	7.1	11.3	18.0	-0.6	-10	-29
1901–1905	10.8	14.0	5.8	10.6	13.1	16.7	-14	-16	-46
1906–1910	9.4	14.9	5.1	8.3	14.2	16.9	-8	-17	-58
1911–1915	10.8	16.9	5.4	7.3	20.5	16.8	+3	-42	-67
1916–1920	15.8	27.6	7.3	13.5	34.6	11.6	-3	-76	-36
1921–1925	15.7	25.8	5.9	17.1	24.4	13.1	-55	-54	-85
1926–1930	14.3	24.0	6.7	17.1	26.7	8.9	-71	-96	-44
1931	13.2	27.4	7.1	22.2	20.0	8.3	-201	-41	-55

Source: Derived from Hsiao Liang-lin, China's Foreign Trade Statistics, pp. 22–24, 148–150, 152–154, 172–163.

Notes: [a]Including reexports.
[b]Excluding Hong Kong and British India.

percent. The share of imports from the United States in total
Chinese imports, on the other hand, advanced with few inter-
ruptions from very small beginnings to parity with exports by
the turn of the century and to higher levels thereafter. As a consequence, the balance of trade with the United States, which
had been marginally positive until the turn of the century, became marginally negative during the following twenty years and
more substantially negative thereafter.

This development, indicative of growing U.S. investment in
China, occurred relatively late. Table 39 shows that it followed
comparable changes in China's trade balances with Britain and
Japan by twenty-five and ten years, respectively. By implication,
the United States held a minor share of the total foreign assets
in twentieth-century China, likewise in contrast with Britain
and Japan. Carl Remer's estimates of foreign investments make
this difference in positions apparent:[11]

Foreign Country	Percent of Total Foreign Investment in China		
	1902	1914	1931
Great Britain	33.0	37.7	36.7
Japan	0.1	13.6	35.1
United States	2.5	3.1	6.1

The minor importance of U.S. commercial involvement in
China is similarly evident from data on the numbers of foreign
firms and foreign residents in China that appear in Table 40.
They show Americans initially in second place behind the British, by 1907 in third place behind the Japanese and British,
and by 1913 in fourth place behind the Japanese, Russian
emigrés, and British. During the 1920s, about 5 percent of all
foreign firms and 3 percent of the foreign population of China
were American.

TABLE 40 Foreign Firms in China, 1875–1931; Foreign Population in China, 1875–1931

Year	American	British	Japanese	Russian	French	German	Total
			Firms				
1875	46	211	1	12	6	52	343
1887	28	252	25	11	18	65	420
1897	32	374	44	12	29	104	636
1907	115	490	1,416	24	99	239	2,595
1913	131	590	1,269	1,229	106	296	3,805
1917	216	655	2,818	2,914	127	132	7,055
1922	377	725	3,940	1,141	229	184	7,021
1931	559	1,021	7,249	1,104	197	340	10,889
			Population				
1875	541	1,611	26	55	311	367	3,579
1887	855	3,604	651	94	515	597	7,905
1897	1,564	4,929	1,106	116	698	950	11,667
1907	2,862	9,205	45,610	479	2,201	3,553	69,852
1913	5,340	8,966	80,219	56,765	2,292	2,949	163,827
1917	5,618	8,479	144,492	51,310	2,262	2,899	220,485
1922	9,153	11,855	152,848	96,727	2,300	1,986	282,491
1931	8,637	13,344	260,621	66,479	8,651	3,444	370,393

Sources: Chong-su See, *The Foreign Trade of China*, p. 395. 1922: Shü-lun Pan, *The Trade of the United States With China*, pp. 92–93. 1931: U.S. Department of Commerce, Bureau of Foreign and Domestic Commerce, *Where China Buys and Sells*, p. 45.

THE RELATIVE IMPORTANCE OF TRADE
IN SPECIFIC COMMODITIES

U.S. Imports

Even if the share of foreign trade in GNP and the share of bilateral trade in foreign trade are small, there remains the possibility that the trade in a specific commodity may account for a large proportion of the bilateral trade as well as for a large part of the commodity's total supply or demand, so that its transaction appears more significant.

Table 41, which lists the relative shares of the continuously more important U.S. import items, indicates that tea and silk dominated for a long time. This was true even during the years prior to 1870, when the composition of trade was not recorded systematically.[12] Raw silk retained its near-30-percent share of total U.S. imports from China into the 1920s, but tea lost its predominant position toward the end of the nineteenth century. Increases in the imports of hides and skins, vegetable oil, and raw wool together tended to offset temporarily the decline of tea. In general, imports from China appeared to become more diverse.

Corresponding to this development, the international sources of supply also became more numerous. At first, tea and raw silk from China accounted for most of the imports of these two items, as shown in tables 42 and 43. In both instances, however, Japan soon challenged the Chinese lead, reduced the Chinese share of the U.S. market, and surpassed China as the principal supplier of silk in the 1880s, and of tea in the 1900s. In the case of tea, China also fell behind England and the British East Indies. In the case of silk, China had to compete in the end not only with Japan but also with U.S. producers of substitute artificial fibers. Similar domestic and foreign competition limited the U.S. market for most other Chinese products even more. During 1926–1931, therefore, when the U.S. government recorded imports by country and by commodity group in the detail of Table 44, China contributed very small shares of most imported groups of items and not more than 10 percent of any. The shares of specific commodities may have been much larger, of course, but it is hard to think of more than a few instances in which it could

TABLE 41 Composition of U.S. Imports from China,
1870–1929
(% of imports)

	Chemicals, Drugs, Dyes	Hides & Skins	Oil, Veg.	Rice & Rice Flours	Silk, Raw	Tea	Wool, Raw
1870	4.4		0.6	3.6	3.3	67.0	
1875	4.0		1.5	6.9	5.1	64.9	
1880	5.0	0.3	0.7	4.5	31.9	45.9	
1885	2.1	2.3	1.2	4.5	23.2	49.3	0.6
1890	2.5	0.8	0.9	3.7	27.5	42.2	5.0
1895	4.9	2.3	0.6	2.4	26.9	36.8	8.3
1901	5.4	7.9	0.7	2.7	34.4	26.5	3.4
1905	6.1	9.1	1.5	1.8	31.6	21.2	11.2
1911	1.3	10.5	8.5	1.4	38.6	8.4	8.7
1915	1.6	13.1	7.2	3.6	28.1	7.7	13.3
1920	4.0	15.1	9.5	0.2	26.4	1.2	2.6
1922	0.0	5.1	6.1	0.0	41.5	1.6	7.2
1929[b]		14.2[a]	?	?	26.6	2.4	0.5

Source: Shü-lun Pan, *Trade of the United States With China,* pp. 42, 65–66, 100–101.

Notes: [a]Including furs.
[b]See Table 44.

TABLE 42 Composition of U.S. Tea Imports, 1865–1922
(% of total value)

Period	China	Japan	Imports From England	British East Indies
1865–1869	77	19		
1870–1874	67	25		
1875–1879	48	41		
1880–1884	52	46		
1885–1889	50	43		
1890–1894	51	44		
1895–1899	54	39	4	2
1900–1904	50	39	5	5
1905–1901	35	44	10	8
1910–1914	24	49	12	11
1915–1919	18	45	9	18
1922	15	37	15	21

Source: Shü-lun Pan, *Trade of the United States with China,* pp. 128–130.

TABLE 43 Composition of U.S. Raw Silk Imports, 1850–1922
(% of total quantity)

Period	Imports from			
	China	Japan	France	Italy
1850–1854	62.0[a]			
1855–1859	54.5[a]			
1860–1864	46.3[a]			
1865–1869	13.1	2.7		
1870–1874	53.0	6.4		
1875–1879	30.4	36.8		
1880–1884	45.0	34.4		
1885–1889	24.3	48.3	5.7	20.4
1890–1894	23.8	53.4	4.3	17.4
1895–1899	28.3	48.5	3.1	17.2
1900–1904	23.8	49.1	3.9	21.5
1905–1909	18.8	55.2	3.3	21.9
1910–1913	22.2	65.6	0.8	10.4
1920	19.7	76.2	0.1	3.7
1922	16.5	79.0	0.3	1.1

Source: Shü-lun Pan, *Trade of the United States with China*, pp. 145–146, 152–153.

Note: [a]Percent of total value.

be said that China had cornered the market for any length of time.

Chinese Exports

Usually, purchases of Chinese goods by the United States did not absorb most of the supplies on the Chinese side either. This would seem to pertain even to the earlier years, when it is difficult to provide breakdowns by commodity, if one argues that, so long as China's total exports of tea and silk each were several times as large as its total exports (of all products) to the United States, the United States obviously could not have bought up most of either tea or silk.[13]

For items with minor shares, of course, such reasoning does not hold, and the United States may well have bought relatively large shares of some of China's less prominent items. Evidently

TABLE 44   U.S. Imports from China by Commodity Groups,
1926–1931
(unweighted average)

Commodity Group	% of Total Imports from China	% of Total Imports of the Group
00 Animals and animal products, edible	5.2	5.8
0 Animals and animal products, inedible, except wool and hair	23.5	9.8
1 Vegetable food products and beverages	4.3	0.7
2 Other vegetable products, except fibers and wood	10.1	2.7
3 Textiles	52.8	8.4
4 Wood and paper	0.3	0.1
5 Nonmetallic minerals	0.5	0.2
6 Metals and manufactures, except machinery and vehicles	2.0	0.8
7 Machinery and vehicles	0.0	0.0
8 Chemicals and related products	0.5	0.5
9 Miscellaneous	1.0	0.7
All commodity groups	100.2	3.4

Source: U.S. Department of Commerce, Bureau of the Census, *Foreign Commerce and Navigation of the United States,* for 1926–1931.

it did toward the end of the period, in 1929, when the United States was the number-one customer for 9 of the 17 items listed in Table 45, which together accounted for 80.5 percent of all exports to the United States in that year. However, the shares of 6 of the 9 items constituted merely 10 percent of all the exports to the United States (and 1.4 percent of all Chinese exports) in that year. The other three, which were bristles, wood oil (tung oil), and hides/skins/furs, together contributed not much more than raw silk did; raw silk continued to account for about one-quarter of all exports to the United States and also of all raw-silk exports from China.

The most persuasive argument for "critical" significance can be made in the case of the wood-oil trade, it seems. China was the world's principal producer of this (sideline) tree crop and

TABLE 45 Commodities Exported by China to the United
States, 1929

Commodity	% of Total Exports to U.S.	% of Total Exports from China
Bristles	4.1	47.0
Eggs and egg products	6.1	16.2
Sausage casings	0.9	29.7
Hides, skins, and furs	14.2	46.2
Wood oil	12.1	70.7
Walnuts	0.6	47.4
Sesame seeds	0.7	7.6
Tea	2.4	10.1
Raw silk	26.6	24.8
Raw cotton	2.7	12.5
Wool	0.5	9.9
Embroideries and laces	2.8	44.0
Carpets, woolen and other	2.8	69.2
Tungsten	0.5	24.0
Antimony	1.2	40.7
Hats, straw and fiber	1.7	45.6
Hairnets	0.6	65.0
Total: 17 items	80.5	

Source: U.S. Department of Commerce, *Where China Buys and Sells*, pp. 52–53.

exported 60–70 percent of the total output. The United States took 40–50 percent of China's entire supply (until the Sino-Japanese War and the Pacific War disrupted trade relations and produced substantial substitution problems for both buyers and sellers). In the case of silk, by comparison, China exported perhaps 40–50 percent of the total output, and the United States acquired no more than 10–12 percent of this production.[14]

United States Exports

During the early years, the United States supplied China mostly with specie and secondarily with cotton cloth. Monetary and nonmonetary silver remained major items throughout the period. Cotton cloth continued to account for a large—at times the largest—share of U.S. exports until the early twentieth

century. It was supplemented in the last quarter of the nineteenth century by petroleum products, especially kerosene,
whose share in exports did not fall before the 1920s. The decline in cloth and oil exports was offset by the rise of metalware
and tobacco exports, according to Table 46. Most staples were
of minor importance, whether they accounted for a fairly constant share, like timber, or for sharply fluctuating shares, like
raw cotton and wheat.

The relative importance of the China market for the major
U.S. merchandise exports to this area is made evident in Table
47. It shows that exports to China accounted for comparatively
large shares of total exports from the United States in the cases
of cotton manufactures and tobacco manufactures. In both instances, however, total exports absorbed relatively small shares
of total domestic production. Moreover, when the commodities
are aggregated into groups, as in Table 48 for the years 1926–
1931, it becomes clear that exports to China constituted less
than 10 percent of the total exports of any group. By implication, it appears that the most significant commodity was silver,
since China absorbed substantial shares not only of the total
exports, but also of the total production of silver by the United
States (see Table 49).

Chinese Imports

The trade in specific commodities did not look very different
from the perspective of the Chinese buyer. Cotton manufactures
were one of the principal exports not only of the United States
but also of Britain and India, which dominated in the China
market until Japan surpassed most of its Western competitors
during World War I. In addition, there occurred a shift from cotton goods to raw cotton in conjunction with the development
of a Chinese cotton textile industry. In the raw-cotton market,
the United States competed mostly with India, and its share of
the China market fluctuated substantially with changes in the
harvests and prices of cotton.[15] The same may be said of wheat
and flour, in which the competitors were Australia, Argentina,
and Canada.

While the United States did not fare so well in the highly

TABLE 46 Composition of U.S. Exports to China, 1870–1929
(% of exports)

| | Cotton Manufactures | Iron and Steel | | Oils, Mineral Refined | Tobacco Manufactures | Unmanufactured Tobacco |
		Manufactures	Machinery			
1870	20.5	3.7		4.7	1.3	
1875	37.7	9.1		28.0	0.8	
1880	30.8	3.7		33.2	0.5	
1885	53.8	12.5		22.7	0.2	
1890	41.8	2.5		44.2	1.4	
1895	47.3	3.3	0.0	32.8	2.9	0.0
1901	42.5	5.1	2.6	22.7	4.9	0.2
1905	51.6	1.9	0.5	15.9	2.7	0.9
1911	26.2	8.5	2.4	36.1	2.8	3.8
1915	7.2	13.8	3.1	36.5	6.8	3.5
1920	6.0	16.3	11.9	12.7	10.5	8.7
1922[b]	2.1	5.7	10.5	20.5	16.1	10.1
1929	0.2	11.8[a]		21.1	15.7	

Source: Shū-lun Pan, Trade of the United States with China, pp. 42, 59–60, 110–111.

Notes: [a]All steel plus machinery and equipment.
[b]See Table 47.

TABLE 47   Share of U.S. Exports to China in Total U.S. Exports, by Commodities, 1870–1922
(% of total exports)

Year	Cotton Manufactures	Iron and steel Manufactures	Machinery	Oil, Mineral, Refined	Tobacco Manufactures	Unmanufactured
1870	15.7					
1875	13.8					
1880	3.4					
1885	28.7	6.7		2.8		
1890	12.3	0.3		2.4		
1895	12.2	0.4		2.4	2.6	
1901	22.8	1.4	0.4	3.1	10.2	0.1
1905	55.5	2.2	0.3	9.7	25.3	1.5
1911	12.9	2.2	0.3	7.0	13.1	2.0
1915	1.7	2.8	0.5	4.3	18.6	1.4
1920	2.3	5.0	2.9	3.3	37.2	5.4
1922	1.7	4.5	4.8	6.3	63.7	7.3

Source: Derived from Shü-lun Pan, *Trade of the United States with China*, pp. 42, 59–60, 100–111; U.S. Department of Commerce, Bureau of the Census, *Foreign Commerce and Navigation of the United States*, 1895–1922 and *Historical Statistics of the United States: Colonial Times to 1970* Part 2, pp. 898–899.

TABLE 48 U.S. Domestic Exports to China by Commodity
Groups, 1926–1931
(unweighted average)

Commodity Group		% of Total Exports from U.S.	% of Total Exports of the Group
00	Animals and animal products, edible	1.2	0.6
0	Animals and animal products, inedible, except wool and hair	1.5	1.5
1	Vegetable food products and beverages	7.3	1.9
2	Other vegetable products, except fibers and wood	23.7	9.5
3	Textiles	22.3	3.3
4	Wood and paper	5.3	3.4
5	Nonmetallic minerals	17.5	2.9
6	Metals and manufactures, except machinery and vehicles	7.4	2.0
7	Machinery and vehicles	6.6	0.6
8	Chemicals and related products	4.0	3.3
9	Miscellaneous	3.4	2.7
All commodity groups		100.2	2.6

Source: U.S. Bureau of the Census, *Foreign Commerce and Navigation of the United States, 1926–1931.*

competitive trade in agricultural staples, it was much more successful in the oligopolistic markets for several modern manufacturing products. In 1926, Trade Commissioner George C. Howard made the following observation with respect to the data reproduced in Table 50:

An examination of these figures brings out strongly the fact that commodities comprising the largest individual items of this trade are those handled by specialized organizations rather than by general import and export houses.

Some outstanding examples of this in connection with American products are kerosene and other mineral-oil products, 85 percent of which business is in the hands of two firms; cigarettes and tobacco, largely controlled by one or two concerns; timber, handled to the extent of 78 percent by five firms; condensed milk, some 90 percent of which is done by two firms; machinery, a large percentage by four houses.[16]

TABLE 49 Production and Exportation of Silver by the
United States, 1846–1930
(million U.S. dollars)

Period	Silver Production	Net Exports of Silver	
		Total	to China[a]
1846–1850		–1	0.3
1851–1855	0.3	1	1.5
1856–1860	0.4	–9	10
1861–1865	39	3	
1866–1870	65	71	
1871–1875	156	112	33
1876–1880	182	48	53
1881–1885	203	52	39
1886–1890	227	66	53
1891–1895	228	100	38
1896–1900	171	134	34
1901–1905	157	113	30
1906–1910	160	71	27
1911–1915	190	115	40
1916–1920	290	428	221
1921–1925	205	49	155[b]
1926–1930	158	92	243[b]

Sources: Silver production: U.S. Bureau of the Census, Historical Statistics, Part 1,
p. 606. Total Net Exports of Silver: ibid., Part 2, pp. 884–885. Net Exports
of Silver to China: Shü-lun Pan, Trade of the United States with China, pp.
22, 43, 70, 119, and U.S. Bureau of the Census, Foreign Commerce and
Navigation of the United States, 1922–1930, pp. 1–3.

Notes: [a]Plus Hong Kong.
[b]These two figures from Foreign Commerce and Navigation.

These few U.S. firms still competed with a few firms of other
nationalities as well as with growing numbers of Chinese firms.
The U.S. shares of total imports tended to diminish in several
instances. This was true of mineral oil, where the competitors
from the Dutch East Indies benefited from their comparative
advantage and reduced America's initial (1870) 100-percent
monopoly on imports to less than half that in the 1920s.[17] It
was also true of tobacco and cigarettes, when a rapid monopo-
lization of the import trade during 1890–1920 was followed by
a period of rapid import substitution.[18]

TABLE 50 Commodities Imported by China from the
United States, 1923

Commodity	% of Total Imports from U.S.	% of Total Gross Imports into China
Kerosene	31.5	71.5
Paraffin wax	1.1	42.4
Gasoline, benzine, naphtha, petrol	0.9	34.6
Liquid fuel	0.8	55.3
Lubricating oil	1.6	74.7
Cigarettes	13.4	72.8
Tobacco	6.8	80.2
Flour	10.6	60.1
Wheat	4.5	76.3
Metals and minerals	6.9	23.2
Machinery	2.9	16.0
Dyes, colors, paints	2.6	14.9
Raw cotton	2.2	6.2
Timber, softwood	1.8	53.7
Tinfoil and other foils	1.2	69.9
Paper	1.2	10.7
Motor cars	0.9	55.3
Electrical materials and fittings	0.9	15.6
Household stores	0.8	26.4
Condensed milk	0.7	52.2
Total: 20 items	93.3	

Source: U.S. Department of Commerce, *China: A Commercial and Industrial Handbook*, p. 53.

The United States appeared in a relatively strong position also in timber and in selected branches of machine manufacturing, which accounted for very small shares of total Chinese imports from the United States but assumed strategic importance toward the end of the period in the context of Kuomintang government efforts to improve transportation by rail, road, and air (see Tables 50 and 51).

The aggregation of Chinese imports from the United States into commodity groups on the pattern of Tables 44 and 48 perhaps obscures this significance. But it does not diminish the importance of the substantial flow of silver from the United

TABLE 51 Commodities Imported by China from the
United States, 1929

Commodity	% of Total Imports from U.S.	% of Total Imports into China
Cotton textiles	0.2	0.3
Raw cotton	15.1	38.2
Iron and steel, ungalvanized	3.0	15.6
Iron and steel, other	0.5	10.7
Electrical machinery	0.2	22.2
Industrial machinery and tools	2.5	19.1
Aircraft and accessories	0.3	40.1
Railway materials and equipment	1.4	29.2
Motor cars, parts and accessories	2.3	46.0
Electric fittings, materials, appliances	1.1	18.4
Telephone and telegraph instruments and materials	0.5	30.3
Chemicals, compounds, medical preparations	0.8	6.0
Dyes, inks, paints, varnishes	2.2	16.1
Gasoline	2.0	50.5
Kerosene	16.4	68.8
Liquid fuel	0.9	52.1
Lubricating oil	1.8	73.5
Newsprint and other papers	1.6	10.8
Hides, leathers, and manufactures	1.0	22.7
Timber and wood, including railway sleepers	6.4	53.1
Tires and tubes	0.6	35.2
Photographic materials	0.5	36.4
Tobacco	15.7	73.2
Condensed milk	0.5	31.9
Fishery and sea products	0.2	2.2
Wheat, flour, cereals	10.4	27.0
Fruits and vegetables	0.4	10.1
Total: 27 items	88.5	

Source: U.S. Department of Commerce, *Where China Buys and Sells,* pp. 49–51.

States, which accounted for most of China's imports of this precious metal, and frequently for more than its net imports of silver. U.S. silver thereby not only increased China's domestic money supply, but also reduced the deficit in its balance of trade with other countries. For both reasons, the silver trade had extraordinary significance for the Chinese side as well. Its great importance became painfully obvious during the early 1930s, when the silver-purchase policy of the U.S. government made it practically impossible for China to remain on the silver standard.[19]

The preceding considerations serve to establish three principal points about the importance of trade relations between the United States and China:

(1) Throughout most of its recorded history, foreign trade in general was of marginal importance to both the United States anc China—if the shares of exports and imports in gross national product (or gross domestic product) are taken as standards.

(2) China was a very minor trading partner of the United States. In comparison, trade with the United States was more important to China. But the U.S. shares of China's total exports and imports placed the United States only in second or third position among the foreign buyers and sellers, behind Britain and Japan. The ranking of the United States among the foreign investors in China was even lower.

(3) There were few instances where the trade in a specific commodity could be called especially or "strategically" important either to China or to the United States. The most significant item for both sides seems to have been silver. Others that might also qualify were tea and silk among the Chinese exports, petroleum and tobacco among the Chinese imports.

In summary, it may be said that trade relations between the United States and China were clearly of minor significance to the United States, and at most times of secondary importance to China. Other measures that could be presented—notably the pattern of U.S.-China shipping and the pattern of migration—would reinforce this conclusion.[20] As other chapters make clear, however, within such aggregate limits, trade relations could be extremely interesting and rewarding for individual business firms.

The Impacts of American Multinational Enterprise on American-Chinese Economic Relations, 1786-1949

MIRA WILKINS

Investment by American international business in China was part of a broader pattern. As United States companies developed, they expanded to reach new markets and new sources of supply. From the early nineteenth century to 1948–1949, China was included in this business expansion.

AMERICAN FIRMS IN CHINA TRADE AND MANUFACTURING

The first investments by Americans in China were in trading outposts. The pattern of American trading-company investments is well documented. In 1786, two years after Canton was opened to American trade, the U.S. Consul in that city, Major Samuel

Shaw, started a company, Shaw & Randall, which acted on behalf of merchants who lacked familiarity with the East. Shaw &
Randall was *based* in Canton. By contrast, and more in keeping
with what would be the general picture of American business
abroad, in 1803 the Boston merchant Thomas Perkins established a branch office in Canton.[1]

Perkins and his brother had been in the China trade for about
a dozen years when they decided to open the branch house. His
biographers give the brothers' reasons:

The opportunity to buy teas and nankeens [a cotton cloth] and china
when the prices were low and competition was absent, storing them until
the ships arrived; the chance to establish better credit and business relations with Hong merchants than the itinerant ships' captains could; and, as
a by-product, to service these captains and thus earn a commission on the
business of their competitors.

The brothers selected a Bostonian apprenticed to the firm for a
number of years to head the new office. Assisting him would be
a Perkins nephew, John P. Cushing, then aged sixteen. The form
of operation was to be a partnership. The managing partner
would be in Canton and would contribute one-quarter of the
capital stock, while the Perkins firm contributed three-quarters.
The chosen partner died, and young Cushing, "8,000 miles from
home, five months away from advice by letter," took over this
branch. The Canton operation was styled Perkins & Co. By
October 1804, Thomas Perkins was instructing his nephew to
purchase an interest in three "factories," warehouses, in China.
Cushing purchased Chinese teas, nankeens, and china in exchange
for American furs and specie.[2]

Perkins & Co. was the first American "branch house" in Canton. Other U.S. trading companies followed, John Jacob Astor's
among them. For Perkins, Astor, and others, the China trade
was of key importance. These firms also often had representa-
tion in London. The Perkins firm dealt in opium, carrying it
from Turkey to China. The China trade was only a part—albeit
a significant part—of the international business. One estimate
puts U.S. investments in Canton in about 1830 at $3 million,
of which five-sixths was silver stocks used to purchase tea and
silk.[3]

In 1833, the British government refused to continue the East India Company's monopoly of the China trade, and the next year the trade was thrown open, providing opportunities for even more diversified U.S. business. By 1836, there were nine American firms in Canton (and about five times as many British houses). By then, Astor had shut his branch (in 1823); Perkins & Co., too, had closed out its business in the winter of 1827–1828. Now the largest American mercantile establishment in China was Russell & Co. (a transplanted Boston firm). Also included were J. P. Sturgis & Co. (the Canton agents of Bryant & Sturgis of Boston) and Olyphant & Co. (a branch of a New York firm).[4]

After 1842, tea and silk continued to be the chief attractions, increasingly paid for with opium. Other American traders established branch houses or made contacts with existing U.S. firms with agencies in China. By 1840, Augustine Heard had broken away from Russell & Co. and had formed a competing mercantile house. Augustine Heard & Co. expanded to become Russell & Co.'s most important rival after 1842. In the 1850s, it opened branches in Hong Kong, Shanghai, and Foochow, with agencies in Amoy and Ningpo. While it did have a Boston-based partner, for all practical purposes Heard & Co. developed its trading activities from its Chinese origins, first from Canton and, after 1856, from British Hong Kong. Historian Stephen Lockwood has described the mid-century U.S.-China trade as carried on by American merchants organized into trading firms that pooled capital, entrepreneurial talent, and business connections. These houses combined the capital of their principals in Boston, and increasingly in New York, with their own specialized knowledge of conditions in China. The Americans associated with the Chinese side of trade were experts in finding the right quality tea and silks at the right price.[5]

Some of these firms developed essentially as "expatriate" enterprises. They were American businesses abroad, but the American principals had become resident in China; their ties to the United States were not those that would meet current definitions prepared by the U.S. Department of Commerce of direct foreign investment (what we look for when we discuss multinational enterprise).[6]

For Americans, the mid-nineteenth-century China trade was essentially an import trade; Americans were buying Chinese tea and silk. In the 1850s and 1860s, while Olyphant & Co. did not deal in opium, its two larger competitors, Russell & Co. and Augustine Heard & Co., did.[7]

In 1869, the first transcontinental railroad crossed the United States, and the Suez Canal opened that same year. From the 1870s, the steamship increasingly replaced the clipper ship, and telegraphic communication connected China with the West. This revolution in transportation and communication began to alter the composition of American business investments in China.

The older trading firms had been particularly successful in communicating information between China and the West, but the new transportation and communication technologies made these firms less essential. Moreover, they were family houses, lacking the management continuity of modern corporations. In the early 1870s, before the exodus of the older firms, there were about 50 American houses in China, the vast majority of them trading enterprises. Estimates of their investments run around $7 million. In 1874, Heard & Co., in 1878 Olyphant & Co., and in 1891 Russell & Co. closed.

Rapidly, these American traders were replaced by a new group, which included Carlowitz & Co., The China and Japan Trading Company, and the American Trading Company. Unlike their predecessors, the new ones specialized in *selling* American goods in China. The 1912 *Export Trade Directory* had one and one-half columns that listed New York export houses in the China trade.[8]

The China and Japan Trading Company had its origins in H. Fogg & Co., an American trading firm organized for trade with China and Japan in the 1850s. The firm was renamed The China and Japan Trading Company in 1876, and by 1908 it had branches in Yokohama, Kobe, Osaka, Nagasaki, Shanghai, and London.

The American Trading Company was another of the new entries, with a different history. In 1877, the American Clock and Brass Work Company (of Connecticut) opened a branch office in Japan to sell clocks and brass work. Its name was changed in 1884 to American Trading Company. By then, it had branches in Japan, China (first opened in Shanghai in 1879), Manchuria, and Korea. In 1900, it merged with Flint, Eddy and Co., whose predecessors had developed business in Latin America since 1857. The $5 million corporation of 1900 was called Flint, Eddy and American Trading Company, which name was changed in 1902 to American Trading Company. By 1920, American Trading Company had branches in fifteen countries and five continents. American Trading Company continued until 1949 in the China trade. In general, however, the trading companies lost some of their importance and many vanished as American industrial enterprises by-passed them and established their own offices.[9]

American trading firms did not confine themselves to imports and exports. For example, from 1862 to 1877, Russell & Co. held controlling interest in the Shanghai Steam Navigation Company, which it then sold.[10]

Some traders invested in manufacturing: American Trading Company had a cotton mill in Shanghai by 1900; others bought control of the Shanghai Rice Mill Company and the Shanghai Paper and Pulp Company.[11] Before World War I, Andersen and Meyer, two Danes, had organized a trading house in Shanghai called Andersen, Meyer & Co. In the 1920s, General Electric, along with other American manufacturers, invested in this firm. Andersen, Meyer & Co. transferred American equipment and methods to China.[12] In the late 1920s, Andersen, Meyer & Co. moved into diversified manufacturing, including window sashes, grease, and bridge construction. It owned a foundry and did casting.[13] In a 1933 volume, economist C. F. Remer referred to the company as an American investment in China and as a "great trading firm" with a long history in China.[14] Trading firms thus were engaged in more than buying and selling goods.

AMERICAN MULTINATIONALS'
DIRECT MARKETING IN CHINA

American industrial enterprises became national and international in the 1870s, 1880s, and 1890s. When they sought to market their new products at home and abroad, they frequently found that the use of independent agents was not the most efficient means of reaching their customers. In their main markets at home and abroad, they appointed exclusive agents and then integrated forward, establishing their own marketing outlets. Since Europe was American business's largest foreign market, U.S. companies tended to develop their first marketing subsidiaries in Europe.[15]

Some large industrial enterprises in the forefront of international sales decided that, for their sales in China, it was wise to move into direct marketing. Just as in Europe, so in China companies with new products took the lead. American Tobacco, Columbia Phonographs, General Electric, International Harvester, Parke-Davis, Sherwin-Williams, Singer Sewing Machine, and Standard Oil of New York were among the U. S. companies that made direct investments in marketing American products in China before World War I.[16]

Standard Oil

Standard Oil (N.Y.) was one of the two largest of these investors. (For the context and details of its growth in China see Chapter 7.) Its interests in Asia in 1905 came to $16 million, a large proportion of which was in China (see Table 52). One estimate gives its 1914 stake in China as $20 million. Standard Oil had started to export oil products to Asia in the 1870s. At first it used merchant firms that bought Standard Oil products in the United States—for example, The China and Japan Trading Company. In the 1880s and 1890s, Standard Oil (N.Y.) devoted increasing attention to this trade. By the 1890s, electricity and gas competed with kerosene in the United States—not so in China. There, the competition was from foreign sources of kerosene, brought in bulk to China by Marcus Samuel & Co. The latter introduced lower-cost kerosene from Russia and in 1897 established The "Shell" Transport and Trading Company, Limited. Royal Dutch, meanwhile, had found oil in the Dutch East Indies, built a refinery in Sumatra, and sold kerosene in China. By 1903, the British-controlled Shell and the Dutch-controlled Royal Dutch cooperated in the Chinese market through Asiatic Petroleum Company. Shell and Royal-Dutch combined on a worldwide basis in 1907.

TABLE 52   Investments of Standard Oil of New York
Entries on Accounts—Asiatic Business

Assets	1903	1904	1905
Real Estate—Asiatic Stations	$ 274,262.11	$ 439,632.23	$ 461,716.56
Construction—Asiatic Stations	332,014.10	460,565.61	894.073.19
Office Furniture—Asiatic Stations	17,033.18	23,727.90	31,277.00
Asiatic Floating Equipment	72,314.58	120,130.34	95,171.87
Accounts Receivable—Asiatic Books	407,989.49	611,867.48	2,431,563.88
Inventories—Asiatic Consignment	7,393,017.00	12,204,410.33	13,059,619.52
Cash—Asiatic stations	314,361.85	424,512.25	1,105,056.01
TOTAL ASSETS	8,810,992.31	14,284,846.14	18,081,478.03
Deduct Accounts Payable	578,317.84	406,969.19	2,080,308.71
NET ASSETS	$8,232,674.47	$13,877,876.95	$16,001,169.26
Profits—Asiatic Consignment	2,228,141.74	1,669,819.64	1,875,432.32

The investment was large primarily owing to the need to carry heavy inventories, which were necessary because of the great quantities of oil in transit between United States and the distant Asiatic points. *Source:* Bureau of Corporations, *Report on Petroleum Industry,* pt. 3, pp. 580–590. Reprinted from Mira Wilkins, *The Emergence of Multinational Enterprise,* p. 210.

Standard Oil, to protect its sales position, in 1893 began to establish its own Asiatic Stations—in Shanghai, Hong Kong, and elsewhere in East Asia. Oil went on consignment from Standard Oil (N.Y.) to resident agents, shipped in cases and cans. In China, the tin cans were used for buckets and roofing, while the wooden cases served as furniture and for use in construction. To encourage kerosene sales, Standard Oil agents sold at low prices (or sometimes gave away) small lamps and wicks. Standard shipped kerosene refined in the eastern or midwestern areas of the United States.

During the 1890s, Standard Oil officials investigated possible supplies of oil closer to Chinese markets. They looked for crude oil sources in China, Sakhalin Island, California, Alaska, and the Dutch East Indies. J. H. Fertig, a Standard Oil production expert, predicted in 1899 that "no material development of petroleum resources of China can be expected for some time." The Dutch East Indies seemed more interesting. Standard Oil attempted to purchase Royal Dutch, an offer the latter rejected. (It also wooed, in vain, Shell, which had oil in Dutch Borneo.)

Standard moved into oil production in Japan in 1900, a short-lived venture. In 1900, it acquired a company that became Standard Oil (California). This gave it a better source of supply for East Asia. Remer notes that Standard Oil Company had in Shanghai in 1898 oil tanks and plants for the tinning of oil. These were part of its Chinese marketing organization, and not related to investment in production.

Standard Oil (N.Y.) functioned despite competition and boycotts. It was affected by the 1905 boycott of U.S. imports into China. In South China, its sales before the boycott had been 90,000 cases of kerosene a month; by November 1905, they were 19,000. Merchants made up the difference by substituting Asiatic Petroleum Company's kerosene from Sumatra. A representative of Standard Oil called on the U.S. State Department, complaining that the boycott "would be a grave disaster to the petroleum industry of the United States." The boycott, was, however, temporary and Standard Oil sales resumed. In 1905, Standard Oil (N.Y.) made a quota agreement that contained "understandings" with Asiatic Petroleum Company in the China market.

The market for Standard Oil in China (excluding sales through Hong Kong) represented 10.3 percent of its 1910 export deliveries of kerosene from the United States. Probably much of the export to Hong Kong went into China. If that total is added, the percentage rises to 15.5 percent. The China market was clearly important; in 1910 Standard's trade in China was the largest in the Orient. (It was, however, substantially smaller than Standard Oil's English or German kerosene trade.) Until 1914, Standard Oil (N.Y.)'s investment in China was related primarily to the distribution of kerosene.[17]

Singer Sewing Machine

Singer Manufacturing Company's London office in the 1880s established sales centers in China, Australia, the Philippines, and Brazil as the last moves in a formidable expansion of that company's international marketing organization. It assigned salaried personnel to the new positions. In 1883, the London office sent E. M. Sang, agent for the company in Brussels, to Shanghai to open the sales center.[18] Before he left, the London office briefed Sang on the results of a talk with the Reverend John McIntyre, the Free Church of Scotland missionary who had recently returned from China. McIntyre reported that the company would need a comprador, who would "act fairly—so long, at least as he is always suspected and closely watched." Singer would experience difficulty with the fluctuating currency exchange rates and would require the assistance of a "shrof," through whom "all money transactions are adjusted and fixed." The London office's briefing indicated that, since McIntyre felt the Chinese were

... steeped in oriental prejudice and with an intense hatred of innovation, our success would probably not be great at first, but at the present time, in consequence of the native tailor coming to the front and cutting out the high charging warehouses and shops, the present seems a most opportune time of getting our m/s into the hands of these tailors.

Based on McIntyre's comments, the London office believed American and English missionaries in China could be used to Singer's advantage, inasmuch as the missionaries "are glad to make use of any *civilizing medium* (such as our sewing m/s eminently are) to help breakdown the conservatism of ages and to knit themselves in bonds of mutual help and sympathy with the people." McIntyre suggested that "a sewing m/s on show at the house of each missionary would ... create a great sensation." The London office explained that there were steamers almost daily from Shanghai to Yokohama and that the Japanese trade could be developed from the Shanghai center.[19]

Sang wrote from China in 1884 on a "very unsettled state of affairs." The London office urged him to make visits "to any other part [of China or Japan] where trade is likely to be done." After Sang had been in Shanghai for two years, the President of the Singer Company, George McKenzie, expressed discontent; Sang had not developed either the Japanese or Chinese business effectively.[20]

On 18 March 1885, McKenzie told the stockholders of Singer Manufacturing Company that the company's foreign trade was doing well, notwithstanding "minor disturbances" such as "war in China." He was referring to the Sino-French War. McKenzie commented that, "in all outlying countries—China and Japan, Brazil, Chile and Cuba, etc. our worst competitors are German imitators . . ."[21] In 1888, the New York office sent London's chief inspector to China, who found that the Chinese style of clothing, with loose seams, was an obstacle to the expansion of sewing-machine sales. On his advice, Singer closed its Shanghai office in June 1888.[22] According to historian Robert B. Davies, for the next sixteen years Singer's business in China was handled by the American Trading Company.[23] Yet, a 1903 trading examiner could refer to a Singer Shanghai office. Indeed, in the late 1890s, Singer paid new attention to the China market and, in 1904, when Singer Manufacturing Company established Singer Sewing Machine Company, the latter took over the worldwide Singer sales organization; in the process it acquired the Singer distribution network in China.[24]

In 1905, a Chinese government commission went to America and Europe to study governmental systems.[25] The New York Singer office wrote to its subsidiary in London on 15 February 1906 that the Chinese Commissioners had just sailed for England. The London office was instructed to entertain them and to take them through Singer's British manufacturing plant at Kilbowie. The letter observed that the Singer Company was "well known" in China and that "we are pretty well established in The Treaty Ports but our hope is of course to be able to extend our business there in the same way as we have in other countries." The writer urged the London office to be particularly cordial to the Commissioners because of "the Chinese boycott which has become quite a serious factor and has affected to some extent the business of all American concerns." The reference here was to the 1905 boycott of U.S. imports in China that, as earlier noted, had adversely affected Standard Oil (N.Y.).[26]

The letter from Singer's New York office continued:

We have taken the position that as a matter of fact the goods which we sell in China are not necessarily American and that the company is in reality broadly International in its scope, and for them [the Chinese Commissioners] to see for themselves that machines practically the same as those which they have seen on this side are manufactured in one of the largest manufacturing concerns in Great Britain [the subsidiary of the U.S. Singer Company] could not help but be of considerable benefit to us in that connection.[27]

The approach was not atypical. Faced with anti-American attitudes, or, alternatively, costs that were lower abroad, U.S.-headquartered multinational corporations had the flexibility to serve any market using third-country manufacturing facilities, that is, plants other than those located in the United States.

While Singer in the 1880s had developed its China trade through its London organization and was later prepared to use its British factory as a supply source, Sherwin-Williams, in a complex corporate structure, handled its China trade through an English subsidiary of its Canadian affiliate. In 1895, the U.S. company adopted the slogan, "Sherwin-Williams Paints Cover the Earth."[28]

Of the large American multinational companies, many of which started or acquired plants in Canada and Europe between 1880 and 1914, few considered China a good place to manufacture. The reason was that direct foreign investment in manufacturing by American-headquartered multinationals was designed almost exclusively to meet the needs of foreign markets. Investments were made in order to cope with patent laws, to jump tariffs, to confront competition, and to fill host-nation market demand that could not be reached satisfactorily by imports. In China, it was generally possible to meet all the limited demand by manufacturing outside and exporting products to that country.

The British-American Tobacco Company

The operations of the British-American Tobacco Company (BAT) were, thus, exceptional. BAT did extensive manufacturing in China. (For details of the company's growth and history in China, see Chapter 6.) Its manufacturing activity preceded that of other U.S. enterprises. American Tobacco was formed in 1890. In 1891, its Chinese agent, Mustard & Co., established a small manufactory in Pootung across from the foreign concession in Shanghai. By 1901, American Tobacco was manufacturing on its own account in Australia, Canada, Japan, and Germany. That year in England it acquired Ogden Ltd., a leading British cigarette maker. The takeover led thirteen British tobacco firms to combine in the Imperial Tobacco Company. For about a year, Imperial and American competed, until, in the fall of 1902, the two agreed that (1) the "territory" of American Tobacco would be the United States and its dependencies; (2) Imperial Tobacco would confine its trade to Great Britain and Ireland; and (3) a new enterprise, British-American Tobacco Company (two-thirds owned by American and one-third by Imperial), would handle the international business outside the territories of its parent companies. American and Imperial transferred their foreign business to British-American Tobacco, and each included its business in China in the transfer.

Originally, BAT was controlled by American Tobacco. In 1911, the stock ownership arrangement was ordered to be dismantled by a U.S. Supreme Court anti-trust decision. Nonetheless, BAT remained under the control of U.S. stockholders until the mid-1920s.

Meanwhile, BAT established a formidable Chinese business. Having acquired the Mustard & Co. plant and the small manufactory of another U.S. firm in 1902, BAT began to manufacture cigarettes in China. Soon, it was expanding in Shanghai and elsewhere. In 1906, BAT's Shanghai facilities were producing 8 million cigarettes a day and had 2,500 Chinese plus about 30 foreign employees. Its plants had British and American machinery, and they initially used leaf tobacco imported from the United States. BAT's motive for manufacturing in China was to save labor and transportation costs. By 1914, British-American Tobacco Company manufactured at Hankow, Newchwang, Mukden, and Shanghai. Economist Remer calls these operations British interests; actually, in 1914, they were U.S. stakes, since the control of the parent, London-headquartered British-American Tobacco Company was at that time American. Indeed, the chief executive officer of BAT was the American entrepreneur, James B. Duke.

In 1908, BAT began to mix Chinese-grown and U.S. tobacco. While its Mukden factory used Manchurian leaf, at Hankow BAT distributed American tobacco seed and encouraged the Chinese to raise the crop. The company introduced Virginia and North Carolina tobacco cultivation. Shantung was found to be particularly suitable for tobacco-growing. Chinese farmers raised the tobacco. Near the tobacco regions, in Weihsien, Hsuchang, and Fengyang, BAT established re-drying plants, which were to be owned in compradors' names, since foreign firms were not permitted to own land outside the treaty ports. Initially, the company gave the peasants seed and fertilizer and supplied building materials for the peasants' curing barns. During the 1920s, as cigarette consumption expanded in China, BAT's Chinese cigarette manufacturing kept pace. As tobacco-growing rose, leaf imports also increased, until 1931. By then—indeed, after the mid-1920s—BAT was a *British*-controlled multinational, which takes it outside our discussion.[29] BAT's presence in China altered the character of the U.S.-China trade in tobacco and tobacco products. U.S. commerce with China in tobacco and tobacco products grew in volume, but U.S. exports changed from predominantly product exports to predominantly leaf-tobacco exports. By the mid-1920s, BAT manufactured more cigarettes in China than it imported.[30]

It has been noted that companies such as Singer, Sherwin-Williams, and American Tobacco were prepared at various times to administer their multinational business in China from London. London was, after all, the world center for foreign trade and investment. British interests in China preceded American and were far more substantial. The effect of such a strategy was that U.S. multinational corporations were not wedded to improving *American* trade. Decisions from London headquarters were responsive to different pressures (pressures to export from Britain, for example) than those coming from an American base.

The large American companies that invested abroad did so in the main to sell. On occasion, they sought raw materials. I have been able to find only one significant foreign investment in Chinese raw materials by an American multinational enterprise (BAT did not actually invest in growing tobacco, although it stimulated Chinese cultivation). In 1914, Standard Oil (N.Y.) sought a cheap *Chinese* source of oil. This effort was in part a response to competition in China from Royal Dutch-Shell's Asiatic Petroleum Co., since the 1905 quota agreement between Standard Oil (N.Y.) and Asiatic had broken down in 1910. It was also related to the 1911 Supreme Court order breaking up Standard Oil, so that Standard Oil of California and Standard Oil of New York were no longer part of a single enterprise. Standard Oil (N.Y.) had to buy California kerosene and then resell it in the Orient. In February 1914, Standard Oil (N.Y.) entered into a contract with the Chinese Government to explore for oil. But the company found little or no oil and in 1917 declared itself convinced oil did not exist in sufficient quantities to warrant commercial development. While Standard Oil (N.Y.)'s initial intentions were to seek oil aggressively, it seems to have discontinued prospecting not so much because of poor results as because of Chinese President Yuan Shih-k'ai's lack of enthusiasm and then, after his death in 1916, because of its own representatives' ineptitude in negotiations.[31]

During 1914–1917, American business often went abroad to fill in gaps created by the involvement of British business in the world war.[32] An American Chamber of Commerce was organized at Shanghai in 1915 with a membership of 32 firms. We would like to have the minutes of this Chamber to document its activity. One can be sure, however, that among the founders were Standard Oil (N.Y.) and the Shanghai branch of the International Banking Corporation (see below).[33] There were 130 U.S. firms in China in 1930, and of those 4 entered before 1900 (Standard Oil, Singer, American Trading Company, among them), 22 before 1913, and 18 in the World War I years.[34]

General Electric appears to have had a small sales organization in China before World War I. The war caused shipping problems, and, in 1917, General Electric started to manufacture lamps on a limited scale in China through a wholly owned subsidiary, China GE.[35]

Western Electric

Another World War I entry into Chinese manufacturing was Western Electric. While the pre-World War I pattern for U.S. multinational corporations was to use a New York or London office to supervise sub-offices in Shanghai and elsewhere in China, a variant on the pattern was evident in the case of Western Electric. Since 1899, this American company had had a Japanese manufacturing affiliate, Nippon Electric.[36]

In June 1905, the Vice-President of Western Electric, H. B. Thayer, wrote Company President E. M. Barton that:

Our Japanese office has been making a successful effort to get some business established in China. It has been apparent for sometime that the Chinese officials prefer to absorb western civilization through the medium of Japanese . . . I should think that it would be proper for the Nippon Electric Company to make a reasonable investment [in Chinese telephone enterprise], if investigation indicated that it would be a safe and proper investment.

In two other letters that June, Thayer enlarged on his plans:

I doubt very much whether it is worthwhile however, to have the Western Electric Company do what is done in its own name or to have the capital furnished as American capital, as you have probably seen by the papers the enforcement of the Chinese Exclusion Act has not increased our popularity in China. It is an iniquitous law and we deserve to lose trade on account of having it on the books.

The plan was that Western Electric would act through Nippon Electric. To the manager of the Japanese affiliate, K. Iwadare, Thayer wrote that "there seems no question but what Japan is the most favored nation with the Chinese. Your judgment however as to how this matter should be handled would be controlling."[37] Compare this strategy with Singer's response to the same situation; Singer went through Britain, Western Electric through Japan.

In October 1905, Thayer wrote Iwadare, "We agree with you the [Chinese] business should be in the name of the Nippon Electric Company and that Western Electric Company should not appear in the transaction."[38] So effective was the implementation that, in January 1906, Thayer was explaining to the president of American Telephone and Telegraph, Western Electric's parent company:

I return herewith Mr. Vaille's letter in regard to the Chinese matter . . . on account of the feeling in China against Americans and in favor of Japanese which seems to exist at the present time we considered it advisable to look after the Chinese business through our Japanese correspondents [affiliate] and I have no doubt, from the reports which I have received, that the Japanese referred to by Mr. Vaille as now getting the business are our own people.[39]

But, by June 1906, Thayer was complaining to Iwadare: "We appear to be losing our hold on the Chinese business. I hope that you will be able to resume close relations. If however, it seems best to handle the business through one of our other houses we will give the matter the best consideration. . . ."[40] By September, Thayer was suggesting that Western Electric's French, German, English, or Belgian house go for the business with the Imperial Chinese Telegraph Administration, since the relations between the latter and Japan "are not of the best [and since] the general prejudices in China against Americans would operate against us."[41]

Because of the panic in the United States in 1907, Western Electric was not prepared to invest in China, directly or indirectly.[42] Plans for manufacturing there were postponed, and, in 1908, Thayer wrote that "with present feeling in China it would be fatal to our prospects to try and handle the business through our Japanese office."[43] In 1909, Arnhold Herbert & Co. was appointed agent for Western Electric in China.[44]

During World War I, Gerard Swope of Western Electric traveled to Japan and arranged to have Mitsui & Co. invest in Nippon Electric. Before Swope left the United States, he made plans for Western Electric to manufacture in China. He elaborated on these plans on his trip to Japan and then to China. In 1918, Swope supervised the formation of China Electric Company, which opened a Peking head office and a Shanghai telephone manufacturing plant. Half the capital for China Electric Company came from the Peking Ministry of Communications, one-quarter from Western Electric, and one-quarter from Western Electric's joint venture in Japan, Nippon Electric. The first manager was Clark H. Minor who, like Swope, soon left for General Electric.[45]

During the 1920s, China wanted to develop its industry, and American multinational corporations were encouraged to participate. General Electric expanded its lamp manufacturing and began to invest in Andersen, Meyer & Co.[46] Western Electric's Chinese manufacturing also continued. Western Electric's one-quarter interest in the Chinese Electric Company (plus notes, advances, and open account receivables) amounted to $1.2 million in 1921; by 1925, however, the investment was only $668,000.[47] That year, Western Electric sold its multinational manufacturing (including operations in China) to International Telephone and Telegraph Corporation (ITT). General Electric and ITT became major manufacturers of electrical goods and equipment in China.[48]

General Electric's manufacturing activities became extensive during the late 1920s and 1930s. The company's subsidiary, China GE, manufactured lamps, and, in the early 1930s, GE acquired controlling interest in Andersen, Meyer & Co., which by then manufactured lathes and planers, other machine tools, and standard electrical apparatus. In the early 1930s, Andersen, Meyer & Co. took a one-third interest in a new firm, China Car & Foundry Company (one-third was owned by the British industrialist Sir Victor Sassoon and one-third by Li Ming, sometime Governor of the Bank of China). In the 1930s, according to W. Rogers Herod, General Electric employed 2,400 persons in China.[49]

Between 1937 and 1941, Shanghai was under Japanese control. A former GE employee in China described his experience: "Our factory [that of Andersen, Meyer & Co.] was under military control. We needed government passes to move cargo, government permits to go to work; we would manufacture equipment for the Japanese, at their request. We had to." The GE lamp factory experienced the same problems. The former GE employee recalled, "All American businesses knew our days were numbered, but we didn't know what was D-Day." General Electric still made profits and could remit them. From December 1941, all the General Electric establishments in China became Japanese.[50]

Ford Motor Company

In late 1921, Henry Ford considered expanding his business in China. He sought information on water-power sites and raw materials, such as iron ore, from Professor Joseph Bailie at Peking University. The latter urged Ford to invest. Arrangements were made for Chinese students to be trained by the company in Detroit. By February 1923, about 100 were there.[51]

In 1924, Sun Yat-sen invited Henry Ford to China and urged him "to express and embody your mind and ideals in the enduring form of a new industrial system." But, at this point, other interests held priority for Ford. During the two years

1925-1926, the Ford Motor Company sold almost 3,000 cars in China, and, in 1928, the company decided to open a sales and service branch in Shanghai to cover China, French Indochina and the Philippines.[52]

In 1929, the first full year of the branch's operation, Ford sales in China rose to 2,263 vehicles. In 1930, Henry Ford considered investing in a Shanghai assembly plant and sent W. C. Cowling to investigate. Cowling reported in August 1930 that "about all you hear in Shanghai is the anti-foreign sentiment on the part of the present government and the danger of investing money in China at the present time. Personally this doesn't disturb me." Cowling continued, "We had martial law in Shanghai two days this past week." Julean Arnold, American Commercial Attaché in Shanghai, talked with Finance Minister T. V. Soong who indicated that the Chinese did not favor American motor cars being assembled in Japan for sale in China. Soong indicated that every possible inducement should be provided to American companies to build assembly plants in China.[53] Cowling also visited other key government officials. He wrote:

If President Chiang Kai-shek, who is now at the war front, gets back to Nanking before I leave, it has been arranged for me to meet him. . . . Should the administration change through the fortunes of war, I have also laid the foundations for this as I have met most of those on the other side. Everyone understands we are not mixing in their politics or wars and that regardless of the outcome we will not be affected.[54]

In 1931, the Japanese moved into Manchuria. On 28 January 1932, the Japanese attacked Chapei, the northernmost section of Shanghai. The Ford service facility (its "plant") was several miles from Chapei. J. V. Crowe, the Ford manager, wrote home on 5 February that the Ford office was carrying on as usual, except for closing part of Friday, 29 January, because of sniping on the river and bullets striking the tender on which some of the company's employees were going to work. None of the employees was hurt. Four members of Ford's staff joined the Shanghai volunteer corps. Crowe reported, "With the bombardment of Woosung and Nanking and trouble at Swatow and Hankow, our business is almost at a standstill."

Business did pick up in 1932, and by year end Ford deliveries reached 1,321 units. Henry Ford had by then decided against a new Chinese factory. In September 1932, when T. V. Soong urged him to "assist us . . . to solve some of our problems" and to establish an assembly and possibly a manufacturing facility, Edsel Ford replied that this might be considered when China's daily demand for cars reached 25 units (in 1932, Ford was delivering fewer than 4 cars a day in that nation). Ford never built an assembly plant in China. The Shanghai sales and service branch continued in business.[55] In August 1937, J. M. Huppman cabled Henry Ford, "PLANT [the service plant] TO DATE IN TACT BUT SURROUNDING TERRITORY SUBJECTED HEAVY BOMBING . . . DO NOT CONSIDER IT NECESSARY CLOSE AND WITHDRAW AT PRESENT." Ford remained there after the Japanese occupation.[56]

General Motors operated similar sales and service facilities in China. In November 1938, General Motors's regional director in East Asia privately indicated that the China market was important, whether dominated by Japan or not. "From the automotive point of view, it is possible that complete domination of China by Japan would mean an upturn in business."[57]

In December 1941, Ford Motor Company had 23 salaried employees in Shanghai, 7 of whom were Americans. Two of these had made it to Manila by 9 December, along with the one Chilean employee. On 15 December, the company had no information on the other 5 Americans, the 2 German, 1 Portuguese, 1 Latvian, and 11 Chinese employees.[58]

Under the rubric "manufacturing," Remer includes among the U.S. investments in China in 1930: "importing, assembling and operating motor vehicles."[59] The "assembling" was undoubtedly attaching wheels or minor assembly at the service "plants" and dealerships. No automobile assembly or manufacturing plants existed in China in the 1920s and 1930s.

The automobile companies did not manufacture in China, nor did the major investors in oil distribution, which did not establish refineries. By the 1920s, there were two significant oil distributors in China and one important, but smaller, network. The big "two" were Shell and Standard Oil of New York. Also selling in China was The Texas Company, which had started direct sales in that nation before World War I.[60] (In addition, Vacuum Oil Company sold specialized petroleum products, mainly lubricants.)

Standard Oil of New York and Vacuum Oil Company merged

in 1931, forming Socony-Vacuum. In 1933, Socony-Vacuum and Standard Oil of New Jersey organized a 50-50 joint venture, Standard-Vacuum Oil Company (Stanvac). Stanvac combined the first parent's East-of-Suez oil-marketing network with the second's Dutch East Indies source of supply; East Asian markets became an outlet for Stanvac's nearby oil. In China, Stanvac marketed under the Standard Oil or Socony name.

In 1936, The Texas Company and Standard Oil of California went into 50-50 joint ventures in Saudi Arabia, Bahrain, and the Dutch East Indies, and into joint marketing East of Suez. For the latter, they organized California Texas Oil Company (Caltex). Despite the formation of Caltex, before World War II Texaco continued to sell in China under the Texaco (China) name.[61]

During the 1920s and 1930s, the oil enterprises weathered the warlords' fighting, the general political disorder in China, problems of local taxes and corruption, Japanese moves, monopolies (short-lived and substantial), as well as currency depreciation and foreign-exchange restrictions. The companies lodged claims with the Department of State against the Chinese government for destruction of their property. When the Manchurian oil monopoly built a refinery, they reluctantly changed from sellers of oil products to suppliers of crude. Operations in China were never "normal" business. Even though the companies did not refine, they still made substantial investments in oil terminals, storage tanks, transport facilities, and inventories.[62]

Sometimes, the oil companies competed with one another; often they cooperated. Frequently, on political questions, the U.S. State Department urged them to act in concert. A memorandum produced for Senator Church's Committee hearings on multinational corporations indicates that, in East Asia, Shell and Stanvac "recognized quota positions on finished products." Another document, of 14 October 1937, reveals that Standard Oil of California (a partner in Caltex) desired to talk with Shell officials about prices in China. H. D. Collier of Standard Oil of California "thinks Shell should agree to higher prices in China," this memorandum reads. Both Stanvac and Caltex continued to sell refined oil products in occupied and unoccupied China until 7 December 1941.[63]

CHINA TRADE CORPORATIONS
OF AMERICAN RESIDENTS IN CHINA

Not all U.S. investors in Chinese industry were part of multinational enterprises. There were also individual American businessmen resident in China, and they frequently used the device of a China trade corporation, a U.S. federal incorporation exempt from U.S. corporate taxes. The U.S. Congress, desiring to encourage American investment in China, passed the China Trade Act of 1922 and amended it in 1925. By 1929, the total capitalization of the 81 China Trade Act companies was estimated by the U.S. Department of Commerce to be between $20 and $30 million. China trade corporations were owned mainly by U.S. citizens *resident* in China.[64] Some of these investors participated in businesses to serve the Chinese market, while others took part in firms that exported from that country. The exact proportions are not clear.

But it is clear that, while the bulk of American multinational corporations' investments in China were market-oriented, that is, designed for the product to be marketed in China, some U.S. stakes were supply-oriented—designed to supply the United States. For instance, Remer describes trading firms that purchased raw furs from Mongolia and brought them to China for preparation and eventual shipment to New York. American investments in Chinese textiles, including investments in Chinese carpet manufacture in Tientsin and Peking, were made to secure export from China. The same was true of U.S. investments in dried eggs and pig bristles.[65] In 1929, Borden Company acquired Amos Bird Company, which maintained a dried-egg plant in Shanghai.[66] In the late 1930s, it was possible to buy 100 eggs for the Chinese equivalent of about U.S. 25 cents, one Shanghai resident recalled.[67] Marshall Field and other large U.S. department stores sent representatives to buy hand-embroidery and other Chinese goods for sale in the United States. Remer describes a great American department store with agents in China who received linen purchased in Ireland, supervised embroidery in China, and shipped the finished products to the United States.[68]

AMERICAN NONINDUSTRIAL ENTERPRISES IN CHINA

In the past, in discussing American multinationals, the literature emphasized industrial enterprises. I have already deviated from this by including trading houses. A further deviation is important. A number of U.S. investments in China were in public utilities (including communication and transportation), construction, insurance, and banking. These were all market-oriented, and many involved multinational businesses.

American Bell and Edison interests appear to have participated in the formation of The Oriental Telephone Company in 1880, which operated telephone systems in Cairo, Alexandria, Hong Kong, Shanghai, and five Indian cities. Apparently, at some early point the Municipal Exchange in Shanghai took over the operations there.[69] Years later, in 1930, International Telephone and Telegraph obtained a franchise to operate the telephone system, The Shanghai Telephone Company, in the International Settlement.[70]

In 1883, Commercial Cable Company was formed in the United States. In 1906, it signed a contract with the Chinese government to develop cable connections. In 1921, the Federal Telegraph Company of California agreed to install wireless telegraph stations.[71] An additional form of communication was the motion picture. Of the 18 distributors of motion picture films in China during the 1920s, 4 were American, 11 Chinese, 2 French, and 1 German.[72]

U.S. direct investments in Chinese railroads began in the 1890s, but they were short-lived. The Chinese government bought out the only large investment, that of the Morgan interests, for $6.75 million in 1905.[73] Participation in the airways was more substantial. On 21 October 1929, China Airways Federal Incorporated formally opened air-mail and passenger service between Shanghai and Hankow via Nanking and Kiukiang; an American enterprise, a subsidiary of the Curtiss companies, participated.[74] In 1931, the China National Aviation Corporation (CNAC) was organized as a joint Sino-American corporation, in which Curtiss Wright Aeroplane Company held a 45-percent interest. Two years later, Curtiss sold out to Pan American Airways. Pan Am thereupon sent men, money, and equipment to the CNAC. At first, the enterprise employed American pilots, then American-born Chinese pilots, and finally, in 1936, native Chinese pilots, but it continued to use American-made planes. [75]

American insurance companies first ventured into the Orient in the 1880s. New York Life Insurance Company started to do business in China in 1884. In 1901, one estimate indicates that nine-tenths of the life insurance business done in China was by New York firms. However, for reasons that had nothing to do with the situation there, U.S. insurance companies did not remain in China. [76]

American banking in East Asia began in 1902 in China with the International Banking Corporation (IBC). By 1914, IBC had 14 branches in the Far East as well as branches in Panama and Mexico. Its board included steel-maker Henry C. Frick, railroadmen E. H. Harriman and Edwin Gould, and mining and smelting executive Isaac Guggenheim. IBC served America's steel export trade. Apparently, before 1915, U.S. Steel had considered and rejected investment in mining in Hunan, Yunnan, and Szechwan. Harriman had dreams of acquiring and building railroads in China. Guggenheim's main foreign business investments were in Mexico, but that family was open to other ventures as well. [77]

In 1915, the National City Bank acquired the International Banking Corporation, an acquisition that gave National City more branches abroad than any bank in the world. National City Bank also established a new company, American International Corporation (AIC). Among the latter's activities were loans to the Chinese Government for surveys of the Grand Canal. AIC cut back on its business after the U.S. recession of 1921, as did National City Bank. Nonetheless, National City Bank remained a giant multinational enterprise. By 1929, it had 93 branches outside the United States, 9 of them in China. [78]

There were in 1930 in China 4 American banks: National City Bank, with 9 branches; American Express Company, with 4; Equitable Eastern Banking Corporation, with 2; and the American Oriental Banking Corporation, with 2. National City Bank was the leader among U.S. banks abroad. American Express, involved in tourism and transport as well as banking, had 47 foreign offices by 1926. Equitable Eastern—with offices in Shanghai, Tientsin, and Hong Kong—was acquired by Chase

Bank in 1930. American Oriental Banking Corporation failed in 1935.[79]

National City Bank adapted well to conditions in China. When the Japanese occupied Manchuria in 1931, the bank placed its branch offices there under a manager located in Tokyo. In 1939, Guy Holman, Assistant Vice-President of National City Bank, visited the State Department to talk about U.S. policies in China. Holman opposed "vigorous official efforts in defense of foreign–'open door' interests in China." He thought "opposing of the Japanese should be avoided." Holman believed that business should do business wherever it could, "without being inhibited by too much consideration or 'theorizing.'" But, by 1941, the bank was closing branches and curtailing its Chinese investment. When war broke out, of the 9 branches a decade earlier, only the Shanghai and Tientsin branches remained.[80]

In the 1920s, American construction companies made contracts with the Chinese government to develop the waterfront in Canton, to build government railways to repair the Yellow River dikes, and to establish highways.[81]

Of all the U.S. investments in China, however, the largest in Shanghai was undoubtedly that of American & Foreign Power Company, a giant multinational enterprise that operated mainly in Latin America. In 1929, it made its first major acquisition in China, buying control of power and light facilities, the largest power station in China, formerly owned by the Shanghai Municipal Council. The company purchased the plant with its franchise, which gave it a monopoly in the foreign settlement for forty years. The U.S. Consul in Shanghai estimated the acquisition would raise U.S. investment in Shanghai by about 40 percent. American & Foreign Power held control but brought in Chinese, British, and Japanese associates in financing this venture.

American & Foreign Power's Chinese investment faced difficulty because depreciating Chinese currency whittled away corporate earnings. When American & Foreign Power made the investment in 1929, a Chinese dollar equaled 42 American cents, in 1939, it equaled 6 cents. This, more than political strife, worried the investors. When the Japanese invaded China in 1937, the company experienced some physical damage and some loss of revenue. But, by 1938, the company was expanding and continued to do so until the events of December 1941 made it necessary for company personnel to leave China.[82]

AMERICAN INVESTMENTS IN CHINA

A census by the U.S. Department of the Treasury in 1943—based on 1 December 1941 data—put American direct investment (controlling interest) in enterprises in China, including Manchuria, at $40.6 million[83] (see Table 53). By that time, trading investments had been reduced to almost nothing, as had banking stakes. It proved, however, impossible to repatriate the bricks and mortar of manufacturing plants, the oil tanks and terminals, and the power facilities. After American entry into World War II, all U.S. business property in China fell under Japanese control. The State Department helped evacuate U.S. company personnel from China and Japan. Many went to the Philippines, where the companies and the State Department mistakenly believed all would be safe. Later, many were interned there.[84]

After the war, Americans returned to China. One General Electric employee recalled later that, during the war years, the Japanese improved the company's manufacturing facilities: "We found a better factory than we left," he remarked. GE found China Car and Foundry functioning well and making all kinds of metal products.[85]

During the war, General Electric in the United States made plans for the postwar expansion of its Chinese business. C. H. Minor of General Electric made the following deal with Li Ming: General Electric, Li Ming, and other Chinese were to form a company called Manufacturing Enterprises of China. GE would hold 60 percent and the Chinese 40 percent. GE's contribution was to be $20 to $40 million. This venture would develop a whole complex of manufacturing activities. The company was formed, but the postwar plans did not materialize. W. Rogers Herod, who visited China in 1948 on behalf of International General Electric, recommended selling all GE holdings. Li Ming urged him not to, as did U.S. government officials in China.

TABLE 53   Value of American Controlling Interests in
           Enterprises in China on 1 December 1941
           (in $US millions)

Type of Business	Value Investment
Manufacturing	16.8
Mining and smelting	—
Petroleum	13.4
Public utilities and transport	8.0
Agriculture	a
Trade	a
Finance	a
Miscellaneous	2.0
	40.6

Source: U.S. Department of the Treasury, *Census of American-Owned Assets in Foreign Countries,* p. 71.

Note: ^aNot available, but included in total.

Although GE did not sell, it refrained from making the pro-
jected new investment.[86] By 1948–1949, GE was worried about
getting its personnel out of China. A committee of Communists
moved into the factory in 1949, and GE feared their manager
would be held for ransom. British diplomatic channels were
apparently more effective than American in evacuating GE
personnel, but the last of GE personnel did not leave until
1951.[87]

Ford also returned to a frustrating situation after World War
II. Imports were limited and foreign-exchange restrictions were
excessive. Ford closed its Shanghai branch in 1948; all sales on
the Chinese mainland (Hong Kong excluded) stopped.[88]

Other companies underwent much the same experience.
Stanvac and Caltex reentered the market. American & Foreign
Power's U.S. management resumed control over its Shanghai
power plant after the war, but, in 1949, its substantial Chinese
investment was expropriated, with no compensation. ITT lost
its telephone factory, as well as its Shanghai telephone system.
On 29 December 1950, the Communists officially took control
of all U.S. property in China.[89]

American business investment in China had had a long history when finally such activities became unfeasible after 1949. Table 54 summarizes the size of that investment, although the figures are rough. Remer's estimates are higher than those of the U.S. Department of Commerce, because he includes investments by American residents in China. The sharp drop from 1930 to 1936 in Department of Commerce figures was due in part to changes in valuation by the Department's compilers and in part to currency depreciation; the 1936–1940 drop reflected the political situation (stimulating repatriation), but in larger measure it was caused by currency depreciation. The rise shown in the table from 1941 to 1949 was apparent rather than real, as a careful reading of the notes will demonstrate.

Looking over the growth and decline of American multinational enterprise in China, one finds the corporations to have been pragmatic. Functioning during stormy times in China, they commented in their dispatches home on "unsettled political conditions," but they seem to have been nonideological in their business decisions.

The major companies were concerned with their own enterprises, not with American trade in general. If they needed to supply China with British or Japanese goods (as in the 1905 boycott), they did not hesitate to do so. If it was more economical to supply China with East Indian oil products, then they sold East Indian oil. If it was cheaper to grow Virginia and North Carolina tobacco in China than to ship it from the United States, that was the strategy they adopted. If manufacture in China was required to hold the market, then corporate considerations prevailed over the American interest in maintaining exports. Ford did not reject the idea of an assembly plant in China in order to save American jobs; rather, the decision was based on business conditions in China. Multinational companies often chose not to manufacture in China because of the low per capita income and thus the absence of a substantial market.

American investment in China peaked in 1930. From that point on, U.S. stakes declined dramatically (see Table 54). Nevertheless, U.S. companies operated in occupied China right up to the American entry into World War II. Many businessmen

TABLE 54   Various Estimates of American Business Investments
in China
(in $US millions)

	Totals According to Different Series				
Year	*(a)*	*(b)*	*(c)*	*(d)*	*(e)*
1830	3				
1875	7				
1900	17.5	5			
1914	42.0				
1929			113.8		
1930	155.1		129.3		
1936			90.6		
1940			46.1		
1941				40.6	
1949					56

Notes: [a]C. F. Remer, *Foreign Investments in China,* pp. 259, 249, 274, 308. Includes investments of Americans resident in China.

[b]Nathaniel T. Bacon, "American International Indebtedness," *Yale Review* 9:276
(November 1900). Includes China, Japan, and the Pacific Islands and portfolio as well
as direct investments.

[c]U.S. Department of Commerce, Bureau of Foreign and Domestic Commerce,
American Direct Investments in Foreign Countries (1930), p. 26; U.S. Department of
Commerce, Bureau of Foreign and Domestic Commerce, *A New Estimate of American
Investments Abroad* (1931), p. 20; U.S. Department of Commerce, Bureau of Foreign
and Domestic Commerce, *American Direct Investments in Foreign Countries—1936,*
pp. 16-17; U.S. Department of Commerce, Bureau of Foreign and Domestic Commerce, *American Direct Investments in Foreign Countries—1940,* p. 16. Excludes investments by Americans resident in China.

[d]U.S. Department of Treasury, *Census of American Owned Assets in Foreign Countries,* pp. 69, 71. Includes American-owned interests in controlled business enterprises.
Other U.S.-owned assets in China came to, in millions of U.S. dollars, nonprofit enterprises (46.5), securities (2.9), bullion, currency, and deposits (1.1), real property
(11.0), estates and trusts (0.1), miscellaneous (20). Add this to the $40,600,000 in
controlled enterprises and the total reaches $122,200,000.

[e]Estimate of Department of State, cited in Legislative Reference Service, Library of
Congress, *Expropriation of American-Owned Property by Foreign Governments in
the Twentieth Century,* p. 16. Represents the "value of U.S. investments in China . . .
not including schools and universities, or U.S. embassy and consular property." The
properties of missionaries do *not* appear to have been excluded from this figure; the
1949 figure apparently also includes securities, bullion, currency, and deposits, real
property, and other miscellaneous stakes. It is clearly *not* comparable to the figures
presented on the table from Remer, the U.S. Department of Commerce, and the U.S.
Department of Treasury.

regarded the Sino-Japanese War as just another skirmish, comparable to past warlord activity, which would eventually subside. Although the U.S. government insisted on treaty rights, the open door, and no monopoly, American enterprises were far more flexible. They looked at the circumstances, *not* the principle.

The impacts of American multinational corporations on U.S.-Chinese economic relations were multifaceted. Clearly, such businesses acted as conduits of U.S.-Chinese trade and, in general, aided in the expansion of this commerce. But multinational corporations were not committed to the acceleration of U.S.-Chinese trade; often they participated in international rather than binational commerce. When they manufactured in China, they sometimes changed the character of the trade (from cigarettes to leaf tobacco, from end products such as lamps to lamp-making equipment). The investments of American & Foreign Power Company in China increased GE's exports of power equipment; Pan Am's investment in Chinese airlines spurred American sales of airplanes.[90]

American multinational companies also introduced U.S. capital into China, but the extent of such influx is not clear. The figures on Table 54 do not reveal the capital flows; rather they indicate the size of direct investment in a particular year and include reinvested profits as well as new monies. Although we have only inadequate records on the profits of multinational corporations, no major U.S. company seems to have faced failure after having lost its income from its Chinese investment.[91]

Certain American multinational corporations transferred U.S. technology to China. They were instrumental in developing cigarette manufacture, tobacco-growing, telephone systems, and airlines. On the other hand, the automobile companies did not manufacture in China, but continued to import. Thus, there was no transfer of American production techniques in the automobile industry. Multinational corporations may have contributed to Chinese "dependence" in the oil industries (the companies never refined in China), but certainly not in the electrical industries (U.S. multinational enterprises made substantial contributions to emerging Chinese manufacturing in electrical products). Moreover, the sewing machine, kerosene, and the motor car had modernizing influences. Other imports of multinational enterprises (from mid-nineteenth-century opium to twentieth-century tobacco) were doubtless less desirable. Perhaps the only legitimate generalization on the impacts is that the American-headquartered multinational corporations tended to bring China into America's economic orbit, even though China was but one nation among many in which these enterprises invested.

APPENDIX: Corporate Members of the American Chamber
of Commerce, Shanghai—1928

Admiral Oriental Line,
Steamship operators.
E. C. Allan,
Exchange and bullion broker.
American Asiatic Underwriters,
Fed. Inc., U.S.A.,
Insurance.
American Bank Note Co.,
Bank note makers.
American Bureau of Shipping,
Classification and record of
American and foreign shipping.
American Drug Co.,
Wholesale, retail and manufac-
turing chemists.
American Express Co., Inc.,
International banking, shipping,
travel and foreign trade.
American Foreign Insurance Assn.,
Inc.,
Fire and marine insurance.
*American Metal Co., Ltd.,
Metals.
American-Oriental Banking Corp.,
Bankers.
American-Oriental Finance Corp.,
Financing.
American Printing Co.,
Printers.
American Trading Co., Inc.,
Engineers, importers and ex-
porters, manufacturers' agents.
The Amos Bird Co., Inc.,
Exporters of egg products.
*Andersen, Meyer & Co., Ltd. (G.E.
affiliate),
Engineers and contractors, ex-
porters, importers, manufac-
turers and insurance agents.

Anderson, Clayton & Co.,
Importers of American raw
cotton.
Asia Life Insurance Co., Inc.,
Insurance.
Asia Realty Co., Fed. Inc., U.S.A.,
Real estate.
*The Ault and Wiborg China Co.,
Importers of paper, inks, print-
ing machinery and supplies,
paints and varnishes.
Belting and Leather Products Assn.,
Inc.,
Importers of leather belting and
leather products
Bill's Motors, Fed. Inc., U.S.A.,
Motor cars.
W. H. Bolton Bristle, Co.,
Sterilization and dressing of
bristle.
H. B. Campbell.,
Paint stocks and paint contract-
ing.
*China Electric Co., Ltd. (ITT sub-
sidiary)
Manufacturers of, and agents
for telephone, telegraph and
electrical equipment.
China Fibre Container Co.,
Manufacturers of fibre boxes
and toilet paper.
China Finance Corp., Fed. Inc., U.S.A.
Holding corporation.
*China General Edison Co., Inc.
(G.E. subsidiary),
Manufacturers of electrical
goods and accessories.
China Motors, Fed. Inc., U.S.A.,
Motor cars.

APPENDIX *(continued)*

The China Press, Inc.,
  Publishers of THE CHINA
  PRESS.
China Realty Co., Fed. Inc., U.S.A.,
  All pertaining to real estate.
The China Weekly Review,
  Weekly publication.
V. Clair,
  Exchange broker.
Commercial and Credit Information
  Bureau,
  Credit service.
Commercial Express and Storage
  Co.,
  Forwarding agents, warehouse-
  men, etc.
Commercial Pacific Cable Co.,
  Pacific cable.
Connell Bros. Company.
  Importers, and exporters food
  products, etc.
The Cosmos Paper Co., Fed. Inc.,
  U.S.A.,
  Importers and dealers, paper
  and printing supplies.
Carl Crow, Inc.,
  Advertising and merchandising
  agents.
R. A. Curry,
  Architect.
Davies & Bryan,
  Attorneys-at-law.
Roy E. De Lay,
  Manufacturers of telephone
  apparatus.
I. Delbourgo,
  Tobacco.
Dodge & Seymour (China) Ltd.,
  Import merchants and manu-
  facturers agents, motor cars,
  typewriters, electrical goods,
  paints.

The Robert Dollar Co.,
  Lumber, shipping and general
  merchants.
C. J. Doughty & Co., Fed. Inc.,
  U.S.A.,
  Heating and sanitary installa-
  tions.
*E. I. Du Pont de Nemours Co., Inc.,
  Importers of indigo, aniline dyes
  and chemicals.
C. K. Eagle Co., Inc.,
  Raw silk export.
*Eastman Kodak Co.,
  Kodak photographic supplies.
Eisler, Reeves & Murphy, Inc.,
  Marine and cargo surveyors and
  naval architects.
Elbrook, Inc.,
  Import, export and carpet
  manufacturers.
Engineering Equipment Co., Fed.
  Inc., U.S.A.,
  Mechanical and electrical
  engineer.
Equitable Eastern Banking Corp.,
  Banking.
L. Everett, Inc.,
  Steamship agent.
The Far Eastern Review,
  Monthly trade and engineering
  journal.
Fessenden & Holcomb,
  Attorneys-at-law.
Fleming, Franklin & Allman,
  Attorneys-at-law.
The Ford Hire Service, Inc.,
  Taxi, or hire business.
Foster-McClellan Company,
  Manufacturing chemists.
Getz Bros. & Co., Inc.,
  Importers of provisions, hard-
  ware, leather, glass, metals, etc.

APPENDIX *(continued)*

A. T. Gillespie,
  Sales brokers, food products.
H. Gulick,
  Exchange broker.
A. R. Hager,
  Business equipment.
Haskins & Sells,
  Certified public accountants.
Elliott Hazzard,
  Architect.
Heacock & Cheek Company,
  Manufacturers' representatives
  and wholesale jewellers.
H. S. Honigsberg & Co., Fed. Inc.,
  U.S.A.,
  Importers and distributors of
  motor cars.
Robert Lang, Fed. Inc., U.S.A.,
  Silks and silk machinery.
V. G. Lyman,
  Export & Import.
*Liggett & Myers Tobacco Co.,
  Tobacco products.
*McKesson & Robbins, Inc.,
  Exporters—Chinese produce.
Mark L. Moody, Fed. Inc., U.S.A.,
  Motor car distributors.
David L. Moss & Co., Inc.,
  Importers and exporters
*National Aniline & Chemical Co.,
  Inc.,
  Manufacturers and importers of
  synthetic indigo, aniline dyes
  and chemicals.
The National City Bank of New
  York,
  Banking.
Oil Export Co.,
  Importers of lubricating oil and
  kerosene.
*Oriental Alcoa Ltd.,
  Aluminum in all forms.

*The Palmolive Peet Company,
  Soaps and toilet preparations
Raven Trust Co., Fed. Inc., U.S.A.,
  Financial agents.
F. V. Reilly,
  Exchange broker.
S. T. Saunders,
  Exchange broker.
*Singer Sewing Machine Co.,
  Sewing machines.
Squires Bingham Co.,
  Sporting goods and gift shop.
*Standard Oil Co. of New York,
  Lubricating oils and petroleum
  products.
L. Suenson & Co., Ltd.,
  Architects and building con-
  tractors.
Sunland Sales Assn., Inc.,
  Agents for Sun-Maid Raisin
  Growers.
*The Texas Company,
  Petroleum products.
*Tobacco Products Corp., (China),
  Tobacco products.
Tobacco Trading Corporation,
  Leaf tobacco merchants.
C. E. Tucker,
  Exchange broker.
*U.S. Rubber Export Co., Ltd.
  (U.S. Rubber subsidiary),
  Importers of rubber goods.
*U.S. Steel Products Co. (U.S.
  Steel subsidiary),
  Products of American steel
  manufacturers.
U.S. Testing Co., Inc.,
  Operating the Shanghai Testing
  House for conditioning silk.
Universal Hire Service, Fed. Inc.,
  U.S.A.,
  Car hire and light hauling.

APPENDIX *(continued)*

Universal Leaf Tobacco Co. of
   China, Inc.,
      Leaf tobacco.
Upson Paint Co., Inc.,
      Decorators, furnishers and
      builders.
*Vacuum Oil Co., Inc.,
      Petroleum products.
Viloudaki & Company,
      Merchants and commission
      agents, public inspectors of
      silk goods.

C. M. Wentworth,
      Exchange broker.
West Coast Life Insurance Co.,
      Life insurance.
*Westinghouse Electric International
   Co.,
      Electrical apparatus for every
      purpose.
York Shipley Incorporated,
      Ice making and refrigerating
      machinery.

Source: American Chamber of Commerce Bulletin, May 1928, 17–18.

Note that the word "Fed" in the name indicates that this was a China Trade Corporation.

*Companies are affiliates or subsidiaries of large U.S. industrial enterprises.

This list does not include Ford, General Motors, Borden, or Shanghai Power (American & Foreign Power), all of which made direct investments in China after it was prepared.

Notes
Bibliography
Glossary
Index

Introduction. Patterns and Problems, by John K. Fairbank

1. For the most recent and authoritative survey of early Sino-American relations, see Michael H. Hunt, *The Making of a Special Relationship: The United States and China to 1914*, especially Chapter 1, "The Rise of the Open Door Constituency 1784–1860" and Chapter 5, "American Policy and Private Interests, 1860–1899." See also his "Bibliographical essays."

2. This thesis is presented in *The Cambridge History of China*, Vol. XIII, *Republican China 1912-1949, Part 2*, ed. J. K. Fairbank and Albert Feuerwerker, Chapter 1 and passim.

Chapter 1. Chinese Teas to America—A Synopsis,
by Yen-p'ing Hao

1. On the early history of tea and of tea drinking in America, see Saeki Tomi, "Cha to rekishi," *Shih-yuan*, p. 5; Peter Kalm, *The America of 1750*, I, 195; William I. Kaufman, *The Tea Cookbook*, p. 89; Rodris Roth, *Tea Drinking in 18th Century America: Its Etiquette and Equipage*, pp. 63, 68; John Paul Brown, *Early American Beverages*, pp. 77–90, 102-103; Margaret Reid, "Tea," pp. 128-129.

2. Samuel Eliot Morison, *The Maritime History of Massachusetts, 1783–1860*, p. 44.
3. Foster R. Dulles, *The Old China Trade*, p. 4; Timothy Pitkin, *A Statistical View of the Commerce of the United States of America*, p. 245; Morison, p. 47.
4. Pitkin, pp. 246–249.
5. Hosea Ballou Morse, *The International Relations of the Chinese Empire*, Vol. I, *The Period of Conflict, 1834–1860*, p. 58; Kenneth Scott Latourette, *The History of Early Relations between the United States and China, 1784–1844*, p. 29.
6. Pitkin, p. 209.
7. Pitkin, p. 301; U.S. Senate *Executive Documents 35*, 37th Congress, 3rd Session, p. 10. Throughout this paper, the sign "$" refers to U.S. dollars when the American statistics are under discussion, and refers to Spanish or Mexican silver dollars when the Chinese end of the trade is mentioned.
8. For a general discussion of tea in China's Western relations, see Yen-p'ing Hao and Erh-min Wang, "Changing Chinese Views of Western Relations, 1840–1895," pp. 142–201; Ch'i Ssu-ho et al., eds., *Ya-p'ien chan-cheng*, II, 144.
9. Morse, *Conflict*, pp. 360–361.
10. Tyler Dennett, *Americans in East Asia*, p. 180.
11. F.W. Taussig, *Tariff History of the United States*, p. 156; I. Smith Homans, Jr., comp., *A Historical and Statistical Account of the Foreign Commerce of the United States*, pp. 181ff.
12. Albert Feuerwerker, *The Chinese Economy, 1870–1911*, p. 51; Hosea Ballou Morse, *The International Relations of the Chinese Empire*, Vol. II, *The Period of Submission, 1861–1893*, pp. 403–405.
13. Dennett, pp. 70–71.
14. Pitkin, p. 251; Latourette, p. 76.
15. Dennett, p. 57.
16. Augustine Heard, Jr., "Old China and New," Box GQ-2, Heard Collection, Baker Library, Harvard University.
17. Robert Fortune, *Three Years' Wanderings in the Northern Provinces of China*, pp. 212–213.
18. Yen-p'ing Hao, *The Comprador in Nineteenth Century China: Bridge between East and West*, pp. 77–81; John Williams (Foochow) to Jardine, Matheson & Co. (Hong Kong), 30 July 1854, Jardine, Matheson & Co. Archives, Cambridge University Library; George V.W. Fisher (Foochow) to Jardine, Matheson & Co. (Hong Kong), 7 December 1855, ibid.
19. Jared Sparks, *The Life of John Ledyard*, pp. 175ff; J.B. Felt, *Annals of Salem*, II, 285, 291; Dennett, pp. 36, 41.
20. Charles C. Stelle, "American Trade in Opium to China, 1821–39," pp. 62, 68; *Chinese Repository* 6:284–286; Dennett, pp. 210–211.

For opium smoking in China during the nineteenth century, see Jonathan Spence, "Opium Smoking in Ch'ing China," pp. 143–173.

21. Morse, *Conflict*, p. 84.
22. See U.S. Department of the Treasury, Bureau of Statistics, *Monthly Summary of Commerce and Finance* (January 1898), pp. 1044–1045, 1618; (June 1901), p. 1042ff. Calculations are mine.
23. James B. Connolly, *Canton Captain*, p. 186.
24. A. J. Sargent, *Anglo-Chinese Commerce and Diplomacy in the Nineteenth Century*, p. 56; Pitkin, p. 303.
25. David Jardine (Canton) to Donald Matheson (Hong Kong), 19 December 1844, Jardine Archives.
26. John Heard, III, (Boston) to Augustine Heard, Jr. (Hong Kong), 12 December 1858, Box EM-7, Heard Collection; Cases 7, 8, 21, Heard Collection; U.S. Department of the Treasury, Bureau of Statistics, *Monthly Summary* (January 1898), pp. 1044–1045.
27. Box EA-1, Heard Collection; Robert Fortune remarked on the tea purchase in Chekiang in the late 1840s: "It sometimes happens that a [Chinese] merchant makes a contract with some of the tea growers before the season commences, in which case the price is arranged in the usual way, and generally a part paid in advance. This, I understand, is frequently the case at Canton when a foreign resident wishes to secure any particular kind of tea." Fortune, *Wanderings*, p. 213; H. G. Bridges (Hankow) to William Dixwell (Shanghai), 15 October 1863, Box HM-23, Heard Collection.
28. Latourette, p. 77.
29. Amasa Delano, *Narrative of Voyages and Travels in the Northern and Southern Hemispheres*, pp. 21–25; Carl C. Cutler, *Greyhounds of the Sea: The Story of the American Clipper Ship*, pp. 43–44.
30. Dennett, p. 10; Alice Morse Earle, *Customs and Fashions in Old New England*, p. 180.
31. M. Daly (Foochow) to A. F. Heard, 7 April 1863, Box HM-25, Heard Collection; Augustine Heard, Jr., "Old China and New," pp. 18–19.
32. Dennett, pp. 56–57; Cutler, p. 169.
33. Samuel Shaw, *The Journals of Major Samuel Shaw*, p. 135; Dennett, p. 11.
34. Cutler, p. 169; Kaufman, p. 23; *Shang-hai ch'ien-chuang shih-liao*, p. 29.
35. Robert B. Forbes, *Personal Reminiscences*, pp. 139–140; William C. Hunter, *The "Fan Kwae" at Canton before Treaty Days, 1825–1844*, pp. 156–157; John Heard, III, "Diary," p. 21, Box FP-4, Heard Collection; Samuel Russell to Augustine Heard, 31 March 1837, Box BM-9, Heard Collection; *Shen pao* (3 July 1875), p. 1; John Heard, III, "Diary," pp. 71, 123.
36. Morse, *Conflict*, p. 86; Hsu Jun, *Hsu Yü-chai tzu-hsu nien-p'u*, pp. 2b, 5b, 34.

37. Henrietta M. Larson, "A China Trader Turns Investor: A Biographical Chapter in American Business History," pp. 346-358.
38. For the life of John M. Forbes, see his *Reminiscences of John Murray Forbes.* For the development of the railroad enterprise, see Thomas C. Cochran, *Railroad Leaders, 1845-1890: The Business Mind in Action;* Arthur M. Johnson and Barry E. Supple, *Boston Capitalists and Western Railroads: A Study in the Nineteenth-Century Railroad Investment Process.*
39. Dennett, p. 12.
40. Hsu Jun later served as a deputy manager of the company. For a general discussion of the steamship companies in China, see Kwang-Ching Liu, *Anglo-American Steamship Rivalry in China, 1862-1874,* passim; Yen-p'ing Hao, *Comprador,* Chapter 6.

Chapter 2. The Boom Years of the Fukien Tea Trade, 1842-1888, by Robert P. Gardella

ABBREVIATIONS

HC I   Heard Collection I (Personal Records and Correspondence) in the Archives of Baker Library, Harvard University Graduate School of Business Administration.

HC II   Heard Collection II (Business Records of Augustine Heard and Company) in the Archives of Baker Library, Harvard University Graduate School of Business Administration, filed and catalogued separately from Heard Collection I.

PP   Great Britain, Parliament, *Sessional Papers, House of Commons* (also: *Parliamentary Papers, House of Commons*).

SKYS   P'eng Tse-i, comp., *Chung-kuo chin-tai shou-kung-yeh shih tzu-liao, 1840-1949* (Peking, 1957), 4 vols.

TEA   China, Imperial Maritime Customs, *Tea, 1888,* 2-Special Series no. 11 (Shanghai, 1889).

USAM   United States Department of State, *Dispatches from U.S. Consuls in Amoy, 1844-1906,* Vols. I-XV.

USFU   United States Department of State, *Dispatches from U.S. Consuls in Foochow, 1849-1906,* Vols. I-X.

1. See Jean Chesneaux, Marianne Bastid, and Marie-Claire Bergère, *China from the Opium Wars to the 1911 Revolution,* tr. Anne Destenay, pp. 326-327. Since this paper was written, several works have appeared that offer fresh and conflicting assessments of the late Ch'ing economy and its involvement in foreign trade. See in particular Ramon H. Myers, *The Chinese Economy: Past and Present;* Rhoads Murphey, *The Outsiders: The Western Experience in India and China;* Francis V. Moulder, *Japan, China and the Modern World Economy;* Lillian M. Li, *China's Silk Trade: Traditional Industry in the Modern World, 1842-1937;* Robert Marks, *Rural Revolution in South China:*

Peasants and the Making of History in Haifeng County, 1570–1930; Philip C. C. Huang, *The Peasant Economy and Social Change in North China.*

2. This paper is based upon my dissertation research begun in Taiwan and Hong Kong in 1971–1972. See "Fukien's Tea Industry and Trade in Ch'ing and Republican China: The Developmental Consequences of a Traditional Commodity Export." A portion of this material appears in my "Reform and the Tea Industry in Late Ch'ing China: The Fukien Case," pp. 71–79. A number of recent publications by Chinese scholars which I have consulted in revising my work for future publication as a monograph are: Li Kuo-ch'i, *Chung-kuo hsien-tai-hua ti ch'ü-yü yen-chiu: Min-Che-T'ai ti-ch'ü, 1860–1916;* Lin Man-hung, "Ch'a, t'ang, chang-nao yeh yü wan-Ch'ing T'ai-wan ching-chi she-hui chih pien-ch'ien 1860–1895"; Ch'en Tzu-yu, "Chin-tai li-ming ch'i Fu-chien ch'a chih sheng-ch'an yü mao-i kuo-tsao."

3. Rev. George Smith, *A Narrative of an Exploratory Visit to Each of the Consular Cities of China,* p. 360, is the source of the population estimate; gentry opposition to foreigners is mentioned in John K. Fairbank, *Trade and Diplomacy on the China Coast: The Opening of the Treaty Ports, 1842–1854,* p. 292.

4. Fairbank, pp. 102, 291–293.

5. Ibid., pp. 288, 301–308.

6. See Yeh-chien Wang, *Land Taxation in Imperial China, 1750–1911,* pp. 114–115.

7. Fairbank, p. 292.

8. Lü Ch'üan-sun, "Min-sheng cheng-shou yun-hsiao ch'a-shui shu."

9. Ibid., p. 1957.

10. See Fairbank, p. 394, and Yen-p'ing Hao, *Comprador,* p. 76.

11. See Fairbank, pp. 394–397; Augustine Heard, Jr., "Old China and New," p. 30 in HC I, GQ-2.

12. Robert B. Forbes, *Personal Reminiscences,* pp. 359–360.

13. Eldon Griffin, *Clippers and Consuls, American Consular and Commercial Relations with Eastern Asia, 1845–1860,* p. 296.

14. Robert Fortune, *A Residence among the Chinese,* pp. 221–223.

15. USFU, Vol. I, Jones to Marcy, no. 11, 21 May 1855.

16. See G. C. Allen and Audrey G. Donnithorne, *Western Enterprise in Far Eastern Economic Development, China and Japan,* pp. 52–55.

17. Stephen C. Lockwood, *Augustine Heard and Company, 1858–1862: American Merchants in China,* p. 6. On Jardine's activities, see Edward Le Fevour, *Western Enterprise in Late Ch'ing China: A Selective Survey of Jardine, Matheson and Company's Operations, 1842–1895.*

18. See Stephen Lockwood, pp. 39–49; Hao, *Comprador,* pp. 75–83, and Sheila Marriner, *Rathbones of Liverpool 1845–73,* pp. 96–98.

19. Heard, "Old China and New," pp. 30–31; Marriner, pp. 96, 98.

20. See Gardella, "Fukien's Tea Industry," Chapter 3.

21. Diary of William Comstock Jr. at Foochow, HC II, Vol. CCLXI, 21 March 1856.

22. Stephen Lockwood, p. 46.
23. Hao, *Comprador,* p. 81; Le Fevour, p. 150.
24. Stephen Lockwood, p. 44.
25. Hao, *Comprador,* pp. 80 and 84.
26. M. Daly (Foochow) to A. F. Heard, HC I, HM-27, 21 March 1866.
27. Stephen Lockwood, pp. 45-46, 113.
28. Ibid., p. 47; and M. Daly (Foochow) to A. F. Heard, HC I, HM-27, 13 February 1863.
29. Heard, "Old China and New," p. 38; also quoted in Hao, *Comprador,* p. 78.
30. Stephen Lockwood, pp. 12-13. See also U.S. Department of State, *Commercial Relations of the U.S.,* no. 1, October 1880, "The Tea Trade of Foochow for 1880," report by Consul DeLano, p. 80; Andrew Shewan, *The Great Days of Sail: Some Reminiscences of a Tea-clipper Captain,* p. 127.
31. HC II, Vol. CCLXXIV contains the tea-tasting book of John Rubb, employed at Foochow during 1861-1862; this is a ledger that lists Congous and Oolongs according to type, quality, and quantity. On tea buying, see Stephen Lockwood, pp. 14-15; and USFU, Vol. IV, no. 123, DeLano to Cadwalader, 28 October 1874.
32. See Stephen Lockwood, p. 33.
33. Ibid., pp. 104-105, 113.
34. David R. MacGregor, *The Tea Clippers: An Account of the China Tea Trade and of Some of the British Sailing Ships Engaged in it from 1849 to 1869,* p. 8; and Alfred Basil Lubbock, *The China Clippers,* p. 188.
35. See Arthur H. Clark, *The Clipper Ship Era: An Epitome of Famous American and British Clipper Ships, Their Owners, Builders, Commanders, and Crews, 1843-1869,* pp. 50, 196-197; Edgar L. Bloomster, *Sailing and Small Craft down the Ages,* pp. 193-194.
36. Shewan, pp. 127-128.
37. MacGregor, *Tea Clippers,* pp. 14-17; and George F. Campbell, *China Tea Clippers,* p. 19.
38. Bloomster, p. 194.
39. David R. MacGregor, *The China Bird: The History of Captain Killick and One Hundred Years of Sail and Steam,* p. 97, quoting letter 10585, Jardine Matheson Archives, 8 October 1869, B6/10/10585.
40. John R. Hanson, II, "The 19th Century Exports of the Less Developed Countries," p. 180; and C. H. Denyer, "Consumption of Tea and Other Staple Drinks in Great Britain," pp. 34-35 and graph, appendix iv.
41. Geoffrey Blainey, *The Tyranny of Distance: How Distance Shaped Australia's History,* p. 202.
42. PP, 1882, LXXII, 18, and T. R. Bannister, "A History of the External Trade of China, 1843-81," p. 142, note 52.

43. Other, less conservative estimates of Foochow tea exports exist for the 1870–1882 period; see PP, 1882, LXXII, 18.
44. USAM, Vol. VII, no. 50, Henderson to Cadwalader, 10 October 1874. Other estimates of Amoy tea exports are available for the 1872–1881 period; see Bannister. Since most of Taiwan's tea was reexported via Amoy, it is difficult to arrive at figures that discount the amount reexported.
45. Taiwan Tea Exporters' Association, *The Historical Brevities of Taiwan Tea Export, 1865–1965,* table facing p. 58; James W. Davidson, *The Island of Formosa, Past and Present,* p. 395.
46. Chou Hsien-wen, *Ch'ing-tai T'ai-wan ching-chi shih,* p. 55.
47. Davidson, p. 373.
48. John Dodd, "Formosa," *The Scottish Geographical Magazine* 11:569 (November 1895).
49. SKYS, II, 108–109 and also Nakanishi Ushiro, *Rikō shōten,* p. 21.
50. Ushiro Nakanishi, *Rikō shōden,* p. 21.
51. Davidson, p. 374; William H. Ukers, *All about Tea,* pp. 232–233.
52. John Dodd, *Journal of a Blockaded Resident in North Formosa during the Franco-Chinese War, 1884–5,* pp. 151–155.
53. Davidson, p. 376.
54. China, Imperial Maritime Customs, *Reports on Trade, 1876,* p. 89.
55. See PP, 1870, LXIV, 654–655, and Francis E. Hyde, *Far Eastern Trade, 1860–1914,* pp. 61–63. On the establishment of the Hongkong and Shanghai Bank, see Maurice Collis, *Wayfoong: The Hongkong and Shanghai Banking Corporation,* pp. 21–35.
56. SKYS, II, 107–108; Chou Hsien-wen, p. 88.
57. SKYS, II, 108; Taiwan Tea Exporters' Association, pp. 49–50 (English text).
58. See Lien-sheng Yang, *Money and Credit in China: A Short History,* p. 83.
59. Davidson, pp. 382–383; Taiwan Tea Exporters' Association, p. 45 (English text).
60. See Taiwan Tea Exporters' Association, p. 45; also Laurent Li-liang Lieou, "Notes sur l'Economie du Thé en Chine."
61. See Nanshi chōsa shiryō, *Fukkenshō no chagyō,* p. 56; "Fukkenshō chagyō no kenkyū," p. 222.
62. Sun Yü-t'ang, *Chung-Jih chia-wu chan-cheng ch'ien wai-kuo tzu-pen tsai Chung-kuo ching-ying ti chin-tai kung-yeh,* pp. 17–18.
63. Andrew Malozemoff, *Russian Far Eastern Policy, 1881–1904, with Special Emphasis on the Causes of the Russo-Japanese War,* p. 7.
64. Sun Yü-t'ang, *Chung-Jih,* pp. 18–19; Allen and Donnithorne, p. 59.
65. Malozemoff, p. 7.
66. Lü Wei-ying, "Min-sheng ch'a-yeh mu-chih ch'ing-hsing," p. 16a.
67. Sun Yü-t'ang, comp., *Chung-kuo chin-tai kung-yeh shih tzu-liao, ti-i chi, 1840–1895,* I, 58, quoting Maritime Customs trade report of 1875, II, 189–199, and also PP, 1880, LXXV, 522.

68. Lü Wei-ying, p. 16a.
69. Sun Yü-t'ang, *Chung-Jih,* pp. 20, 85–86.
70. See Ellsworth C. Carlson, *The Foochow Missionaries, 1847–1880,* pp. 94–95, 104, 115–128.
71. USFU, Vol. V, no. 154, DeLano to Cadwalader, 30 March 1876, quoting an article in the *Foochow Herald* (30 March 1876) entitled "Our Treaty Rights—What are they?"
72. See ibid., Vol. V, no. 154, enclosure no. 19, DeLano to Seward (U.S. Minister to Peking), 26 January 1880.
73. On the issue of sovereignty, see Saundra Sturdevant, "Imperialism, Sovereignty, and Self-Strengthening: A Reassessment of the 1870's."
74. See Bannister, p. 125; Allen and Donnithorne, pp. 58–60.
75. Sun Yü-t'ang, *Kung-yeh shih,* I, 60–61, quoting the 4 October and 13 December 1881 issues of the *North China Herald.*
76. See Sun Yü-t'ang, *Chung-Jih,* pp. 70, 85–86; also Chi-ming Hou, *Foreign Investment and Economic Development in China, 1840–1937,* pp. 79–80.
77. Boris P. Torgashev, *China as a Tea Producer,* p. 31.
78. USFU, no. 10, Dunn to Cass, 30 June 1859; Griffin, p. 297.
79. Ramon Myers, "Taiwan under Ch'ing Imperial Rule, 1684–1895: The Traditional Economy," p. 377.
80. William M. Speidel, "The Administrative and Fiscal Reforms of Liu Ming-ch'uan in Taiwan, 1884–1891: Foundation for Self-Strengthening," pp. 453–454, note 63.
81. Edgar B. Wickberg, "Late Nineteenth Century Land Tenure in North Taiwan," pp. 83–84.
82. Ibid., p. 82.
83. C. Imbault-Huart, *L'Isle Formosa: Histoire et Description,* pp. 207, 230–231.
84. Davidson, p. 379.
85. Pien Pao-ti, *Pien chih-chün cheng-shu,* chüan 3:2b–3a and 4:1a–3a.
86. Chiang Heng, "Chin-k'ai ch'a-shan i," pp. 304–305, 430–431.
87. TEA, pp. 96, 103 (Chinese text).
88. Rev. Justus Doolittle, *Social Life of the Chinese,* I, 46.
89. TEA, pp. 139–140, 163 (English text).
90. Lo Ju-tse, re-comp., *Hsia-p'u-hsien chih,* chüan 18, 6b; *Fu-an-hsien chih.*
91. USAM, Vol. VII, no. 50, Henderson to Cadwalader, 10 October 1874.
92. Ibid., Vol. VI, no. 23, Henderson to Davis, 2 April 1874.
93. Chiang Heng, pp. 21–22.
94. Maeda Katsutaro, "Min Shin no Fukken ni okeru nōka fukugyō," p. 584, quoting *Min shang shih hsi-kuan tiao-ch'a pao-kao lu.*
95. TEA, pp. 142, 161 (English text); and John Thomson, *Through China with a Camera,* pp. 149–150.
96. Wickberg, pp. 82, 85.
97. Ibid., pp. 83–84.

98. SKYS, II, 109, quoting an article in *Nung-hsueh pao,* no. 22 (February-March 1898).

99. On the *ta-tsu,* see Wickberg, pp. 80–81, and 90, note 7.

100. See T'ai-wan yin-hang ching-chi yen-chiu shih, comp., *T'ai-wan ssu-fa wu-ch'üan pien,* VI, 1059–1062 (documents 5-1, 5-2, 5-3), 1069–1073 (documents 12–15), 1076–1078 (document 18), and 1086 (document 19).

101. TEA, pp. 95, 99, 110.

102. China, Imperial Maritime Customs, *Reports on Trade,* 1875, p. 197.

103. Myers, "Taiwan," p. 378.

104. SKYS, II, 109–110, quoting *Nung-hsueh pao,* no. 22.

105. Fu I-Ling, *Ming-Ch'ing nung-ts'un she-hui ching-chi,* p. 158, note 2, quoting *Nan-p'ing-hsien chih,* chüan 10, *shih-yeh-chih.* On the "shack people," see Evelyn S. Rawski, "Agricultural Development in the Han River Highlands."

106. TEA, p. 95 (Chinese text).

107. Chan Hsuan-yu, re-comp., *Chien-ou hsien chih,* chüan 25, p. 3a.

108. See Chung-kuo jen-min ta-hsueh Chung-kuo li-shih chiao-yen-shih, comp., *Ming-Ch'ing she-hui ching-chi hsing-t'ai ti yen-chiu,* p. 301, quoting Lu Ch'i-kuang, *Nan-feng feng-su wu-ch'an chih;* H. Stübel, "Der Wu-i schan"; Lin Fu-ch'üan, comp., *Wu-lung ch'a chi pao-chung ch'a chih-tsao hsueh,* p. 181.

109. TEA, p. 112 (Chinese text).

110. See Chou Hsien-wen, pp. 55–56; Nakanishi, p. 21; Davidson, p. 379.

111. Wolfram Eberhard, *Taiwanese Ballads: A Catalogue,* p. 26.

112. Davidson, pp. 379, 385.

113. See "Regulations of the Canton Guild at Foochow," in Rev. Justus Doolittle, *A Vocabulary and Hand-book of the Chinese Language Romanized in the Mandarin Dialect,* II, 399–402.

114. Tseng Nai-shuo, "Ch'ing-chi Ta-tao-ch'eng chih ch'a-yeh," pp. 101–102.

115. Davidson, p. 385.

116. See Justus Doolittle, *Social Life of the Chinese,* I, 49, and Artemas Ward, *The Encyclopedia of Food,* pp. 517–518, quoting an undated article from the *Foochow Herald* describing the operation of tea-packing firms.

117. See "Terms Concerning Tea and the Tea Business" in Doolittle, *Vocabulary,* II, 632–633.

118. H. Parkes, "An Account of the Paper Currency and Banking System of Fuhchowfoo."

119. See Wang Hsiao-ch'üan, comp., *Fu-chien ts'ai-cheng shih kang,* II, 394–395; "The Dai Fook Dollar of Foochow"; "Native Banks in Foochow."

120. See "Dai Fook Dollar," pp. 132–133; An Ch'un, "Wu-i ch'a ti kuo-ch'ü ho hsien-tsai."

121. T'ai-wan yin-hang ching-chi yen-chiu shih, *Fu-chien sheng-li,* IV,

pp. 584–587, quoting a communication of Governor-General Wang I-te and Governor Ch'ing Tuan dated 23 October 1857.

122. This phenomenon receives more extensive discussion in Yen-p'ing Hao, "Commercial Capitalism along the China Coast during the Late Ch'ing Period," pp. 303–327. The reader may question the omission of a discussion of the opium imports which also paid for tea exports in the early stages of direct trade, and whose impact on Fukien's population was hardly beneficial. Yet specie was far more important as a means of financing tea exports than opium, and the opium trade was a separate commerce in itself after the end of the upcountry purchase system. Little opium was thereafter bartered for tea (see PP, 1870, LXIV, 640). In any case, by the last quarter of the nineteenth century, domestic opium was rapidly ousting foreign imports; see Spence, pp. 152–153. The same cannot be said for Taiwan, however. Opium importation there continued to be important up to 1895, and peasants often bartered tea for the drug. Local opium consumption reportedly exceeded that on the mainland. See Lin Man-hung, pp. 166–167.

123. See Mary C. Wright, *The Last Stand of Chinese Conservatism: The T'ung-chih Restoration, 1862–1874,* pp. 149, 178–179.

124. See Yeh-chien Wang, *Land Taxation,* pp. 12, 80–81.

125. For examples of this shift, see Spence, pp. 170–172, which notes Ch'ing reliance on opium likin during the late nineteenth century; and Britten Dean, *China and Great Britain: The Diplomacy of Commercial Relations, 1860–1864,* which describes the Sino-British disputes over likin and export duties in the Yangtze Valley.

126. Lo Yü-tung, *Chung-kuo li-chin shih,* I, 322. On the origin of the likin tax, see Edwin George Beal, Jr., *The Origin of Likin, 1853–1854.*

127. Lo Yü-tung, I, 325.

128. Ibid.

129. Ibid., and also Ching-chi hsueh-hui, comp., *Fu-chien ch'üan-sheng ts'ai-cheng shuo-ming-shu, ch'a-shui,* p. 4.

130. See TEA, p. 133 (English text).

131. See a memorial discussing this problem by Foochow Tartar General Yu-feng dated 29 June 1856, in Kuo T'ing-i, comp., *Tao-kuang Hsien-feng liang-ch'ao ch'ou-pan i-wu shih-mou pu-i,* pp. 385–387.

132. Lo Yü-tung, I, 326.

133. Ibid. See also Ching-chi hsueh-hui, *ch'a-shui,* p. 10.

134. China, Imperial Maritime Customs, *Reports on Trade,* 1864, p. 61.

135. Tso Tsung-t'ang, *Tso wen-hsiang kung ch'üan-chi,* Vol. III, chüan 19, 61a.

136. See Chou Hsien-wen, pp. 109–110; Lo Yü-tung, I, 338; Speidel, p. 456.

137. TEA, pp. 99–100 (English text).

138. See Hsiao Liang-lin, *China's Foreign Trade Statistics, 1864–1949,* p. 132, Table 5.

139. Lo Yü-tung, I, 332. Lo notes that the *ching-hsiang* levy was larger for Fukien than for other provinces because of the magnitude of Fukien's tea taxation.

140. Ibid., I, 334; II, 575–576, Table 87.
141. Ibid., I, 337; II, 575–576, Table 87.
142. See Kobayashi Kazumi, "Chūgoku han-shokuminchika no keizai katei to minshū no tatakai—rikin o megutte, jūkyūseiki kōhan." This article is summarized in K. H. Kim, *Japanese Perspectives on China's Early Modernization*, pp. 95–96.
143. See Philip Kuhn, *Rebellion and its Enemies in Late Imperial China: Militarization and the Social Structure, 1796–1864;* also Jean Chesneaux, *The Chinese Labor Movement, 1919–1927,* tr. H. M. Wright, pp. 142–143.
144. Chu Wen-djang, *The Moslem Rebellion in Northwest China, 1862–1878,* pp. 112–113.
145. John L. Rawlinson, *China's Struggle for Naval Development, 1839–1895,* pp. 53, 99–102.
146. See Yeh-chien Wang, *An Estimate of the Land-tax Collection in China, 1753 and 1908,* Tables 13, 27.
147. Taiwan Tea Exporters' Association, p. 3 (Chinese text); and T'ai-wan yin-hang, *T'ai-wan ssu-fa,* VI, 1056–1057, document dated 20 October 1876.
148. E. H. Parker, "A Journey from Foochow to Wenchow through Central Fukien."
149. "Proclamation Relating to the Tea Business at Foochow," in Doolittle, *Vocabulary,* II, 437–438.
150. See United States Department of State, *Commercial Relations,* no. 136, Wingate to Dept. of State, 16 September 1885, and also PP, 1874, LXVIII, 41.
151. Sir Percival Griffiths, *The History of the Indian Tea Industry,* pp. 35–82.
152. Ibid., pp. 35–37, 41; see also Sir George Watt, *The Commercial Products of India,* pp. 213–214.
153. See F. Hung, "La Geographie du Thé," pp. 109–110; Stanley Szu-yee Tsou, "The World Tea Industry and China," p. 57.
154. Griffiths, p. 120.
155. Ibid., pp. 487–504; also H. A. Antrobus, *A History of the Assam Company, 1839–1953,* pp. 289–304.
156. Donald R. Snodgrass, *Ceylon: An Export Economy in Transition,* pp. 32–35, 37.
157. See Edward Money, *The Cultivation and Manufacture of Tea,* pp. 174–175; also Samuel Philips Day, *Tea: Its Mystery and History,* p. xiv.
158. TEA, pp. 98–99, 120 (English text).
159. Griffiths, p. 579; Money, p. 207.
160. TEA, p. 2 (English text).
161. Ibid., pp. 2–5.
162. Ibid., p. 5.
163. Hsueh Fu-ch'eng, "Ch'ou-yang ch'u-i," II, 11b; see also Chesneaux, pp. 245–246.
164. On the proponents of commercial reform in late Ch'ing China, see Yen-p'ing Hao and Erh-min Wang, "Changing Chinese Views of Western

Relations, 1840–85," pp. 171–172, 190–194; Paul A. Cohen, "Littoral and Hinterland in Nineteenth Century China: The 'Christian' Reformers," pp. 197–225; Chao Feng-t'ien, *Wan-Ch'ing wu-shih nien ching-chi ssu-hsiang shih.*

165. See Liu Kuang-ching, "Cheng Kuan-yin *I-yen:* Kuang-hsu ch'u-nien chih pien-fa ssu-hsiang"; Yen-p'ing Hao, "Cheng Kuan-ying: The Comprador as Reformer."

166. See Ma Chien-chung, "Fu-min shuo," pp. 1–4; also Hayashi Yōzō, "Ba Ken-chū no keizai shisō: 'fumin' shisō no seiritsu oyobi sono yakuwari," *Tezukayama daigaku kiyo,* 2:191–219 (1966), summarized in Kim, pp. 80–81.

167. China, Imperial Maritime Customs, *Decennial Reports,* 1892–1901, II, 99.

168. Ibid., pp. 124–125; Torgashev, pp. 35–36; Remer, *Foreign Trade of China,* p. 142.

169. TEA, pp. 95, 99, 110 (Chinese text).

170. Ibid., p. 106 (Chinese text).

171. There were 183,695 tea-growing households in Fukien in 1915, according to the earliest government survey; by 1939, the number had fallen to about 106,000. See Hu Hao-ch'uan and Wu Chueh-nung, *Chung-kuo ch'a-yeh fu-hsing chi-hua,* p. 30; T'ang Yung-chi and Wei Te-tuan, *Fu-chien chih ch'a,* II, 200. On the decline in tea production, see Dwight Perkins, *Agricultural Development in China, 1368–1968,* p. 285, Table D.28.

172. See O. E. Nepomnin, *Genezis kapitalizma v sel'skom khoziastve Kitaia,* pp. 55–62; also Chesneaux, pp. 218, 326. I am indebted to Professor Gilbert Rozman of Princeton University for a summation of Nepomnin's work.

Chapter 3. The Silk Export Trade and Economic Modernization in China and Japan, by Lillian M. Li

The Chinese side of this chapter is based on material from my book, *China's Silk Trade: Traditional Industry in the Modern World, 1842–1937.* I am grateful to Cheng-lung Ch'en for research assistance on the Japanese side of this project in the initial stages, and to Kazuko Yoshida for assistance in the final stages. Ms. Yoshida, a graduate student in the Department of International Relations at Tokyo University, has published her undergraduate thesis on the Japanese silk industry (see note 55 below). I am grateful also to Professor Richard J. Smethurst, Department of History, University of Pittsburgh, for his comments on this paper. Swarthmore College and the Fairbank Center for East Asian Research at Harvard University have given me generous institutional support over the years. This chapter has appeared in somewhat altered form under the title "Silks by Sea: Trade, Technology, and Enterprise in China and Japan," *Business History Review* 56.2:192–217 (Summer 1982).

1. Silk Association of America, *Annual Report,* 1919, p. 706.
2. Silk Association of America, *Annual Report,* 1906, p. 69; 1913, p. 36; and 1914, p. 15.
3. Jesse W. Markham, *Competition in the Rayon Industry,* p. 33. In fact, during the 1920s and 1930s, the consumption of silk in the United States increased steadily, even as rayon gained great popularity. See textile consumption figures in *Sen'i kōgyō* (*Chōki keizai tōkei* Vol. XI), comp. Fujino Shōzaburō et al., pp. 144, 311. See also Table 16.
4. Tuan-liu Yang, Hou-pei Hou, et al., comps., *Statistics of China's Foreign Trade during the Last Sixty-five Years,* p. 41, and Hsiao Liang-lin, pp. 109-111. I have deducted Hsiao's "Raw Silk, Miscellaneous" from his totals for "Total Raw Silk" to make the latter consistent with Yang's and Hou's figures for the earlier period. I have converted piculs to kilograms: 1 picul = 60 kilograms.
5. G. C. Allen, *A Short Economic History of Modern Japan, 1867-1937,* p. 172. 1 kwan or kan = 3.75 kilograms.
6. Data for China from Lillian M. Li, Table 9, and Hsiao Liang-lin, pp. 24, 109-111. For Japan, see Takisawa Hideki, *Nihon shihonshugi to sanshigyō,* p. 79.
7. Based on data provided by Union des Marchands de Soie de Lyon, *Statistique de la production de la soie en France et à l'étranger,* 1880-1928, annual. Actual percentages for China and Japan may have been even higher, since this set of data compares Chinese and Japanese trade to European and other output figures.
8. C. F. Remer, an economist, observed, "Chinese raw silk is either excellent or rather poor in quality. . . . Japanese raw silk is of more uniform quality, but the best Chinese silk is said to be superior to the Japanese product." *The Foreign Trade of China,* p. 140.
9. Ishii Kanji, *Nihon sanshigyōshi bunseki,* p. 41; and Charles Joseph Huber, *The Raw Silk Industry of Japan,* p. 31.
10. China, Maritime Customs, *Reports and Returns of Trade,* annual until 1920; after 1920, *Quarterly Trade Returns.* These data are summarized in Table 15, Chapter 3 of Lillian M. Li. Data for Canton can also be found in "Canton Exports of Raw Silk and Silk Waste in 1927."
11. William W. Lockwood, *The Economic Development of Japan,* expanded ed., p. 94.
12. See, for example, Miyohei Shinohara, "Economic Development and Foreign Trade in Pre-War Japan," p. 227; and Masao Baba and Masahiro Tatemono, "Foreign Trade and Economic Growth in Japan: 1858-1937," pp. 162-182.
13. Kenzō Hemmi, "Primary Product Exports and Economic Development: The Case of Silk," p. 308.
14. This point is made by William Lockwood, pp. 370-378.
15. Lillian M. Li, Chapter 4; Shinohara, p. 226, compiled from Ministry of Agriculture and Commerce and Ministry of Finance statistics. Do-

mestic consumption of silk in Japan also expanded markedly in these years. See *Sen'i kōgyō*, p. 142.

16. A critique of the Western stimulus-Chinese response approach may be found in Paul A. Cohen, "Ch'ing China: Confrontation with the West, 1850–1900," pp. 29–61.

17. The modernization approach to modern Japanese history finds its fullest expression in a series of conference volumes put out by Princeton University Press. The introductory volume is Marius B. Jansen, ed., *Changing Japanese Attitudes Toward Modernization*. A sharp attack on the modernization approach is made by John W. Dower in his introduction to the *Origins of the Modern Japanese State: Selected Works of E. H. Norman*, pp. 3–102.

18. Ezra F. Vogel's *Japan as Number One: Lessons for America* has attracted a greal deal of attention for emphasizing the superiority of Japanese management techniques over American techniques.

19. Perhaps the most notable of the "cultural" explanations is Robert N. Bellah, *Tokugawa Religion: The Values of Pre-industrial Japan*, which in effect finds in Japanese religion and thought a counterpart to the Protestant ethic.

20. Economic historians have used the silk industry to ask theoretical questions about the origins of capitalism in Japan. Some stress the leading role of the government and big business in developing the silk trade, while others stress the importance of grass-roots initiatives. The leading proponents of the former view are Ishii Kanji (see above, n. 9), and his professor, Yamaguchi Kazuo, editor of *Nihon sangyō kin'yūshi kenkyū: seishi kin'yūhen*. The leading proponent of the latter view is Yagi Haruo. See for example his *Nihon kindai seishigyō no seiritsu—Nagano-ken Okaya seishigyōshi kenkyū*.

21. The following discussion is summarized from Chapter 1 of Lillian M. Li.

22. The Silk Association of America and the Shanghai International Testing House, comp., *A Survey of the Silk Industry of Central China*, pp. 8–9.

23. Kenzō Hemmi stresses the importance of constant technological improvement in maintaining the relative profitability of mulberry as opposed to other crops; pp. 318–321. Since the Meiji era, the yields of silk from cocoons have more than doubled in Japan.

24. Lillian M. Li, Chapter 1. In fact, the data in Ch'en Heng-li, *Pu Nung-shu yen-chiu*, strongly suggest a steady decline in yields from the late Ming to the 1950s.

25. These developments are more extensively discussed in Lillian M. Li, Chapter 4.

26. Based on figures from H. D. Fong, "China's Silk Reeling Industry," p. 491, Table V.

27. In 1925, 81% of the cocoon output of Kiangsu was sold to filatures, whereas only 18% of the Chekiang output was. See The Silk Association of America, *A Survey*, pp. 5–6, 93.

28. Suzuki Tomoo, "Shinmatsu Minsho ni okeru minzoku shihon no tenkai katei: Kanton no seishigyō ni tsuite," pp. 47–49; China, Imperial Maritime Customs, *Decenniel Reports, 1882-1891, 1892-1901,* as reproduced in Min-hsiung Shih, *The Silk Industry in Ch'ing China,* tr. E-tu Zen Sun, p. 17.
29. Leo Duran, *Raw Silk: A Practical Handbook for the Buyer,* 2nd ed., p. 147; Charles Walter Howard and K. P. Buswell, *A Survey of the Silk Industry of South China,* p. 144.
30. *Taikei Nihonshi sōsho,* comp. Yamakawa shuppansha, XI, 91, 278; also Yagi Haruo, "Seishigyō," I, 223; also Fujimoto Jitsuya, *Nihon sanshigyōshi,* I, 147-149 passim.
31. *Taikei Nihonshi sōsho,* XI, 50-51.
32. The sericultural manuals in the early Tokugawa period were largely based on Chinese works, but those of the mid-Tokugawa period were often based on Japanese technological innovations. Uchida Hoshimi, *Nihon bōshoku gijitsu no rekishi,* pp. 54–55.
33. The names used here are those of current prefectures. Traditionally, Ōshu corresponded roughly to Fukushima, Joshu to Gumma, and Shinshu to Nagano.
34. A summer crop was developed in Nagano in the 1830s; *Nihon sanshigyō taikei,* V, 186. For discussion of other Tokugawa technological advances, see Yagi, "Seishigyō," p. 240; and Uchida, pp. 57-66.
35. *Nihon sanshigyō taikei,* IV, 260-261; and Yagi, "Seishigyō," p. 227.
36. For a description in English of such activity in Saitama-ken, see William Jones Chambliss, *Chiaraijima Village: Land Tenure, Taxation, and Local Trade, 1818-1884,* pp. 17-22.
37. *Taikei Nihonshi sōsho,* XII, 60.
38. Keishi Ohara, comp., *Japanese Trade and Industry in the Meiji-Taishō Era,* pp. 229-233; and Thomas C. Smith, *Political Change and Industrial Development in Japan: Government Enterprise, 1868-1880,* pp. 58-61.
39. See for example, *Taikei Nihonshi sōsho,* XII, 226-229.
40. See below, n. 80.
41. Ohara, pp. 243-249. Yagi, "Seishigyō," p. 240, notes that the Japanese technique was yet unknown in Europe or China. In Kiangnan, rereeled silk did not become an important export item until the 1910s.
42. Ishii, pp. 57-83. His analysis of the financing of the silk industry is based on the difference between these two types of silk, which he terms Type I and Type II. See below, n. 82.
43. *Taikei Nihonshi sōsho,* XII, 399-401. Some Japanese filatures also used electric power. See *Sen'i kōgyō,* pp. 179-180.
44. Ishii, p. 88; Ohara, pp. 275-276.
45. Based on output data in *Sen'i kōgyō,* pp. 294-295, which does not include waste silk. According to *Nihon sen'i sangyōshi,* comp. Nihon sen'i kyōgikai, I, 942, only 75% of total output in 1925 was machine-reeled if waste silk is included. For export data, see *Nihon boeki*

seiran, comp. Tōyō keizai shimposha, pp. 53–55; and also *Sen'i kōgyō*, p. 308.

46. Huber, p. 42.
47. For Japan, see pp. 41–42, and map (end fold-out) in Huber, and also *Sen'i kōgyō*, p. 139. For China, see Lillian M. Li, Chapter 4. In the Republican period, wild silk, known as Tussah, from Shantung and Manchuria became extremely popular for export. The provinces of Szechwan and Hupeh also produced a substantial amount of raw silk, but mostly inferior yellow silk for the domestic market.
48. *Sen'i kōgyō*, p. 306; and William Lockwood, p. 45, for Japan in general. Data for Yamanashi prefecture are from *Yamanashi-ken tōkeisho* and have been generously shared with me by Professor Richard J. Smethurst, who is preparing a manuscript on tenancy disputes in that area. For data on the value of sericultural products in total agricultural production, see *Noringyō (Chōki keizai tōkei* Vol. XI), comp. Umemura Mataji et al., pp. 146–149. For data on mulberry acreage, see *Sen'i kōgyō*, pp. 306–307.
49. Data from Chapter 5, Table 25 of Lillian M. Li.
50. Johannes Hirschmeier, *The Origins of Entrepreneurship in Meiji Japan*, p. 95, makes this point, as do others. The continuing strength of the rural sector in the Japanese silk industry, even into the twentieth century, is at least one reason to be cautious about adopting the commonly held view that Japan had evolved a "dual economy" in the late nineteenth and early twentieth century, in which the traditional-rural sector of the economy experienced a declining rate of growth, while the modern-urban sector advanced quickly. This idea is best expressed by Kazushi Ohkawa and Henry Rosovsky, in "A Century of Japanese Economic Growth," pp. 47–92, where they characterize the period 1906–1930 as one in which a differential structure was created.
51. For example, in Gumma. *Nihon sanshigyō taikei*, IV, 277–278.
52. For example, in Yamanashi. See Nakamura Masanori, "Seishigyō no tenkai to jinushisei," pp. 46–71.
53. Allen, p. 110. On the low wages of filature employees in Yamanashi, see Arlon Tussing, "The Labor Force in Meiji Economic Growth: A Quantitative Study of Yamanashi Prefecture," pp. 70–92.
54. The Silk Association of America, *A Survey*, p. 2; Ohara, p. 276.
55. Yoshida Kazuko, "Meiji shoko no seishi gijitsu ni okeru dochaku to gairai," pp. 17–18.
56. Ishii, pp. 422ff.
57. Thomas C. Smith, "Pre-Modern Economic Growth: Japan and the West," p. 158. The shift from urban-centered marketing to town- and village-centered commerce in the cotton industry is described in William B. Hauser, *Economic Institutional Change in Tokugawa Japan: Osaka and the Kinai Cotton Trade*, Chapters 6 and 7.

58. Yagi Haruo, *Nihon keizaishi gaisetsu*, p. 217; also Yamaguchi, pp. 10–11.
59. *Nihon sanshigyō taikei,* IV, 280–283; Ohara, pp. 244–249.
60. Ibid., pp. 292–294; also, Huber, p. 17.
61. Allen and Donnithorne, p. 68.
62. The most famous silk cooperative in China is well described by Fei Hsiao-t'ung, in his *Peasant Life in China.*
63. Sanshigyō dōgyōkumiai chūōkai, comp., *Shina sanshigyō taikan,* pp. 235–236, shows that the average size of filatures in the Kiangan area was 261 basins. The ones in Canton tended to be larger.
64. The varieties of arrangements were many. This institution is discussed in Lillian M. Li, Chapter 6.
65. Ibid.
66. *Taikei Nihonshi sōsho,* XII, 56–57.
67. Suzuki Tomoo, p. 62. Also, Marianne Bastid, "Le Développement des filatures de soie modernes dans la province du Guangdong avant 1894," pp. 175–188, discusses the issue of native capital.
68. There is debate among scholars about whether the scarcity of capital invested in modern enterprises was due to an absolute scarcity, or to the unwillingness of individuals to risk investment of their wealth in new enterprises.
69. See Lillian M. Li, Chapter 5.
70. Horie Eiichi, *Keizai ni kansuru Shina kankō chōsa hōkokusho Shina sanshigyō ni okeru torihiki kankō,* pp. 129–131.
71. *Shina shōbetsu zenshi,* comp. Tōa dōbunkai, XIII, 600–601; XV, 735–736.
72. Tseng T'ung-ch'un, *Chung-kuo ssu-yeh,* pp. 96–97; and Ralph E. Buchanan, *The Shanghai Raw Silk Market,* pp. 24–28.
73. *Shina shōbetsu zenshi,* XV, 685–88.
74. Howard and Buswell, p. 121; Lillian M. Li, Chapter 6.
75. Suzuki Tomoo, p. 62.
76. Buchanan, p. 7.
77. Yueh Ssu-ping, *Chung-kuo ts'an-ssu,* pp. 110–111, 201–202.
78. See William Hauser, pp. 47–48, on the abolition of the *kabu-nakama* during the Kansei reforms; and *Taikei Nihon sōsho,* XII, 55, 240.
79. On peasants, see *Taikei,* XI, 91, and XII, 55, 240; on ex-samurai, see XII, 191–194, and Hirschmeier, pp. 93–94.
80. Yoshida, p. 19. Regional differences are also explored in Ebato Akira, *Sanshigyō chiiki no keizai chirigakuteki kenkyū.*
81. Yagi, *Nihon kindai seishigyō no seiritsu—Nagano-ken Okaya seishigyō-shi,* pp. 10–11.
82. According to Ishii Kanji's analysis, these new districts produced what he calls Type I silk, factory-reeled silk of high quality; see Ishii, p. 62.
83. Yamaguchi, pp. 8–9.
84. Ibid., pp. 25–34.
85. Ishii, pp. 373, 413.

86. Ohara, pp. 276–281.
87. Yagi, "Seishigyō," p. 233.
88. Yamaguchi, p. 10.
89. *Yokohama shishi,* IIIA, 633. Maeda Masana and Kawaze Hideharu both were active in the direct-export movement after serving in France as diplomats. Hoshino Chōtarō of Gumma and Hasegawa Hanshichi were important rural leaders.
90. Ishii, p. 64; Yagi, *Nihon keizaishi gaisetsu,* pp. 282–283; Yamaguchi, pp. 10–11.
91. Nakamura, p. 56; Ishii, pp. 424–425.
92. Allen and Donnithorne, p. 227.
93. Ohara, p. 262; Hemmi, p. 316; Yamaguchi, pp. 514–623 passim.
94. Ishii, p. 413.
95. Yagi, *Nihon keizaishi gaisetsu,* p. 260; Hemmi, p. 316.
96. Ohara, p. 263; and Hugh T. Patrick, "Japan, 1868–1914," p. 279.
97. Hemmi, p. 316, estimates, on the basis of Yamaguchi's data, that bank loans amounted to 25–30,000,000 yen in 1907, a year when sericultural production amounted to 192,000,000 yen. Patrick, p. 249, believes that government leadership in developing the banking system has been exaggerated. He prefers to stress the importance of private initiative.

Chapter 4. The Chinese-American Cotton-Textile Trade, 1830–1930, by Kang Chao

1. Based on the trade returns given by the Chinese Customs, the cumulated trade volumes of the four big trading partners are as follows (in million HKT):

	1871–1900	1901–1930
Britain	1,421	3,589
India	555	1,511
Japan	424	8,416
United States	468	4,924

See Hsiao Liang-lin, pp. 137–163.
2. Ibid., pp. 162–163.
3. This should be even clearer in the breakdown of trade statistics. For instance, the values of various commodity groups exported by the United States to China in 1860 were (in $1,000):

Cotton goods	3,897
Meats and dairy products	269
Wheat flour	302
Coal	118
Drugs and medicines	51

Ginseng	296
Iron and steel products	88
Tobacco products	98
Others	508
Total	5,627

See Shü-lun Pan, *The Trade of the United States with China,* p. 29.

4. M. T. Copeland, *The Cotton Manufacturing Industry of the United States,* p. 5.
5. Ibid.
6. W. P. Strassman, *Risk and Technological Innovation,* p. 87.
7. Copeland, p. 141. However, mills in the southern states were somewhat smaller than those in New England.
8. Ibid., p. 153.
9. National Bureau of Economic Research, *Output, Employment, and Productivity in the United States after 1800,* Studies in Income and Wealth, XXX, 231.
10. Copeland, p. 267.
11. C. F. Ware, *The Early New England Cotton Manufacture: A Study in Industrial Beginnings,* p. 190.
12. Ibid.
13. See, for example, "The Report by U.S. Vice Consul General Bailey of Shanghai on the Commerce, Navigation, and Industry of China, its Trade with the United States and Other Foreign Countries for the Year 1878," in the U.S. Government, *U.S. Commercial Relations 1878,* p. 209.
14. Copeland, p. 227.
15. Ibid., p. 221.
16. China, Maritime Customs, *Trade Reports, 1877,* pp. 30–31, and *Decennial Reports, 1922–31,* I, 140.
17. Pitkin, pp. 138–144.
18. Ware, pp. 49, 193, 194.
19. China, Maritime Customs, *Decennial Reports,* 1922–31, I, 96.
20. Ibid., p. 191, and "The Report of U.S. Consul DeLano at Foochow for the Year 1878," in *U.S. Commercial Relations,* p. 245.
21. China, Imperial Maritime Customs *Trade Reports, 1877,* pp. 30–31.
22. China, Imperial Maritime Customs *Trade Reports, 1881,* p. 12, and *Decennial Reports,* 1892–1901, pp. 152, 228, 231, 274, 477.
23. "The Report of Vice-Consul General Bailey," p. 211.
24. "The Report of U.S. Consul DeLano," p. 253.
25. Before Newchwang was opened up as a treaty port, shipments of American fabrics usually landed at Shanghai as the port of entry, and the goods were then distributed to dealers who carried them to Manchuria and other parts of North China.
26. Yen Chung-ping, *Chung-kuo mien-fang-chih shih-kao,* p. 76.

27. Ibid., p. 120.
28. China, Imperial Maritime Customs, *Decennial Reports, 1892–1901,* p. 534.
29. Griffin, p. 309.
30. Ibid., p. 304.
31. China, Imperial Maritime Customs, *Monthly Reports, 1866,* reprint, (Taipei: 1971) July 1866, Foochow, p. 13.
32. For instance, the Customs Office reported in June 1866:

    News from Europe foretelling further reduction in the price of cottons and woollens caused the native merchants to buy nothing out of their absolute wants.

    See China, Imperial Maritime Customs, *Monthly Reports 1866,* June 1866, Hankow, p. 23.
33. China, Imperial Maritime Customs, *Monthly Reports 1866,* August 1866, Tientsin, p. 27.
34. China, Imperial Maritime Customs, *Decennial Reports, 1882–1891,* pp. 46, 416.
35. "The Report by American Consul Edward C. Lord, of Ningpo, on the Trade and Commerce in 1878," in *U.S. Commercial Relations 1878,* p. 271.
36. Copeland, p. 226.
37. For a detailed discussion on the evaluation of the Chinese handicraft textile production in the past hundred years or so, see Kang Chao, "The Growth of a Modern Cotton Textile Industry and the Competition with Handicrafts."
38. H. D. Fong, *Chung-kuo chih mien-fang-chih-yeh,* p. 4.
39. Kang Chao, *The Development of Cotton Textile Production in China,* Chapter 9, Table 9-4.
40. Ibid., Appendix Tables A-3 and A-4.
41. Freda Utley, *Lancashire and the Far East,* p. 191.
42. Keizō Seki, *The Cotton Industry of Japan,* p. 70.
43. Utley, pp. 207–209.
44. Seki, p. 124.
45. Ibid., p. 125.
46. Ibid., p. 68.
47. W. A. Graham Clark, *Cotton Goods in Japan,* p. 103.
48. Only 1.9% of cotton goods imports came to China via Antung in 1913, but the figure rose to 15.7% by 1929. See Fong, *Chung-kuo chih,* p. 302.
49. Ibid., p. 255.
50. Ralph M. Odell, *Cotton Goods in China,* p. 63.
51. Arno S. Pearse, *Cotton Industry of Japan and China,* p. 142.
52. Odell, p. 113.
53. Ibid., p. 112.

54. *U.S. Census of Manufactures, 1905,* U.S. Government Bulletin, No. 74, p. 35.
55. There was a tremendous boom in the Chinese imports of machinery of all kinds, especially equipment of factories, in 1919–1921. In the next decade (1922–1931), imports of machinery jumped to the first place on the commodity list of imports. See China, Maritime Customs, *Decennial Reports, 1922–31,* I, 177.

Chapter 5. The East Asian "Textile Cluster" Trade, 1868–1973: A Comparative-Advantage Interpretation, by Bruce L. Reynolds

1. Seki, p. 6.
2. Ibid., p. 5.
3. G. E. Hubbard, *Eastern Industrialization and its Effect on the West,* pp. 217–218.
4. Sung-jae Koh, *Stages of Industrial Development in Asia,* p. 254.
5. Ibid., p. 229.
6. Seki, p. 19.
7. Ibid., p. 31: 2.09 billion square yards vs. 2.03 billion.
8. Ibid., p. 31.
9. Ibid., p. 49.
10. See, for example, works by G. T. Jones, A. Marshall, T. Veblen, J. Hobson, D. S. Landes, and D. H. Aldcroft cited in Lars G. Sandberg, *Lancashire in Decline.*
11. Aldcroft, pp. 116–123, as cited in ibid., pp. 9–10.
12. Seki, p. 307, in value terms.
13. See Sandberg.
14. R. Robson, *The Cotton Industry in Britain,* p. 321.
15. Actually, the argument is slightly more complex than this. See Bruce L. Reynolds, "The Impact of Trade and Foreign Investment on Industrialization: Chinese Textiles, 1875–1931," pp. 160–164.
16. For further discussion of this point, see ibid., pp. 81–82.
17. Maheshi Chand, "A Note on the Cotton Industry in India."
18. Jacquard and other "advanced" but non-power looms probably required yarns of higher counts as well, which would have moved the pattern of yarn demand in an upward direction in the late nineteenth and twentieth centuries.
19. Japanese cloth imports did not decline until World War I. Table 25 shows net imports, which declined earlier due to the growth in cloth exports.
20. Seki, p. 24.
21. U.S. Department of Commerce, Bureau of Foreign and Domestic Commerce, *Where China Buys and Sells,* pp. 54–55.
22. See Table 24.
23. I assume, for Japan, that all yarn produced domestically was handicraft

yarn, since in 1882 Japan had only 29,000 machine spindles (Seki, p. 311); and, second, that domestic cotton output was 50 million pounds. Seki, p. 8, gives 49 million for the late Tokugawa. Given these assumptions, then all cotton goes to hand-spinning, and hand-spun yarn is (50+3)/(50+3±37) or 53/90 or 59%. Koh, p. 306, says that annual cotton output before 1886 was "no more than" 200 million pounds. The fact that in 1893–1897 Japan absorbed 223 million pounds (202+7+14) in imports when domestic cotton output was negligible lends credence to the higher figure, which would imply hand-spun yarn output of 203/240 or 83%. On the other hand, some cotton was used for wadding and other non-yarn purposes, which reduced the percentage.

24. Kaneko Kentarō, Japanese Vice-Minister for Agriculture and Commerce, stated that handspinning "has almost gone out of use" in 1892. Koh, p. 23.

25. Yang Tuan-lin, et. al., *Liu-shih-wu nien lai Chung-kuo kuo-chi mao-i t'ung-chi*, pp. 43–44, gives cotton imports for 1925–28 by country as United States, 2.9 million piculs; India, 5.7; Japan, .1; total, 9 million piculs.

26. Figures in this paragraph are from Seki, p. 304, Koh, p. 24, and Table 28.

27. Information in this paragraph is from Reynolds, Appendix C.

28. But not, of course, the highest counts produced by Britain, and sold, for example, in the United States. Japan was probably not able to produce, and certainly not able to compete in, the highest counts— say, over 100.

29. See the introduction to this chapter.

30. Koh, p. 139.

31. Average manufactured yarn output was 149 million (Seki, p. 311), and average exports were 34 million (Table 25) in 1893–1897.

32. Seki, p. 22.

33. Ibid., p. 20, referring to British exports to Japan ca. 1905.

34. Koh, p. 247.

35. Ibid., p. 137.

36. Ibid., p. 138.

37. See below for argument that exports of 111 million pounds in 1905 were 15% of the cotton crop (and thus 15/85 or 18% of domestic consumption). Population in 1821–1830 was much lower, and cotton cloth use was less widespread; 50 million pounds would surely have bulked larger in that decade than 111 million pounds in 1905.

38. Domestic cloth production was about 2,000 million yards (Table 24). This required 850,000,000 pounds of cotton (at 17 pounds per 40-yard piece of hand cloth—see Reynolds, Appendix E). Of this, 300 million was imported in the form of yarn (Table 24). Then domestic cotton production supplied the remaining 550, plus 111 for

export (Table 27), plus perhaps 100 for wadding and other purposes, totaling 760 million pounds. 111/760=15%.

39. Koh, pp. 137-138; and Seki, p. 328.
40. See Table 25.
41. Average annual output of handwoven and machine cloth in 1919-1931 was 2,300 million yards (Table 24). This required 920 million pounds of yarn (at 16 pounds per 40-yard piece). Cotton wadding and other uses probably took about 150 million pounds, raising total consumption to 1,070 million pounds of cotton. Yarn imports filled on average 50 million pounds of this demand during 1919-1921 (Table 24). The remaining 1,020 must have been supplied by China's cotton crop. The imports were 190/1020 or 19% of the domestic cotton crop and 190/(1020+190) or 16% of the domestic cotton consumption. This falls close to Fong's statement that 17.6% of the total cotton consumed in Tientsin in the years 1919-1929 was foreign; H. D. Fong, *Cotton Industry and Trade in China*, p. 37.
42. Seki, p. 8.
43. Chinese cotton imports were as follows:

Year	United States %	India %	Total (million lbs.)
1917	6	94	40
1925	32	63	271
1931	43	56	620
1934	59	33	256

Sources: Totals from Reynolds, p. 232 and Hsiao, p. 39. Distribution from Julean Arnold, *Commercial Handbook of China*, p. 48; Yang Tuan-lin, p. 43; and U.S. Department of Commerce, *Where China Buys and Sells*, p. 49. Koh, p. 137-138, describes Indian cotton exports to China in the nineteenth century.

44. Koh, p. 139.
45. Grover Clark, *Economic Rivalries in China*, p. 18.
46. Koh, p. 248.
47. Seki, p. 328; and Koh, p. 252.
48. Arnold, *Commercial Handbook*, I, 278-279.
49. Ch'en Chen et al., comps., *Chung-kuo chin-tai kung-yeh shih tzu-liao*, col. 4, p. 823.
50. Reynolds, Appendix B.
51. Spindleage in operation was 1.1 million in 1919, and 4.1 million in 1931. Reynolds, Appendix B. The sale by Saco-Lowell of 781,000 spindles is in Charles J. Ferguson, ed., *Andersen, Meyer and Company Ltd. of China*, p. 24.
52. The evidence that Japanese sold textile machinery to China during World War I is inferential. Total textile-machinery imports were 4.8 million HKT, 1916-1918, of which the U.S. provided no more than

0.5 million (see Arnold, *Commercial Handbook,* p. 47). Japanese total exports of machinery to China rose sharply in those years, from an average of 0.8 million HKT in 1912–1915 to an average of 2.8 million in 1916–1918 (Ts'ai Cheng-ya, *Chung-Jih mao-i t'ung-chi,* p. 175). Therefore, it seems likely that a substantial part of the textile machinery imports in 1916–1918 was Japanese.

53. Sandberg, p. 172.
54. Sandberg, for example, stresses the "unwillingness" of other countries to allow continued imports from the U.K., of a "strong determination to resist them," pp. 203–206.
55. If 20% of the price of 16-count yarn was value added, and 40% of the price of 60-count yarn was value added, and if the price of 60-count yarn was 1.2 times the price of 16-count yarn, then a 10% tariff, for example, if it was ad valorem, imposed an effective burden on the yarn industry of the exporting country which was twice as heavy for 16-count as for 60-count.
56. Sandberg, p. 216.
57. Ibid., p. 217.

Chapter 6. Commercial Penetration and Economic Imperialism in China: An American Cigarette Company's Entrance into the Market, by Sherman Cochran

ABBREVIATIONS

Chang Yu-i	Chang Yu-i et al., comp., *Chung-kuo chin-tai nung-yeh shih tzu-liao, ti-erh-chi, 1912–1927* (Historical materials on modern Chinese agriculture, second collection, 1912–1927; Peking, 1957).
Ch'en Chen, col. 1	Ch'en Chen, comp., *Chung-kuo chin-tai kung-yeh shih tzu-liao, ti-i-chi* (Historical materials on modern Chinese industry, first collection), 2 vols. (Peking, 1957).
Ch'en Chen, col. 2	———, comp., *Chung-kuo chin-tai kung-yeh shih tzu-liao, ti-erh-chi* (Historical materials on modern Chinese industry, second collection), 2 vols. (Peking, 1958).
Ch'en Chen, col. 4	———, comp., *Chung-kuo chin-tai kung-yeh shih tzu-liao, ti-ssu-chi* (Historical materials on modern Chinese industry, fourth collection), 2 vols. (Peking, 1961).
FO	Great Britain, Records of the British Foreign Office, Public Record Office, London, England.

Li Wen-chih	Li Wen-chih, comp., *Chung-kuo chin-tai nung-yeh shih tzu-liao, ti-i-chi, 1840–1911* (Historical materials on modern Chinese agriculture, first collection, 1840–1911; Peking, 1957).
NA	National Archives of the United States, Washington, D.C.
Nanyang	Chung-kuo k'o-hsueh yuan Shang-hai ching-chi yen-chiu so Shang-hai she-hui k'o-hsueh yuan ching-chi yen-chiu so (The Shanghai economic research institute of the Chinese academy of sciences and the economic research institute of the Shanghai academy of social sciences), comps., *Nan-yang hsiung-ti yen-ts'ao kung-ssu shih-liao* (Historical materials on the Nanyang Brothers Tobacco Company; Shanghai, 1958).
NCH	*The North China Herald and Supreme Court and Consular Gazette.*
P'eng Tse-i	P'eng Tse-i, comp., *Chung-kuo chin-tai shou-kung-yeh shih tzu-liao, 1840–1949* (Historical materials on modern Chinese handicraft industries, 1840–1949), 4 vols. (Peking, 1957).
Wang Ching-yü	Wang Ching-yü, comp., *Chung-kuo chin-tai kung-yeh shih tzu-liao, ti-erh-chi, 1895–1914* (Historical materials on modern Chinese industry, second collection, 1894–1914), 2 vols. (Peking, 1957).

1. Paul A. Varg, "The Myth of the China Market," Chapter 3 in his *The Making of a Myth: The United States and China, 1897–1912;* Marilyn Blatt Young, *The Rhetoric of Empire: American China Policy, 1895–1901;* Dennett, Chapter 30; George F. Kennan, *American Diplomacy, 1900–1950,* Chapters 2, 3.
2. Richard P. Dobson, *China Cycle,* p. 18.
3. James A. Thomas, *A Pioneer Tobacco Merchant in the Orient,* p. 42.
4. FO 371/3189, no. 126013, Rickards of BAT to Grey, 17 July 1918; U.S. Department of Commerce, Bureau of the Census, *Stocks of Tobacco Leaf,* Bulletins 139–165 (1919–1929). On consumption in the United States, see Richard B. Tennant, *The American Cigarette Industry,* pp. 4, 16.
5. FO 371/3189, no. 126013, Rickards of BAT to Grey, 18 July 1918; *Tobacco,* 7 January 1915, p. 4.
6. On the cigarette industry in China before 1902, see China, Imperial Maritime Customs, *Decennial Reports, 1892–1901,* pp. 12, 45; Wang Ching-yü, pp. 206–207, 209–211.
7. The full text of the agreement between the American Tobacco

Company and the Imperial Tobacco Company has been reproduced in Bureau of Corporations, *Report of the Commissioner of Corporations on the Tobacco Industry,* pt. 1, pp. 440–447. For details on the negotiations, see B. W. E. Alford, *W. D. & H. O. Wills and the Development of the U.K. Tobacco Industry, 1786–1965,* pp. 268–269; Maurice Corina, *Trust in Tobacco: The Anglo-American Struggle for Power,* pp. 101–103, 129; and Mira Wilkins, *The Maturing of Multinational Enterprise,* pp. 146–151. See also her account in Chapter 9 below.

8. BAT stockholders' newsletter called *The Times,* 17 January 1928, pp. 2–3, in the William H. Brown Collection; John K. Winkler, *Tobacco Tycoon: The Story of James Buchanan Duke,* p. 147. Duke is quoted by Patrick G. Porter, "Origins of the American Tobacco Company," p. 76 n70.

9. Patrick Fitzgerald, *Industrial Combination in England,* pp. 145–146; British American Tobacco Company, *Report of the Directors* for 1923, Brown Collection; Wilkins, *Maturing,* p. 152; Winkler, pp. 147–148. See also Chapter 9 below by Mira Wilkins. Duke delegated the position of chairman to W. R. Harris from 1902 to 1912 and held it himself from 1912 until 1923.

10. Alfred D. Chandler, Jr., *The Visible Hand,* p. 382.

11. Thomas, *Pioneer,* p. 49.

12. Ibid., p. 50.

13. *B.A.T. Bulletin,* new series, 17.73:25–31 (May 1926); ibid., 19.97:18 (May 1928); Wang Ching-yü, pp. 207–208, 212–213; Bureau of Corporations, *Report,* pt. 1, p. 443.

14. Thomas, *Pioneer,* p. 5.

15. Robert Easton, *Guns, Gold & Caravans,* p. 106.

16. James Lafayette Hutchison, *China Hand,* p. 268.

17. Thomas, *Pioneer,* p. 7.

18. James A. Thomas, "Selling and Civilization," p. 896.

19. Thomas, *Pioneer,* p. 24; Corina, p. 101; Easton, p. 106; Carl Crow, *Foreign Devils in the Flowery Kingdom,* p. 60.

20. Report by Alexander Hosie, *British Diplomatic and Consular Reports on Trade: Foreign Trade in China, 1906,* 3943, p. 46.

21. Bureau of Corporations, *Report,* pt. 1, pp. 16 and 306; FO 371/3189, Rickards of BAT to Grey, 17 July 1918.

22. Wang Hsi, "Ts'ung Ying-Mei yen kung-ssu k'an ti-kuo chu-i ti ching-chi ch'in-lueh," p. 93; Hou, p. 102.

23. Remer estimates that foreign investment in manufacturing in China in 1914 was $110.6 million. See his *Foreign Investments in China,* p. 70.

24. Ch'en Chen, col. 2, pp. 93–94; Wu Ch'eng-lo, *Chin-shih Chung-kuo shih-yeh t'ung-chih,* II, 74–75; Wang Ching-yü, pp. 215, 217–218, 1183–1192; report by Wang Shih-jen, *Nanyang,* July 1915, pp. 40, 67; China, Imperial Maritime Customs, *Decennial Reports, 1902–1911,*

p. 358; Thomas, "Selling and Civilization," p. 949; Thomas, *Pioneer,* p. 50. (I have revised Wang Ching-yü's figures on BAT employment in light of the evidence cited in this note.)

25. It seems safe to assume that all cigarettes imported into China from the United States and Great Britain in 1916 (about 4.7 billion) belonged to BAT; this constituted slightly more than one-third of the company's total sales for the year. If it is assumed that all imports from Hong Kong also belonged to BAT (when in fact probably only some unknown fraction of these belonged to it), the company's total imports amounted to about 5.6 billion, slightly less than one-half its total sales for the year. See China, Imperial Maritime Customs, *Returns of Trade and Trade Reports,* pt. 3, I, 268.

26. On the significance of Duke's innovations, see Chandler, *The Visible Hand,* pp. 382–391.

27. William Ashley Anderson, *The Atrocious Crime (of Being a Young Man),* p. 1. See also Hutchison, Chapter 1.

28. Thomas, *Pioneer,* pp. 85–86.

29. Ibid., pp. 103–106; Hutchison, p. 5. For examples of the loneliness and sense of cultural isolation from which young American BAT representatives sometimes suffered, see ibid., pp. 18–19, 43–45, 49–50, 106–107, 114–115, 189–191, 243–244; *B.A.T. Bulletin,* 2.35 (December 11, 1915), p. 133, and passim; and, for the most poignant characterization, W. Somerset Maugham, *On a Chinese Screen,* Chapter 23.

30. Hutchison, pp. 199, 230. One of BAT's Chinese competitors visited BAT branches north of Peking and testified to two Western BAT representatives' fluency in the local dialect. (Chien Chao-nan to Chien Yü-chieh, 13 September 1916, *Nanyang,* pp. 59–60.) The language proficiency of many English BAT representatives was also evident in their assignment during World War I. Of the 80 who returned from China to be in the military, many applied to the British government to serve as bilingual interpreters with the Chinese Labor Corps in Europe, passed the required language examinations, and were assigned to the Chinese Labor Corps for the duration of the war. See *B.A.T. Bulletin* 4-8 (1917–1919, paginated consecutively), pp. 789, 1325, 1391, 1579, 1652–1653, 1699, 1725, 1756, 1782, 1821, 1887, 1951, 1981–1982, 2005, 2027, 2062, 2111, 2203, 2310, 2326. On the role of interpreters in the Chinese Labor Corps, see Judith Blick, "The Chinese Labor Corps in World War I," *Harvard Papers on China* 9: 117, 123.

31. Lee Parker and Ruth Dorval Jones, *China and the Golden Weed,* p. 11.

32. FO 228/2154, Jordan to the Ministry of Foreign Affairs, 31 May 1912.

33. Wang Ching-yü, p. 229; *B.A.T. Bulletin* 16.69:268–270 (January 1926); Thomas, *Pioneer,* p. 237; Thomas, "Selling and Civilization," pp. 948–949.

34. BAT relied, for example, on the *S.S. Cigarette* to carry goods on the Upper Yangtze. See FO 228/1946, Hewlett to Jordan, 7 July 1915. On the origins of Western shipping privileges, see Westel W. Willoughby, *Foreign Rights and Interests in China,* pp. 161–163.

35. For an excellent analysis of these regional systems, see G. William Skinner, "Regional Urbanization in Nineteenth Century China," in Skinner, ed., *The City in Late Imperial China,* pp. 211–249.

36. On North China, see Wang Ching-yü, pp. 215–216; H. T. Montague Bell, and H. G. Woodhead, *China Yearbook,* p. 47; FO 371/2332, no. 156279, report by Walker; T'ung Hsu Photography Shop to Nanyang, 1914, *Nanyang,* p. 59. On the northwest, see Chien Chao-nan to Chien Yü-chieh, 13 September 1916, *Nanyang,* pp. 59–60; Wang Shih-jen to Nanyang, April 1916, *Nanyang,* p. 64; Anderson, pp. 99–112; Hutchison, Chapters 13–16; FO 371/1608, no. 51903, Alston to Grey, 1 November 1913. On the Yangtze regions, see FO 228/1659, Tours to Jordan, 15 February 1907; FO 228/1630, Werner to Jordan, 1 November 1906; FO 228/1663, Smith to Jordan, 27 March 1907; FO 228/1695, Phillips to Jordan, 12 October 1908; FO 228/1628, Giles to Jordan, 10 November 1906; Wang Ching-yü, p. 227. On the southeast, see Wang Ching-yü, p. 229. On South China, see FO 371/1349, no. 47131, Sly to FO, 5 November 1912; Wang Ching-yü, pp. 229 and 234; Arnold Wright, ed., *Twentieth Century Impressions of Hong Kong, Shanghai and other Treaty Ports in China,* III, 795–796; U.S. Department of Commerce, Bureau of Foreign and Domestic Trade, *Tobacco Trade of the World,* p. 31. On the southwest, see Thomas, *Pioneer,* p. 327; Wang Ching-yü, pp. 229–230; FO 371/640, no. 26840, Cunliffe-Owen of BAT to Grey, 14 July 1909; no. 33459, Stanley to Grey, 11 September 1909; no. 36339, Carnegie to Grey, 30 September 1909; FO 371/864, no 39392, O'Brien-Butler to Jordan, 25 September 1910; Edwin J. Dingle, *Across China of Foot,* pp. 100–101. On the northeast, See FO 371/1349, nos. 43817 and 51150, Jeffress of BAT to FO, 17 October and 29 November 1912; FO to Jeffress, 20 October 1912; no. 47141, Sly to FO, 5 November 1912; FO 371/1688, Campbell to BAT, 27 June and 31 August 1905; FO 371/180, no. 244, Cunliffe-Owen of BAT to FO, 1 January 1906; no. 6685, Fulford to Satow, 11 December 1905; nos. 12656 and 13164, MacDonald to Grey, 13 April and 15 March 1906; no. 13338, Hood of BAT to Grey, 18 April 1906; no. 15220, Satow to Grey, 19 March 1909; Wang Ching-yü, pp. 225–227; Dana G. Munro, "American Commercial Interests in Manchuria," p. 157n8; T'ung Hsu to Nanyang, 1914, *Nanyang,* p. 59. On Japanese and Russian competition in Manchuria, see Wang Ching-yü, pp. 234–235.

37. Quoted by Patrick G. Porter, pp. 64–65.

38. Thomas, *Pioneer,* pp. 10–23, 36.

39. Ch'en Chen, col. 2, p. 125.

40. FO 371/180, nos. 2370 and 6685, Fulford to Satow, 11 December

1905; Livingston in *The Tobacco Leaf,* 14 November 1905, enclosed in FO 17/1690, Hood to Landsdowne, 4 December 1905. The Japanese administration tore down this number of posters in Yingkow. The number left up was not recorded. For additional examples of BAT advertising in Manchuria, see Wang Ching-yü, pp. 222–227; and Liu Ai-jen to Chien Chao-nan, 1914, *Nanyang,* p. 68.

41. *NCH,* 14 June 1907, p. 669; and 27 January 1911, p. 198. For additional examples of BAT advertising in North China, see *NCH,* 17 January 1908, p. 124; and 7 November 1908, p. 313; J.W. Sanger, *Advertising Methods in Japan, China, and the Philippines,* photograph opposite, p. 74; Thomas, *Pioneer,* pp. 161–162.

42. Arnold Wright, III, 795–796.

43. Report by H. H. Fox, acting British Consul in Wuchow, 7 September 1904, republished in *Journal of the American Asiatic Association* 4.11:345 (December 1904).

44. FO 371/864, no. 24094, Playfair to Jordan, 8 June 1909; Dingle, p. 100. On BAT advertising in Tengyueh, Yunnan, see Wang Ching-yü, pp. 228 and 230. On Kueiyang, Kweichow, see *NCH,* 10 June 1911, p. 679; and 13 June 1914, pp. 822–823.

45. FO 371/864, no. 8889, O'Brien-Butler to FO, 4 February 1919; Wang Ching-yü, p. 230.

46. On Shanghai, Hangchow, Nanking, Anking, Hankow, Changsha, Shashi, Chungking, and Chengtu, see FO 228/1660, Fox to Jordan, 20 June 1907; FO 228/1631, Smith to Satow, 19 January 1906; FO 228/1663, Smith to Jordan, 27 March 1907; FO 228/1695, Phillips to Jordan, 15 January 1908; and Hewlett to Jordan, 24 October 1908; Wang Ching-yü, pp. 216, 227–228; *B.A.T. Bulletin,* 14.37:835 (May 1923); *NCH,* 17 June 1906, p. 377; 5 September 1908, p. 581; 12 December 1908, p. 641; 7 October 1910, p. 18; 1 April 1911, p. 31.

47. Arnold to Thomas, 19 December 1915, James A. Thomas Papers, Manuscript Department, William R. Perkins Library, Duke University.

48. U.S. Department of Commerce, Bureau of the Census, *Stocks of Tobacco Leaf: 1918,* Bulletin no. 139, p. 30; Wang Ching-yü, pp. 211, 216, 219; Ch'en Chen, col. 2, pp. 104, 122; FO 228/1632, Fraser to Satow, 9 January 1906; *British Diplomatic and Consular Reports on Trade No. 4366, Report on the Trade of Shanghai 1908,* p. 7; Chang Yu-i, p. 152; and R. H. Gregory's records of his travel and research in China, June–August 1906, in the Richard Henry Gregory Papers, Manuscript Department, William R. Perkins Library, Duke University.

49. Ch'en Chen, col. 2, pp. 140–141; *British Diplomatic and Consular Reports, China, Report on the Trade of Hankow, 1913,* pp. 5–6; Gregory to Jeffress, 12 November and 22 December 1915, and Thomas to Seeman, 11 August 1928, Thomas Papers; FO 228/1953, Pratt (in Tsinan) to Jordan, 5 April 1915; Charles E. Gage, U.S. Department of Agriculture *Yearbook* for 1926; A. Sy-hung Lee,

"The Romance of Modern Chinese Industry," p. 160. On efforts to transplant bright tobacco on five continents, see Nannie May Tilley, *The Bright Tobacco Industry, 1860-1929*, pp. 385-386.

50. See Chandler, *The Visible Hand*, pp. 382-391.
51. Ernest O. Hauser, *Shanghai: City for Sale*, p. 100.
52. China, Imperial Maritime Customs, *Decennial Reports 1902-1911*, p. 358.
53. "Tobacco Growing in Shantung," *The Weekly Review* 22:98 (23 September 1922).
54. Julean Arnold, et al., *China: A Commercial and Industrial Handbook*, p. 75.
55. Ernest Hauser, p. 101.
56. Thomas, *Pioneer*, pp. 41-42.
57. Patrick G. Porter, pp. 62, 68-70.
58. Wang Hsi, p. 89; Jean Chesneaux, pp. 59, 72, 95, 427; Harold Isaacs, *Five Years of Kuomintang Reaction*, pp. 59-68.
59. Thomas to Russell, 18 September 1915, Thomas Papers.
60. Thomas to Straight, 2 August 1915, Thomas Papers.
61. Thomas, *Pioneer*, p. 40.
62. Han-Seng Chen, *Industrial Capital and Chinese Peasants*, pp. 6, 11, 26, 28; FO 371/3180, no. 2564, Kennett of BAT to Jordan, 22 October 1917; Chang Yu-i, p. 502; Thomas, *Pioneer*, pp. 66-69; Ch'en Chen, col. 2, pp. 141-142; Huang I-feng, "Kuan-yü chiu Chung-kuo mai-pan-chieh-chi ti yen-chiu," pp. 103, 107.
63. Ping-ti Ho, *Studies on the Population of China, 1368-1953*, p. 203; several relevant excerpts from local gazetteers have been republished in Li Wen-chih, pp. 440-442; the study was by Hsu Shu-lan, "Chung yen-yeh fa" in *Nung-hsueh pao*, No. 14, republished in Li Wen-chih, pp. 609-611.
64. Gregory to Thomas, 3 April 1922; Gregory to Jeffress, 12 November 1915, Thomas Papers.
65. Chen Han Seng, p. 8; Ping-ti Ho, p. 203; *Journal of the China Branch of the Royal Asiatic Society*, p. 97; FO 228/1589, report by Rose, 5 July 1905; FO 228/1595, Fraser to Satow, 4 January 1905; FO 228/1632, Fraser to Satow, 9 January and 7 April 1906; and Chang Yu-i, p. 160. Lacking figures on farm prices between 1913 and 1915, I have inferred that prices were lower in China on the basis of figures that show this was the case in a slightly later period, 1919-1936. See Chen, p. 94; and Pettitt to Thomas, 14 March 1921, Thomas Papers.
66. L. Carrington Goodrich, "Early Prohibitions of Tobacco Smoking in China and Manchuria," pp. 648-657; Spence, pp. 146-154, 161-167; Li Wen-chih, pp. 140-141.
67. I have found no direct evidence that Duke, Thomas, or others invested in China because they perceived the Chinese as opium smokers who would substitute cigarettes for drugs, but circumstantial evidence

suggests that they might well have seen a connection between the two commodities. In the nineteenth century, prior to BAT's investment in China, American officials in China expressed the hope that American tobacco might replace opium. And later, eulogizing Duke at his death in 1925, a BAT executive claimed that Duke had deliberately combined "business with humanity by weaning the Chinese . . . from opium by teaching them to smoke North Carolina cigarettes." This quotation is from *B.A.T. Bulletin* 15.58:281 (February 1925); for a similar claim, see FO 371/3701, no. 171045, Hood of BAT to Amery, 6 January 1920. Officials' references to the possibility of American tobacco replacing opium are in Dennett, p. 185; and Wang Ching-yü, p. 227. On anti-opium campaigns in the early 1900s, see Mary C. Wright, "Introduction," to *China in Revolution*, pp. 14–15; Roger V. DesForges, *Hsi-liang and the Chinese National Revolution*, pp. 93–102; Edward J. M. Rhoads, *China's Republican Revolution*, pp. 94–97, 124–125, 151, 253, 268.

68. Dingle, pp. 100–101.
69. U.S. Department of Commerce, *Tobacco Trade of the World*, p. 31.
70. Wang Ching-yü, pp. 214–215, 231–232.
71. Ibid., pp. 231–234.
72. *Who's Who in China*, I, 240–241; Thomas, *Pioneer*, p. 131; report by Thomas, 23 February 1927, Thomas Papers; Arnold Wright, III, 433. On Chekiang as a birthplace for compradors and a financial elite, see Yen-p'ing Hao, *Comprador*, pp. 174–175; and Susan Mann Jones, "Finance in Ningpo: The 'Ch'ien Chuang,' 1750–1880," pp. 47–77.
73. Thomas, *Pioneer*, p. 131.
74. FO 228/2154, Savage to Jordan, 23 October 1912; Huang I-feng, p. 103.
75. Arnold Wright, III, 662.
76. FO 228/1631, Smith to Satow, 19 January 1906.
77. Wang Ching-yü, pp. 223–224, 228–229, 231–232; Hutchison, Chapters 14–15 and passim.
78. Wang Ching-yü, pp. 222–223, 225–226, 228–229; FO 228/2154, Cobbs of BAT to Fraser, 15 July 1912; K'ung Hsiang-hsi, "The Reminiscences of K'ung Hsiang-hsi (1880–)," pp. 37–39; Howard L. Boorman and Richard C. Howard, eds., *Biographical Dictionary of Republican China*, II, 263–264; Easton, p. 116. On the development of guilds (including tobacco guilds) in China before 1850, see Peter J. Golas, "Early Ch'ing Guilds."
79. Hutchison, p. 221. Hutchison gives numerous examples from firsthand experience of his and other Westerners' lack of close supervision or control over Chinese BAT dealers. See ibid., pp. 47, 107–108, 135, 137, 219–220, 281–283, 305–306, 320–321, 343.
80. Parker and Jones, p. 33.
81. Thomas, "Selling and Civilization," p. 948; Thomas to Wolsiffer,

22 April 1923, Thomas Papers; Canton branch of the Nanyang Brothers Tobacco Company to Nanyang's main office in Hong Kong, June 1915, *Nanyang*, p. 77.

82. Ch'en Chen, col. 2, I, 121. The amount received for "handling charges" varied. Around 1920 it was 4 yuan per case (of 50,000 cigarettes). See ibid., p. 122.

83. Liu Ai-jen in Manchuria to Chien Chao-nan, 1914, *Nanyang*, p. 68.

84. The British American Tobacco Company, *The Record in China of the British-American Tobacco Company, Limited*, p. 32.

85. Ōi Senzō, "Shina ni okeru Ei-Bei Tabako Torasuto no keiei keitai, zai-Shi gaikoku kigyō no hatten to baiben soshiki no ichikōsatsu," pp. 12–13, 24. Cf. Hao, *Comprador*, p. 208.

86. Hao, *Comprador*, Chapters 2 and 4.

87. The British-American Tobacco Company, *Record in China*, p. 33.

88. FO 371/10940, no. 5505, Cunliffe-Owen to FO, 13 November 1925; China, Maritime Customs, *Decennial Reports, 1922–31*, p. 361.

89. Lu Yao-chen to Nanyang, 23 January 1915, *Nanyang*, pp. 40–43; Teh-lung Shop to Nanyang, July 1915, *Nanyang*, p. 58. While testifying under oath in a court of law, Thomas Cobbs, a BAT representative in China, admitted that the company maintained these exclusive dealing arrangements. See *NCH*, 27 September 1907, p. 765.

90. Arnold, *China: A Commercial and Industrial Handbook*, p. 75; FO 371/10297, no. F3405, Rose of BAT to the British Minister, 24 August 1924. BAT was exceptional among foreign firms in its willingness to extend credit to its Chinese agents and to set its prices in silver dollars (rather than gold or the currency of its own country). See Crow, pp. 56–58.

91. On Chungking, see FO 228/1695, Phillips (in Chungking) to Jordan, 15 January 1908; U.S. Department of Commerce, *Tobacco Trade of the World*, no. 68, p. 33; Wang Ching-yü, p. 219. On Shanghai, see Wang Shih-jen to Chien Chao-nan and Chien Yü-chieh, March 1916, *Nanyang*, pp. 65–66. On Hangchow, see FO 228/1663, Smith (in Hangchow) to Jordan, 27 March 1907. On Peking, Tientsin, Chinwangtao, Changli, and Liaoyang, see Wang Ching-yü, pp. 223–224. On Foochow, see FO 371/638, no. 24094, Playfair to Jordan, 21 May 1909. On Kunming, see Wang Ching-yü, p. 229, and FO 371/864, no. 39392, O'Brien-Butler (in Kunming) to Jordan, 25 September 1910. On Canton, see Arnold Wright, III, 796.

92. Albert Feuerwerker, *The Chinese Economy, ca. 1870–1911*, p. 17; see also his *The Chinese Economy, 1912–1949*, p. 13.

93. P'eng Tse-i, comp., II, Appendix 4, Table 1; Ta-chung Liu and Kung-chia Yeh, *The Economy of the Chinese Mainland*, pp. 143, 152, 428, 513, 535; and Wu Pao-san, "Chung-kuo kuo-min so-te 1933 hsiu cheng," p. 140. For nonstatistical impressions that cigarettes were competing with hand-made tobacco products in Kwangtung, Fukien,

and Chekiang provinces, see Wang Hsi, p. 88; and "Tobacco Crops of Chekiang." Cf. Dwight H. Perkins, "Growth and Changing Structure of China's Twentieth Century Economy," p. 121.

94. This publication apparently originated in BAT's "Training School" for Chinese agents in Peking. Founded in 1921, it was called *Ying-Mei yen kung-ssu yueh-pao* (BAT monthly). Six thousand copies of this first issue were published, and, according to BAT, were circulated "from the Yellow Sea to the borders of Tibet; from Hong Kong to Siberia." See *B.A.T. Bulletin*, 12.13:288 (May 1921). The references to Wang Ching-yü, pp. 223–229, in the following notes are to excerpts from this publication.

95. Wang Ching-yü, pp. 223–224.

96. Spence, p. 167.

97. Wang Ching-yü, p. 223.

98. Ibid., pp. 224–226, 228–229.

99. Nanyang Brothers Tobacco Company agent in Manchuria to Nanyang in Hong Kong, 1914, *Nanyang*, p. 59.

100. Chien Chao-nan to Chien Yü-chieh, 13 September 1916, and 28 October 1917, *Nanyang*, pp. 51, 59–60.

101. Hutchison, p. 102. On Hutchison's travels in rural North China in 1912 and 1913, see ibid., Chapters 14–18 and pp. 320–322.

102. Rural consumption of industrial goods (including kerosene, cotton yarn, and other commodities, as well as cigarettes) is a subject in need of further research. According to one isolated statistic, in the year 1935, of Chinese farm families, 19% purchased tobacco of some kind. See Albert Feuerwerker, "The Foreign Establishment in China in the Early Twentieth Century," p. 89.

103. Sanger, pp. 44–83; Arnold, *Commercial Handbook of China*, II, 393; Thomas, *Pioneer*, pp. 160–161; U.S. Department of Commerce, *Tobacco Trade of the World*, no. 68, p. 33.

104. Sun Chia-chi, "Cigarette Cards," pp. 58–67, 71, 74; The Cartophilic Society of Great Britain, Ltd., comp., *The British American Tobacco Company Booklet* (1952), pp. 59, 61, 66, 90–92, 183–189, 195–204; Arnold, *Commercial Handbook of China*, II, 392–393; and Arnold et al., *China: A Commercial and Industrial Handbook*, p. 344. For examples of posters in which anti-Christian Chinese propagandists depicted mid-nineteenth-century foreign missionaries as cuckolds wearing green hats, see illustrations in Paul A. Cohen, *China and Christianity*, pp. 140ff.

105. Arnold, *China: A Commercial and Industrial Handbook*, p. 195.

106. See Henry Doré, *Researches into Chinese Superstitions*, V, 714–715; and Lu Hsun's amusing comparison of Chinese and Western attitudes toward bats in "On Bats," *Selected Works of Lu Hsun* (Peking, 1956), III, 281–282.

107. Sun Chia-chi, pp. 59, 67; Cartophilic Society, pp. 195–196.

108. Hutchison, pp. 266–267.

109. *NCH,* 27 September 1907, p. 763; Crow, pp. 58–59; Edward Alsworth Ross, *The Changing Chinese,* p. 86; U.S. Department of Commerce, *Tobacco Trade of the World,* p. 33; Sanger, p. 57; Chung Hua Tobacco Company in Manchuria to Nanyang, August 1914, *Nanyang,* p. 68; report of Lu Yao-chen to Nanyang, 23 January 1915, *Nanyang,* p. 40.
110. Thomas, "Selling and Civilization," pp. 949–950.
111. Bureau of Corporations, *Report,* pt. 1, p. 335; Robert F. Durden, "Tar Heel Tobacconist in Tokyo, 1899–1904," p. 354. On the parallel case of Americans investing for the same reason in Europe, see Mira Wilkins, "An American Enterprise Abroad: American Radiator Company in Europe, 1895–1914," p. 342.
112. Sumiya Mikio, *Dai-Nihon teikoku no shiren,* p. 129; *Nichi-Bei bunka kōshō-shi,* II, *Tsūsho sangyo-hen,* pp. 428–429; Bureau of Corporations, *Report,* pt. 1, pp. 83–84, 183, 335, 443. Cf. Robert F. Durden, *The Dukes of Durham, 1865–1929,* p. 74. The total foreign capital imported into Japan between 1897 and 1903 was only 194 million yen; during the subsequent decade (1904–1914), it rose to 1,857 million. See Baba and Tatemoto, p. 178.
113. Parrish to Komura, 20 April 1904, and Parrish to Murai Kichibei, 25 April 1903, Edward J. Parrish Papers, Manuscript Department, William R. Perkins Library, Duke University; Bureau of Corporations, *Report,* pt. 2 (1911), p. 300. On Murai Brothers' advertising techniques, see Suzuki Tsutomu, ed., *Nisshin Nichi-Ro sensō,* pp. 134–135, 156–157; and Durden, *Dukes of Durham,* p. 75.
114. For a summary of the advertising wars, see Sumiya, pp. 130–131. The largest of the Japanese tobacco companies, Chiba, earned 7,984 yen in 1901, 40,679 in 1902, and 72,915 in 1903; see Parrish to Komura, 20 April 1904, Parrish Papers. The quotation is used by Durden in "Tar Heel Tobacconist," p. 358. On late Meiji attitudes toward foreign investment, see Dan Fenno Henderson, *Foreign Enterprise in Japan,* pp. 11–12. In the transaction with the government, Murai Brothers' stockholders absorbed a relatively small loss, receiving 11,286,949 yen as compensation, 713,051 less than their investments (which by 1904 totaled 12 million yen). For details of the negotiations over compensation, see Durden, "Tar Heel Tobacconist," pp. 355–363. For provisions of the Tobacco Monopoly Law, see *Laws and Regulations of the Government Monopoly of Japan.*
115. As early as 1904—before Japan's annexation of Korea—Duke's representatives in East Asia were resigned to the loss of the Korean market, but they fought for a share of it between 1904 and 1914 and, after finally withdrawing, demanded full compensation for their factory at Chemulpo (Inchon). See Fiske to Parrish, 16 September 1904. Though excluding American manufacturers from Japan, the Japanese continued to purchase bright tobacco from the United States. In 1909, Japan was the world's second largest importer of this commodity

(behind Great Britain), but by 1923 it imported less than 5% of the bright tobacco exported from the United States. See Tilley, pp. 334–335.

116. For the period 1903–1928, the decline of the gold value of the HKT reduced the effective rate of the tariff below 4% ad valorem. See Yen Chung-p'ing, ed., *Chung-kuo chin-tai ching-chi shih t'ung-chi tzu-liao hsuan-chi*, p. 61.

117. For the English text, see William F. Mayers, comp., *Treaties between the Empire of China and Foreign Powers*, p. 28; for the Chinese text, see Huang Yueh-po et al., comps., *Chung-wai t'iao-yueh hui-pien*, p. 10.

118. Stanley F. Wright, *China's Struggle for Tariff Autonomy, 1843–1938*, pp. 361–362; Ch'eng Shu-tu et al., comps., *Yen-chiu shui shih*, II, ch. 7, pt. 1, p. 1; FO 371/861, no. 2875, Willis to Jordan, 17 August 1909; FO 371/180, no. 18884, Prince Ch'ing to Satow, 26 December 1904; Satow to Warren, 29 December 1904; Keily of BAT to Warren, 14 January 1905; Warren to Satow, 16 January 1905; Satow to Prince Ch'ing, 8 February 1905; Wai-wu pu to Satow, 23 February 1905. See also Nien Ch'eng, *Hung-p'u-chiang-pan hua tang-nien*, p. 95.

119. Quoted by Willis to Jordan in FO 371/861, no. 2875, 17 August 1909.

120. FO 371/861, no. 2875, Jordan to the Ministry of Foreign Affairs (Wai-wu pu), 15 September 1909. On the diplomacy of Hsu and Hsi-liang, see DesForges; Michael H. Hunt, *Frontier Defense and the Open Door*.

121. FO 371/1082, no. 1593, Jordan to Grey, 16 October 1911. The Chung-hua Tobacco Company complained that total taxes on its cigarettes in Manchuria were "half again more" than taxes on BAT goods and gave this as the reason why it could not compete with BAT. Chung-hua Tobacco Company to Nanyang Brothers Tobacco Company, September 1914, *Nanyang*, p. 63.

122. Thomas, *Pioneer*, p. 48.

123. FO 371/1945, no. 9845, Hood of BAT to Grey, 4 March 1915, outlines the scheme in detail.

124. FO 371/1945, no. 21554, Stanley to FO, 13 May 1914; no. 18349, Jordan to Grey, 11 April 1914; no. 27274, Musgrave to Grey, 16 June 1914.

125. FO 371/1945, no. 56433, Jordan to Grey, 28 July 1914; BAT to Chou Tzu-chi and Liang Shih-i, 10 June 1914; FO 371/2329, no. 34426, Hood of BAT to FO, 23 March 1915; no. 37366, Jordan to Grey, 31 March 1915; *Who's Who in China*, I, 241. Negotiators for the Chinese government later privately revealed that they and BAT had discussed the possibility of BAT's paying 3 million yuan for its share of control over tobacco tax stamps. According to American

sources, the two sides also considered forming a joint corporation with 55% of the stock to be held by BAT and 45% by the Chinese government. See James C. Sanford, "Tobacco Taxation on the Eve of Tariff Autonomy," p. 22; Chien Chao-nan to Chien Yü-chieh, 27 September 1916, *Nanyang*, pp. 122–123.

126. Ch'eng Shu-tu et al., eds., *Chuan-yen t'ung-shui shih*, Chapter 2, p. 7; Chi-ming Hou, pp. 104–105.

127. Mary Wright, "Introduction," pp. 1–30; Rhoads, Chapters 3 and 4.

128. FO 228/2155, English translation of the original Chinese document enclosed in Thomas of BAT to Pelham-Warren, 15 August 1905.

129. Ho Tso, "1905–nien fan-Mei ai-kuo yun-tung," pp. 24, 28; Chu Shih-chia, *Mei-kuo p'o-hai Hua-kung shih-liao*, pp. 155–156; Wang Ching-yü, pp. 737, 1004.

130. English translations of the three posters are enclosed in FO 228/2155, Thomas of BAT to Pelham-Warren, 2 August 1905; Proclamation of the Mixed Court of the International Settlement of Shanghai, 29 August 1905.

131. FO 228/2155, Harvey of BAT to Satow, 26 September 1905.

132. A photographic reproduction of this poster appears in Wang Ching-yü, second plate following p. 732.

133. Several songs of this type were sung during the boycott and are recorded in Ting Yu, "1905–nien Kuang-tung fan-Mei yun-tung."

134. On the marketing of American-made bicycles in China at the time of the boycott, see Raymond F. Crist and Harry R. Burrill, *Trade with China*, pp. 89–90.

135. Che Lang (pseud.), "Tiao yen-tsai," p. 14.

136. Cecil Clementi, *Cantonese Love Songs*, p. 1.

137. Cf. Arthur Waley, *The Life and Times of Po Chu-i, 772–846 A.D.*, pp. 62–63.

138. Ting Yu, pp. 18, 23, 33. On the role students and merchants played in the boycott at Canton, see Rhoads, pp. 83–90.

139. FO 228/2155, Hopkins to Pelham-Warren, 27 July 1905; report by Arnold enclosed in Rodgers to Loomis, 17 August 1905, NA; Margaret Field, "The Chinese Boycott of 1905," p. 95.

140. Shih-shan Tsai, "Reaction to Exclusion: Ch'ing Attitudes toward Overseas Chinese in the United States, 1848–1906," p. 307; FO 228/2155, Harvey to Satow, 26 September 1905; Field, p. 74; Howard K. Beale, *Theodore Roosevelt and the Rise of America to World Power*, p. 228.

141. Quoted by Beale, p. 235.

142. Ibid.

143. Roosevelt condemned these companies for creating monopolies through unethical practices; he distinguished them from "natural" trusts, which had also created monopolies but which (in his estimation) had behaved more ethically. See John Morton Blum, *The Republican*

Roosevelt, p. 118; and Gabriel Kolko, *The Triumph of Conservatism,* pp. 122-127.

144. FO 17/1689, Jeffress of BAT to the Colonial Office, 13 September 1905; and NA, Heintzleman's consular dispatches, 4 December 1905. On American businessmen in China and their efforts to reform immigration laws in the United States, see James J. Lorence, "Business and Reform: The American Asiatic Association and the Exclusion Laws." On American businessmen's promotion of progressive domestic legislation in this period, see Robert Wiebe, *Businessmen and Reform: A Study of the Progressive Movement.*

145. NA, Rodgers to Loomis, 12 and 22 September 1905; FO 228/2155, Fraser to Satow, 5 December 1905; FO 228/1632, Fraser to Satow, 9 January 1906; FO 228/1631, Smith to Satow, 1 April 1906; *Kuang-chou tsung-shang-hui pao,* quoted in Ting Yu, p. 39; Rhoads, pp. 90–91.

146. I have based the latter two explanations on interpretations advanced by C. F. Remer, *A Study of Chinese Boycotts,* p. 238. The cigarette firms were founded in Peking (3), Tientsin (1), Yingkow (1), Yentai (5), Shanghai (9), Hangchow (1), Hankow (2), Ichang (1), Chungking (1), Chengtu (1), T'ang-hsia (1), Hong Kong (1). See Wang Ching-yü, pp. 810–811, 912–913; P'eng Tse-i, II, 338–340; Hsu Yen-cho, ed., *Chung-kuo kung-i yen-ko shih-lueh,* p. 29; Ting Yu, p. 19; FO 228/1628, Smith to Satow, 26 July 1906. In addition, a few foreign tobacco companies entered Chinese markets at this time: the Japanese Imperial Tobacco Monopoly in South Manchuria; the Alliance Tobacco Company of Tientsin (established in 1904) and the Express Cigarette Company of Shanghai (established in 1906), both operated by Greeks; and the San-lin Tobacco Company of Fengtien (established in 1907), a Sino-Japanese venture. On these, see Wu Ch'eng-lo, II, 74–75.

147. Chang Ts'un-wu, *Kuang-hsu sa-i-nien Chung-Mei kung-yueh feng-ch'ao,* pp. 245-246; Bureau of Corporations, *Report,* pt. 1, p. 306; Wang Ching-yü, p. 913; Wang Hsi, p. 86. For details on the Pei-yang Tobacco Company and a discussion of the *shang-pan* and *kuan-shang ho-pan* modes of operation, see Wellington K. K. Chan, *Merchants, Mandarins, and Modern Enterprise in Late Ch'ing China,* pp. 104–105 and Chapters 5-7.

148. P'eng Tse-i, II, 339-340; FO 228/1631, Smith to Satow, 26 July 1906; FO 228/1628, Giles to Jordan, 10 November 1906; FO 228/1663, Smith to Jordan, 27 March 1907.

149. Quoted by Wang Hsi, pp. 86-87. For additional evidence of the collapse of the Chinese cigarette industry in the aftermath of the boycott, see Wang Ching-yü, pp. 810,1004; Wu Ch'eng-lo, II, 72; *Nanyang,* p. 254.

150. For additional evidence of BAT's use of coercive tactics against

Chinese companies in this period, see "Memoirs of Chien Yü-chieh," *Nanyang*, p. 3. On Duke's techniques in the United States, see Tennant, pp. 28, 41–44; and William H. Nicholls, *Price Policies in the Cigarette Industry*, pp. 27–28. On tactics used in the "tobacco war" of 1902 in England, see Alford, pp. 264–269. On BAT's subversion of an American company interested in China, see Winkler, pp. 222–223.

151. Urban protests against BAT advertising can be documented for almost every region: Manchuria (Yingkow), the Middle Yangtze (Changsha), the southeast coast (Foochow), and the southwest (Chaotung). See FO 371/180, no. 6685, Fulford to Satow, 11 December 1905; FO 371/180, no. 2370, Jeffress of BAT to FO, 18 January 1906; FO 371/180, no. 15212, Hosie to Satow, 14 March 1906; FO 371/476, no. 19630, Partlett to MacDonald, 16 April 1908; FO 228/1695, Hewlett to Jordan, 24 October 1908; FO 371/638, no. 19976, Hood of BAT to Grey, 27 May 1909; FO 371/638, no. 24094, Playfair to Jordan, 21 May 1909; FO 371/638, no. 36459, Jordan to Grey, 20 August 1909; Dingle, p. 100. On antismoking campaigns, see *NCH*, 14 October 1910, p. 106; 17 June 1911, pp. 737, 754; 9 August 1911, p. 476; 26 August 1911, p. 539; 29 June 1912, p. 940; 24 May 1913, p. 564; 13 June 1914, p. 823. On rural protests against BAT agricultural policies in Hupeh province in 1914, see Ch'en Chen, col. 2, p. 141; and Chang Yu-i, p. 505.

152. Parrish to Fiske, 12 October 1904, Parrish Papers.

153. On the rivalry between these two companies, see Sherman Cochran, *Big Business in China: Sino-Foreign Rivalry in the Cigarette Industry, 1890–1930*.

154. Paul A. Cohen, *Between Tradition and Modernity*, pp. 196–208; Hou, pp. 93–94, 131, 254; Wang Hsi, pp. 92–94.

155. Wang Hsi, p. 93. Admitting that his figures may not be representative, Hou has calculated that 56.3% of foreign manufacturing firms reinvested 30% or more of their profits in China between 1872 and 1936. Cf. Hou, p. 102.

156. David S. Landes, "Some Thoughts on the Nature of Economic Imperialism."

157. Wang Hsi, p. 89; John Gittings, *The World and China, 1922–1972* p. 23.

158. Ernest Mandel, *Marxist Economic Theory*, II, 459–465.

159. Figures for bright tobacco are from Chen Han Seng, p. 20. Percentages of land occupied by bright tobacco have been estimated on the basis of figures in Perkins, *Agricultural Development in China*, p. 236, Table B.14; and p. 262, Table C.17.

160. See Mira Wilkins, *The Emergence of Multinational Enterprise*, pp. 215–216; and Wilkins, *Maturing*, p. 92.

161. Stephen Lyon Endicott, *Diplomacy and Enterprise: British China Policy, 1933–1937*, p. 177.

162. For application of this argument to the cigarette industry, see Wang

Hsi, pp. 78-80, 85-89. As Hou Chi-ming has pointed out, Mao Tse-tung, Chiang Kai-shek, Sun Yat-sen, and other leaders have also made this argument. See Hou, pp. 1-3.

163. FO 371/3189, no. 126013, Rickards of BAT to Grey, 17 July 1918. See Hou, pp. 112-118; and Tennant, p. 5.

164. Several historians have argued that the unfavorable effects of imperialism in China were primarily political and psychological rather than economic. For a review article that makes this point and cites the major works on the subject, see Andrew J. Nathan, "Imperialism's Effects on China."

165. BAT used similar tactics against non-Chinese (mostly American) competitors in China, but its opposition to these rivals does not fit any commonly accepted definition of imperialist exploitation. See Thomas to Pettitt, 9 January and 9 May 1922; Thomas to Allen, 10 April 1922; and Pettitt to Thomas, 13 March 1922, all in the Thomas Papers; NA 693.1112/104, Cunningham to State, 20 July 1925; *NCH*, 29 October 1927, p. 206; Reavis Cox, *Competition in the American Tobacco Industry, 1911-1932*, pp. 300-301; Crow, pp. 60-61.

Chapter 7. The United States Petroleum Trade with China, 1876-1949, by Chu-yuan Cheng

Research work for this paper was financed by a faculty research grant from Ball State University and was also supported by the College of Business at Ball State. The author is indebted to Professors Robert Jost and Irvine H. Anderson for their helpful comments.

1. For instance, Gunnar Myrdal theorizes that trade between advanced and underdeveloped countries results in increased discrepancies between their productivities with "backwash effects" on the underdeveloped nation. See Myrdal, *Economic Theory and Underdeveloped Regions*, pp. 13, 28, 29.

2. Erh-wen Yen, "Oil to Dominate Old China"; also Chun P'u, "Shih-chiu-shih-chi hou-pan-ch'i chi-chung yang-huo he t'u-huo tsai kuo-nei-shih-ch'ang-shang te ching-cheng." On the growth of Standard Oil as an American multinational firm in China, see Chapter 9 below.

3. Ida M. Tarbell, *The History of the Standard Oil Company*, II, 213.

4. Ibid., p. 217.

5. During the 1912-1937 period for which price data are available, a calculation of price elasticity of demand between years shows that, with the exception of 4 years (1914-1915, 1924-1925, 1925-1926, and 1928-1929), there is a clear inverse relationship between quantity imported and price change.

6. China, Imperial Maritime Customs, *Report*, Hankow, 1879, p. 29.

7. China, Imperial Maritime Customs, *Report*, Ningpo, 1884, p. 201.

8. A regression analysis of import price (customs price) and the quantity of kerosene imported during the 1912–1935 period shows that $Q=208.41-88P$, $R^2=0.20$, $F=0.2148$. This indicates that the customs price did not seem to have an effect on the quantity imported. However, during the 1923–1935 period, when market price of kerosene differed materially from the customs price, there is a significant relationship between market price and quantity import as measured by the F-test: $Q=315.72-299.87P$, $R^2=0.60$, $F=4.048$.

9. Yu-kwei Cheng, *Foreign Trade and Industrial Development of China*, pp. 53–56.

10. Ch'en and Huang, p. 417.

11. Cheng, p. 70.

12. *China Monthly Trade Report*, Shanghai, 1 March 1930, p. 21.

13. John K. Chang, *Industrial Development in Pre-Communist China*, p. 92.

14. Ch'en and Huang, p. 134.

15. Ralph W. Hidy and Muriel H. Hidy, *Pioneering in Big Business, 1882–1911*, p. 132.

16. Glyn Roberts, *The Life of Sir Henri Deterding*, pp. 99–102.

17. Anton Mohr, *The Oil War*, pp. 61–62.

18. Ibid., p. 63.

19. These percentages are derived from shipment figures supplied by the Texaco Company and are compared with total U.S. shipments to China in various years.

20. *The Chinese Nation*, Shanghai, 11 November 1931, p. 768.

21. Wei Ching-chuan, pp. 132–133.

22. Ch'in Pen-li, *Mei-ti ching-chi ch'in-hua-shih*, p. 56.

23. *The China Weekly Review*, Shanghai, 30 January 1926, pp. 244–246.

24. Rawleigh Warner Jr., *Mobile Oil: A View from the Second Century*, p. 19.

25. The recruiting and forwarding process for those young salesmen was described in Alice Tisdale Hobart's novel *Oil For the Lamps of China*. Hobart went out to China to visit her sister, stayed on and married an American oil man, whose experiences were narrated in the novel. See Richard O'Connor, *The Oil Barons*, p. 119.

26. Gerald T. White, *Formative Years in the Far East: A History of Standard Oil Company of California and Predecessors through 1919*, p. 281.

27. Statement of Walter L. Faust, Vice President, Director, Socony-Vaccum Oil Co., in *American Petroleum Interests in Foreign Countries*, hearing before a special committee investigating petroleum resources, U.S. Senate 1945, pp. 114–115.

28. Erh-wen Yen, p. 16.

29. Arnold Wright, IV, 213–214.

30. Huang I-feng, p. 99.

31. The list is not complete. Data are gathered mainly from Chien Tsai

and Yu-kwei Cheng, *Statistics of Foreign Trade of Different Chinese Ports with Various Foreign Countries.*

32. Reconstruction Committee, Institute for Investigating Economy of Chekiang Province, *Investigation Report on Economic Conditions at Hangchow,* 1932, p. 366.
33. This information was supplied by the Texaco Company in New York in December 1975.
34. Erh-wen Yen, pp. 15–16.
35. Allen and Donnithorne, p. 101.
36. Ibid.
37. *Investigation Report on Economic Conditions at Hangchow,* 1932, pp. 672–673.
38. Ibid., p. 672.
39. Allen and Donnithorne, p. 101.
40. Huang I-feng, p. 97.
41. Hidy and Hidy, p. 549.
42. G. S. Gibb and E. H. Knowlton, *The Resurgent Years 1911–1927, History of the Standard Oil Company (New Jersey),* p. 499.
43. Tarbell, II, 273.
44. Fung Hua-nien.
45. China, Imperial Maritime Customs, *Report,* Chefoo, 1886, p. 41.
46. China, Imperial Maritime Customs, *Decennial Reports, 1892–1901,* Hankow, p. 298.
47. China, Imperial Maritime Customs, *Decennial Reports, 1892–1901,* Chinkiang, p. 443.
48. *Chang-wen-hsiang-kung ch'üan-chi,* Vol. CCXVII, letter 4, pp. 6–7, 23 April 1887.
49. *Yin-hang Chou-pao* 2.37:14.
50. Ministry of Industries, *Chung-kuo shih-yeh-chih,* VIII, 153.
51. Chu-yuan Cheng, *China's Petroleum Industry: Output Growth and Export Potential,* pp. 1–2.
52. Leonard M. Fanning, *The Rise of American Oil,* pp. 40–41.
53. Peiping Geological Society, "General Statement," No. 3 (1929).
54. *Chinese Treaties and Agreements,* No. 1914/3, 10 February 1914, pp. 1190–1111.
55. Note of Ministry for Foreign Affairs, Republic of China, regarding cancellation of Standard Oil Company's Prospecting Agreement of 1914, issued on 7 April 1917.
56. *The Science of Petroleum,* I, 139.
57. *Transactions,* American Institute of Mining and Metallurgical Engineering, 1922. LXVIII, 1109.
58. Erh-wen Yen, pp. 15–16.
59. Boris P. Torgashev, "China's Petroleum Mysteries."
60. Helen Smyth, "China's Petroleum Industry," p. 188.
61. Torgashev, "China's Petroleum Mysteries."
62. H. Foster Bain, "A Note on China's Petroleum Possibilities," p. 359.

63. *Chung-hang Yueh-pao,* Shanghai, 7.1:127–128 (July 1933).
64. Erh-wen Yen.
65. Remer, *Foreign Trade of China,* p. 202.
66. Fan Po-chuan, "Chung-kuo shou-kung-yeh tsai wai-kuo tzu-pen-chu-i ch'in-ju-hou ti tsao-yü he ming-yun."
67. *The Chinese Nation,* 16 September 1931, p. 447.
68. Chih Tsang, *China's Postwar Markets,* pp. 48–49.

Chapter 8. The Minor Significance of Commerical Relations Between the United States and China, 1850–1931, by Peter Schran

1. Ta-chung Liu, *China's National Income, 1931–1936: An Exploratory Study.*
2. Chung-li Chang, *The Income of the Chinese Gentry,* Supplement 1, pp. 291–325, esp. p. 296.
3. Feuerwerker, *The Chinese Economy, ca. 1870–1911,* p. 2.
4. Derived from Chung-li Chang, p. 323, plus notes 2 and 3.
5. Liu and Yeh, p. 66.
6. Derived from ibid., and Hsiao Liang-lin, p. 24.
7. See Ta-chung Liu, and Hsiao Liang-lin.
8. On the relation between balance of trade deficits and foreign investment, see Yu-kwei Cheng, pp. 90–93.
9. Shü-lun Pan, pp. 15, 22, 43, 69, 114.
10. See ibid., plus pp. 32, 50, 84.
11. See Remer, *Foreign Investments in China,* p. 76, as quoted in Chiming Hou, p. 17. Note also that the U.S. holdings of $196.8 million in 1931 accounted for perhaps 2% of all net foreign assets of the United States and for merely 0.05% of its total national wealth. See U.S. Bureau of the Census, *Historical Statistics of the United States, Colonial Times to 1970,* I, 255.
12. Shü-lun Pan, pp. 18, 30.
13. Cf. Yu-kwei Cheng, pp. 19, 20.
14. Derived from Table 45 and T. H. Shen, *Agricultural Resources of China,* pp. 251, 319.
15. U.S. Department of Commerce, Bureau of Foreign and Domestic Commerce, *Where China Buys and Sells,* p. 9.
16. U.S. Department of Commerce, Bureau of Foreign and Domestic Commerce, *China: A Commercial and Industrial Handbook,* pp. 53–54.
17. See Shü-lun Pan, p. 230, and Department of Commerce, *Where China Buys and Sells,* pp. 19–20.
18. See Shü-lun Pan, p. 239, and Department of Commerce, *Where China Buys and Sells,* pp. 23–24.
19. For a discussion of this relation, see Michael B. Russell, "American Silver Policy and China, 1933–1936."
20. On shipping, see Hsiao Liang-lin, pp. 199ff. Regarding migration, al-

though Chinese nationals in the United States were many times more numerous than U.S. nationals in China and also more prone to stay, they nevertheless accounted for extremely small shares of both the total and the foreign-born U.S. population at all times. Census data indicate that the fraction of Chinese-born residents rose to 1.6% of all foreign-born residents, and to 0.2% of the total U.S. population in 1880 (*Historical Statistics of the United States, Colonial Times to 1970*, I, 14). Immigration data suggest that both shares peaked within a few years thereafter (ibid., pp. 108–109). Moreover, even more than most immigrant groups and unlike the Japanese, the Chinese were severely unbalanced in favor of men. As a consequence, the U.S. population of Chinese "race" apparently declined from the 1890s until the 1920s. Surprisingly, however, the census data also imply a most unusual sex ratio for the U.S.-born population of Chinese ancestry, which suggests an extreme underenumeration of females that would serve to exaggerate the decline.

Chapter 9. The Impacts of American Multinational Enterprise on American-Chinese Economic Relations, 1786–1949, by Mira Wilkins

1. Wilkins, *Emergence of American Business*, p. 7.
2. Carl Seaburg and Stanley Paterson, *Merchant Prince of Boston: Colonel T. H. Perkins 1764–1854*, pp. 155–156, 163, 166.
3. Ibid., p. 155; Wilkins, *Emergence*, p. 7; Remer, *Foreign Investments*, p. 66.
4. Remer, *Foreign Investments*, pp. 242, 340; Wilkins, *Emergence*, p. 9, 254n13; Kenneth Wiggins Porter, *John Jacob Astor*, II, 614; Seaburg and Paterson, p. 359; Stephen Lockwood, p. 4.
5. Stephen Lockwood, pp. 5 ff.
6. See John Stopford, "The Origins of British Based Multinational Manufacturing Enterprises," p. 305, on expatriate investments. Definitions from the U.S. Department of Commerce.
7. Stephen Lockwood, pp. 21 ff.
8. Ibid., p. 117; Remer, *Foreign Investments*, pp. 67, 246, 250; American Exporter, *Export Trade Directory*.
9. Cleona Lewis, *America's Stake in International Investments*, pp. 176–177; *Amtraco Bulletin*, March 1920, pp. 1–5; *Japan Times*, 12 April 1957.
10. Remer, *Foreign Investments*, pp. 67, 247. See the major study by Kwang-Ching Liu, *Anglo-American Steamship Rivalry in China, 1862–1876*, and William D. Wray, *Mitsubishi and the N.Y.K., 1870–1914: Business Strategy in the Japanese Shipping Industry*, p. 98–99.
11. Kwang-Ching Liu, p. 252.
12. Interview with W. Rogers Herod, New York, 1 March 1964, and with

J.W. Whiteside, Bombay, September 1965. On Saco-Lowell's investment in Andersen, Meyer, see George Sweet Gibb, *The Saco-Lowell Shops: Textile Machinery Building in New England, 1813-1949,* pp. 481-482, 794n26.

13. Herod interview, 1 March 1964.
14. Remer, *Foreign Investments,* p. 281.
15. Alfred D. Chandler, "The Beginnings of 'Big Business' in American Industry," pp. 1-31; Wilkins, *Emergence,* chapters 3-5.
16. Wilkins, *Emergence,* pp. 208-209.
17. Noel H. Pugach, "Standard Oil and Petroleum Development in Early Republican China," p. 453, indicates that Standard Oil invested more than $20 million in China. Pugach seems to suggest that this was the size of the investment by 1914, but he is vague on the date. Hidy and Hidy, pp. 137, 259-267, 341, 343, 498, 528, 731n11, 750n46. Mira Wilkins, "The Internationalization of the Corporation—the Case of Oil," p. 280. Remer, *Foreign Investments,* p. 251. In 1882, the Chinese Exclusion Act was passed; in 1902, the exclusion was extended for the indefinite future; U.S. Statutes at Large, 32 (1902), p. 176. In San Francisco, anti-Chinese sentiment was strong, and the 1902 law was strictly and perhaps arbitrarily enforced. Moreover, an earlier 10-year Chinese-American Exclusion Treaty of 1894, which specifically exempted Chinese merchants, teachers, students, and travelers from exclusion, was not renewed in 1904. The Chinese reacted with a boycott in May 1905. Rhoads, pp. 83-91 (effects on Standard Oil, p. 89, Chinese imports from Sumatra, p. 85). Also on the boycott, see Beale, pp. 191-223 ("grave disaster" to the U.S. petroleum industry, p. 204). On the 1905 quota agreement, see Hidy and Hidy, p. 549, and Robert Henriques, *Bearsted: A Biography of Marcus Samuel First Viscount Bearsted and Founder of "Shell" Transport and Trading Company,* p. 521.
18. London Committee Minutes, 11 June 1885, Acq. 2, Box 41, Singer Mss., State Historical Society of Wisconsin. On Sang, see E.M. Sang to George R. McKenzie, 31 December 1881, Acq. 2, Box 5, Singer Mss.
19. J. Whitie, London, to E.M. Sang, Brussels, 6 March 1883, Acq. 2, Box 7, Singer Mss.
20. London Committee Minutes, 29 September 1884, and 11 June 1885, Acq. 4, Box 41, Singer Mss.
21. Report in Acq. 1, Box 159, Singer Mss.
22. Robert B. Davies, "Peacefully Working to Conquer the World: The Singer Manufacturing Company in Foreign Markets, 1854-1889," p. 324. See also Robert B. Davies, *Peacefully Working to Conquer the World: Singer Sewing Machines in Foreign Markets 1854-1920,* Chapter 7.
23. Davies, *Peacefully Working,* p. 193.

24. Memo, 28 November 1904, Acq. 1, Vol. IX, Singer Mss.
25. Nathaniel Peffer, *The Far East,* p. 202.
26. On the boycott, see note 17 above. On the impact of Singer, see also Beale, p. 204.
27. New York Office to F. A. Park, 15 February 1906, Acq. 1, Vol. X, Singer Mss.
28. Wilkins, *Emergence,* p. 146; *Fortune,* August 1935, p. 73.
29. Sherman Cochran, "Big Business in China: Sino-American Rivalry in the Tobacco Industry, 1890–1930," and his *Big Business in China: Sino-Foreign Rivalry in the Cigarette Industry, 1890–1930.* See also Wilkins, *Emergence,* pp. 91–92; Remer, *Foreign Investments,* p. 360; Allen and Donnithorne, pp. 169–172.
30. See Cochran, "Big Business," p. 274, on rise of Chinese manufacturing vis-à-vis imports.
31. Wilkins, *Maturing,* pp. 15–16; Pugach, pp. 457–473. There were other exploration *plans* that never amounted to anything. For example, Harry Hussey's American syndicate got a contract in 1922 to establish an oil industry in Szechwan. See U.S. Department of State, *List of Contracts of American Nationals with the Chinese Government.*
32. Wilkins, *Maturing,* Chapter 1.
33. Remer, *Foreign Investments,* p. 264n, suggests this was the first American Chamber abroad. He is wrong. There was an American Chamber of Commerce in Liverpool in 1801! See Richard Heathcote Heindel, *The American Impact on Great Britain 1894–1914,* p. 206. While we do not have a 1915 membership list, a 1928 one is included as an Appendix. We are indebted to David Wilson for locating this list for us.
34. Remer, *Foreign Investments,* p. 283.
35. Wilkins, *Maturing,* 28 and interview with W. Rogers Herod, New York, 24 February 1964. Always called China GE in the United States, this company was known in China as China General Edison Co.
36. Data on Nippon Electric from Western Electric Archives, New York.
37. H. B. Thayer to E. M. Barton, 1 June 1905; Thayer to W. E. Welles, 29 June 1905; Thayer to K. Iwadare, 30 June 1905, Western Electric Archives.
38. Thayer to Iwadare, 6 October 1905, Western Electric Archives.
39. Thayer to F. P. Fish, 29 January 1906, Western Electric Archives.
40. Thayer to Iwadare, 29 June 1906, Western Electric Archives.
41. Thayer to Iwadare, 21 September 1906, Western Electric Archives.
42. Thayer to R. C. Dodd, 17 December 1907, Western Electric Archives.
43. Thayer to Welles, 17 August 1908, Western Electric Archives. On Chinese-Japanese relations and the anti-*Japanese* boycott of 1908, see Rhoads, pp. 135–141.
44. See Chronology in Western Electric Archives. Arnhold Herbert & Co. may have been a German firm. On occasion, American manufacturing

the Far East before World War I. See Mira Wilkins and Frank Ernest Hill, *American Business Abroad: Ford on Six Continents,* p. 58. On the German background of Markt & Hammacher, interviews with V. A. Dodge, New York, 23 and 29 November 1960.

45. Wilkins, *Maturing,* p. 28; Gerard Swope, "Reminiscences."
46. Herod interviews, 24 February 1964, and 1 March 1964.
47. Financial records in Western Electric Archives.
48. On the sale, see Wilkins, *Maturing,* p. 71.
49. Herod interview, 1 March 1964. Another General Electric executive put the figure at 2,500. Interview with P. M. Markert, Johannesburg, 3 August 1965.
50. Interview with J. W. Whiteside, Bombay, September 1965.
51. E. G. Liebold to Joseph Bailie, 2 December 1921, Acc. 285, Box 84; Bailie to Liebold, 22 February 1922, Acc. 285, Box 84; Liebold to Bailie, 28 February 1923, Acc. 285, Box 736; all in Ford Archives, Dearborn, Mich.
52. Wilkins and Hill, pp. 150-159. Sales figures in Acc. 713, Box 54, Ford Archives.
53. Acc. 713, Box 54, Ford Archives; Wilkins and Hill, p. 203; W. C. Cowling to Edsel Ford, 18 August 1930, Acc. 689, Ford Archives; Julean Arnold to Bureau of Foreign and Domestic Commerce, Washington, 15 August 1930, copy in Acc. 689, Ford Archives.
54. Cowling to C. E. Sorensen, 10 September 1930, Acc. 689, Ford Archives.
55. J. V. Crowe to Roberge, 5 February 1932, Acc. 689; sales figures, Acc. 713, Box 54, Ford Archives; Wilkins and Hill, pp. 242-243.
56. Cable, 19 August 1937, in Acc. 285, Box 2025, Ford Archives.
57. E. M. Vorhees, "Political and Economic Conditions and Japan," 22 November 1938.
58. W. W. Townsend, Memorandum, 15 December 1941, Acc. 6, Box 369, Ford Archives.
59. Remer, *Foreign Investments,* p. 290.
60. Standard Oil (N.Y.) and Shell's Asiatic Petroleum Company had far more extensive distribution networks in China than Texaco.
61. Wilkins, *Maturing,* pp. 212-217.
62. By the mid-1920s, Standard Oil (N.Y.) was clearly the most important American enterprise in China. For some of Stanvac's experiences in occupied and unoccupied China 1937-1941, see Mira Wilkins, "The Role of U.S. Business," p. 366. State Department and British foreign office records are rich in material on Standard Oil in China. See Irvine H. Anderson, *The Standard-Vacuum Oil Company and United States East Asian Policy 1933-1941* for additional useful data.
63. U.S. Senate, Committee on Foreign Relations, Subcommittee on Multinational Corporations, *Multinational Corporations and United*

States Foreign Policy, 93rd Cong., 2nd sess. (1974), pt. 8, Exhibit 8, n.d., and Memorandum, 14 October 1937, both on p. 74. See also Wilkins, "The Role of U.S. Business," p. 366.

64. Wilkins, *Maturing,* p. 53.

65. Remer, *Foreign Investments,* pp. 293-294, 289.

66. The Borden Company. *Annual Report for the Fiscal Year, 1929.*

67. Interview with Frank Lees, Tokyo, 26 September 1965.

68. Ibid.; Remer, *Foreign Investments,* p. 293.

69. Wilkins, *Emergence,* pp. 49-50; Julien Brault, *Le Téléphone en 1888,* p. 243; H. B. Thayer to Leggett, 25 May 1905, Western Electric Archives. In 1905, Oriental Telephone was still functioning in Hong Kong. It appears *not* to have involved American capital at that time.

70. Wilkins, *Maturing,* p. 168.

71. Wilkins, *Emergence,* p. 48. U.S. Department of State, *List of Contracts of American Nationals with the Chinese Government.*

72. U.S. Department of Commerce, Bureau of Foreign and Domestic Commerce, *Motion Pictures in China,* pp. 2-3.

73. Wilkins, *Emergence,* p. 204n; Remer, *Foreign Investments,* pp. 258-259.

74. Department of Overseas Trade, London, *Economic Conditions in China,* p. 38.

75. Dorothy Borg, *The United States and the Far Eastern Crisis,* p. 143.

76. Data from New York Life Insurance. U.S. Department of the Treasury, Bureau of Statistics, *Monthly Summary of Commerce and Finance 1901,* p. 2919 (1901 business). Beale, p. 204, discusses the impact of the 1905 boycott on the agents of New York Life Insurance Co. On the reasons for the retreat, see Wilkins, *Emergence,* p. 106, and Wilkins, *Maturing,* pp. 43-44.

77. Wilkins, *Emergence,* pp. 107, 204, 116, 215; Wilkins, *Maturing,* p. 13. See also F. A. Vanderlip to James Stillman, 29 October 1915, Vanderlip Papers, Special Collections, Columbia University Library. The Guggenheim facilities in Mexico produced silver, and this might well have been associated with their interest in China. Mexican silver went to China.

78. Wilkins, *Maturing,* pp. 20, 52, 136. Report of Chinese receipt of $250,000, A. A. Adee (2nd Assistant Secretary of State) to Vanderlip, 22 May 1918, A.I.C. Box 2, Vanderlip Papers.

79. Remer, *Foreign Investments,* p. 289; Wilkins, *Maturing,* pp. 136, 169, 203.

80. Wilkins, "Role of U.S. Business," pp. 359-360.

81. In order cited, 1921 James A. Rabbit Engineering Corp.; 1922, General American Car Co.; 1922, Asia Development Co.; 1923, C. H. Kettering. U.S. Department of State, *List of Contracts.*

82. Wilkins, *Maturing,* pp. 131-134, 201-202; Remer, *Foreign Investments,* pp. 286-288.

83. U.S. Department of the Treasury, *Census of American-Owned Assets in Foreign Countries,* p. 71.
84. Herod interview, 11 March 1964.
85. Markert interview, 3 August 1965.
86. Herod interview, 11 March 1964.
87. Ibid. and Markert interview, 3 August 1965.
88. See 1947 data in Acc. 507, Box 37, Folder 70, Ford Archives.
89. Wilkins, *Maturing,* pp. 302, 304, 313.
90. A Federal Trade Commission report, *Report on Cooperation in American Export Trade,* p. 222, notes investment of foreign capital in local industries (cotton mills, paper mills) "guarantees" the use of imported machinery from the country of the foreign investor.
91. Remer, *Foreign Investments,* p. 166, indicated that U.S. remittances from China in 1930 were between $5 and 10 million, that is between 3.2 and 6.4% of the $155 million investment, hardly a dramatic return on investment. We do not know how representative these 1930 figures are.

BIBLIOGRAPHY

Alford, B. W. E. *W. D. & H. O. Wills and the Development of the U.K. Tobacco Industry, 1786-1965*. London, Methuen, 1973.

Allen, G. C. *A Short Economic History of Modern Japan*. London, Allen & Unwin, 1946.

—— and Audrey G. Donnithorne. *Western Enterprise in Far Eastern Economic Development*. New York, Macmillan; London, Allen & Unwin, 1954.

American Exporter. *Export Trade Directory*. New York, 1912.

An Ch'un 安椿. "Wu-i ch'a ti kuo-ch'ü ho hsien-tsai" 武夷茶的過去和現在 (The past and present of Bohea tea), *Shen pao yueh-k'an* 4.8:87 (August 1935).

Anderson, Irvine H. *The Standard-Vacuum Oil Company and United States East Asian Policy 1933-1941*. Princeton, Princeton University Press, 1975.

Anderson, William Ashley. *The Atrocious Crime (of Being a Young Man)*. Philadelphia, Dorrance, 1973.

Antrobus, H. A. *A History of the Assam Company, 1839-1953*. Edinburgh, Constable, 1957.

Arnold, Julean et al. *Commercial Handbook of China*. Department of Commerce, Bureau of Foreign and Domestic Commerce, Miscellaneous Series No. 84. Washington, D.C., 1919.

———. *China: A Commercial and Industrial Handbook.* Department of Commerce, Bureau of Foreign and Domestic Commerce, Trade Promotion Series No. 38. Washington, D.C., 1926.

Baba, Masao, and Masahiro Tatemoto. "Foreign Trade and Economic Growth in Japan: 1858-1937," in Lawrence Klein and Kazuchi Ohkawa, eds., *Economic Growth: The Japanese Experience Since the Meiji Era.* Homewood, Irwin, 1968.

Bacon, Nathaniel T. "American International Indebtedness," *Yale Review* 9 (November 1900).

Bain, H. Foster. "A Note on China's Petroleum Possibilities," *Far Eastern Survey,* 20 November 1946.

Bank of Japan, Statistics Department. *Hundred-year Statistics of the Japanese Economy.* Tokyo, 1966.

Bannister, T. R. "A History of the External Trade of China, 1843-81," in China, The Maritime Customs, *Decennial Reports, 1922-1931.* Shanghai, 1933.

Bastid, Marianne. "Le Développement des filatures de soie modernes dans la province du Guangdong avant 1894," in *The Polity and Economy of China: The Late Professor Muramatsu Yuji Commemoration Volume.* Tokyo, Tōyō keizai shinposha, 1975.

B.A.T. Bulletin. Vols. I-XX, 1915-1930. (Available in the British Library.)

Beal, Edwin George, Jr. *The Origin of Likin, 1853-1854.* Cambridge, East Asian Research Center, Harvard University, 1958.

Beale, Howard K. *Theodore Roosevelt and the Rise of America to World Power.* Baltimore, Johns Hopkins University Press, 1956; reprint New York, Collier Books, 1962.

Bell, Henry Thurburn Montague, and Henry George Wandesforde Woodhead. *China Yearbook.* London, Routledge, 1912.

Bellah, Robert N. *Tokugawa Religion: The Values of Pre-industrial Japan.* Glencoe, Free Press, 1957.

Blainey, Geoffrey. *The Tyranny of Distance: How Distance Shaped Australia's History.* Melbourne, Sun Books, 1967.

Blick, Judith. "The Chinese Labor Corps in World War I," *Harvard Papers on China* 9. 1955.

Bloomster, Edgar L. *Sailing and Small Craft down the Ages.* Annapolis, U.S. Naval Institute, 1940.

Blum, John Morton. *The Republican Roosevelt.* Cambridge, Harvard University Press, 1954.

Boorman, Howard L., and Richard C. Howard, eds. *Biographical Dictionary of Republican China.* 4 vols. New York, Columbia University Press, 1967–1971.

Borden Company, The. *Annual Report for the Fiscal Year.* 1929.

Borg, Dorothy. *The United States and the Far Eastern Crisis.* Cambridge, Harvard University Press, 1964.

Brault, Julian. *Le Téléphone en 1888.* Paris, 1888.

The British-American Tobacco Company. *The Record in China of the British-American Tobacco Company, Limited.* n.p., 1925 (?).

——. *Report of the Directors for 1923.* William H. Brown Collection, Sterling Memorial Library, Yale University.

British Diplomatic and Consular Reports, China. *Report on the Trade of Shanghai, 1908.* London, 1909.

——. *Report on the Trade of Hankow, 1913.* London, 1914.

Brown, John Paul. *Early American Beverages.* Rutland, Vt., Tuttle, 1966.

Brown, William H. Collection. Sterling Memorial Library, Yale University, New Haven.

Buchanan, Ralph E. *The Shanghai Raw Silk Market.* New York, The Silk Association of America, Inc., 1929.

Bureau of Corporations. *Report of the Commissioner of Corporations on the Tobacco Industry.* Washington, D.C., 1909.

Campbell, George F. *China Tea Clippers.* New York, David McKay, 1974.

"Canton Exports of Raw Silk and Silk Waste in 1927," *Chinese Economic Journal* 2.6:529–532 (June 1928).

Carlson, Ellsworth C. *The Foochow Missionaries, 1847–1880.* Cambridge, East Asian Research Center, Harvard University, 1974.

Cartophilic Society of Great Britain, Ltd., comp. *The British American Tobacco Company Booklet.*

Chambliss, William Jones. *Chiaraijima Village: Land Tenure, Taxation, and Local Trade, 1818–1884.* Tucson, University of Arizona Press, 1965.

Chan Hsuan-yu 詹宣猷, re-comp. *Chien-ou hsien chih* 建甌縣志 (A gazetteer of Chien-ou). Taipei, Ch'eng-wen reprint, 1967.

Chan, Wellington K. K. *Merchants, Mandarins, and Modern Enterprise in Late Ch'ing China.* Cambridge, East Asian Research Center, Harvard University, 1977.

Chand, Maheshi. "A Note on the Cotton Industry in India," *Indian Journal of Economics* 30.116:47–48 (July 1949).

Chandler, Alfred D., Jr. "The Beginnings of 'Big Business' in American Industry," *Business History Review* 33 (Spring 1959).

——. *The Visible Hand.* Cambridge, Harvard University Press, 1977.

Chang Chia-yü 張家佑. "Fei-ch'ang shih-ch'i ying-ch'ü chih shih-yu cheng-t'se" 非常時期應取之石油政策 (Petroleum policy for the period of emergency), *Chung hang yueh-k'an* (The Bank of China monthly). Shanghai, August-September, 1939.

Chang, Chung-li. *The Income of the Chinese Gentry.* Seattle, University of Washington Press, 1962.

Chang, John K. *Industrial Development in Pre-Communist China.* Chicago, Aldine, 1969.

Chang Ts'un-wu 張存武 . *Kuang-hsu sa-i-nien Chung-Mei kung-yueh feng-ch'ao* 光緒卅一年中美公約風潮 (The storm in 1905 over the Sino-American labor treaty). Taipei, Institute of Modern History, Academia Sinica, 1965.

Chang-wen-hsiang-kung ch'üan-chi 張文襄公全集 (The complete works of Chang Wen-hsiang kung). Ed. Wang Shu-nan 王樹枏 . 228 chüan in 120 vols. Peiping, Wen-hua-chai, 1928.

Chang Yu-i 章有義 et al., comps. *Chung-kuo chin-tai nung-yeh shih tzu-liao, ti-erh-chi, 1912–1927* 中國近代農業史資料 第二輯 (Historical materials on modern Chinese agriculture, second collection, 1912–1927). Peking, 1957.

Chao Feng-t'ien 趙豐田 . *Wan-Ch'ing wu-shih nien ching-chi ssu-hsiang shih* 晚清五十年經濟思想史 (History of economic thought during the last fifty years of the Ch'ing period). Peiping, Harvard-Yenching Institute, 1939.

Chao, Kang. "The Growth of a Modern Cotton Textile Industry and the Competition with Handicrafts," in D. H. Perkins, ed., *China's Modern Economy in Historical Perspective.* Stanford, Stanford University Press, 1975.

——. *The Development of Cotton Textile Production in China.* Cambridge, East Asian Research Center, Harvard University, 1977.

Che Lang 哲郎 (pseud). "Tiao yen-tsai," 弔煙仔 (Farewell to the American cigarette), in A Ying 阿英 (Ch'ien Hsing-ts'un 錢杏邨), comp., *Fan-Mei Hua-kung chin-yueh wen-hsueh chi* 反美華工禁約文學集 (Collected literature on opposition to the American treaty excluding Chinese laborers). Peking, Chung-hua shu-chü, 1960.

Chen, Han-Seng. *Industrial Capital and Chinese Peasants.* Shanghai, Kelly & Walsh, 1939.

Ch'en Chen 陳真 et al., comps. *Chung-kuo chin-tai kung-yeh shih tzu-liao* 中國近代工業史資料第一輯 (Historical materials on modern Chinese industry. Ti-i-chi (1st collection), 2 vols., 1957; ti-erh-chi (2nd collection), 2 vols., 1958; ti-san-chi (3rd collection), 2 vols., 1961; ti-ssu-chi (4th collection), 2 vols., 1961. Peking, San-lien shu-tien.

Ch'en Heng-li 陳恒力 . *Pu Nung-shu yen-chiu.* 補農書研究 (Studies on the enlarged version of agricultural treatise of 1643). Peking, Chung-hua shu-chü, 1958.

Ch'en, Po-chuang and Y. L. Huang. *Statistics of Commodity Flow of Chi-*

nese Maritime Customs and Railways, 1912–1936. Changai, Chiao-tung University, 1937.

Ch'en Tz'u-yü 陳慈玉 "Chin-tai li-ming ch'i Fu-chien ch'a chih sheng-ch'an yü mao-i kou-tsao" 近代黎明期福建茶之生產與貿易構造 (Production and trade of Fukien tea in early modern times), *Shih-huo yueh-k'an* 食貨月刊 (Food and commodities monthly) 6.9:516–534 (December 1976) and 6.10:553–573 (January 1977).

Cheng, Chu-yuan. *China's Petroleum Industry: Output Growth and Export Potential*. New York, Praeger, 1976.

Cheng, Yu-kwei. *Foreign Trade and Industrial Development of China*. Washington, D.C., The University Press of Washington, D.C., 1956.

Ch'eng Shu-tu 程叔度 et al., eds. *Chüan-yen t'ung-shui shih* 捲菸統稅史 (A history of the consolidated cigarette tax). Shanghai, Hsin-kuo-min yin-shu-kuan, 1929.

—— et al., comps. *Yen-chiu shui shih* (A history of tobacco and wine taxes). Shanghai, Ta-tung shu-chü, 1929.

Chesneaux, Jean. *The Chinese Labor Movement, 1919–1927*. Tr. H. M. Wright. Stanford, Stanford University Press, 1968.

——, Marianne Bastid, and Marie-Claire Bergère. *China from the Opium Wars to the 1911 Revolution*. Tr. Anne Destenay. New York, Pantheon, 1976.

Ch'i Ssu-ho 齊思和 et al., eds. *Ya-p'ien chan-cheng* 鴉片戰爭 (The Opium War). 6 vols. Shanghai, Shen-chou-kuo-kuang-she, 1954.

Chiang Heng 蔣衡 . "Chin-k'ai ch'a-shan i" 禁開茶山議 (On prohibiting the cultivation of tea in the mountains), from his *Yun-liao shan-jen sen-ch'ao* (Writings of a mountain man alone in the clouds), in P'eng Tse-i, comp., *Chung-kuo chin-tai shou-kung-yeh shih tzu-liao, 1840–1949*, Vol. I.

Chih, Tsang. *China's Postwar Markets*. New York, Macmillan, 1945.

Ch'in Pen-li 欽本立 . *Mei-ti ching-chi ch'in-Hua-shih* 美帝經濟侵華史 (History of economic invasion of China by U.S. imperialism). Peking, Shih-chieh chih-shih she, 1950.

China, [Imperial] Maritime Customs Service. *Decennial Reports on the Trade, Navigation, Industries, etc., of the Ports Open to Foreign Commerce in China and on the Condition and Development of the Treaty Port Provinces, 1892–1901, 1902–1911, 1922–1931*.

——. *Reports on Trade, 1871–1872*. The Statistical Department of the Imperial Maritime Customs, Shanghai, 1873.

——. *Reports on Trade, 1875*. Shanghai, 1876.

——. *Reports on Trade, 1876*. Shanghai, 1877.

——. *Returns of Trade*. Shanghai, Imperial Maritime Customs Press, 1867.

China, [Imperial] Maritime Customs Service. *Tea, 1888.* Shanghai, 1889.

———. *Monthly Reports on Trade at the Ports in China Open by Treaty to Foreign Trade.* 1864, 1866, 1871–1872, 1875, 1876, 1877, 1878, 1879, 1881. Shanghai.

———. *Quarterly Returns of Trade.* Annual after 1920. The Statistical Department of the Inspectorate General of Customs, Shanghai.

———. *Returns of Trade and Trade Reports, 1918.* 3 vols. The Statistical Department of the Inspectorate General of Customs, Shanghai, 1918–1919.

———. *Synopsis of External Trade of China, 1882–1931.*

China, Ministry of Industries. *Chung-kuo shih-yeh-chih* 中國實業誌 (Chinese industrial gazette). Vol. VIII. Shanghai.

Chinese Repository, The. Vol. VI, May 1837–April 1838. Canton, printed for the proprietors, 1838.

Chinese Treaties and Agreements. No. 1914/3. 10 February 1914. Shanghai, Commercial Press.

Ching-chi hsueh-hui 經濟學會 (Society for Economics), comp. *Fuchien ch'üan-sheng ts'ai-cheng shuo-ming-shu* 福建全省財政說明書 (Fukien financial report). Peking, Ministry of Finance, 1915.

Chou Hsien-wen 周憲文. *Ch'ing-tai T'ai-wan ching-chi shih* 清代臺灣經濟史 (An economic history of Taiwan during the Ch'ing). Taipei, Bank of Taiwan, 1957.

Chu Shih-chia 朱士嘉. *Mei-kuo p'o-hai Hua-kung shih-liao* 美國迫害華工史料 (Historical materials on the persecution of Chinese coolies by the U.S.). Peking, Chung-hua shu-chü, 1959.

Chu, Wen-djang. *The Moslem Rebellion in Northwest China, 1862–1878.* The Hague, Mouton, 1966.

Chun P'u 君樸. "Shih-chiu-shih-chi hou-pan-ch'i chi-chung yang-huo he t'u-huo tsai kuo-nei-shih-ch'ang-shang ti ching-cheng" 十九世紀後半期幾種洋貨和土貨在國內市場上的競爭 (The competition among several Western and indigenous commodities in the Chinese market during the latter half of the nineteenth century, *Ching-chi yen-chiu* 2:121–137 (1956).

Chung-hang yueh-pao 中行月報 (Bank of China monthly review). Shanghai. 7:127–128 (July 1933).

Chung-kuo jen-min ta-hsueh Chung-kuo li-shih chiao-yen-shih 中國人民大學中國歷史教研室 (Chinese History Teaching and Research Section, Chinese People's University), comp. *Ming-Ch'ing shehui ching-chi hsing-t'ai ti yen-chiu* 明清社會經濟形態的研究 (Research on the character of Ming-Ch'ing society and economy). Shanghai, Shang-hai jen-min ch'u-pan-she, 1957.

Chung-kuo jen-min yin-hang Shang-hai-shih fen-hang 中國人民銀行上海市分行 (The Shanghai branch of the People's Bank of China), comp. *Shang-hai ch'ien-chuang shih-liao* 上海錢莊史料 (Historical materials of the native banks in Shanghai). Shanghai, Shang-hai jen-min ch'u-pan-she, 1961.

Chung-kuo k'o-hsueh yuan Shang-hai ching-chi yen-chiu so Shang-hai she-hui k'o-hsueh yuan ching-chi yen-chiu so 中國科學院上海經濟研究所上海社會科學院經濟研究所 (The Shanghai Economic Research Institute of the Chinese Academy of Sciences and the Economic Research Institute of the Shanghai Academy of Social Sciences), comps. *Nan-yang hsiung-ti yen-ts'ao kung-ssu shih-liao* 南洋兄弟烟草公司史料 (Historical materials on the Nanyang Brothers Tobacco Company). Shanghai, Shanghai jen-min ch'u-pan-she, 1958.

Clark, Arthur H. *The Clipper Ship Era: An Epitome of Famous American and British Clipper Ships, Their Owners, Builders, Commanders, and Crews, 1843–1869.* New York, Putnam, 1920.

Clark, Grover. *Economic Rivalries in China.* New Haven, Yale University Press, 1932.

Clark, W. A. Graham. *Cotton Goods in Japan.* Department of Commerce, Special Agents Series no. 86. Washington, D.C., 1914.

Clementi, Cecil, tr. *Cantonese Love Songs.* Oxford, Clarendon Press, 1904.

Cochran, Sherman. "Big Business in China: Sino-American Rivalry in the Tobacco Industry, 1890–1930," PhD dissertation, Yale University, 1975.

———. *Big Business in China: Sino-Foreign Rivalry in the Cigarette Industry, 1890–1930.* Cambridge, Harvard University Press, 1980.

Cochran, Thomas C. *Railroad Leaders, 1845–1890: The Business Mind in Action.* Cambridge, Harvard University Press, 1953.

Cohen, Paul A. *China and Christianity.* Cambridge, Harvard University Press, 1963.

———. "Ch'ing China: Confrontation with the West, 1850–1900," in James B. Crowley, ed., *Modern East Asia: Essays in Interpretation.* New York, Harcourt, Brace & World, 1870.

———. *Between Tradition and Modernity.* Cambridge, Harvard University Press, 1974.

———. "Littoral and Hinterland in Nineteenth Century China: The 'Christian' Reformers," in John K. Fairbank, ed., *The Missionary Enterprise in China and America.* Cambridge, Harvard University Press, 1974.

Collis, Maurice. *Wayfoong: The Honkong and Shanghai Banking Corporation.* London, Faber and Faber, 1965.

Connolly, James B. *Canton Captain.* Garden City, Doubleday, 1942.

Copeland, M. T. *The Cotton Manufacturing Industry of the United States.* Cambridge, Harvard University Press, 1923.

Corina, Maurice. *Trust in Tobacco: The Anglo-American Struggle for Power.* New York, St. Martin's, 1975.

Cox, Reavis. *Competition in the American Tobacco Industry, 1911–1932.* New York, Columbia University Press, 1933.

Crist, Raymond F., and Harry R. Burrill. *Trade with China.* U.S. Department of Commerce and Labor, Bureau of Manufactures, Washington, D.C., 1906.

Crow, Carl. *Foreign Devils in the Flowery Kingdom.* New York and London, Harper, 1940.

Cutler, Carl C. *Greyhounds of the Seas: The Story of the American Clipper Ship.* New York, 1920. 1930 ed. published by Putnam.

"The Dai Fook Dollar of Foochow," *Chinese Economic Journal* 1.2: 127–141 (February 1927).

Davidson, James W. *The Island of Formosa, Past and Present.* Shanghai, Kelly & Walsh, 1903.

Davies, Robert B. "Peacefully Working to Conquer the World: The Singer Manufacturing Company in Foreign Markets, 1854–1889," *Business History Review* 43 (Autumn 1969).

———. *Peacefully Working to Conquer the World: Singer Sewing Machines in Foreign Markets 1854–1920.* New York, Arno Press, 1976.

Day, Samuel Philips. *Tea: Its Mystery and History.* London, Simpkin, Marshall, 1878.

Dean, Britten. *China and Great Britain: The Diplomacy of Commercial Relations, 1860–1864.* Cambridge, East Asian Research Center, Harvard University, 1974.

Delano, Amasa. *Narrative of Voyages and Travels in the Northern and Southern Hemispheres.* Boston, printed by E. G. House for the author, 1817.

Dennett, Tyler. *Americans in Eastern Asia: A Critical Study of the Policy of the United States with Reference to China, Japan, and Korea in the 19th Century.* New York, Macmillan, 1922.

Denyer, C. H. "Consumption of Tea and Other Staple Drinks in Great Britain," *Economic Journal* 3.9:34–35 and graph appendix iv (March 1893).

DesForges, Roger V. *Hsi-liang and the Chinese National Revolution.* New Haven, Yale University Press, 1973.

Dingle, Edwin J. *Across China on Foot: Life in the Interior and the Reform Movement.* New York, Holt, 1911.

Dobson, Richard P. *China Cycle.* London, Macmillan, 1946.

Dodd, John. *Journal of a Blockaded Resident in North Formosa during the Franco-Chinese War, 1884–5.* Hong Kong, 1888.

———. "Formosa," *The Scottish Geographical Magazine* 11:569 (November 1895).

Doolittle, Justus. *A Vocabulary and Hand-book of the Chinese Language Romanized in the Mandarin Dialect.* Foochow, 1872.

———. *Social Life of the Chinese.* 2 vols. in 1. New York, Harper, 1876.

Doré, Henry. *Researches into Chinese Superstitions.* Tr. M. Kennelly. 10 vols. in 7. Shanghai, T'usewei Printing Press, 1914-1938.

Dower, John W. *Origins of the Modern Japanese State: Selected Works of E. H. Norman.* New York, Pantheon, 1975.

Dulles, Foster R. *The Old China Trade.* Boston and New York, Houghton Mifflin, 1930.

Duran, Leo. *Raw Silk: A Practical Handbook for the Buyer.* 2nd rev. ed. New York, Silk Publishing Co., 1921.

Durden, Robert F. *The Dukes of Durham, 1865-1929.* Durham, Duke University Press, 1975.

———, "Tar Heel Tobacconist in Tokyo, 1899-1904," *North Carolina Historical Review* 53.4 (October 1976).

Earle, Alice (Morse). *Customs and Fashions in Old New England.* London, D. Nutt; New York, Scribner's, 1893.

Easton, Robert. *Guns, Gold and Caravans: The Life and Times of Fred Schroder, Frontiersman and Soldier of Fortune, in California, Mexico, Alaska, and China, including his Discovery of the Mysterious Pyramids of Shensi and Rescue of the Boy Emperor.* Santa Barbara, Capra Press, 1978.

Ebato Akira 江波戶昭. *Sanshigyō chiiki no keizai chirigakuteki kenkyū* 蚕糸業地域の経済地理学的研究 Research on the economic geography of sericultural districts. Tokyo, Kokon sho-in, 1969.

Eberhard, Wolfram. *Taiwanese Ballads: A Catalogue.* Taipei, Orient Cultural Service, 1972.

Economic Conditions in China. London, Department of Overseas Trade, 1930.

Endicott, Stephen Lyon. *Diplomacy and Enterprise: British China Policy, 1933-1937.* Toronto, University of British Columbia Press, 1975.

Fairbank, John K. *Trade and Diplomacy on the China Coast: The Opening of the Treaty Ports, 1842-1854.* Reprint. Stanford, Stanford University Press, 1969.

———, and Albert Feuerwerker, eds. *Republican China 1912-1949, Part 2. The Cambridge History of China,* Vol. XIII. Cambridge, Cambridge University Press, forthcoming.

———, and Kwang-Ching Liu, eds. *Late Ch'ing, 1800-1911, Part 2. The Cambridge History of China,* Vol. XI. Cambridge, Cambridge University Press, 1980.

Fan Po-Ch'uan 樊百川. "Chung-kuo shou-kung-yeh tsai wai-kuo tzu-pen-chu-i ch'in-ju-hou ti tsao-yü he ming-yun," 中國手工業在外國

資本主義侵入後的遭遇和命運 (The fate of Chinese handicraft industries after the invasion of foreign capital), *Li-shih yen-chiu* 3:88–115 (June 1962).

Fanning, Leonard M. *The Rise of American Oil.* New York, Harper, 1936.

———. *American Oil Operations Abroad.* New York, McGraw-Hill, 1947.

Fei Hsiao-t'ung. *Peasant Life in China.* London, Routledge and Kegan Paul, 1939.

Felt, J. B. *Annals of Salem.* Salem, Mass., 1845–1849.

Ferguson, Charles J., ed. *Anderson, Meyer and Company Ltd. of China.* Shanghai, Kelly and Walsh, 1931.

Feuerwerker, Albert. *The Chinese Economy, 1912–1949.* Michigan Papers in Chinese Studies No. 1. Ann Arbor, Center for Chinese Studies, University of Michigan, 1968. Chapter 2 in *The Cambridge History of China,* Vol. XII, ed. John K. Fairbank.

———. *The Chinese Economy, ca. 1870–1911.* Michigan Papers in Chinese Studies No. 5. Ann Arbor, Center of Chinese Studies, University of Michigan, 1969. Chapter 1 in *The Cambridge History of China,* Vol. XI, ed. John K. Fairbank and Kuang-Ching Liu.

———. "The Foreign Establishment in China in the Early Twentieth Century." Ann Arbor, Center for Chinese Studies, University of Michigan, 1976. Chapter 3 in *The Cambridge History of China,* Vol. XII, ed. John K. Fairbank.

Field, Margaret. "The Chinese Boycott of 1905," *Papers on China* 11. Cambridge, East Asian Research Center, Harvard University, 1957.

Fitzgerald, Patrick. *Industrial Combination in England.* London, Pitman, 1927.

Fong, H. D. *Cotton Industry and Trade in China.* Tientsin, Chihli Press, 1932.

———. "China's Silk Reeling Industry," *Monthly Bulletin on Economic China* (Nankai Institute of Economics) 7.12 (December 1934).

——— 方顯廷 . *Chung-kuo chih mien-fang-chih-yeh* 中國之棉紡織業 (China's cotton textile industry). Shanghai, Commercial Press, 1934.

Forbes, John M. *Reminiscences of John Murray Forbes.* Ed. Sarah Forbes Hughes. Boston, Ellis, 1902.

Forbes, Robert B. *Personal Reminiscences.* Boston, Little Brown, 1878. 2nd rev. ed., Boston, Little, Brown, 1882.

Ford Archives. Dearborn, Michigan.

Fortune, Robert. *Three Years' Wanderings in the Northern Provinces of China.* London, John Murray, 1847.

———. *A Residence Among the Chinese.* London, John Murray, 1852.

Fox, E. H. Report republished in *Journal of the American Asiatic Association*. December 1904.

Fu I-ling 傅衣凌 . *Ming-Ch'ing nung-ts'un she-hui ching-chi* 明清農村社會經濟 (Peasant society and economy in Ming and Ch'ing). Peking, San-lien shu-tien, 1961.

Fujimoto Jitsuya 藤本實也 . *Nihon sanshigyōshi* 日本蠶絲業史 (History of Japan's silk industry). 3 vols. Tokyo, 1933.

Fujino Shōzaburō 藤野正三郎 et al., comps. *Sen'i kōgyō (Chōki keizai tōkei* Vol XI) 纖維工業 (The textile industry long-term economic statistics). Tokyo, Tōyō keizai shimposha, 1979.

Fung Hua-nien 馮華年 ."T'ien-chin-ti-ch'ü shou-kung-yeh-chia-t'ing sheng-huo-fei chih fen-hsi" 天津地區手工業家庭生活費之分析 (An analysis of the living expenditures for handicraft families in the Tientsin area), *Ching-chi t'ung-chi chi-k'an* 1.3:505–525 (1932).

Gage, Charles. *Yearbook*. U.S. Department of Agriculture, 1926.

Gardella, Robert. "Fukien's Tea Industry and Trade in Ch'ing and Republican China: The Developmental Consequences of a Traditional Commodity Export." PhD dissertation, University of Washington, 1976.

———. "Reform and the Tea Industry in Late Ch'ing China: The Fukien Case," in Paul A. Cohen and John E. Schrecker, eds., *Reform in Nineteenth Century China*. Cambridge, Council on East Asian Studies, Harvard University, 1976.

Gibb, George Sweet. *The Saco-Lowell Shops: Textile Machinery Building in New England, 1813–1949*. Cambridge, Harvard University Press, 1950.

——— and E. H. Knowlton. *The Resurgent Years 1911–1927: History of the Standard Oil Company (New Jersey)*. New York, Harper, 1956.

Gittings, John. *The World and China, 1912–1972*. London, Methuen, 1974.

Golas, Peter J. "Early Ch'ing Guilds," in G. William Skinner, ed., *The City in Late Imperial China*. Stanford, Stanford University Press, 1977.

Goodrich, L. Carrington. "Early Prohibitions of Tobacco Smoking in China and Manchuria," *Journal of the American Oriental Society* 58 (1938).

Great Britain. Records of the British Foreign Office. Public Record Office, London.

Great Britain, Parliament. *Sessional Papers, House of Commons*. Vol. LXVII, 1867; Vol. LXVIII, 1868; Vol. LXXII, 1872.

Gregory, Richard Henry. Papers. Records of his travel and research in China, June–August 1906. Manuscript Department, William R. Perkins Library, Duke University.

Griffin, Eldon. *Clippers and Consuls, American Consular and Commercial*

Relations with Eastern Asia, 1845-1860. Ann Arbor, Edwards Brothers, 1938.

Griffiths, Sir Percival. *The History of the Indian Tea Industry.* London, Weidenfeld and Nicolson, 1967.

Hanson, John R., II. "The 19th Century Exports of the Less Developed Countries." PhD dissertation, University of Pennsylvania, 1972.

Hao, Yen-p'ing. "Cheng Kuan-ying: The Comprador as Reformer," *Journal of Asian Studies* 29.1:20 (November 1969).

———. *The Comprador in Nineteenth Century China: Bridge between East and West.* Cambridge, Harvard University Press, 1970.

———. "Commercial Capitalism along the China Coast during the Late Ch'ing Period," in Chi-ming Hou and Tzong-shian Yu, eds., *Modern Chinese Economic History.* Taipei, The Institute of Economics, Academia Sinica, 1979.

——— and Erh-min Wang. "Changing Chinese Views of Western Relations, 1840-1895," in John K. Fairbank and Kwang-ching Liu, eds., *The Cambridge History of China,* Vol. XI. Cambridge, Cambridge University Press, 1978.

Hatano Yoshihiro 波多野善大 . Chūgoku kindai kōgyōshi no kenkyū 中國近代工業史の研究 (Studies on the early industrialization of China). Kyoto, Tōyōshi kenkyūkai, 1961. Cited in Sung-jai Koh, *Stages of Industrial Development in Asia.* Philadelphia, University of Pennsylvania Press, 1966.

Hauser, Ernest O. *Shanghai: City for Sale.* New York, Harcourt Brace, 1940.

Hauser, William B. *Economic Institutional Change in Tokugawa Japan: Osaka and the Kinai Cotton Trade.* Cambridge, Cambridge University Press, 1974.

Hayashi Yōzō 林要三 . "Ba Ken-chū no keizai shisō: 'fumin' shisō no seiritsu oyobi sono yakuwari" 馬建忠の経済思想—富民思想の成立及びその役割) The economic thought of Ma Chien-chung: The development and role of the concept of "enriching the people"), *Tezukayama daigaku kiyo* 2:191-219 (1966).

HC I. Heard Collection I (Personal Records and Correspondence) in the Archives of Baker Library, Harvard University Graduate School of Business Administration.

HC II. Heard Collection II (Business Records of Augustine Heard and Company) in the Archives of Baker Library, Harvard University Graduate School of Business Administration. Filed and catalogued separately from Heard Collection I.

Heindel, Richard Heathcote. *The American Impact on Great Britain 1894-1914.* Philadelphia, University of Pennsylvania Press, 1940.

Hemmi, Kenzō. "Primary Product Exports and Economic Development: The Case of Silk," in Kazushi Ohkawa et al., eds., *Agriculture and Economic Growth: Japan's Experience.* Princeton, Princeton University Press, 1970.

Henderson, Dan Fenno. *Foreign Enterprise in Japan.* Chapel Hill, University of North Carolina Press, 1973.

Henriques, Robert. *Bearsted: A Biography of Marcus Samuel First Viscount Bearsted and Founder of "Shell" Transport and Trading Company.* New York, Viking, 1960.

Hidy, Ralph Willard and Muriel E. Hidy. *Pioneering in Big Business, 1882–1911.* Vol. I of *History of Standard Oil Company (New Jersey).* New York, Harper, 1955.

Hirschmeier, Johannes. *The Origins of Entrepreneurship in Meiji Japan.* Cambridge, Harvard University Press, 1964.

Ho Ping-hsien 何炳賢 . *Chung-kuo ti-kuo-chi mao-i* 中國的國際貿易 . (The foreign trade of China). Shanghai, the Commercial Press, 1937.

Ho, Ping-ti. *Studies on the Population of China, 1368–1953.* Cambridge, Harvard University Press, 1959.

Ho Tso 和作 . "1905-nien fan-Mei ai-kuo yun-tung" 1905年反美愛國運動 (The 1905 anti-U.S. patriotic movment), *Chin-tai shih tzu-liao* 近代史資料 (Source materials on modern history), Vol. I. 1956.

Homans, Isaac Smith, Jr. *A Historical and Statistical Account of the Foreign Commerce of the United States.* New York, Putnam, 1857.

Horie Eiichi 堀江英一 . *Keizai ni kansuru Shina kankō chōsa hōkokusho, Shina sanshigyō ni okeru torihiki kankō* 経濟に關する支那慣行調查報告書—支那蠶絲業における取引慣行 (A report of investigation of economic customs in China, on the trade customs in the sericulture and silk-spinning industry in China). Tōa kenkyūjo, 1944.

Hosie, Alexander. *British Diplomatic and Consular Reports on Trade: Foreign Trade in China, 1906.* London, Harrison and Sons, 1907.

Hou, Chi-ming. *Foreign Investment and Economic Development in China, 1840–1937.* Cambridge, Harvard University Press, 1965.

Howard, Charles Walter, and K. P. Buswell. *A Survey of the Silk Industry in South China.* Hong Kong, The Commercial Press, 1925.

Hsiao Liang-lin. *China's Foreign Trade Statistics, 1864–1949.* Cambridge, East Asian Research Center, Harvard University, 1974.

Hsu Jun 徐潤 . *Hsu Yü-chai tzu-hsu nien-p'u* 徐愚齋自敘年譜 (Chronological autobiography of Hsu Jun). Hsiang-shan, the Hsu family, 1927.

Hsu Shu-lan 徐樹蘭. "Chung yen-yeh fa" 種烟葉法 (Techniques for the cultivation of tobacco), *Nung-hsueh pao* 農學報 (Journal of agricultural science), No. 14 (1898).

Hsu Yen-cho 許衍灼, ed. *Chung-kuo kung-i yen-ko shih-lueh* 中國工藝沿革史略 (A brief history of the technological evolution in China). Shanghai, Commercial Press, 1917.

Hsueh Fu-ch'eng 薛福成. "Ch'ou-yang ch'u-i" 籌洋芻議 (A rough discussion of the management of foreign affairs), in *Hsueh Fu-ch'eng ch'üan-chi* 薛福成全集 (Collected works of Hsueh Fu-ch'eng). Taipei, Kuang-wen reprint, 1963.

Hu Hao-ch'uan 胡浩川 and Wu Chueh-nung 吳覺農. *Chung-kuo ch'a-yeh fu-hsing chi-hua* 中國茶葉復興計劃 (A plan for the rehabilitation of China's tea industry). Shanghai, Commercial Press, 1935.

Huang I-feng 黄逸峯. "Kuan-yü chiu-Chung-kuo mai-pan-chieh-chi ti yen-chiu 關於舊中國買辦階級的研究 (A study of the comprador class in old China), *Li-shih yen-chiu* 歷史研究 (Historical research), 3 (June 1964).

Huang, Philip C. C. *The Peasant Economy and Social Change in North China*. Stanford, Stanford University Press, 1985.

Huang Yueh-po 黄月波 et al., comps. *Chung-wai t'iao-yueh hui-pien* 中外條約彙編 (Compendium of treaties between China and other countries). Shanghai, The Commercial Press, 1935.

Hubbard, Gilbert Ernest. *Eastern Industrialization and its Effect on the West, with Special Reference to Great Britain and Japan*. London, Oxford University Press, 1935.

Huber, Charles Joseph. *The Raw Silk Industry of Japan*. New York, The Silk Association of America, 1929.

Hung, F. "La Geographie du Thé." PhD dissertation, Faculty of Letters, University of Lyon, 1932.

Hunt, Michael H. *Frontier Defense and the Open Door: Manchuria in Chinese-American Relations, 1895–1911*. New Haven, Yale University Press, 1973.

————. *The Making of a Special Relationship: The United States and China to 1914*. New York, Columbia University Press, 1983.

Hunter, William C. *The "Fan Kwae" at Canton before Treaty Days, 1825–1844*. London, Paul, Trench and Co., 1882.

Hutchison, James Lafayette. *China Hand*. Boston, Lothrop, Lee and Shepard, 1936.

Hyde, Francis Edwin. *Far Eastern Trade, 1860–1914*. New York, Harper and Row, 1973.

Imbault-Huart, C. *L'Isle Formosa: Histoire et Description*. Paris, E. Leroux, 1893.

Isaacs, Harold. *Five Years of Kuomintang Reaction.* Shanghai, China Forum Publishing Co., 1932.

Ishii Kanji 石井寛治 . *Nihon sanshigyōshi bunseki* 日本蚕糸業史分析 (Analysis of the history of the Japanese sericulture and silk-spinning industry). Tokyo, Tokyo daigaku shuppansha, 1972.

Jansen, Marius B., ed. *Changing Japanese Attitudes Toward Modernization.* Princeton, Princeton University Press, 1965.

Japan Times, 12 April 1957.

Jardine, Matheson & Co. Archives. Cambridge University Library.

Johnson, Arthur M., and Barry E. Supple. *Boston Capitalists and Western Railroads: A Study in the Nineteenth-Century Railroad Investment Process.* Cambridge, Harvard University Press, 1967.

Jones, Susan Mann. "Finance in Ningpo: The 'Ch'ien Chuang,' 1750–1880," in W. E. Willmott, ed., *Economic Organization in Chinese Society.* Stanford, Stanford University Press, 1972.

Journal of the China Branch of the Royal Asiatic Society. Vol. XXIII (1889).

Kalm, Peter. *The America of 1750.* New York, Wilson-Erickson, 1937.

Kaufman, William I. *The Tea Cookbook.* Garden City, Doubleday, 1966.

Kennan, George F. *American Diplomacy, 1900–1950.* Chicago, University of Chicago Press, 1951.

Kim, Kwan Ho. *Japanese Perspectives on China's Early Modernization.* Ann Arbor, Center for Chinese Studies, University of Michigan, 1974.

Kobayashi Kazumi 小林一美. "Chūgoku han-shokuminchika no keizai katei to minshū no tatakai—rikin o megutte, jūkyūseiki kōhan" 中國半殖民地化の経済過程と民衆の闘い－厘金をめぐって, 19世紀後半 (The economic process of China's semi-colonization and popular struggle—with reference to the likin in the second half of the nineteenth century), *Rekishigaku kenkyū* 398:1–18 (February 1971).

Koh, Sung-jae. *Stages of Industrial Development in Asia: A Comparative History of the Cotton Industry in Japan, China, and Korea.* Philadelphia, University of Pennsylvania Press, 1966.

Kolko, Gabriel. *The Triumph of Conservatism: A Re-interpretation of American History, 1900–1916.* New York, Free Press of Glencoe, 1963.

Kuhn, Philip. *Rebellion and its Enemies in Late Imperial China: Militarization and the Social Structure, 1796–1864.* Cambridge, Harvard University Press, 1970.

K'ung Hsiang-hsi. "The Reminiscences of K'ung Hsiang-hsi (1880–)" as told to Julie Lien-ying How. Manuscript in the Special Collections Library, Butler Library, Columbia University. 1961.

Kuo T'ing-i 郭廷以 , comp. *Tao-kuang Hsien-feng liang-ch'ao ch'ou-pan i-wu shih-mo pu-i* 道光咸豐兩朝籌辦夷務始末補遺 (Supplement to the complete account of the management of barbarian affairs during the Tao-kuang and Hsien-feng periods). Nankang, Taipei, Institute of Modern History, Academia Sinica, 1966.

Landes, David S. "Some Thoughts on the Nature of Economic Imperialism," *The Journal of Economic History* 21.4:499–500 (1961).

Larson, Henrietta M. "A China Trader Turns Investor: A Biographical Chapter in American Business History," *Harvard Business Review* 12: 346–358 (1933–1934).

Latourette, Kenneth Scott. *The History of Early Relations between the United States and China, 1784–1844.* New Haven, Yale University Press, 1917.

Laws and Regulations of the Government Monopoly of Japan. 1906.

Lee, A. Sy-hung. "The Romance of Modern Chinese Industry," *China Review,* November 1923.

Lees, Frank. Interview. Tokyo, 26 September 1965.

LeFevour, Edward. *Western Enterprise in Late Ch'ing China: A Selective Survey of Jardine, Matheson and Company's Operations, 1842–1895.* Cambridge, East Asian Research Center, Harvard University, 1968.

Lewis, Cleona. *America's Stake in International Investments.* Washington, D.C., The Brookings Institution, 1938.

Li Kuo-ch'i 李國祁 . *Chung-kuo hsien-tai-hua ti ch'ü-yü yen-chiu: Min-Che-T'ai ti-ch'ü, 1860–1916* 中國現代化的區域研究：閩浙臺地區 (Modernization in China 1860–1916: A regional study of Fukien, Chekiang, and Taiwan provinces). Nankang, Taipei, Institute of Modern History, Academia Sinica, 1981.

Li, Lillian M. *China's Silk Trade: Traditional Industry in the Modern World, 1842–1937.* Cambridge, Council on East Asian Studies, Harvard University, 1981.

Li Wen-chih 李文治 et al., comps. *Chung-kuo chin-tai nung-yeh shih tzu-liao* (Historical materials on modern Chinese agriculture). Ti-i-chi (1st collection), 1840–1911; ti-erh-chi (2nd collection), 1912–1927. Peking, San-lien shu-tien, 1957.

Lieou, Laurent Li-liang. "Notes sur l'Economie du Thé en Chine," *Bulletin de l'Université l'Aurore,* 3rd series, pp. 855–860 (1942).

Lin Fu-ch'uan, comp. *Wu-lung ch'a chi pao-chung ch'a chih-tsao hsueh* 烏龍茶及包種茶製造學 (A study of the manufacture of Oolong and Paochung tea). Taipei, 1956.

Lin Man-hung 林滿紅 . "Ch'a, t'ang, chang-nao yeh yü wan-Ch'ing T'ai-wan ching-chi she-hui chih pien-ch'ien 1860–1895" 茶糖樟腦業與晚清臺灣經濟社會之變遷 (The tea, sugar, and camphor industries and economic and social change in late Ch'ing Taiwan, 1860–1895). MA thesis, National Taiwan University, 1976.

Liu Kuang-Ching 劉廣京 . "Cheng Kuan-ying *I-yen:* Kuang-hsu ch'u-nien chih pien-fa ssu-hsiang" 鄭觀應易言—光緒初年之變法思想 (Cheng Kuan-ying's *I-Yen:* Reform proposals of the early Kuang-hsu period), *Tsing Hua Journal of Chinese Studies* 8.1/2:373–425 (1970).

Liu, Kwang-Ching. *Anglo-American Steamship Rivalry in China, 1862–1874*. Cambridge, Harvard University Press, 1962.

Liu, Ta-chung. *China's National Income, 1931–1936: An Exploratory Study*. Washington, D.C., Brookings Institution, 1946.

——— and Kung-chia Yeh. *The Economy of the Chinese Mainland: National Income and Economic Development, 1933–1959*. Princeton, Princeton University Press, 1965.

Lo Ju-tse 羅汝澤 , re-comp. *Fu-an-hsien chih* 福安縣志 (A gazetteer of Fu-an, 1884), quoted in Nanshi chōsa shiryō 南支調查資料 (Data for investigation concerning South China), "Fukkenshō chagyō no kenkyū" 福建省茶葉の研究 (A study of the tea industry in Fukien), p. 235.

———, re-comp. *Hsia-p'u-hsien chih* 霞浦縣志 (A gazetteer of Hsia-p'u). Chüan-shou plus 40 chüan. 1929.

Lo Yü-tung 羅玉東 . *Chung-kuo li-chin shih* 中國釐金史 (A history of the likin tax in China), Vols. I, II. Shanghai, Commercial Press, 1936.

Lockwood, Stephen C. *Augustine Heard and Company, 1858–1862: American Merchants in China*. Cambridge, East Asian Research Center, Harvard University, 1971.

Lockwood, William W. *The Economic Development of Japan*. Expanded edition. Princeton, Princeton University Press, 1968.

Lorence, James J. "Business and Reform: The American Asiatic Association and the Exclusion Laws," *Pacific Historical Review* 39: 421–438 (November 1970).

Lü Ch'üan-sun 呂佺孫 . "Min-sheng cheng-shou yun-hsiao ch'a-shui shu" 閩省征收運銷茶稅疏 (On taxing the conveyance of tea in Fukien), in Wang Yen-hsi 王廷熙 and Wang Shu-min 王樹敏 , comps., *Huang-ch'ao (Ch'ing) Tao-Hsien-T'ung-Kuang tsou-i* 皇朝道咸同光奏議 (Memorials of the Tao-kuang, Hsien-feng, T'ung-chih, and Kuang-hsu reigns), in Shen Yun-lung 沈雲龍 , ed., *Chin-tai Chung-kuo shih-liao ts'ung-k'an* 近代中國史料叢刊

(Collected sources of modern Chinese history, Vol. 331, Part 3, pp. 1956-1957. Taipei, Wen-hai Publishing House, 1969.

Lü Wei-ying 呂渭英 . "Min-sheng ch'a-yeh mu-chih ch'ing-hsing" 閩省茶業木植情形 (The condition of the tea industry and lumbering in Fukien), *Shang-wu kuan-pao*, 12 January 1908.

Lubbock, Alfred Basil. *The China Clippers.* Glasgow, J. Brown and Son, 1914.

Lunt, Carroll. *Some Builders of Treaty Port China.* Los Angeles, Everett Stockton Trade Press, 1965.

Ma Chien-chung 馬建忠 . "Fu-min shuo" 富民説 (Proposals for enriching the people), in *Ma, Shih-k'o-chai chi-yen* 適可齋記言 (Notes from the Shih-k'o Studio). Peking, Chung-hua shu-chü reprint, 1960.

MacGregor, David R. *The Tea Clippers: An Account of the China Tea Trade and of Some of the British Sailing Ships Engaged in it from 1849 to 1869.* London, Percival Marshall, 1952.

———. *The China Bird: The History of Captain Killick and One Hundred Years of Sail and Steam.* London, Chatto and Windus, 1961.

Maeda Katsutarō 前田勝太郎 . "Min Shin no Fukken ni okeru nōka fukugyō 明清の福建における農家副業 (On the subsidiary industries of peasant households in Fukien during the Ming and Ch'ing), in *Suzuki Shun kyōju kanreki kinen Tōyōshi ronsō* 鈴木俊教授還暦記念東洋史論叢 (Collected articles on Far Eastern history commemorating Professor Suzuki Shun's 60th birthday). Tokyo, Daian, 1964.

Malozemoff, Andrew. *Russian Far Eastern Policy, 1881–1904, with Special Emphasis on the Causes of the Russo-Japanese War.* Berkeley, University of California Press, 1958.

Mandel, Ernest. *Marxist Economic Theory.* Tr. Brian Pearce. 2 vols. New York, Monthly Review Press, 1968.

Markham, Jesse W. *Competition in the Rayon Industry.* Cambridge, Harvard University Press, 1952.

Marks, Robert. *Rural Revolution in South China: Peasants and the Making of History in Haifeng County, 1570–1930.* Madison, University of Wisconsin Press, 1984.

Marriner, Sheila. *Rathbones of Liverpool 1845–73.* Liverpool, Liverpool University Press, 1961.

Maugham, W. Somerset. *On a Chinese Screen,* New York, Doran, 1922.

Mayers, William F., comp. *Treaties between the Empire of China and Foreign Powers.* Shanghai, North China Herald, 1906.

Mohr, Anton. *The Oil War.* New York, Harcourt Brace, 1926.

Money, Edward. *The Cultivation and Manufacture of Tea.* 4th ed. London, W. B. Whittingham & Co., 1883.

Morison, Samuel Eliot. *The Maritime History of Massachusetts, 1783–1860.* Boston, Houghton Mifflin, 1930.

Morse, Hosea Ballou. *The International Relations of the Chinese Empire.* Vol. I, *The Period of Conflict, 1834–1860.* Vol. II, *The Period of Submission, 1861–1893.* London, Longmans Green, 1910 and 1918.

Moulder, Francis V. *Japan, China and the Modern World Economy.* Cambridge, Cambridge University Press, 1977.

Munro, Dana G. "American Commercial Interests in Manchuria," *The Annals of the American Academy of Political and Social Science* 39. 128 (January 1912).

Murphey, Rhoads. *The Outsiders: The Western Experience in India and China.* Ann Arbor, University of Michigan Press, 1977.

Myers, Ramon H. "Taiwan under Ch'ing Imperial Rule, 1684–1895: The Traditional Economy," *Journal of the Institute of Chinese Studies of the Chinese University of Hong Kong* 5.2:377 (December 1972).

———. *The Chinese Economy: Past and Present.* Belmont, California, Wadsworth, 1980.

Myrdal, Gunnar. *Economic Theory and Underdeveloped Regions.* London, Duckworth, 1957.

Nakamura Masanori 中村政則 . "Seishigyō no tenkai to jinushisei" 製糸業の展開と地主制 (The development of silk-spinning industry and landlordism), *Shakai keizai shigaku* Nos. 5 and 6 combined in one.

Nakanishi Ushiro 中西牛郎 . *Rikō shōden* 李公小傳 (A short biography of Li Ch'ung-sheng). Taihoku, 1908.

Nanshi chōsa shiryō 南支調査資料 (Data for investigation concerning south China). "Fukkenshō chagyō no kenkyū 福建省茶葉 の研究 (Research on the Fukien tea industry), in *Nanshi chōsa shiryō, Fukken kensetsu no hōkoku* (Fukien reconstruction report). Taihoku, Nan'yō kyokai Taiwan shibu, 1938.

———. *Fukkenshō no chagyō* 福建省の茶葉 (The Fukien tea industry). Taihoko, Nan'yo kyōkai Taiwan shibu, 1938.

Nathan, Andrew J. "Imperialism's Effects on China," *Bulletin of Concerned Asian Scholars* 4.4:3–8 (December 1972).

National Bureau of Economic Research. *Output, Employment, and Productivity in the United States after 1800.* New York, Columbia University Press, 1966.

"Native Banks in Foochow," *Chinese Economic Journal* 10.5:440–448 (May 1932).

Nepomnin, O. E. *Genezis kapitalizma v sel' skom khoziaistve Kitaia*. Moscow, 1966.

Nicholls, William H. *Price Policies in the Cigarette Industry: A Study of "Concerted Action" and its Social Control 1911–50*. Nashville, Vanderbilt University Press, 1951.

Nien Ch'eng 念澄 . *Huang-p'u-chiang-p'an hua tang-nien* 黄浦江畔話當年 (Talking about the past on the bank of the Huangpu River). Hong Kong, Chih-ch'eng ch'u-pan-she, 1971.

Nihon bōeki seiran 日本貿易精覽 (A brief guide to the trade of Japan). Comp. Tōyō keizai shimpōsha. Reprint, Tokyo, 1975.

Nihon sanshigyō taikei 日本蠶糸業大系 (An outline of the sericulture and silk-spinning industry in Japan). Comp. Tōdai shuppansha. Tokyo, 1961.

Nihon sen'i sangyōshi 日本纖維産業史 (A history of the Japanese textile industry). Comp. Nihon sen'i kyōgikai. Tokyo, Nihon sen'i kyōgikai sen'i nenkan kankōkai, 1958.

O'Connor, Richard. *The Oil Barons*. Boston, Little, Brown, 1971.

Odell, Ralph M. *Cotton Goods in China*. Department of Commerce. Washington, D.C., 1914.

Ohara Keishi 小原敬士 , ed. *Tsūshō sangyō-hen* 通商産業篇 (Section on commerce and industry). Vol. II in Kaikoku hyakunen kinen bunka jigyōkai 開國百年記念文化事業會 (Society for cultural work in commemoration of the 100th anniversary of the opening of Japan), comp. *Nichi-Bei bunka kōshōshi* 日米文化交渉史 (History of Japanese-American cultural exchange). Tokyo, Yōyōsha, 1954.

——, comp. *Japanese Trade and Industry in the Meiji-Taishō Era*. Tokyo, Ōbunsha, 1957.

Ohkawa, Kazushi, and Henry Rosovsky. "A Century of Japanese Economic Growth," in William W. Lockwood, ed., *The State and Economic Enterprise in Japan*. Princeton, Princeton University Press, 1965.

Ōi Senzō 大井專三 . "Shina ni okeru Ei-Bei Tabako Torasuto no keiei keitai, zai-Shi gaikoku kigyō no hatten to baiben soshiki no ichikōsatsu 支那に於ける英米煙草トラストの經營形態.——在支外國企業の發展と買辦組織の一考察 (Form of management of the British-American Tobacco Trust in China—One view of the development and comprador organization of foreign enterprises in China), *Tōa kenkyūsho hō* 26 (February 1944).

Pan, Shü-lun. *The Trade of the United States with China*. New York, China Trade Bureau, 1924.

Parker, E.H. "A Journey from Foochow to Wenchow through Central

Fukien," *Journal of the North China Branch, Royal Asiatic Society* 19:1, 13 (1883).

Parker, Lee, and Ruth Dorval Jones. *China and the Golden Weed.* Ahoskie, N.C., Herald Publishing Co., 1976.

Parkes, H. "An Account of the Paper Currency and Banking System of Fuhchowfoo," *Journal of the Royal Asiatic Society of Great Britain and Ireland* 13.179–189 (1852).

Parrish, Edward J. Papers. Manuscript Department, William R. Perkins Library, Duke University.

Patrick, Hugh T. "Japan, 1868–1914," in Rondo E. Cameron, ed., *Banking in the Early Stages of Industrialization.* New York, Oxford University Press, 1967.

Pearse, Arno S. *Cotton Industry of Japan and China.* Manchester, England, Taylor, Garnett, Evans, 1929.

Peffer, Nathaniel. *The Far East.* Ann Arbor, University of Michigan Press, 1958.

P'eng Tse-i 彭澤益, comp. *Chung-kuo chin-tai shou-kung-yeh shih tzu-liao, 1840–1949* 中國近代手工業史資料 (Historical materials on modern Chinese handicraft industries, 1840–1949). 4 vols. Peking, San-lien shu-tien, 1957.

Perkins, Dwight H. *Agricultural Development in China, 1368–1968.* Chicago, Aldine, 1969.

——. "Growth and Changing Structure of China's Twentieth Century Economy," in Perkins, ed., *China's Modern Economy in Historical Perspective.* Stanford, Stanford University Press, 1975.

Pien Pao-ti 卞寶第. *Pien chih-chün cheng-shu* 卞制軍政書 (Official records of Pien Pao-ti). 4 chüan in Shen Yun-lung 沈雲龍, gen. ed., *Chin-tai Chung-kuo shih-liao ts'ung-k'an* 近代中國史料叢刊 (A compendium of materials on modern Chinese history), Series No. 20. Taipei, Wen-hai ch'u-pan-she, 1968.

Pitkin, Timothy. *A Statistical View of the Commerce of the United States of America.* New Haven, Durrie and Peck, 1835.

Porter, Kenneth Wiggins. *John Jacob Astor: Business Man.* Cambridge, Harvard University Press, 1931.

Porter, Patrick G. "Origins of the American Tobacco Company," *Business History Review* 43.1 (Spring 1969).

Pugash, Noel H. "Standard Oil and Petroleum Development in Early Republican China," *Business History Review* 45 (Winter 1971).

Rawlinson, John L. *China's Struggle for Naval Development, 1839–1895.* Cambridge. Harvard University Press, 1967.

Rawski, Evelyn S. "Agricultural Development in the Han River Highlands," *Ch'ing shih wen-t'i* 3.4:71–73 (December 1975).

Reconstruction Committee, Institute for Investigating the Economy of Chekiang Province, comp. *Investigation Report on Economic Conditions at Hangchow.* 1932.

Reid, Margaret. "Tea," in Maggie Keswick, ed., *The Thistle and the Jade: A Celebration of 150 Years of Jardine, Matheson & Co.* London, Octopus Books, 1982.

Remer, Charles F. *The Foreign Trade of China.* Shanghai, Commercial Press, 1926. Taipei, Ch'eng-wen reprint, 1967.

——. *A Study of Chinese Boycotts.* Baltimore, Johns Hopkins Press, 1933.

——. *Foreign Investments in China.* New York, Macmillan, 1933.

"Report by U.S. Vice Consul General Bailey of Shanghai on the Commerce, Navigation, and Industry of China, its Trade with the United States and Other Foreign Countries for the Year 1878," in U.S. Government, *U.S. Commercial Relations 1878.* Washington, D.C. 1879.

"Report by U.S. Consul DeLano at Foochow for the year 1878," in *U.S. Commercial Relations 1878.* Washington, D.C., 1879.

"Report by the U.S. Consul Edward C. Lord, of Ningpo, on the Trade and Commerce in 1878," in *U.S. Commercial Relations 1878.* Washington, D.C., 1879.

Reynolds, Bruce L. "The Impact of Trade and Foreign Investment on Industrialization: Chinese Textiles, 1875–1931." PhD dissertation, University of Michigan, 1975.

Rhoads, Edward J. M. *China's Republican Revolution: The Case of Kwangtung, 1895–1913.* Cambridge, Harvard University Press, 1975.

Roberts, Glyn. *The Life of Sir Henri Deterding.* New York, Covici Friede, 1938.

Robson, R. *The Cotton Industry in Britain.* New York, Macmillan, 1957.

Ross, Edward Alsworth. *The Changing Chinese: The Conflict of Oriental and Western Culture in China.* New York, Century, 1911.

Roth, Rodris. *Tea Drinking in 18th Century America: Its Etiquette and Equipage.* Washington, D.C., Smithsonian Institution, 1961.

Russell, Michael B. "American Silver Policy and China, 1933–1936." PhD dissertation, University of Illinois, 1972.

Saeki Tomi 佐伯富 . "Cha to rekishi" 茶と歴史 (Tea and history), *Shih-yuan.* Taipei, 6 October 1975.

Sandberg, Lars G. *Lancashire in Decline: A Study in Entrepreneurship, Technology, and International Trade.* Columbus, Ohio State University Press, 1974.

Sanford, James C. "Tobacco Taxation on the Eve of Tariff Autonomy." Seminar paper, Harvard University, 1971.

Sanger, J. W. *Advertising Methods in Japan, China, and the Philippines.* Department of Commerce Special Agent Series No. 209. Washington, D.C., 1921.

Sanshigyō dōgyōkumiai chūōkai 蠶絲業同業組合中央會 (Central Association of the Cooperative Unions for the Sericulture and Silk-Spinning Industry), comp. *Shina sanshigyō taikan* 支那蠶絲業大觀 (A general survey of the sericulture and silk-spinning industry in China). Tokyo, Okada Nichieidō, 1929.

Sargent, Arthur J. *Anglo-Chinese Commerce and Diplomacy in the Nineteenth Century.* Oxford, Oxford University Press, 1907.

Science of Petroleum, The. 4 vols. London, Oxford University Press, 1938.

Seaburg, Carl, and Stanley Paterson. *Merchant Prince of Boston: Colonel T. H. Perkins, 1764-1854.* Cambridge, Harvard University Press, 1971.

See, Chong-su. *The Foreign Trade of China.* New York, Columbia University Press, 1919.

Seki, Keizō. *The Cotton Industry of Japan.* Tokyo, Japan Society for the Promotion of Science, 1956.

Shapiro, Seymour. *Capital and the Cotton Industry in the Industrial Revolution.* Ithaca, Cornell University Press, 1967.

Shaw, Samuel. *The Journals of Major Samuel Shaw, The First American Consul at Canton.* Ed. Josiah Quincy. Boston, Crosby and Nichols, 1847.

Shen, Tsung-han. *Agricultural Resources of China.* Ithaca, Cornell University Press, 1951.

Shewan, Andrew. *The Great Days of Sail: Some Reminiscences of a Tea-clipper Captain.* London, Heath, Cranton, 1972.

Shih Min-hsiung. *The Silk Industry in Ch'ing China.* Tr. E-tu Zen Sun. Ann Arbor, University of Michigan Center of Chinese Studies, 1976.

Shina shōbetsu zenshi 支那省別全誌 (Encyclopedia of the Chinese provinces). Comp. Tōa dōbunkai. 18 vols. Tokyo, 1917-1920.

Shinohara, Miyohei. "Economic Development and Foreign Trade in Pre-War Japan," in C. D. Cowan, ed., *The Economic Development of China and Japan.* London, Allen and Unwin, 1964.

Silk Association of America. *Annual Report.* 1906. 1913. 1914. 1919.

Silk Association of America and the Shanghai International Testing House, comp. *A Survey of the Silk Industry of Central China.* Shanghai, Printed by the *Shanghai Times,* 1925.

Singer Manuscripts. State Historical Society of Wisconsin.

Skinner, G. William. "Regional Urbanization in Nineteenth Century China," in Skinner, ed., *The City in Late Imperial China.* Stanford, Stanford University Press, 1977.

Smith, George. *A Narrative of an Exploratory Visit to Each of the Consular*

Cities of China, and to the Islands of Hong Kong and Chusan, in Behalf of the Church Missionary Society, in the years 1844, 1845, 1846. London, Seeley, Burns, 1847.

Smith, Thomas C. *Political Change and Industrial Development in Japan: Government Enterprise, 1868–1880.* Stanford, Stanford University Press, 1955.

———. "Pre-Modern Economic Growth: Japan and the West," *Past and Present* 60:158 (August 1973).

Smyth, Helen. "China's Petroleum Industry," *Far Eastern Survey* 15.12: 187–190 (19 June 1946).

Snodgrass, Donald R. *Ceylon: An Export Economy in Transition.* Homewood, Irwin, 1966.

Sparks, Jared. *The Life of John Ledyard: The American Traveller.* Cambridge, Mass., Hilliard and Brown, 1828.

Speidel, William M. "The Administrative and Fiscal Reforms of the Liu Ming-ch'uan in Taiwan, 1884–1891: Foundation of Self-Strengthening," *Journal of Asian Studies* 35.3:453–454 (May 1976).

Spence, Jonathan. "Opium Smoking in Ch'ing China," in Frederic Wakeman, Jr., and Carolyn Grant, eds., *Conflict and Control in Late Imperial China.* Berkeley, University of California Press, 1975.

Stelle, Charles C. "American Trade in Opium to China, 1821–39," *Pacific Historical Review* 10.1 (March 1941).

Stopford, John. "The Origins of British Based Multinational Manufacturing Enterprises," *Business History Review* 48 (Autumn 1974).

Strassman, W. P. *Risk and Technological Innovation: American Manufacturing Methods during the Nineteenth Century.* Ithaca, Cornell University Press, 1959.

Stübel, H. "Der Wu-i schan," *Mitteilungen der Deutschen Gesellschaft für Natur- und Volkerkunde Ostasiens* 30.39 (1937).

Sturdevant, Saundra. "Imperialism, Sovereignty, and Self-Strengthening: A Reassessment of the 1870s," in Paul A. Cohen and John E. Schrecker, eds., *Reform in Nineteenth-Century China.* Cambridge, East Asian Research Center, Harvard University, 1976.

Sumiya Mikio 隅谷三喜男 . *Dai-Nihon teikoku no shiren* 大日本帝国の試煉 (Ordeal of the Japanese Empire). Vol. XXII of *Nihon no rekishi.* Tokyo, Chūō kōronsha, 1966.

Sun Chia-chi. "Cigarette Cards." Tr. Robert Christensen. *Echo of Things Chinese* 6.4 (January 1977).

Sun Yu-t'ang 孫毓棠 . *Chung-Jih chia-wu chan-cheng ch'ien wai-kuo tzu-pen tsai Chung-kuo ching-ying ti chin-tai kung-yeh* 中日甲午戰爭前外國資本在中國經營的近代工業 (Modern industries controlled by foreign capital in China before the Sino-

Japanese War of 1894–1895). Shanghai, Shanghai jen-min Ch'u-pan-she, 1955.

———, comp. *Chung-kuo chin-tai kung-yeh shih tzu-liao, ti-i-chi, 1840–1895* 中國近代工業史資料第一輯 (Source materials on the history of modern industry in China, first collection, 1840–1895). Peking, K'o-hsueh ch'u-pan-she, 1957.

Suzuki Tomoo 鈴木智夫 . "Shinmatsu Minsho ni okeru minzoku shihon no tenkai ketei: Kanton no seishigyō ni tsuite," 清末民初における民族資本の展開過程—広東の生糸業について— (The process of development of "native capital" during the late Ch'ing and early Republican period), *Tōyō shigaku ronshū*, Vol VI. 1960.

Suzuki Tsutomu 鈴木勤, ed. *Nisshin Nichi-Ro sensō* 日清日露戦争 (The Sino-Japanese and Russo-Japanese Wars), in Shimomura Fujio 下田富士男, gen. ed., *Nihon rekishi shirizu* 日本歴史シリーズ (Series in Japanese history), Vol. XIX. Tokyo, Seikai bunkasha, 1967.

Swope, Gerard. "Reminiscences." Oral History Collection, Columbia University Library.

T'ai-wan yin-hang ching-chi yen-chiu shih 臺灣銀行經濟研究室 (The Economic Research Department of the Bank of Taiwan), comp. *T'ai-wan ssu-fa wu-ch'üan pien* 臺灣司法物權編 (Documents from *Judicial System in Taiwan* pertaining to the "right over things" [property rights]). Taipei, 1963.

———. *Fu-chien sheng-li* 福建省例 (Sub-statutes of Fukien). Vol. IV. Taipei, 1964.

Taikei Nihonshi sōsho 体系日本史叢書 (A systematic Japanese history series). Comp. Yamakawa shuppansha. Tokyo, 1965.

Taiwan Tea Exporters' Association. *The Historical Brevities of Taiwan Tea Export, 1865–1965*. Taipei, 1965.

Takisawa Hideki 瀧澤秀樹. *Nihon shihonshugi to sanshigyō* 日本資本主義と蚕糸業 (Japanese capitalism and the sericulture and silk-spinning industry). Tokyo, Miraisha, 1978.

T'ang Yung-chi 唐永基 and Wei Te-tuan 魏德端. *Fu-chien chih ch'a* 福建之茶 (Fukien tea). Yung-an, Fukien, Fukien-sheng cheng-fu t'ung-chi-ch'u, 1941.

Tarbell, Ida M. *The History of the Standard Oil Company*. 2 vols. New York, McClure, Phillips, 1904.

Taussig, Frank W. *Tariff History of the United States*. New York and London, Putnam, 1931.

Tennant, Richard B. *The American Cigarette Industry.* New Haven, Yale University Press, 1950.

Thomas, James A. "Selling and Civilization," *Asia* 23.12 (December 1923).

———. *A Pioneer Tobacco Merchant in the Orient.* Durham, Duke University Press, 1928.

———. Papers, Manuscript Department, William R. Perkins Library, Duke University.

Thomson, John. *Through China with a Camera.* London, Harper, 1899.

Tilley, Nannie May. *The Bright Tobacco Industry, 1860–1929.* Chapel Hill, University of North Carolina Press, 1948.

Ting Yu. 丁又 "1905-nien Kuang-tung fan-Mei yun-tung" 1905年廣東反美運動 (The 1905 anti-American movement in Kwangtung), *Chin-tai shih tzu-liao* 5 (October 1958).

"Tobacco Crops of Chekiang," *Chinese Economic Journal* 5.3:806–810 (September 1929).

"Tobacco Growing in Shantung," *The China Weekly Review* 22 (23 September 1922).

Torgashev, Boris P. *China as a Tea Producer.* Shanghai, Commercial Press, 1926.

———. "China's Petroleum Mysteries," *Chinese Nation,* 8 October 1930, pp. 350–352.

Tsai, Chien and Yu-kwei Cheng. *Statistics of Foreign Trade of Different Chinese Ports with Various Foreign Countries.* Shanghai, Commercial Press, 1936.

Tsai, Shih-shan. "Reaction to Exclusion: Ch'ing Attitudes toward Overseas Chinese in the United States, 1848–1906." PhD dissertation, University of Oregon, 1970.

Ts'ai Cheng-ya 蔡正雅 . *Chung-Jih mao-i t'ung-chi* 中日貿易統計 (Statistics on Sino-Japanese trade). Shanghai, Chinese Economic Society, 1933.

Ts'ai Feng-chi 蔡鳳機 , re-comp. *Nan-p'ing-hsien-chih* 南平縣志 (A gazetteer of Nan-p'ing). 24 *chüan* in 20 *ts'e. Chüan* 10, *Shih-yeh-chih* 實業志 (The section on industry). 1928.

Tsang, Chih. *China's Postwar Markets.* New York, Macmillan, 1945.

Tseng Nai-shuo 曹迺碩 . "Ch'ing-chi Ta-tao-ch'eng chih ch'a-yeh" 清季大稻埕之茶葉 (The tea industry of Ta-Tao-ch'eng in the Ch'ing), *T'ai-pei wen-wu* 5.4.101–102 (June 1957).

Tseng T'ung-ch'un 曹同春 . *Chung-kuo ssu-yeh* 中國絲業 (The Chinese silk industry). Shanghai, Commercial Press, 1933.

Tso Tsung-t'ang 左宗棠 . *Tso wen-hsiang kung ch'üan-chi* 左文襄公全集 (Collected works of Tso Tsung-t'ang). 100 chüan in 97 ts'e. Changsha, 1888–1897.

Tsou, Stanley Szu-yee. "The World Tea Industry and China." PhD dissertation, Harvard University, 1947.

Tussing, Arlon. "The Labor Force in Meiji Economic Growth: A Quantitative Study of Yamanashi Prefecture," *Journal of Economic History* 26. 1:70-96 (March 1966).

Uchida Hoshimi 内田星美 . *Nihon bōshoku gijutsu no rekishi* 日本紡織技術の歴史 (History of Japanese textile technology). Tokyo, Chijinshukan, 1960.

Ukers, William H. *All about Tea.* New York, The Tea and Coffee Trade Journal Company, 1935.

Umemura Nataji 梅村又次 et al., comps. *Noringyō* 農林業 *(Chōki keizai tōkei* 長期経済統計) (Agriculture and forestry; Long-term economic statistics). Tokyo, Tōyō keizai shimposha, 1966.

Union des Marchands de Soie de Lyon. *Statistique de la production de la soie en France et à l'étranger.* 1880-1928, annual.

U.S. Census of Manufactures, 1905. U.S. Government Bulletin No. 74.

U.S. Department of Commerce, Bureau of the Census. *Foreign Commerce and Navigation of the United States,* 1895-1922, 1926-1931. Washingtion, D.C.

――――. *Stocks of Tobacco Leaf.* Bulletins 139-165 (1919-1929).

――――. *Historical Statistics of the United States: Colonial Times to 1957.* Washington, D.C., 1960.

――――. *Historical Statistics of the United States: Colonial Times to 1970.* Washington, D.C., 1976.

U.S. Department of Commerce, Bureau of Foreign and Domestic Commerce. *Tobacco Trade of the World.* Special Consular Report no. 68. Washington, D.C., 1915.

――――. *China: A Commercial and Industrial Handbook.* Washington, D.C., 1926.

――――. *Motion Pictures in China.* Washington, D.C., 1930.

――――. *American Direct Investments in Foreign Countries.* Trade Information Bulletin No. 731. Washington, D.C., 1930.

――――. *A New Estimate of American Investments Abroad.* Trade Information Bulletin No. 767. Washington, D.C., 1931.

――――. *Where China Buys and Sells.* Trade Information Bulletin No. 827. Washington, D.C., 1935.

――――. *American Direct Investments in Foreign Countries—1936.* Economic Series 1. Washington, D.C., 1938.

――――. *American Direct Investments in Foreign Countries—1940.* Economic Series 20. Washington, D.C., 1942.

U.S. Department of State. *Commercial Relations of the United States.* "Report of U.S. Consul DeLano at Foochow for the Year 1878."

——. *Commercial Relations of the United States* No. 1. "The Tea Trade of Foochow for 1880." Report by Consul DeLano. October 1880.

——. *Commercial Relations of the United States: Reports from the Consuls of the United States* No. 94 (21 March 1884); No. 122 (17 March 1885); No. 136 (16 September 1885); No. 152 (12 March 1886).

——. *Dispatches from U.S. Consuls in Amoy, 1844–1906.* Vols. I–XV.

——. *Dispatches from U.S. Consuls in Foochow, 1849–1906.* Vols. I–X.

——. *List of Contracts of American Nationals with the Chinese Government.* Washington, D.C., 1925.

U.S. Department of the Treasury. *Census of American Owned Assets in Foreign Countries.* Washington, D.C., 1947.

U.S. Department of the Treasury, Bureau of Statistics. *Monthly Summary of Commerce and Finance.* January 1898 and June 1901.

——. *Annual Reports, Commerce and Navigation.* 1860– .

U.S. Federal Trade Commission. *Report on Cooperation in American Export Trade.* Washington, D.C., 1916.

U.S. Library of Congress, Legislative Reference Service. *Expropriation of American-Owned Property by Foreign Governments in the Twentieth Century.* Washington, D.C., 1963.

U.S. Register of the Treasury. *Commerce and Navigation of the United States, for the Year Ending June 30, 1860.* Washington, George W. Bowman, 1860.

U.S. Senate. *Executive Document 31,* 19th Congress 1st Session, 6 February 1826; *Executive Document 35,* 37th Congress, 3rd Session, 9 February 1863.

U.S. Senate hearing. *American Petroleum Interests in Foreign Countries.* Washington, D.C., 1945.

U.S. Senate, Committee on Foreign Relations, Subcommittee on Multinational Corporations. *Multinational Corporations and United States Foreign Policy.* 93rd Congress, 2nd Session, 1974.

University of Michigan Project on Chinese Economic Studies. Data Bank on Chinese Trade.

Utley, Freda. *Lancashire and the Far East.* London, Allen and Unwin, 1931.

Vanderlip Papers. Special Collections, Columbia University Library.

Varg, Paul A. "The Myth of the China Market," in Varg, *The Making of a Myth: The United States and China, 1897–1912.* East Lansing, Michigan State University Press, 1968.

Vogel, Ezra F. *Japan as Number One: Lessons for America.* Cambridge, Harvard University Press, 1979.

Vorhees, E. M. "Political and Economic Conditions in Japan," 22 November 1938. Lamont Papers, Box 184, Folder 15, Harvard Business School Library.

Waley, Arthur. *The Life and Times of Po Chu-i, 722–846 A.D.* London, Allen and Unwin, 1949.

Wang Ching-yü 汪敬虞 , comp. *Chung-kuo chin-tai kung-yeh shih tzu-liao, ti-erh-chi, 1895–1914* 中國近代工業史資料.第二輯 (Historical materials on modern Chinese industry, second collection, 1895–1914). 2 vols. Peking, K'o-hsueh ch'u-pan-she, 1957.

Wang Hsi 汪熙 . "Ts'ung Ying-Mei yen kung-ssu k'an ti-kuo chu-i ti ching-chi ch'in-lueh" 從英美煙公司看帝國主義的經濟侵略 (Economic aggression of imperialism as seen [in the activities of] British and American Tobacco Company), *Li-shih yen-chiu* 4 (August 1976).

Wang Hsiao-ch'üan 王孝泉 , comp. *Fu-chien ts'ai-cheng shih kang* 福建財政史綱 (An outline history of Fukien financial administration). 2 vols. Foochow, Yuan-tung yin-shu-chü, 1935–1936.

Wang Shih-jen 王世仁 . Report in *Nan-yang hsiung-ti yen-ts'ao kung-ssu shih-liao* 南洋兄弟烟草公司史料 (Historical materials on the Nanyang Brothers Tobacco Company). Shanghai, Shanghai jen-min ch'u-pan-she, 1958.

Wang Tzu-chien 王子建 . *Ch'i-sheng hua-shang sha-ch'ang tiao-ch'a pao-kao* 七省華商紗廠調查報告 (Report on Chinese spinning mills in seven provinces). Shanghai, Commercial Press, 1935.

Wang, Yeh-chien. *An Estimate of the Land-tax Collection in China, 1753 and 1908.* Cambridge, East Asian Research Center, Harvard University, 1973.

———. *Land Taxation in Imperial China, 1750–1911.* Cambridge, Harvard University Press, 1973.

Ward, Artemas, ed. *The Encyclopedia of Food.* New York, Peter Smith, 1941.

Ware, Caroline F. *The Early New England Cotton Manufacture: A Study in Industrial Beginnings.* New York, Russell & Russell, 1966.

Warner, Rawleigh, Jr. *Mobile Oil: A View from the Second Century.* New York, Newcomers Society in North America, 1966.

Watt, Sir George. *The Commercial Products of India, being an Abridgment of "The Dictionary of the Economic Products of India."* London, John Murray, 1908.

Wei Ching-ch'üan 韋鏡權 . "Ying-Mei-Ngo chih shih-yu-chan yü wo-kuo chih kuo-chi-min-sheng 英美俄之石油戰與我國之國計民生 (Petroleum war between the British, Americans, and

Russians and the effects on China's economic welfare), *Tung-fang tsa-chih* 31.14:125-139.

Western Electric Archives. New York.

White, Gerald T. *Formative Years in the Far East: A History of Standard Oil Company of California and Predecessors through 1919.* New York, Appleton-Century-Crofts, 1920.

Who's Who in China. Shanghai, 1920.

Wickberg, Edgar B. "Late Nineteenth Century Land Tenure in North Taiwan," in Leonard H. D. Gordon, ed., *Taiwan: Studies in Chinese Local History.* New York, Columbia University Press, 1970.

Wiebe, Robert H. *Businessmen and Reform: A Study of the Progressive Movement.* Cambridge, Harvard University Press, 1962.

Wilkins, Mira. "An American Enterprise Abroad: American Radiator Company in Europe, 1895-1914," *Business History Review* 43.3 (Autumn 1969).

————. *The Emergence of Multinational Enterprise: American Business Abroad from the Colonial Era to 1914.* Cambridge, Harvard University Press, 1970.

————. "The Role of U.S. Business," in Dorothy Borg and Shumpei Okamoto, *Pearl Harbor as History.* New York, Columbia University Press, 1973.

————. "The Internationalization of the Corporation—the Case of Oil," in K. I. Lindgren et al., eds., *The Corporation and Australian Society.* Sydney, Law Book Co., 1974.

————. *The Maturing of Multinational Enterprise: American Business Abroad from 1914 to 1970.* Cambridge, Harvard University Press, 1974.

———— and Frank Ernest Hill. *American Business ABroad: Ford on Six Continents.* Detroit, Wayne State University Press, 1964.

Willoughby, Westel W. *Foreign Rights and Interests in China.* Baltimore, John Hopkins Press, 1920.

Winkler, John K. *Tobacco Tycoon: The Story of James Buchanan Duke.* New York Random House, 1942.

Wray, William D. *Mitsubishi and the N.Y.K., 1870-1914: Business Strategy in the Japanese Shipping Industry.* Cambridge, Council on East Asian Studies, Harvard University, 1984.

Wright, Arnold, ed. *Twentieth Century Impressions of Hong Kong, Shanghai, and Other Treaty Ports of China.* London, Lloyd's Great Britain Publishing Co., 1908.

Wright, Mary C. *The Last Stand of Chinese Conservatism: The T'ung-chih Restoration, 1862-1874.* New York, Athenaeum, 1966.

————. *China in Revolution: The First Phase, 1900-1913.* New Haven, Yale University Press, 1968.

Wright, Stanley F. *China's Struggle for Tariff Autonomy, 1843–1938*. Shanghai, Kelly & Walsh, 1938.

Wu Ch'eng-lo 吳承洛 . *Chin-shih Chung-kuo shih-yeh t'ung-chih* 今世中國實業通志 (Industrial gazette of present-day China). Shanghai, Commercial Press, 1933.

Wu Pan-nung 吳半農 . *T'ieh mei ho shih-yu* 鐵煤和石油 (Iron, coal, and petroleum). Peiping, Institute of Social Survey, 1932.

Wu Pao-san 巫寶三 . "Chung-kuo kuo-min so-te 1933 hsiu cheng," 中國國民所得, 一九三三修正 (Corrections to "China's national income in 1933"), *She-hui k'o-hsueh tsa-chih* 9.2: 92–153 (December 1947).

Yagi Haruo 矢木明夫 . *Nihon kindai seishigyō no seiritsu—Nagano-ken Okaya seishigyōshi kenkyū* 日本近代製糸業の成立 — 長野県岡谷製糸業史研究 (The establishing of modern silk-spinning industry in Japan: A study of the history of silk-spinning industry in Okaya, Nagano prefecture). Tokyo, Ochanomizu shobō, 1960.

———. "Seishigyō" 製絲業 , in Chihōshi kenkyū kyōgikai 地方史研究協議會 (Council for local history studies), comp., *Nihon sangyōshi taikei: Sōron hen* 日本產業史大系 ： 総論篇 (An outline of the industrial history of Japan: General remarks). Tokyo, Tokyo daigaku shuppankai, 1961.

———. *Nihon keizaishi gaisetsu* 日本經濟史概説 (A general survey of the economic history of Japan). Tokyo, Hyōronsha, 1974.

Yamaguchi Kazuo 山口和雄 , ed. *Nihon sangyō kin'yūshi kenkyū: seishi kin'yūhen* 日本產業金融史研究 ： 製糸金融篇 (Research on the history of Japanese industrial finance: Section on silk-spinning finance). Tokyo, Tokyo daigaku shuppankai, 1966.

Yang, Lien-sheng. *Money and Credit in China: A Short History*. Cambridge, Harvard University Press, 1952.

Yang Tuan-liu 楊端六 et al. *Liu-shih-wu nien lai Chung-kuo kuo-chi mao-i t'ung-chi* 六十五年來中國國計貿易統計 (Statistics on China's foreign trade during the last sixty-five years). Nanking, Academia Sinica, 1931.

———, Hou-pei Hou, et al., comps. *Statistics of China's Foreign Trade during the Last Sixty-five Years*. Nanking, 1931.

Yen Chung-p'ing 嚴中平 , ed. *Chung-kuo chin-tai ching-chi shih t'ung-chi tzu-liao hsuan-chi* 中國近代經濟史統計資料選輯 (Selected statistical materials on modern Chinese economic history). Peking, K'o-hsueh ch'u-pan-she, 1955.

———. *Chung-kuo mien-fang-chih shih-kao* 中國棉紡織史稿

(Draft history of China's cotton textile industry). Peking, K'o-hsueh ch'u-pan-she, 1963.

Yen, Erh-wen. "Oil to Dominate Old China," *China Reconstructs* 15.4:15–16 (April 1966).

Yokohama shishi 横浜市史 (History of the city of Yokohama). Yokohama, Yūrindō, 1961.

Yoshida Kazuko 吉田和子. "Meiji shoki no seishi gijutsu ni okeru dochaku to gairai" 明治初期の製糸技術における土着と外来 (Silk-spinning technology in the early Meiji period: indigenous and imported), *Kagakushi kenkyū* 2.16:16–24 (Spring 1977).

Young, Marilyn Blatt. *The Rhetoric of Empire: American China Policy, 1895–1901.* Cambridge, Harvard University Press, 1968.

Yueh Ssu-ping 樂嗣炳. *Chung-kuo ts'an-ssu* 中國蠶絲 (Chinese sericulture). Shanghai, Shih-chieh shu-chü, 1935.

Bōseki Rengōkai
紡績連合会

ch'a-chan 茶棧
ch'a chuang 茶莊
ch'a-fan 茶販
ch'a-kuan 茶館
ch'a-k'o 茶客
ch'a-liao 茶寮
ch'a-shih 茶師
ch'a-shui 茶稅
ch'a-shui chü-k'a (ch'ia)
茶稅局卡
ch'a-yeh li-chin 茶葉釐金
ch'an-mien 纏綿
Chang Chih-tung 張之洞

chen 鎮
Cheng Kuan-ying 鄭觀應.
Cheng Po-chao (Cheang Park
Chew) 鄭伯昭
ch'eng-chen 城鎮
Chiang Heng 蔣衡
Chiang Kai-shek 蔣介石
chiao-ch'ing 交情
Chien Chao-nan 簡照南
Chien Yü-chieh 簡玉階
ch'ien-chuang 錢莊
chin (33 lbs.) 斤
chin (25-chin boxes) 斤
Ch'in Sung-k'uan 秦松寬
ching-hsiang 京餉
ching-shih 經世
Chou Tzu-ch'i 周自齊

Chung-hua Tobacco Co. 中華

Dai Fook dollar 台伏

Erh-shih-ssu hsiao 二十四孝

fu-ch'iang 富強
"Fu-min shuo" 富民說
fu-t'ou chiao 佛頭角

han 藩
hang 行
Hao Yen-p'ing 郝延平
Hasegawa Hanshichi 長谷川半七
Hemmi Kenzō 逸見謙三
hong 行
Hoshino Chōtarō 星野長太郎
Hou Chi-ming 侯繼明
Hsi-liang 錫良
Hsi-yu chi 西遊記
Hsia Hsien-lun 夏獻倫
hsiang 鄉
Hsiao Ling-yü 蕭令裕
Hsieh I-ch'u 謝益初
Hsu Jun 徐潤
Hsu Lo-t'ing 徐樂亭
Hsu Shih-ch'ang 徐世昌
Hsueh Fu-ch'eng 薛福成
Hu-pu 戶部
hui-kuan 會館

hui-tui-kuan 匯兌館

I-k'uang 奕劻

Jen Po-yen 任伯彥

kabu-nakama 株仲間
Katakura 片倉
Kawaze Hidehara 河瀨秀治

k'o-hu 客戶
k'o-mang 客詷
Koofunsing (Ku Feng Sheng) 顧豐盛
k'uai fa-ts'ai 快發財
kuan-shang ho-pan 官商合辦
kumi 組
Kung, H. H. 孔祥熙
Kwang Hwa Petroleum Co., Ltd. 光華

Li Ch'un-sheng 李春生
li-jun tsai-t'ou-tzu lü 利潤再投資率
Li Wen-chung (Li Wang-chang) 李文仲
Liang Ching-kuo (Kinqua) 梁經國
Liang Shih-i 梁士詒
Lin Tse-hsu 林則徐
Lin Wei-yuan 林維源
Liu Ai-jen 劉藹仁
Liu Chin-sheng 劉金聲

Liu Ming-ch'uan 劉銘傳
Lu Yao-ch'en 盧堯臣
Lü Ch'üan-sun 呂佺孫

ma-chen-kuan 媽振館
Ma Chien-chung 馬建忠
Ma Yü-ch'ing 馬玉清
Maeda Masana 前田正名
mao-ch'a 毛茶
Mei-fu (Mei-foo) 美孚
Mitsui Bussan Kaisha
　　三井物產会社
mou 畝
Murai Kichibei 村井吉兵衛
Murai Brothers Co.
　　村井

Nanyang Brothers Tobacco
　Co. 南洋兄弟煙草公司
Nei-wu fu 內務府
Nihon Menka 日本綿花

Pai-she 白蛇
Pai-tzu t'u 百子圖
Pan Ku 班固
Pao Shih-ch'en 包世臣
Peiyang Tobacco Co. 北洋
p'eng-min 棚民
*P'eng-min yü shan-chu huo
　　wei yeh* 棚民與山主伙為業

p'ien 片
Pien Pao-ti 卞寶第
Po Chü-i 白居易

San Hsing Tobacco Co. 三星
San-lin Tobacco Co. 三林
San-pai liu-shih hang
　　三百六十行
shang-chan 商戰
shang-pan 商辦
Sheng Hsuan-huai 盛宣懷
shou-hsu fei 手續費
Shui-hu chuan 水滸傳
Soong, T.V. 宋子文

ta-tsu 大祖
ta-yang 大洋
taotai 道台
Tong King-sing 唐景星
tonya 問屋
tou-ping 豆餅
Tōyō Menka 東洋綿花
Tsai-tse 載澤
Tso Tsung-t'ang 左宗棠
Ts'ui Tsun-san 崔尊三
t'u-yeh 土業
T'ung-chih Restoration
　　同治中興
T'ung-shang tsung-chü
　　通商總局

urikomitonya 売込問屋

Wai-wu pu 外務部
Wang-hsia 望廈
Wang I-te 王懿德
Wang Shih-jen 王世仁

Wu Chien-chang (Samqua)
吳健彰
Wu K'o-chai 吳克齋
Wu Ping-chien (Houqua)
伍秉鑑
Wu T'ing-sheng 鄔挺生

Yang Kuei-fei 楊貴妃
Yang Teh-fu 楊德富
Yeh Ch'eng-chung 葉澄衷

Ying-Mei yen kung-ssu yueh-pao 英美烟公司月報
Ying-Mei yen-ts'ao kung-ssu
英美烟草公司
Yu Shao-tseng 尤少增
Yü-sheng-ho (house) 玉盛合
Yueh Fei 岳飛
Yung-t'ai-ho (Company) (Wing Tai Vo) 永泰和

zaguri 座繰ll